JAINISM IN INDIAN PHILOSOPHY

JAINISM IN INDIAN PHILOSOPHY

By

DIBAKAR MOHANTY

BHARATIYA KALA PRAKASHAN
DELHI (INDIA)

First Published : 2006

Published by **C.P. Gautam**
BHARATIYA KALA PRAKASHAN
3421-A, IInd Floor, Narang Colony, Tri Nagar, Delhi-110035.
Phone : 27393083, 32967505 (O), 32492129 (R)

ISBN : 81-8090-125-4

Laser Type Setting by
A-ONE GRAPHICS
JD-18C, IInd Floor, Pitampura, Delhi-110088

Printed By :
Tarun Offset Printer
Delhi-53.

DEDICATED

TO

MY BELOVED PARENTS

FOREWORD

I have great pleasure in introducing Dr. Divakar Mohanty's works Jainism as Presented in Indian Philosophy which is the modified and revised version of his doctotial thesis submitted to the Centre of Advanced Study in Sanskrit, University of Pune in 2003. I have been associated with work right from the beginning as the guide and have noticed how the scholar has meticulously identified and collected the references from the vast literature of Nyāya, Vedānta and Mīmāṁsā texts. The scholar has spent full four years in identifying the references by going through the original texts of these three systems line by line since there was no other way. **For the first time references of jain doctrines in other systems are collected and critically examined**. Keeping in mind the true sprit of Jainism the scholar has not entered into controversies in refuting the doctrine of others except in few cases. It is a fact that Jainism as a system of philosophy has not received the importance it deserves in early period and even in recent times.

The method of the presentation of the scholar has been comparative and analytical. The candidate has tired to compare the Jaina doctrines with that of rival schools by putting their texts side by side. The subjects have been arranged on the basis of the concepts and doctrines. In the introduction the candidate has presented basic doctrines of Jaina philosophy, which is rather a reappraisal of the outcome of studies available in early secondary literature to facilitate smooth discussions from the point of view of their systems. The scholor has tired to verify the reference with the original text in most cases while discussing the treatment of Jaina doctrines by other systems. He has quoted profusingly from the original texts from the rival schools. At times it is noticed that the scholar has failed to give a critical analysis of the arguments and satisfied himself only by giving the translation of the text. The observation of the scholar in his conclusion is from different aspects, from the aspect of their presentation by the rival systems, from the point of view of their accuracy and adequacy and also from the point of view of correctness or otherwise of the refutation of the rival systems in the background of Jaina philosophy.

The work is well documented and is good piece of research based on original text of these systems. I hope the readers in general and scholars of Indian Philosophy would welcome this work of Dr. Mohanty.

B.K. Dalai
CASS, Pune University

PREFACE

In India there are six orthodox systems of Philosophy viz. Nyāya, Vaīśeṣīka, Vedānta, Sāṁkhya, Yoga and Māmāṁsā and three heterdox system of philosphy viz. Jainism, Buddhism and Cārvāka Philosophy. It is a fact that, all these philosophical systems are developed by the process of mutual dialogue. Therefore it is obvious that , when one system is emerging that has to interact with other philosophical system. I happen with all the systems of Indian philosophy. Having this idea in mind I have taken this endeavour to show the references of Jainism in other systems of Indian philosophy, particularly in Buddhism, in Nyāya and Vaiśeṣika system of philosophy and all the major schools of Vedanta system of Indian philosophy. It is a critical and comparative type of study between Jainism VS other systems of Indian Philosophy.

Basically, the idea of such type of study is of my revered teacher Dr. Bata Kishore Dalai, CASS, University of Pune, whose sincere guidance, love and blessing enabled me complete this study. I am extremely thankful to our beloved Vice-Chancellor Prof. Dr. Pankaja Chande for his blessings.

I am obliged to Prof. V.N. Jha, Director, CASS, University of Pune, Prof. S.S. Gedam HOD, GVISH, Amravati and all of my colleagues, Dr. P.C. Panda, A.D. Mohanty, B.K. Agasthi and all of my teachers for their love and valuable suggestions.

To carry out this study ICPR (Indian council of Philosophical Research) has awarded me a Fellowship, for that, I record my obligation to ICPR.

Similarly, I am thankful to Late Dr. U.K. Pungulia, Ex-chairman, Sanmati Teerth, Pune, for giving a Fellowship at the early study of my research.

I am also obliged to Late Sivannāth Sahu, for his kindness and love.

I hardly find words to express my indebtedness to my parents, brothers and my better-half, whose love and encourgement inspired me a lot to complete this work. I sincerely thank Dr. Ekanta Patel P.G.T. Kendriya Vidyālaya, Ganeshkhind, Pune for going throuth the work and suggesting improvements. I also thank Mr. C.P. Gautam, Bhāratīya Kalā Prakāśana for accepting this work for Publication.

Amravati, **Divakar Mohanty**
Caitra Rāmanavami, 2006.

CONTENTS

INTRODUCTION

Problem and Nature of the work

Prof. E. Frauwallner in his forward to "*Jaina* theories of Reality and Knowledge" observes:

"During the whole period of Indian philosophy, Jainism has not been attended to very much by the other systems. Whatever the causes for this negligence might have been, the history of Jainism during this time is still a potential object of thorough research, the facts are that the schools like *Nyāya, Mīmāṁsā,* hardly mention Jainism in their polemics. It is only since the time of *Akalaṅka* that the Buddhists pay more attention to *Jainism*".

On the backdrop of this introduction it becomes adequately evident that no research has been conducted yet from this point of view to study the *Jaina* philosophy as presented in the other systems of Indian philosophy like Buddhism, *Nyāya, Mīmāṁsā, Vedānta* and *Sāṁkhya-Yoga*.

A peep into the text of any system of Indian philosophy reveals the fact that it has developed by the process of mutual dialogue amongst the various systems of Indian philosophy. The *Jainas* have their own theories and have developed various concepts in favour of their philosophical speculations. The Buddhists are the worst enemy of the *Jainas* in this regard. Therefore, they, in their respective texts, while expounding and establishing their own theories try to refute the theories of the *Jainas*. Most importantly the *Jaina* theory of *Anekānta,* theory of reality, Soul, Omniscience, Concept of *Pramāṇas (pratyakṣa, aṇumāna, pratyabhijñāna, smṛti, tarka)* and many more philosophical concepts, to mention a few, of Jainism are quoted and refuted.

An attempt has been made here to make a critical and comparative analysis of those cases, where the *Jaina* doctrines are quoted in the texts of Indian philosophical systems and are refuted or otherwise. It also tries to evaluate the appropriateness and correctness of the refutations from the point of view of Jainism in particular and Indian philosophy in general.

Further, one of the prime concerns of the present endeavour would be to verify the doctrines of the Jainism as presented in the texts of other systems by making a comparison by putting side by side the original texts of *Jaina* philosophy with that of the rival schools.

When Jainism is quoted by some philosophers it is probable that it is quoted without any bias, it is also possible that it is misquoted or though quoted properly, is interpreted differently as suitable to the need of the concerned system, for, he has to refute those. Further, if it is quoted properly and properly understood and interpreted as well, one has to examine the grounds and arguments provided by the concerned philosopher in favour of the doctrines of the opponents. Thus, care will be taken to examine critically the depth, the completeness and the accuracy of the prima-facie arguments of the opponents against the doctrines of Jainism, which are quoted and refuted by respective systems of Indian philosophy. An attempt has also been made to bring out the contribution of Jainism in the development of Indian philosophy.

Survey of the researches already conducted

We have made an exhaustive survey of the research works conducted on this topic. As stated in the beginning, we do not find any systematic and complete work, where the treatment of *Jaina* philosophy by the rival schools of Indian philosophy is discussed, except a very few research articles, two or three to be specific and a book on some aspects of Buddhism by Bhagchandra Jain Bhasker. We present here, a brief comment on that book to which a full chapter is devoted in the present thesis. This book 'Jainism in Buddhist literature' by Bhagchandra Jain Bhasker, published by *Alok prakāśana, Nagpur* in 1972 is presented in five chapters. In the first chapter he describes the historical background of *Jaina* philosophy by giving a brief summary on *Jaina* literature and Buddhist literature in some one hundred pages. The second and third chapters are devoted to the general discussion and analysis of *Jaina* philosophy and *Jaina* ethics. Only in the fourth and fifth chapter he considers the treatment of *Jaina* doctrines in Buddhist literature. There too, real treatment of *Jaina* doctrine by Buddhist philosopher is very scanty. As a matter of fact, whole of the text seems to be oriented as an attempt to present the doctrines and philosophical concept of the Jainas. No attempt has been made to study the view of the Jainism as presented in the Buddhist literature from the point of view of comparison and criticism. In very few cases the author has drawn something from the original texts of the Buddhist literature to develop the argument against the Jainism. Again the treatment seems to be more like giving the summary of the tenets than a picture of philosophical debates between two opposite traditions. We have gone through this work very carefully. Apart from this, we do not have any work where the treatment of *Jaina* doctrines by Buddhists is analyzed.

There is an article by K. V. Apte, titled 'Criticism of Jainism in *Brahmasūtra Śrikara Bhāṣya'* published in Journal of the Asiatic Society of Bombay, where the treatment of Jainism by *Rāmānuja* is presented. Though *Śankara, Rāmānuja, Madhva, Nimbārka* and *Ballhahba* have discussed some of the important aspects of the *Jaina* philosophy in their respective texts, nothing has been written on them. This survey explains and justifies the present endeavour to study the treatment of the *Jaina* doctrines by the other schools of Indian philosophy.

Scope and limitation of the work

In the present work we have concentrated on three different schools of thought namely *Nyāya, Vedānta* and Buddhism, for their treatment of *Jaina* doctrines. The reason of selecting these three systems is that, we find the treatment of *Jaina* doctrine to some considerable extent in these systems. We have gone through the literature of *Mīmāṁsā* and *Sāṁkhya-Yoga* philosophy as well very carefully and do not find much reference to *Jaina* doctrines in these texts. Though it was planned to study Jainism in all systems of Indian philosophy, due to lack of materials and references in *Mīmāṁsā* and *Sāṁkhya-Yoga* we restricted our study to *Nyāya, Vedānta* and Buddhism. There was no way to identify the occurrences of the *Jaina* doctrines in *non-jaina* texts without going through individual texts of different systems. After examining thoroughly most of the primary texts of *Nyāya, Vedānta* and Buddhism we noticed that the Buddhists have taken the Jainism very seriously for critical examination. Again among the Buddhists *Dignāga, Dharmakīrti, Nāgarjuna, Śāntarakṣita, Prajṃākaragupta,* etc. have tried to refute the position of the Jainas, in their respective texts, which we have referred to.

In the *Nyāya* system we have examined *Nyāyasūtra Bhāṣya, Vārtika, Tātparyaṭīkā* along with almost all important texts like *Nyāyamajṃarī* of *Jayantabhaṭṭa, Nyāyasāra* and *Nyāyabhuṣaṇa* of *Bhāṣarvjña, Nyāyasiddhantamajṃaī* of *Janakinnatha, Nyāyasiddhāntamuktāvallī* of *Viśvannātha paṃcānana Bhaṭṭācārya* and *Tarkasaṁgraha, Deepikā* of *Annabhaṭṭa* to identify the *Jaina* doctrines there. We have also gone through *Vaiśeṣika* texts like *Sūtra* of *Kaṇāda, Prasatha-padabhāṣya, Kandalī* of *Śridhara* and *Upaskāra* of *Śankara Mishra* along with other texts like *Sapta Padārthi* of *Sivādaitya Mishra*.

The *Vedānta* texts like *Śankara Bhāṣya* on *Brahmasūtra* along with *Bhāmatī* of *Vācaśpati Mishra* and *Kalpaṭaru* of *Appya Dixit,* all the important texts of *Dvaita* school of *Madvācārya, Viśiṣṭādvaita* school of *Rāmānuja, Daitādvaita* school of *Nimbārka* and *Śuddhādvaita* school *of Vallabhācārya* are considered for framing the objections of the *Vedāntins* against the basic doctrines of the *Jainas*. It must be stated that a work of the present type being very vast, a limitation covering some restricted literature are to be determined and hence, will never be complete. There is every possibility of missing or non-identifying a case of the treatment of *Jaina* doctrine by some systems due to negligence of over sightedness.

Methodology

The method of our presentation is governed by the principle of comparison and criticism. To do justice to this objective we have tried to show the comparison of the *Jaina* doctrines with that of rival schools by putting their texts side by side, sometimes in the body of the texts and at times in the footnotes as far as possible. Very meticulously the occurrences of *Jaina* doctrines in the texts of different schools of Indian philosophy have been gathered initially. They have been arranged on the basis of the concepts and doctrines. In the introduction a presentation of *Jaina* doctrines, which is rather a reappraisal of discussion available in early secondary literature, is presented to facilitate smooth discussion afterwards, while examining them from the point of view of other systems at the time of refutation. Here also, we have identified some important philosophical concepts and doctrines, which are later criticized by other systems. While discussing the treatment of *Jaina* doctrines by other systems we have tried to verify the references with the original text in most cases. For convenience, we have even quoted profusingly from the original texts of the rival systems with reference to original *Jaina* texts in the footnotes. While dealing with a concept we have taken the view of different authorities belonging to a system mostly chronologically, who have bothered to explain or analyze the *Jaina* concepts in the rival camp. We have tried to make observation from two aspects: from the aspect of their presentation by the rival systems, from the point of view of their accuracy and adequacy, and also from the point of view of the correctness or otherwise of the refutation of the rival systems in the background of the *Jaina* philosophy. The detailed organization of the work is as follows:

Introduction:

Problem and nature of the work.

A survey of the recourses already conducted.

Scope and limitation of the present work.

Methodology.

Chapter I

A brief sketch of the important doctrines of the *Jaina*.

Chapter II

Jaina philosophy as presented in *Nyāya* and *Vaiśeṣika* system.

Chapter III

Jaina philosophy as presented in *Vedānta* system.

Chapter IV

Jaina philosophy as presented in Buddhist literature.

Conclusion/Observations.

Chapter 1

A BRIEF SKETCH OF THE IMPORTANT DOCTRINES OF THE JAINA

Introduction

In this chapter we propose to present a brief outline of the important tanents of the Jaina Philosophy, which are later criticized and refuted by other systems of Indian Philosophy. Even otherwise, to aquaint the presuppositions and their doctrines which are related to logical, epistemological and metaphysical problems are chosen for presentation. The topic discussed here are: .

1. Pramāṇa.
2. Classification of Pramāṇa.
3. Validity of Pramāṇa.
4. Pratyakṣa Pramāṇa and its classification.
5. Sāṃvyavahārika pratyakṣa.
6. Īhā, Avagraha, Avāya and Dhāraṇā.
7. Pāramārthika Pratyakṣa.
8. Smṛti Pramāṇa.
9. Pratybhijṃā Pramāṇa.
10. Tarka Pramāṇa.
11. Anumāna Pramāṇa.
12. Āgama Pramāṇa.
13. Anekāntavāda.
14. Syādvāda.
15. Nayavāda.
16. Nikṣepa.

17. Anekāntavāda.
18. Dravya.
19. Jīva.
20. Ajīva.
21. Dharma.
22. Saṃbara.
23. Baṅdha.
24. Āśrava.
25. Pudgala.
26. Ākāśa.
27. Mokṣa.
28. Mind.
29. Sense organs
30. Omniscience
31. Karma.

Pramāṇa: [The (means of) valid knowledge]

Many *Jaina* logicians, right from Umaswati (1-85 A.D) till Yaśovijaya (1608-88A.D) have defined it differently. Though the definition differs in terms of expression, conceptually they are same. Let us record a few definitions of *Pramāṇa,* from some selected text of *Jaina* logic:

1. सम्यज्ञानं प्रमाणम्।[1]
2. प्रमाणं स्वपराभासि ज्ञानं बाधवर्जितम्।[2]
3. तत्त्वज्ञानं प्रमाणं ते युगपत्सर्वभासनम्।[3]
4. प्रमाणादिष्टसंसिद्धिरन्यथातिप्रसंगत:।[4]
5. प्रमाणमविसंवादि ज्ञानमनधिगतार्थाधिगम लक्षणत्वात्।[5]
6. स्वापूर्वार्थव्यवसायात्मकं ज्ञानं प्रमाणम्।[6]
7. स्वपरव्यवसायि ज्ञानं प्रमाणम्।[7]

8. प्रकर्षेण संज्ञायादिव्यवच्छेदेन मीयते परिच्छिद्यते वस्तुतत्त्वं येन तत् प्रमाणम्।[8]

9. प्रमीयते परिच्छिद्यतेऽर्थो अनेकान्तविशिष्टोऽनेनेति प्रमाणम्।[9]

10. स्वपरव्यवसायि ज्ञानं प्रमाणम्।[10]

As we notice here the *Jainas* have defined *Pramāṇa* in terms of knowledge unlike the other systems of Indian Philosophy, who differentiated jñāna from *Pramāṇa*. Here we intend to discuss a primary question: what was the need or rather what was the reason for the *Jainas* to define *Pramāṇa* in terms of knowledge?

A carefully observation of these definitions suggest two basic things:

1. There is a historical development of the concept. The definition seems to be refined *(pariṣkṛta)* in course of time by adding qualifications, keeping the essence of the definition intact, in subsequent period.
2. There is clear-cut influence of other systems of Indian philosophy on the *Jainas'* definitions of *Pramāṇa* particularly the *Nyāya*.

Let us analyze these definitions to identify the historical development. The earliest definition of *Pramāṇa* belonging to logical tradition is of *Samantabhadra,* who defines *Pramāṇa* in term of valid knowledge, which illuminates itself and its object. It is Siddhasena Divākara who adds the qualification *'bādhavarjita' i.e.* devoid of any obstacle, and thus, modified it. Some of the definitions of *Pramāṇa* are based on derivation as given by Pujjyapāda, for example, "*Pramīyate pramīṇoti pramīti mātraṁ vā Pramāṇan*" or as given by Hemacandra, which I have already quoted. It may be recorded here that *Nyāyasūtrakāra* Gautama has not defined *Pramāṇa,* suggesting that it has to be understood by derivation and Bhāṣyakāra Vātsyāyana fills this lacuna by providing a derivative definition. He defines *Pramāṇa* as *upalbdhi sādhanāni pramāṇānīti samākhyānirvacanasāmarthyāt bodhavyaṃ pramiyate aneneti karaṇārthābhidhānao hi pramāṇa śabda.* Vidyānanda probably following Umāsvāti, has defined *Pramāṇa* in terms of valid knowledge: *samyagjñānaṃ Pramāṇaṃ*. In the later time, *Pramāṇa* is defined in terms of knowledge with the additions of following qualifications like:

1. *Bādhavarjitaḥ:* (without any obstruction) as given by Siddhasena Divākara.
2. *Svaparavyavasāyī:* (that reveals both the self and the object) as given by Vādidevasuri and Jasovijayagani.
3. *Avisamvādi:* (uncontradicted) as given by Vidyānanda.
4. *Anadhigatattval Apūrvārthattva:* (not known before or novel) as given by Māṇikyanandi and Prabhacandra.
5. *Vyavasāyātmakaḥ:* definite knowledge as given by Māṇikyanandi and Prabhacandra.

From this it is clear that the simple definition of *Pramāṇa* in terms of knowledge has developed into some complex definitions presenting new theories. In all these definitions, qualifications are added in later period, which present a view of the historical development.

If we make a comparison between the definitions of *Pramāṇa* we can notice that, there are some similarities between the *Jaina* definition of Pramāṇa and other systems. For example, the ideas of *anadhigatārtha* or *apūrvārthatva* etc. are introduced in *Jaina* logic in the text of *Parīkṣāmukha* of Vidyānandi and *Aṣṭasahasrī* of Māṇikyanandi. As a matter of fact, the ideas *of anadhigatārtha* or *apūrvūrthttva* are already existent in the definition of *Pramāṇa* as given by Kumārilabhaṭṭa. His definition of *Pramāṇa* is as follows:

> ***'tatrāpūrvārthavijñānaṃ niścitaṃ vādhavarjitaṃ aduṣṭakāraṇārabdhaṃ pramāṇaṃ lokasammataṃ'.***

Thus, it is clear that the *Jaina* logicians have borrowed this idea of *bādhavarjita, anadhigatārtha* and *apūrvārtha* from Kumārila. Further, the idea of *avisaṁvādakatva* is definitely taken from Buddhist source that defines *Pramāṇa* as follows: '*pramāṇaṃavisamvādi jñānam*' [Pramāṇavārtika of Dharmakirti-24].

Classification of Pramāṇa

The problem of classification of the *Pramāṇa* has been treated in *Jaina* tradition in two ways viz. based on the agamic classification and based on logical classification. We have stated that in *Jaina* logical tradition there is no distinction between *Pramāṇa* and knowledge. So, the classification of *Pramāṇa* means classification of knowledge. The treatment where knowledge is divided into *mati, śṛta* etc. is the one based on *agamic* classification. The treatment where it is divided into *Pramāṇa* like perception, inference etc, is based on the logical classification. An unmixed instance of the first type treatment is found in *Āvaśyaka niryukti,* where as an instance of the second type can be noticed in the text of *Nyāyāvatāra.*

If we see the history of development of the *Jaina* theory of knowledge, we observe that during agamic period the idea was pure and unalloyed. At that time, there were five-fold divisions of knowledge. And at the stage of *Niryukti* the idea of two-fold division usurps in, which is an external influence. [u] Yet the predominance of *āgama* was there. But at the state of *Aṇuyoga,* where the five-fold division of the *āgama* takes a back seat and the four-fold division of *Nyāya* comes into prominence.[12] Umāsvāti reverts to the position of the *Niryuktis* and stresses upon the two-fold division, which was finally accepted.[13] In *Nāndisūtra* another development is seen where the sense cognition is included into *Pratyakṣa*[14] Jinabhadra and Akalaiika designated it as *Sāṁvyavahārika Pratyakṣa i.e.* perception according to the common usage, just to avoid its contradiction with the *Niryukti* or *Tattvārthasūtra i.e.* agamic authority. Māṇīkyanandi and Vādidevasuri again adopted the logical division and try to formulate the agamic conceptions into their own style.[15] The logic of Siddhasena divides *Pramāṇa* in three types only.[16] Thus, the development of *Jaina* division of knowledge passes through various stages or phases. In the initial stage it was free from external influence, and in later period slightly mixed with external influences and losing its originality and ultimately establishing its originality and then constructing a parallel system of logical development. Thus,

Paṇḍit Sukhalāljee has arranged these developments into seven stages[17]

(1) Purely agamic,
(2) Based on the Niryuktis,
(3) Presented by the Anuyogadvāra,
(4) Based on the Tattvārthasūtra,
(5) Contribution of Siddhasena Divākara,
(6) Contribution of Jinabhadra,
(7) Contribution of Akalanka and his followers.

We present here various classificatioins of *Pramāṇa* on the basis of different *Jaina* authority by table and diagram.

Division based on *Bhagavatisūtra:*

Jñāna

- abhinibodhika
  - avagraha
  - īhā
  - avāya
  - dhāranā
- śruta
- avadhi
- manahparvāva
- kevala

Division based on Prajñāpanāsūtra:

Upayoga

- nirākāra
  - caksudarśana
  - acaksudarśana
  - avadhidarśana
  - kevaladarśana
- sākāra
  - matijñāna
  - matiajñāna
  - śrutajñāna
  - avadhijñāna
  - manaparyāya
  - kevalajñāna
  - śrutājñāna
  - vibhangājñāna

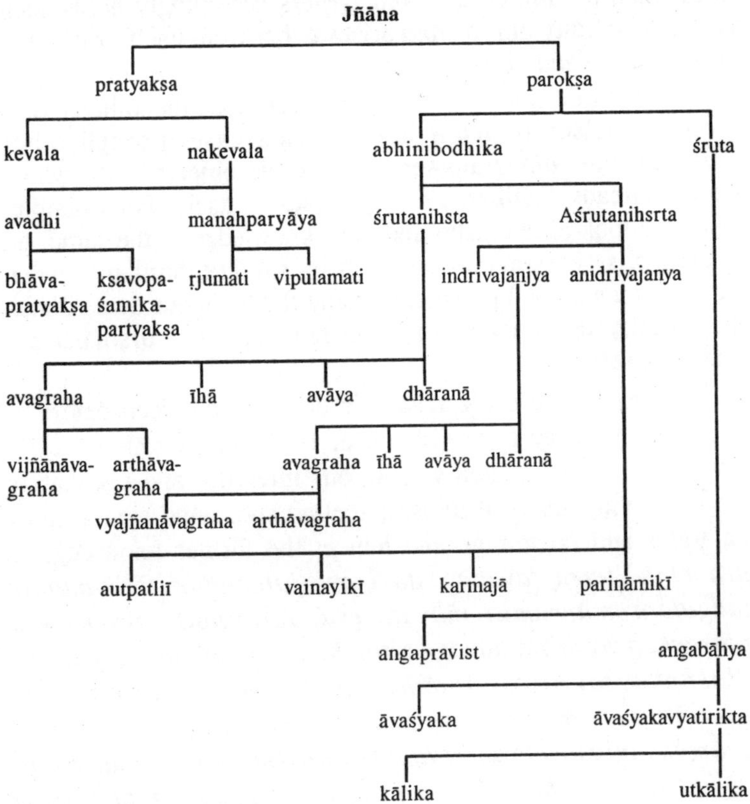

Validity of Knowledge

With regard to the validity *of pramāṇa,* it is stated that the validity arises from itself or through another *'tat prāmāṇyam svataḥ parataśca'.*

In *Nyāya* philosophy, it is postulated that the validity of *pramāṇa* arises through other means. *Bhāṣyakāra* Vātsyāyana says that through inference, the validity of *pramāṇa* is established. An objection may be raised: if an inference, which is itself a *pramāṇa,* confirms another *pramāṇa* to establish its validity, how will this inference be validated. If it is said that another inference will validate this, the result would be an end less chain of infinite regress. So we must accept that in some cases *pramāṇa* validates itself and in other cases, its validity is established by inference. *Jaina* writers accordingly holds such view that validity of *pramāṇa* arises either from itself or through another *pramāṇa* like inference.

To the question as to, in what case does the validity of a *pramāṇa* arises of itself and in what case through other *pramāṇa,* the *Jainas* answer: in case,the objects, with which we are already familiar, *pramāṇa* rises of itself. For example, when we look at our palm and have knowledge of the same, no inference is necessary to establish its validity. Similarly, when we have seen a pond previously many times, in our own village, the validity does not require the help of other pramāṇa but arise of itself.

But when we see a reservoir of water not seen before at any time, we may have a doubt at first whether this is really water or a mirage. Then we use our inference and say that as we are having smell of lotuses, feeling cool wind etc., it must be water and no mirage and hence, the former knowledge is *pramāṇa 'tatra tavabhyastaviṣaye jalamidamiti jñanejāte tadgataprāmānyamiti jñāyata eva. Anyathottarakṣaṇa eva nihsankapravṛttirabhāvāt, asthi hi jalajñānottarakṣaṇa eva nihsankapravṛttih. Anabhyasthetuviṣaye jalajñānejāte jalajñānam mama jātamite jñānaśvarūpa nirnayepi prāmāṇyanirnayenyata eva. Anyathottarakāle samdehanupāpatteh, asthi hi samdeho jalajñānam mama jatam, tatkim jalamutamariciketi? Tataḥ kamalaparimalasitlamahdamarutpracāraprabhriravadhārayati, pramāṇaṃ prāktanam jalajñānenam, kamalaparimalādyanyathānupāpatteh'.*[18]

'Prāmāṇyatuḥ svataḥ sidhamabhyāsāt parotonyathā'.[19]

In *Pramāṇanayatattvāloṅkāra,* it is stated that *prāmāṇya* and *aprāmāṇya* arises through others, where their knowledge arises by both, *i.e.* by themselves and by others, *'tadubhayamutpattau parata eva jñaptautu svataḥ parataśca'.*[20]

Pratyakṣa pramāṇa:

Pratyakṣa pramāṇa is defined as follows:

1. जदि केवलेण णादं हवदि हि जीवेण पच्चक्खं।[21]
2. अक्षणोति व्याप्नोति जानातीत्यक्ष आत्मा। तमेव......प्रतिनियतं प्रत्यक्षम्।।[22]

3. प्रत्यक्षलक्षणं प्राहुः स्पष्टं साकारमञ्जसा। द्रव्यपर्यायसामान्यविशेष-र्थात्मवेदनम्।[23]
4. प्रत्यक्षं विशदं ज्ञानम्।[24]
5. इन्द्रियानिन्द्रियानपेक्षमतीतव्यभिचारं साकारग्रहणं प्रत्यक्षम्।[25]

In the tradition of *Jaina* philosophy the treatment of problem of knowledge can be discussed at two levels. The treatment as found in *agamic* literature and based on *agamic* classification and treatment based on later logical literature and the classification based on it. By logical literature, what we intend is the systematic logical texts from *Akalaṅka* (750 A. D.) downwards or even from *Siddhasena Divākara* (480-550 A. D.). The treatment where knowledge is divided into *mati, śruta,* etc., is one, based on the agamic literature and where it is divided into *pramāṇas* like perception etc., is one based on logical classification which we have already recorded. Here we discuss the concept of *Pratyakṣa* on the light of the discussion made by the later Jaina logicians. Before doing so, it would not be out of place to peep into the agamic literature to know the historical development with a view to acquaint ourselves on the stand taken by them and thus form a ground for further analysis, m^s are *twa^rahs,*

The *Bhagavatisūtra* enumerates five types of knowledge, namely, *abhinibodhika* etc. *Abhinibodhika* is further divided into six kinds on the basis of five sense organs and mind. *Abhinibodhika jñāna* arising due to sense organs are sense perceptions whereas *Abhinobodhika jñāna* dependent on mind includes in it all the knowledge ordinarily known as *parokṣa,* with the exception to *Sṛta.* In *Sthānṅgasūtra* the five kinds of knowledge beginning with *abhinobodika* is brought under *parokṣa.* The reason for this contention of the *Jainas* is not far to seek. *Āgama* considers only those cognitions to be *pratyakṣa* for which self has not to depend on anything else. *Abhinibodha jñāna* due to five sense organs and *avadhi, manaḥparyāya, kevala* are categorized as *praytyakṣa* in *Nāndisūtra.* Out of these, the first five are *indriya pratyakṣa* and *avadhi* etc., are *noindriya pratyksa.* Each of the five *abhinibodhika jñāna* is accepted to have four stages namely *avagraha, īhā, avāya* and *dhāraṇā.*

Alike *Nāndisūtra, Anuyogadvārasūtra* also divides *pratyakṣa* into two: *indriya* and *noindriya pratyksa.* Jinabhadra (484-588 A. D.) accepts the knowledge due to sense organs as *pratyakṣa.* Umāsvāti (185 A.D.) however, regards such knowledge as *parokṣa* following agamic viewpoint. It is only in the work of Divākara that we find a systematic and logical treatment of the problem. He defines *pratyakṣa* as *aparokṣa,* other than or different from *parokṣa.* The sensuous perception, which is called *Parokṣa* in agamic period and is called *saṁvyavahārika* in later logical period, is stated to be of four kinds or it is presented in four stages. The four stages are *avagraha, īhā, avāya* and *dhāraṇā.* It is maintained that each stage is an independent knowledge and subsequently they produce collective knowledge. What is meant is: in a sense *avagraha* is independent, *īhā* supported by *avagraha* is another independent knowledge, *avāya* supported by *avagraha* and Īhā is still another independent knowledge and finally *dhāraṇā* on the basis of the succeeding three knowledge forms another independent knowledge of the same object. We may now take for discussion the four stages of *indriya pratyakṣa.*

JAINA CONCEPT OF SENSUOUS PERCEPTION

Avagraha:

We do not have a definition of *avagraha* in *Nāndisūtra.* It records two types of *avagraha: vynjanavagraha* and *arthavagraha.* It is pointed out that *vynjanavagraha* is not possible in the case of visual sense organs. Umāsvāti records the synonyms of *avagraha* and states that *avagraha* is an inderminate cognition *avagraho-graho-grahanam-dlocanam-avadhāraṃ ity anarhdntarani)*[26]. Pujjyapāda defines it as the first cognition after the contact of the object of sense organs *(viṣaya viṣayi sannipāta samānāntaraṁ ādyagrahaṇaṇ avagrahaḥ)*[21] Two steps are pointed out: when the sense organ is contacted with the object, there occurs *darśana.* And in the second stage, the cognition arising thereafter is *avagraha.* He gives the example of the cognition of white color by the organ of sight *(viṣaya viṣ ayi sannipāte* sati *darśanaṁ bhāvatitad anantaraṁ arthagrahaṇṁ avagrahaḥ, yathā cakṣusā śuklaṁ itirūpaṁ avagrahaḥ.)*[28]. It is significant to record that pujjyapāda accepts *vya-*

ñjanāvagraha as indeterminate cognition. He writes: *arthāvagraha-vyañjanāvagrahayor vyaktāvyakta kṛto viśeṣaḥ*[29].

On *avagraha,* Jinabhadra makes some significant points. On the expression of *Nāndisūtra* the *avagraha* is instantaneous. He observes that this *avagraha* of *Nāndisūtra* refers to *arthavagraha*. According to him, *arthavagraha* is instantaneous whereas *vyañjanāvagraha* involves a more lengthy process[30]. It is evident that Jinabhadra proposes to refute the view of Pujjyapāda, namely *avagraha* is determinate.

Īhā

Coming to *īhā',* *Nāndisūtra* describes it to follow from *avagraha* knows the object distinctly. In *avagraha,* for example, a person simply hears a sound while in *īhā* he cognizes the nature of the sound "se *jahā nāmakei purise avvattaṁ saddaṁ suṇijja, teṇaṁ saddo iti uggahie nò ceva jāṇai ke saddo.... tao jāṇai amuge esa sadde"*[31] It further states that the process of *īhā* never exceeds one *muhūrta.* It records the following synonyms of *īhā: abhogantā, mārgaṇatā, gaveṣaṇatā, cintā* and *vimaarśa.* Umāsvāti adds four more to this list of synonyms of *īhā* namely *tarka, parikṣā, vicāraṇā* and *jījñāsā*[32].

Pujjyapāda defines *īhā* as the striving for a specific characteristic of the object cognized by *avagraha.* He writes: *"avagraha gṛhite arthe tad ciśeṣākāṅṣāṇāṁ īhā"*[33]. Thus to him *īhā* means inquiring for the distinctive characteristics.

Avāya/Apāya:

In *Āvaśvaka niryukti, apāya* is defined as determinate cognition *"vyavasāyaṁ ca avāyam"*[34]. *Nāndisūtra* records the following synonyms of *apāya: buddhi, vijñāna*[35]. Umāsvāti adds further to the list *avarthnatā, apanoda, apavyādha, apeta, apagata, apavidhha, apaṇutha.* Umāsvāti defines *avāya* as the end of the process, characterized by *īhā.* It can be gathered from the synonyms as recorded by Umāsvāti that according to him *avāya* consists in excluding the non-existing character of the object cognized.[36]

Dhāraṇā:

According to *Nāndisūtra, avāya* is followed by *dhāraṇā,* which means the retention of the perceptual judgment for a number of instances *"tao dhāraṃ pavisai taoṇaṃ dhārai saṃkhejjaṃ vā kālaṃ, asaṃakhejjaṃ vā kālaṃ"*[31]. The following synonyms are recorded in *Nāndisūtra* as *dhāraṇā, sthāpanā, pratistā, koṣṭa. Āvaśyaka Niryukti also defines dharana* as retention. Umāsvāti defines *dhāraṇā* to be the final determination of non-forgetting in subsequent period.

It is significant to remember that except in *Jaina* logic, we nowhere find that knowledge derived from the senses being called *parokṣa*. In *Nyāya* philosophy knowledge derived from senses is known as *praytyakṣa.*[38]

Akalaṅkadeva, the greatest of *Jaina* logicians attempted to reconcile this in the following way. He divided *Pramāṇa* into two, *praytyakṣa* and *parokṣa,* but instead of dividing *praytyakṣ a* into *'sakala'* and *'vikala'* as is done in early period, he laid down two hitherto unknown divisions, namely: *Sarhvyavahdrika* and *Mukhya Pratyakṣa.*

pratyakṣaṃ viśadaṁ jñānaṁ mukhyasāṁvyavahārikaṁ parokṣaṁ śeṣavijñānaṁ pramāṇaṃiti saṁgrahaḥ'.[39]

The Jaina theory of non-sensuous perception

As stated above, the *Jaina* classifies perception into two types: the *saṁvyavahārika* and the *mukhya pratyakṣa.* The first one is empirical perception, which depends on the sense organs and mind. The *mukhya* or the non-sensuous perception is direct knowledge, which arises directly in the self without the assistance of sense organs and mind. It arises when the obstruction of *'karma'* is destroyed.

The word *'mukhya'* means *pradhāna, i.e.* superior in comparison to rest of the *knowledges.* As the face has a superior status in comparison to other parts of body, *Mukhya Pratyakṣa* is also superior amongst all knowledges.

Māṇikyanandi and Hemacandra have also defined it as a perfect knowledge arising in the self without the instrumentality of the sense organs. To Māṇikyanandi *'mukhya'* is that clear, nor-sensuous and infinite knowledge from which all veils are removed by special condition *(sāmagrī viśeṣa- viślesita-akhilāvaraṁ atindriyaśeṣato mukhyaṃ)*.[40] On the peculiar nature of such infinite knowledge Prabhacandra notes that it arises when all the veils of *karma* are removed completely under special conditions. Right knowledge, right faith and right conduct are the internal condition, while space, time etc., are external conditions. When all the conditions are favourable, the karmas are removed completely, and there arises *mukhya pratyakṣa*. It is clear and right knowledge. It is *atindriya i.e.* it does not depend on mind and sense organs. So it is perfect and infinite.

Kinds of mukhya pratyakṣa

According to *Jainas,* there are three types of *Mukhya Pratyakṣa,* namely, *avadhi jñāna,* maṇaḥparyāya and *keval jñāna.*

The first two are called *deśa pratyakṣa (vikala)* and the last one is called *sarva pratyakṣa (sakala).*

Avadhi Jñāna

The *'avadhi jñāna'* is non-sensuous knowledge. It means limitation/limited. Though *avadhi jñāna* is non-sensuous, it is limited. In this knowledge, one can perceive the objects, which possess form *(rūpa).* All the objects, which have form, are manifested in *avadhi* but all their modes cannot be manifested. It apprehends objects that possess form, although the objects are of the past, future are distant. It can apprehend very fine objects, such as the atoms and the karmic matter. *Avadhi jñāna* is divided into many types. All types of *avadhi jñāna* cannot apprehend all objects of all space and of all time. This faculty differs in different being on account of the development of their spiritual discipline. The highest type of *avadhi jñāna* is able to apprehend the material objects of all time and all space. The lower type of *avadhi jñāna* extends to a very small fraction of space and time. With regard to its possessor, the *avadhi jñāna* is of two types: *bhāva pratyakṣa* and *guṇa pratyakṣa.* This may also be interpreted as the knowledge, which is associated with the person right from his birth due to his previous karmas in his earlier births. This seems to us more logical than the traditional view. The former is that which arises in a person due to his birth, for example, beings of heaven and hell acquiring this kind of *avadhi jñāna* right from their birth.

The *guṇa pratyakṣa avadhi jñāna* is that which has to be acquired as a result of special merit. Everybody can acquire it when his *avadhi jñānāvaraṇa* is destroyed by meditation and discipline. Although both the type of avadhi jñāna arises by destruction and subsidence of its karmic veil, yet for the *bhāva pratyakṣa-avadhi jñāna,* the birth is the *nimitta kāraṇa,* who possesses it.

Manaḥparyāya Jñāna

The changing modes of minds are called *manaḥparyāya.* According to *Jainas,* mind is a material substance. Its modes are its different changing states. Depending on the change of state of thought, the mode also changes. And the knowledge, which knows the modes of thinking of the mind of other persons, is called manaḥparyāya *jñāna (parakīya manogatārtha jñānam manaḥparyāyaḥ).*[41] *A* person possessing manaḥparyāya *jñāna* directly knows the other mental states without the help of sense organs and mind. Such knowledge arises by the destruction and subsidence of *manaḥparyāya jñānavaraṇa: 'parakīya manogatārtha jñānam manaḥparyāyaḥ'.*[42]

There are different views on the nature of *manaḥparyāya jñāna.* According to *Jinabhadra,* in *manaḥparyāya jñāna,* one perceived the state of mind substance directly, but the external objects of thoughts of another mind are known only by inference. Because the external objects of thought may be material or non-material and the non-material object cannot be apprehended by *manaḥparyāya* (The *amūrtas* are known directly only in *kevala).* Akalarika rejects this and points out that manaḥparyāya *jñāna* also apprehends directly that object of other thought. The knowledge of such objects cannot be an inference: it is perceptual knowledge. Akalarika holds that the external objects also are directly apprehended by *manaḥ-paryāya,* as they are associated with mind. However, mind is not the cause of manaḥparyāya. Akalaṅka argues that mind is only the *apekṣā* in this knowledge, and not the cause. For example, when one sees the moon in the sky, one cannot see the moon without perceiving the sky. The sky is only the *apekṣ ā* and not the cause in the knowledge of moon. It is of two types: *ṛjumati* and *vipulamati*. They are different in respect of 'purity' and 'duration'. *Ṛjumati* is less pure and it sometimes flatters. *Vipulamati* is purer, cleaner and more enduring. It lasts upto the rise of omniscience. Man can possess both types of *manaḥparyāya*.

Kevala Jñāna

It is the perfect and infinite knowledge. We may call it omniscience. When the obstructions of all the *karmas* are destroyed, the self attains *kevala*. In this knowledge one apprehends simultaneously all substances and all the qualities without the assistance of sense organs and mind. Nothing remains to be known and nothing is unknown. It is perfect and eternal knowledge. The causes of omniscience are two: internal and external.

A question frequently asked is : whether the other knowledge like *avadhi* etc., are present or not, in the state of omniscience. According to some, all other knowledge exist, but is over powered by *kevala*. For example, the stars are not seen during the daytime. However, according to Umāsvāti, this view is not correct, because, *kevala* arises due to the total destruction of all karmic matter, while the other knowledge arises by the destruction and subsistence of their own *jñānāvaraṇa*. When there is the total destruction of karmic matters the other knowledge also could not arise. There would only be the state of omniscience.

We may now make some observations on the basis of the aforestated discussioin.

1. The *Jaina* view that the sense organs are not capable to apprehend the objects with all its permanent and changing qualities seems to be reasonable since sense organs have limited capacities.

2. According to *Jainas, pratyakṣa* is that type of knowledge, which is able to apprehend the objects with all its permanent and changing qualities and that is possible only by the self. Therefore, *pratyakṣa* means, the knowledge arising in the self directly.
3. The knowledge of the object derived from the sense organs is called *sarhvyavaharika pratyakṣa*. The *Jaina* not only defines *saṁvyavahārika pratyakṣa* but also analyzes the process involved in it. The process consists in the four stages of *avagraha, īhā, avāya and dhāraṇā*. The idea of four states is original to this system. Though other systems of Indian philosophy distinguish between *nirvikalpaka* and *savikalpaka* perception, their distinction is not as thorough as that of the *Jainas*. No other system has given us such an account of the different states of sense perception.
4. The concept of non-sensuous knowledge of the *Jaina* philosophy is based on their metaphysics. According to *Jainas,* knowledge is the essential quality of the self. The pure self possesses infinite knowledge, but due to the veil of the karmic matters, it cannot realize its true nature. When the obstruction of true nature is destroyed knowledge arises in the self. The self can know objects directly without the help of the sense organs.
5. Regarding the nature of non-sensuous perception, the *Jainas* are not very clear. They simply say that in *avadhi jñāna* one apprehends material objects directly by the self. In *manaḥparyāya* the knowledge of other mind is acquired and in *keval jñāna,* the self possesses the knowledge of all things past, present and future and also of its own pure nature. The *Jainas* do not say much about the nature of it. How does the self apprehend the object? Does it apprehend the objects as done by the sense organs? Do other objects come in contact with the self only in the shape of ideas, in this knowledge purely subjective experience like the

pleasure and pain! These questions are left unanswered.

6. The *Jainas* hold that everybody can become an omniscient, while most other schools believe only in God as the omniscient being. According to *Nyāya,* a Yogi can acquire omniscience, this is not permanent, owing the state of release, and there would be no knowledge. Only God's omniscience is eternal.

7. Regarding the nature of omniscient or *kevala jñāna,* the *Jainas* are not very clear. They simply say that in *kevala jñāna,* the self possesses knowledge of all.

This may be compared with the Yogic perception of the *Nyāya* and other systems. In *Nyāya,* there are three types of extra ordinary perception. The first two, *sāmānya lakṣaṇā* and *jñāna lakṣaṇā* cannot be called atindriya *pratyakṣa* from *Jaina* point of view. *Atindriya pratyakṣa* is not caused by the sense organs and mind whereas *sāmānya lakṣaṇā* and *jñāna lakṣaṇā* arise with the help of the senses. Though there is no direct sense object contact, there is indirect contact. The *Jaina* also would argue that *sāmānya lakṣaṇā* is not *pratyakṣa* at all, for the *'pratyakṣa'* is a clear knowledge. The *Yogi pratyakṣa* of the *Naiyāyikas* may be called as *atindriya pratyakṣa.* It may be compared with *kevala jñāna* of *Jainas.*

The *Brahmānda* of *Advaitins* is *atindriya jñāna* but there is no knowledge of the object of the past, present and future. There is no question of direct apprehension of all objects of the world is in Brahma *jñāna.* There is the direct apprehension of the self, only that is called *Brahma.* They also accept the direct apprehension of the pure self in the stage of *kevala.* The *Yogi patyaksa* of the Buddhist may be called *atindriya pratyakṣa,* because it is not caused by sense organs. It is the direct intuition of transcendental reality. But the *Jaina* does not accept the *Nirvikalpaka* character of it. According to *Jaina,* knowledge must be determinate. As mentioned above, determinate-ness is the criterion of the right knowledge.

Smṛti: (Recollection)

We have already recorded that *parokṣa pramāṇa* is divided into five types viz. *smṛti, pratyabhijñāna, tarka, aṇumāna* and *āgama,* because these *pramāṇas* are dependent on other means of knowing *i.e.* perception.

Recollection is accepted as valid and independent means of knowing in Jainism alone. It is defined as:

1. स्मरणं स्मृतिः।[43]
2. तत्तोल्लोखिज्ञानं स्मरणम्।[44]
3. संस्कारोदबोधानिबन्धना तदित्याकारा स्मृतिः। स देवदत्तो यथा।[45]
4. स्मृतिजीवादितत्त्वानां यथात्म्यानुस्मृतिः स्मृताः। गुणानुसरणं वा स्यात् सिद्धार्हत्परमेष्टिनाम्।।[46]

Recollection is a cognition, which has for its condition the stimulation of a memory impression (retention *i.e. vasanā* or *samskāra)* and which refers to its content by a form of the pronoun 'that' *(tad)*.

When requisite conditions such as the elimination and subsidence of obstructive veils, observation of similar objects and the like (similarity, contiguity and contrast of modern psychology) are at work to bring it to maturation, recollection occurs. And so the clause, 'which has for is condition the stimulation of a memory impression' has been stated. The phrase, which refers to its content by a form of the pronoun 'that' is inserted for its mode of communication.

Other systems of Indian philosophy including Buddhism deny to accept it as a independent *pramāṇa*. But all have accepted it and explained it as a helping factor in the process of various *pramāṇas*. On the contrary, *Jaina* philosophers have accepted it as a valid means of knowing by asserting that the *samskāras* recall for any particular purpose the things experienced in the past. The memory of such things is a source of knowledge obtained through senses. Therefore, it has to be accepted as a *pramāṇa,* since it is true of facts *'samvādin'* just as perception.

Pratyabhijñāna: (Recognition)

Pratyabhijñāna i.e. recognition is a synthetic judgment, which is the result of observation and recollection as specified by such forms as 'that necessarily is it' *(tadavedaṁ),* 'he is that same *Devadatta' (soyaṁ devadattaḥ),* 'it is like that' *(tadśādṛsaṃ),* 'that is dissimilar to that' (*tadvilakṣaṇaṁ*), this is different from that' *(tad pratiyogī)* and the like. It is defined thus:

1. तदेवेदमिति स्मरणं प्रत्यभिज्ञानम्। तदकस्मान्नभवतीति योऽस्य हेतुः स तद्भावः। भवनं भावः। तस्य भावस्तद्भावः। येनात्मना प्रग्हष्टं वस्तु तेनैवात्मना पुनरपि भावात्तदेवेदमिति प्रत्यभिज्ञायते।[47]

2. अनुभवस्मृतिहेतुकं तिर्यमूधर्वतासामान्यादिगोचरं संकलनात्मकं ज्ञानं प्रत्यभिज्ञानम्। यथा तज्जातीय एवायं गोपिण्डः गोशदृशो गवयः स एवायं जिनदत्त इत्यादि।[48]

3. अनुभवस्मृतिर्व्यैतिरिक्तं प्रत्यभिज्ञानं नास्तीति तदसत् अनुभवस्य वर्तमानकालवर्तिविवर्तमात्रप्रकाशत्वम् स्मृतेश्चातीतविवर्त्तद्योतकत्वमिनि नावद्वस्तुगतिः। कथं नाम तयोरतीतवर्त्तमान।[49]

Recognition is a complex mode of cognition. It includes both perception and recollection. Perception is the direct observation of the objects existing before our sense organs. Recollection is reproduction of the latent mental trace. These two are the condition of recognition. Thus, recognition is a kind of synthetic judgment. When perception and recollection are combined in particular form, recognition emerges. It delivers its contents in forms like the following: 'that necessarily is it' is one of the forms. It is the judgement of identity. All such judgment as 'this is necessarily jar, cloth, that man etc. are the cases of this type. When the same object is cognized on different occasions, such judgments occur. 'This is like that' is the judgment of similarity. When we happen to come across an object, which is similar to another one that has already been experienced, such judgments as 'this is like that' emerges. All such judgments as 'this book is like that one' 'my house is like that of yours' etc. are the cases of the judgment of similarity.

There are certain judgments that are just reverse to the judgments of the similarity. 'The buffalo is dissimilar to the cow', 'the horse is dissimilar to the ass' and the like can be mentioned as examples of the variety of judgment. This is called the judgment of dissimilarity. There is also the judgment of difference. All such judgments as 'ten is less than twenty', 'five is more than three', 'the elephant is heavier than camel' etc. are the cases of the judgments of difference.

Tarka: (Reasoning)

Reasoning helps us in arriving at certain conclusions in our experience. It elaborates and expands the materials collected and conserved by the processes like sensation, speculation and perception etc. It is an immense extension of the bounds of our experiences. It helps us in getting a glimpse of the remote past, unseen present and distant future. It is through reasoning that we discover mutual relations of different concepts. It is the power of reasoning upon which our inferential judgments are based. It is defined in the tradition as:

1. ईहा, ऊहा, तर्क परीक्षा विचारणा जिज्ञासा इत्यनर्थान्तरम्।[50]
2. साध्यसाधानसंबन्धाज्ञानविवृत्तिरूपेसाक्षात् स्वार्थनिश्चयने फले साधकतमस्तर्कः।[51]
3. व्याप्तिज्ञानं तर्कः। साध्यसाधनयोर्गम्यगमकभावप्रयोजको व्यभिचार-गन्धासहिष्णुः संबन्धविशेषो व्याप्तिरविनाभाव इति च व्यपदिश्यते तत् सामर्थ्यात् खल्वग्न्यादिधूमादिरेव गमयाति न तु घटादि तदभावात्। तस्याश्चाविनाभावापरनाम्न्याः व्याप्तेः प्रमितौ यत्साधकतमं तदिदं तर्काख्यं प्रमाणमित्यर्थः। यत्र यत्र धूमवत्त्वं तत्र तत्राग्निमत्वमिति।[52]
4. उपलम्भानुपलम्भसंभव त्रिकालीकलितसाध्यसाधनसंबन्धाद्या-लम्बनमिदमस्मिन् सत्येव भवतीत्याद्याकारं सवेदनमूहस्तर्कापरपर्यायः। यथा यावान् कश्चिद् घूमः स सर्वो वह्नौ सत्येव भवतीति तस्मिन्नसति असौ न भवत्येवेति वा।[53]

Reasoning is the knowledge of invariable concomitance conditioned by observation *(upalambha)* and non-observation *(aṇupaiambha)*. Observation means the knowledge of existence of *sādhya i.e.* the thing to be proved, on the existence of the *linga* or *sādhana*. Non-observation stands for the knowledge of non-existence of the *sādhana* or *linga* where there is no *sādhya,* or it can be given judgments to a new one. For example, we observe smoke and fire together in our day-to-day experience. This observation is not confined to one or two cases only. We observe the same on many occasions and reach the final conclusion that smoke is necessarily related to fire. On the basis of this, we infer the existence of fire from the sight of smoke. Our inferential judgment develops through the process of reasoning somewhat in the following manner: 'I saw smoke and fire together so many times and I never saw smoke without fire although I sometimes saw fire without smoke. Thus, we infer, because here is smoke, therefore, here must be fire'. In short, our reasoning derives the conclusion that whatever is a case of smoke is invariably the product exclusively of fire.

It should not be maintained that such knowledge of invariable concomitance is derived exclusively from perceptual cognition. It is beyond the capacity of perception to derive the knowledge of universal concomitance, since our empirical perception is limited, whereas the knowledge of invariable concomitance is unlimited. In other words perception is not discursive and owes its genesis to the influence exerted by a datum that is present in a limited sense.

Nor, it can be maintained that such knowledge is obtained by inference, since, inference itself is not possible in the absence of invariable concomitance has been apprehended as an antecedent condition of inference. Such being the case, how is it possible that the knowledge of invariable concomitance *i.e.* the reasoning can be obtained by inference? It follows, therefore, that the reasoning or *'tarka'* is a separate means of knowledge of invariable concomitance, which is not apprehended by other recognized means.

Anumāna: (Inference)

In Jainism *Anuman pramāṇa* is included in the *parokṣa pramāṇa,* owing to its dependence on other cognition *i.e.* perceptual cognition *(pratyakṣa)*. It is defined as follows:

1. साधानात्साध्यविज्ञानमनुमानं तदत्यये विरोधान्त्क्वचिदेकस्य विधानप्रति-षेधयो:।[54]

2. साधनात्साध्यज्ञानुमानम्।[55]

Inference is the knowledge of the probandum *(sādhya)* on the strength of the probans *(sādhana)*. Or in other words, the knowledge of the probandum in which is the nature of authentic cognition of a real fact and which arises from a probans either observed or expressly stated is called inference. It means, the cognition of *sādhya i.e.* that what is to be known, produced by *sādhana i.e.* the instrument to prove the *sādhya* is called *aṇumāna,* which follows *lingagrahaṇa* (*i.e.* apprehension of the predicate of proposition and *vyāptismarana i.e.* the remembrance of invariable concomitance). And because it is *avisambādin i.e.* non-discrepant in its own subject and removes the obstacles arising due to doubt *(samsaya),* perversion *(viparyaya)* and indecision *(anadhyavasāya)*. Thus, it should be considered as *apramāṇa*.

It is of two kinds; for one's own self *i.e. svārthānumāṇa* or subjective and for the sake of others *i.e. parārthānumāna* or syllogistic.

Subjective inference is defined as:

1. अत्रान्यथानुपपत्त्येकलक्षणहेतु ग्रहणसंबन्धस्मरणकारणकं साध्यविज्ञानं स्वार्थम्।[56]

2. परोपदेशमनपेक्ष स्वयमेव निश्चितात्प्राक्तकानुभूतव्याप्तिस्मरणसह-कृताद्धूमादे: साधनादुत्पन्नपर्वतादौ धर्मिण्यग्न्यादे: साध्यस्य ज्ञानं स्वार्थानुमानमित्यर्थ:।[57]

It consists in the knowledge of the prodbandum from the probans ascertained by one's own self as having the sole and solitary characteristic of standing in necessary concomitance with the probandum. Necessary concomitance with the probandum means the impossibility of the probans apart from the probandum. The knowledge of the probandum from such a probans definitely cognized by the arguer himself as having for sole and solitary characteristic of inseparable relation with the probandum is called *Svārthānumāna*.

Parārthānumāna or syllogistic inference is defined as definite cognition resulting from a statement of a probans having the characteristic of necessary concomitance with the probandum. It is defined thus:

1. परार्थतु तदर्थपरामार्शिवचनाज्जातम्। तद्वचनमपि तद्धेतुत्वात्।[58]

2. परोपदेशमपेक्ष्य साधनात्साध्यविज्ञानं परार्थनुमानम्। प्रतिज्ञाहेतुरूप परोपदेशवशाच्छ्रोतुरुपपन्नं साधनात्साध्यविज्ञानं परार्थानुमानमित्यर्थः।[59]

The definite authentic cognition of a fact that arises from a statement of a person having the sole and solitary characteristic of necessary concomitance with the probandum is called *Parārthānumāna.* In other words, it is the knowledge of the probandum derived from the communication made by another person.

Invariable concomitance *i.e. vyāpti* is the main feature of *aṇumāna.* It is defined thus:

1. व्याप्तिर्हि साध्ये वह्न्यादौ सत्येव साधनं धूमादिरस्ति। असति तु नास्तीति साध्यसाधननियतसाहचर्य लक्षणां। एवमेवं साध्यं विना साधनस्याभावादविना भावमिति च व्यपदिश्यन्ते।[60]

2. व्याप्तित्वं साहचर्यस्यनियमः स यथा मिथः। सति यत्र यः स्यादेव न स्यादेवासतीह यः।[61]

Avinābhāva, anyathānupannatva, vipakṣavyāvṛtti and *nityasāhacarya* are well known characteristics of *vyāpti*. Thus, Akalaṅka very precisely says that *sahabhāvaniyamaḥ i.e.* having co-relation and *kramabhāvaniyamaḥ i.e.* having successive relation and *tadutpatti i.e.* identical cause or origination serve the grouond for inference. But it can also be applied to those things, which do not possess of the *tādāmya* and *tadutpatti* relation. For example, we can make an inference about the taste of something looking of its form, which has no *tādātmya* relation.

Regarding the organs or the constitution of syllogism of *parāsthānumāna* there is no unanimity views of the *Jaina* tradition. They have accepted the number of *avayavas* with regards to the *pramātṛ i.e.* to whom it is addressed, of a particular inferential cognition. In other words, the capability or the standard of *pramātṛ* determines the number of the member of syllogism. That is the reason why we find in Jainism sometimes ten *avayavas,* sometimes five, or three or even one. In *agamic* period particularly Bhadrabahu has accepted the number upto ten but in the logical period we find the philosopher like Akalaṅka has restricted it up to five being influenced by the *Nyāya* school of philosophy.

Āgama Pramāṇa:

'Word', according to *Jainas,* is a material stuff like earth. It exists even when it is not heard. Thus, the *Jainas'* view go with the *Mīmāṁsā* theory that 'word' is eternal whether perceived or otherwise. But unlikely the *Mīmāṁsakas,* the *Jainas* do not maintain that the word stuff is unchangingly real. A change is the form of a word from its unperceived form to perceive form involves a change in the character of word.

It is defined.as follows:

1. आप्तोपज्ञमनल्लडध्यंदृष्टविरोधकम्। तत्वोपदेशकृत्सार्वशास्त्रंकापथ घट्टनम्।[62]
2. पूर्वापरविरुद्धादेर्व्यापेतो दोषसंहते। द्योतक: सर्वभावनामाप्तव्याहरिागम:। आगमो ह्याप्तवचनमाप्तं दोषक्षयंविदु: त्यक्तदोषोऽनृतं वाक्यं नब्रूयाद्धेत्व-संभावात्।[63]
3. आप्तेन हि क्षीणदोषेण प्रत्यक्षाज्ञानेनप्रणीत आगमो भवति न सर्व:। यदि सर्व: स्यात् अविशेषस्यात्।[64]
4. आप्तवाक्यनिबन्धनमर्थज्ञानामागम:।[65]
5. आसामस्त्येनानन्तधर्मविशिष्टतया ज्ञायन्तेऽववुद्धयन्ते जीवाजीवादय: पदार्था यया सा प्रज्ञा आगम: शासनम्।[66]

The concept of omniscient being is very much important in the context of verbal testimony. In this regard, the *Jainas* point out that the *āgama* is *'pauruṣeya'.* The *Jainas* deny the existence of 'God' as an Omniscient Being who creates *āgama,* but they do not deny the existence of *Tīrthaṅkaras* as omniscient Beings.

The words of an *āpta* are called *āgama*. *Āpta* means a person of superior intellect and character, who is non-discrepant (*i.e. avisaṁvādin)* in his respective subjects. The *Jainas* believe that their prophets were *āptas* and therefore they accept *āgamas* as an independent *pramāṇa*. An *āpta* is a person who knows the real nature of a thing about which he speaks and who speaks according to his correct knowledge. Only words of such a person established without any opposition are *pramāṇa*. Such an *āpta* can be of two types:

(a) Laukika

(b) Alaukika or *Lokottara*.

An *āpta* is free from all faults. Regarding the nature of *āpta* Kundnakundạcārya observes: he who is free from all defects and is possessed of all pure attributes in the supreme authority. The defects are: hunger, thirst, fear, anger, attachment, perspiration, fatigue, pride, indulgence, surprise, sleep, birth, and restlessness. A person freld from all these defects is called a perfect one. Being freed from faults he reveals the scripture. He is of highest status and is of unpassed splendor. He is free from attachment and devoid of impurities. He has no beginning, middle and end and is a friend and teacher of all living beings. [67] Just as a drum sounds being struck by a drummer without any desire of its own, so an *āpta* reveals the truth for the benefit of all people without any personal motive.[68] That alone is true scripture, which flows spontaneously out of the āpta, which is irrefutable, which is salutary for the well being of all beings, which is capable of undermining the perverse path and lastly which reveals the objective nature of things.

The most salient and central of all the above features are the belief in the seven *tattvas*. The *Jaina ācāryas* are of the opinion that belief in an *āpta,* the guru, the scripture etc., is valid if it engenders belief in the *tattvas*.

To overcome the difficulty arising from the scriptural texts propounding contradictory theories, the *Jaina* philosophers distinguish between valid and invalid scriptures. Akalaṅkadeve uses consistency *i.e. avisaṁvadatva* as the criterion of a valid scripture. But on this criterion, the validity of other scriptures cannot be denied. Consistency cannot be claimed to be the special prerogative of the *Jaina* scriptures alone. We have a very interesting objection raised by Santaraksita, a Buddhist philosopher: 'If *Saugata* is omniscient, why not Kapila also, and if both are omniscient, why are there difference of opinion between them.[69] Any reply to this will only be a shifting of position or a dogmatic assertion of one's own position.

According to the *Jainas, Tīrthaṅkaras* like Mahāvīra are *āptas,* whose statements being the source of valid knowledge are taken to be the verbal testimony. An *āpta* is a *Kevalin i.e.* he has the knowledge of things from all points of view. He is possessed of both *jñāna* (knowledge) and *darśana* (intuition). The question, whether *jñāna* and *darśana* of *kevalin* occur simultaneously or successively is a matter of controversy among different *Jaina* philosophers.

Digaṁbara ācārya unanimously holds that the *jñāna* and *darśana* of a *kevalin* occur simultaneously. Umāsvāti and his followers, Pujyapāda, Akalaṅkadeva, Vidyānanda etc., also support this view. Kundakunda too believes that *jñāna* and *darśana* are simultaneous. Jinabhadra, a great upholder of the agamic view bases his objections on the scriptural texts and established traditions, which unanimously recognize alternate occurrence *of jñāna* and *darśana.*

The *Anuyogadvāra* recognizes two types of *āgamas* (scripture), which we have already recorded,

(a) Empirical *(Laukika)* and

(b) Transcendental *(Alaukika).*

The *non-Jaina Śāstras* like the Vedas, the *Mahābhāratas,* the seventy-two sciences and arts are included in the first category.

The second type comprises the *Jaina Śāstra* only. It seems that in the early period the words of *"Jīna" i.e.* omniscient persons were regarded as *pramāṇa* but gradually even the words of *'śruta kevalin'* came to be regarded as *pramāṇa,* not independently, but on the ground that they were always in consonance with the *āgamas*.

Kinds of verbal testimony

Verbal testimony may be personal or scriptural. A young man coming to the side of a river cannot ascertain whether the river is fordable or not. And immediately an experienced old man of the locality, who has no enmity with him comes and tells him that the river is easily fordable. The word of the old man is to be accepted as a source of valid knowledge. It is personal testimony or *laukika śabda.*

Scripture is also a source of valid knowledge, for it lays down injunctions on matters, which baffle perceptions and inference. For instance, it teaches that misery is the consequence of vice. Knowledge derived from this source is called scriptural testimony. Scripture is defined as that which was first cognized or composed by a competent person and which is not such as to be passed over by others. And which is not incompatible with the truth derived from perception, which imparts true instructions and which is profitable to all men and is preventive of all evil paths.[70]

Validity of Verbal Testimony

The *prāmāṇya* and *aprāmāṇya* of *āgama* depends on the right and wrong attitude of the author. All words are neutral, hence, neither *prāmāṇa* nor *apramāṇa.* The validity or invalidity of words depends upon the attitude of this knower. If his attitude is right, whatever he knows becomes right, and if his attitude is wrong, his knowledge also becomes wrong. Siddhasena Divākara defines *śabda* or verbal testimony as a valid knowledge, which arises from a right understanding of the words that come from the mouth of an *āpta,* express the real object, and not contradicted by perception. The purpose of verbal testimony is to instruct, to relate the nature of reality, to be beneficial to all and to remove false notion. But is it not possible to speak the untruth consistently? Again, is it not possible to have coherence in the body of the knowledge, in spite of its being wholly wrong? So, it seems that Siddhasena Divākara has taken a step forward in the right direction when he states that verbal testimony to be *pramāṇa* must be self consistent, and coherent and also must not be in conflict with other *pramāṇa* like perceptions. Later philosophers like Samantabhadra, Akalaṅka follow his view in this regard.

He elaborates further that words expressing the real objects and consistent with the whole body of the speaker's knowledge generate valid knowledge in the hearer, provided he understands the import rightly. Even the words of an *āpta* may cause wrong knowledge if the hearer is not a suitable receiver. For valid knowledge in the listener, word should not only come from.

Verbal testimony: an independent pramāṇa

The Buddhists and the *Vaiśeṣikas* do not consider verbal testimony as an independent *pramāṇa.* The *Jaina* philosophers do not subscribe to this view. On the contrary, they along with the *Naiyāyikas,* the *Sāṁkhya-Yoga* philosophers, the *Mīmāṁsakas* and the *Vedāntins* maintain that verbal testimony is an independent *pramāṇa.*

The Jainism differs from the *Cārvākas,* Buddhism, and *Vaiśeṣikas* in accepting *śabda* as a *pramāṇa. Cārvāka's* denial of *śabda* as a *pramāṇa* is unconditional, whereas Buddhism and *Vaiśeṣika* do not deny the attainment of knowledge through it, but they do not consider it as an independent source of knowledge. Instead, they take it as a case of inference. But Jainism has completely positive attitudes in this regard. According to it, *śabda* as a source of valid knowledge is independent of other *pramāṇas.*

Once *śabda* in general is accepted to be a *pramāṇa,* it becomes difficult to differentiate the valid authority from the invalid one. None of the criteria, namely, consistency, coherence, and verifiability through perception can be made basis for rejecting other scriptures as untrue or invalid.

If the validity of verbal testimony is not intrinsic but subject to its verification by perception etc., the independence-ness of *śabda pramāṇa,* as claims the *Jainas* falls flat.

In the end it is worth mentioning in favour of the *Jaina* philosophers that though the *Jainas* describe the testimony of *Tīrthṅkaras* as transcendental, or *lokottara,* it is not in fact super mundane and super human. The *Tīrthṅkaras* are not other-worldly or super natural deities, but the human beings, liberated from the clutches of the bondage *of karma.* The ideal *of Tīrthṅ-kara* hood is common to all. Anybody, through self efforts and self discipline can queer the karma, can attain the state of *kevalin,* and thus can become an *āpta* whose statement qualify for being true or valid verbal testimony. In this respect the *Jaina* concept of verbal testimony is more appealing than the orthodox concept in which a super mundane divine Being in the name of God is generally accepted to be the ultimate source of the verbal testimony.

Anekāntavāda:

Anekāntavāda is the foundation of the *Jaina* philosophy, on which the mansion of *Jaina* philosophy stands. According to Jainism, the reality is dynamic, which is having innumerable characteristic, hence cannot be perceived or known at once by an ordinary man. Different people look at from different aspects of the same reality and therefore, their partial findings seem to be contradictory to one other. Hence, they indulge in debates claiming that each of them was completely true. The *Jaina* philosophers thought over this conflict and tried to reveal the whole truth by establishing a theory of non-absolutist standpoint *i.e. Anekāntavāda,* based on two theories, namely, *Nayavāda* and *Syādvāda.*

To understand the reality there are two mutually distinct and fundamental standpoints from which all things can be considered. They are universalization and particularization. Universalization starts with the observation on a synthetic basis of similarities and gradually reacts the level where distinction exists and finally concludes that any object of consciousness is in reality an element. On the other hand, particularization is based on observation of dissimilarities, which finally leads on to the conclusion that the universe is, but a conglomeration of completely dissimilar existence.

These two standpoints have given rise to several other conceptions in Indian philosophy. They can be classified into five principal categories viz.

(i) The conception of identity.

(ii) The conception of difference.

(iii) The conception of subordinating difference to identity.

(iv) The conception of subordinating identity to difference.

(v) The conception of identity-in-difference.

Out of these five conceptions the last one viz. the conception of identity-in-difference is developed by the *Jaina* philosophers, which plays a great role to understand the theory of *anekānta*.

About the nature of reality there are many conflicting views and heated arguments, which confused the minds of the people to such a degree that it becomes essential to reconsider this burning philosophical question in a conciliatory spirit. This important steps was taken by the *Jainas* and the result was the theory of *anekāntavdda,* which, postulates a theory of manifold methods of analysis *i.e. Nayavāda* and synthesis *i.e. Syādvāda.*

The nature of reality, according to his theory, is permanent in change. It possesses three common characters viz. *utpāda i.e.* origination, *vyaya i.e.* destruction and *dhrauvya i.e.* permanence through birth and decay.[71] It also possesses the attributes *i.e. guṇas* which is called *anvayl* and which co-exist with substance *(drávya)* and modifications *(parydya)* which is called *vyatirekl,* and which succeed each other.[72] And productivity and destructivity constitute the dynamic aspect of an entity and permanence is the enduring factor.[73]

Ankekantavada is a theory by which one is able to know the real nature of the many-faced reality. It is defined as:

अनेकवहवोन्ता अंशा धर्मा वा आत्मनः स्वरूपाणि यस्य तदनेात्मकम्।[74]

Syādvāda (The conditional Dialectic)

or

Saptabhahgi (The Theory of Sevenfold Predication)

Saptabhaṅgī, or the theory of sevenfold predication, is treated as synonymous with *syādvāda* owing to the fact that the number of possible or alternative truths under the conditional method of *syādvāda* are, as will be noticed hereafter, seven only.

The fact that the term '*syādvāda*' is often treated as standing for the entire Jaina philosophy is due to the dread importance attached to the method of the conditional dialectic with which it (the term) is most intimately connected. The controversy as to whether '*syādvāda'* is a synonym of *'saptabhangī'* or of the entire *Jaina* philosophy is, therefore, a needlessly scholastic one, at any rate from the philosophical standpoint.

Syādvāda or *Saptabhaṅgī* is defined in the tradition as follows:

1. धर्मिणोऽनन्तरूपत्वं धर्माणां न कथंचन। अनेकन्तोऽप्यनेकान्त इति जैनमतं मतः।[75]

2. स्यात्कथचिंत् विविक्षितप्रकारेणनेकान्तरूपेण वदनं वादो-जल्पः कथनं प्रतिपादनमिति स्याद्वादः।[76]

3. उत्पाद्यते उत्पाद्येत येनासौ वादः, स्यादिति वादो वाचकः शब्दो यस्यानेकान्तवादस्यादौ स्याद्वादः।[77]

4. णियमणिसेहणसीलो णिपादणदो य जोहु खलु सिद्धो, सो सियसहो भणियो जो सावेक्खं पसाहेदि।[78]

5. एकस्मिन् वस्तुनि प्रश्नवाशाद् दृष्टेनेष्टेन च प्रमाणेनाविरुद्धा विधिप्रतिषेध विकल्पना सप्तभंगी विज्ञेया।[79]

6. एकस्मिन्नविरोधेन प्रमाणनयवाक्यतः। सदादिकल्पना या च सप्तभंगीति सा मता।

7. प्रश्निकप्रश्नज्ञानप्रयोज्यत्वे सति एकवस्तुविशेष्यकाविरुद्धविधि-प्रतिषेधा-त्मक धर्मप्रकारकबोधजनकसप्तवाक्यं पर्याप्तिसमुदायत्वम्।[80]

Syādvāda or *Saptabhaṅgī* is that conditional method in which the modes, or predications *(bhaṅgāḥ)* affirm *(vidhi)*, negate *(niṣedha)* or both affirm and negate, severally, *(pṛthagbhūta)* or jointly *(samudita)*, in seven different ways, a certain attribute *(dharma)* of a thing (*vasta*) without incompatiblity ·*(avirodhena)* in a certain context *(praśnavaśāt)*. That is, no modal assertion, or proposition, simple or complex; affirmative, negative or both, can, at once, express anything other than an aspect *(prakāra)* of the truth of a thing. The full truth, or rather the synthesis of truths, can result only from a well-ordered scheme of propositions *(vacanavinyāsa)*. Each proposition is, therefore, relative to, or alternative with, the other propositions, which, in their totality, present the full of the thing with respect to the particular attribute, predicated of it. The *Jaina* maintains that *saptabhaṅgī* offers such a well-ordered scheme in which the modes *(bhaṅgas)* are exclusive of one another, but are at the same time, in their totality, exhaustive of the many-sided truth of the indeterminate real under discussion.

It is difficult to translate *syādvāda* into English or any modern Indian languages. Some of the suggested English equivalents like 'probably', may be', 'perhaps', 'indefinitely' and so forth are inadequate, if not somewhat misleading. Its main significance lies in its emphasis on the indeterminate or manifold nature of the real, which like all other reals, comes within its purview. Indeterminateness or manifoldness means that the reals cannot be determined as possessing only such and such attributes and not the rest. The nature of reality is expressed completely by none of them for in its concrete richness it admits all predicates. Every proposition is therefore in strictness only conditional. Absolute affirmation and absolute negation are both erroneous. It is this conception of reality 'as extremely indeterminate in nature' that is suggested or 'illumined' by the term *'syāt'*. A phrase which will approximately bring out this in-deterministic significance of *'syāt'* would be 'from a certain point of view', or 'in a certain sense', or some other equivalent form.

Another Sanskrit word which is used to suggest that each of the conclusions signified by the seven modes is exclusive—

that is, does not encroach upon the province of the conclusions pointed out by the other modes is ' eva' which may be translated as 'only' or 'certainly' (or in some equivalent form such as 'there is no doubt', or 'without doubt'). For instance, the first mode, syādastyeva ghaṭaḥ, means: "In a certain sense, the jar exists without doubt." This sense of exclusion *(vyāvṛtyartham)* seems to be more prominent than implies the other and both the functions, which may also be, described as restrictive force and the definitive force, respectively—which are inherent in the word.

The *syādvāda* warns us against allowing *'eva'* to proceed beyond its prescribed limits of exercising the restrictive and deterministically articulating influence on the mode within which it functions. That is, its force *(sāmarthya)* is confined to the avoidance of intrusions from the other modes and to the bringing of a definitive articulation into the mode with which it is connected.

Let us present the seven modes with the help of the example of a 'jar' or 'pot'. The seven modes are:

(1) In a certain sense, the jar is *(syādastī ghaṭaḥ)*.

(2) In a certain sense, the jar is not *(syānnāsti ghaṭaḥ)*:-

(3) In a certain sense, the jar is and is not *(syādasti nāsti caghaṭaḥ)*.

(4) In a certain sense, the jar is inexpressible *(syādavaktavyo ghaṭaḥ)*.

(5) In a certain sense, the jar is and is inexpressible *(syādastyavaktavyaśca ghaṭaḥ)*.

(6) In a certain sense, the jar is not and is inexpressible *(syānnāstyavaktavyaśca ghaṭaḥ)*.

(7) In a certain sense, the jar is, is not and is inexpressible *(syādastināsti cāvaktavyaśca ghaṭaḥ)*.

The first mode, represented by the proposition, "In a certain sense the jar is", asserts the existent or positive aspect of the jar. By virtue of the fact that the existence of the jar is inseparably bound up with the non- existence of linen *(paṭa)* etc. in it. What the proposition signifies is that for some reason at the moment of our making the assertion, our attention is being focused primarily *(pradhānatayā)* on the existent aspect of the jar is to be understood in terms of its self-quaternary, and the non-existent aspect, in terms of the other-quaternary. If, on the contrary, the jar is understood to be capable of being the linen as well *(itararūpāpattyāpi),* then it will surely lose its very nature *(svarūpahāniprasaṅgaḥ)* as a distinctive existent, viz., a jar. This claim for a distinctive existence is guaranteed by implicitly understood term 'eva' in the proposition.

The second fundamental concept is 'non-being' *(asat).* It is embodied in the second predication, viz., 'the jar not'. It is the negative *(niṣedha)* element in the determinate context of the concrete nature of the full make-up of the jar. The main significance of the second mode lies not in the false statement that the jar does not exist as the jar but in the irrefutable statement that the jar does not exist as linen or anything else.

The third mode offers successive presentation *(kramār-paṇa)* and the fourth one offers a simultaneous presentation *(sahārpaṇa)* of the two concepts. Although the third mode appears to be one proposition, it entails, in actual fact, two propositions, which are expressed as one owing to a certain verbal facility. But the verbal togetherness does not signify a logical co-presence of the propositions, or the concepts they embody.

No such difficulties arise in the case of the third predication which is concerned with presenting, consecutively *(kramār-paṇayā),* the two aspects of 'being' and non-being', although it is expressed in the shortened form of a single proposition.

The remaining three modes are derived from combining the three primary concepts in such a way that these three, combined with the four modes hitherto expounded, exhaust all the possible or alternative aspects of truth concerning the object in question (the jar in the present instance).

The fifth mode, viz., "In a certain sense, the jar is, and is inexpressible", asserts the truth of the 'being' of the jar conjointly with the inexpressible truth of the competence of the being and the non-being of the same object. This is a combined mode derived from bringing together the first and the fourth predicates in a complex expressed judgement.

The sixth mode, viz., "In a certain sense, the jar is not, and is inexpressible", asserts the truth of non-being of the jar conjointly with the inexpressible truth of the competence of the 'being' and the 'non-being' of the same object. This again, is a combined mode resulting from bringing together the second and the fourth predicates a complex expressed judgement.

The seventh and last mode, viz., "In a certain sense, the jar is, is not, and is inexpressible", combines the consecutive presentation of the 'being' and the 'non-being', conjointly with the co-presentation or co-presence, of the 'being' and the 'non-being' of the jar. This mode is evidently a resultant of bringing together, within its fold, the third and the fourth predicates of the conditional dialectic.

Unlike the first two and the fourth predications, each of which contains a simple predicate involving one of the three primary concepts, the fifth, the sixth and seventh predications are, severally, complex in structure, the last one being the most complex among them. This is so because they are assertions of complex judgements.

These are seven modes each, which contain one alternative truth, while all together contain the total truth of a situation in which any feature predicated of a real is investigated.

Nayavāda: (The Theory of Standpoints)

Nayavāda and syādvāda are two complementary processes of the relativistic presupposition of the Jaina metaphysics, forming a scheme, which is pre-eminently one of correlative methods.

Nayavāda is principally an analytical method investigating a particular standpoint of a factual situation according to the purpose and the level of equipment of the experiment *(jñātṛ)*.

The particular standpoint thus investigated is one among a multitude of different viewpoints which, in their totally, reflect the full nature of the situation. *Syādvāda,* or *saptabhaṅgī,* is essentially a synthetically method designed to harmonize the different viewpoints arrived at by *nayavāda.*

A naya is defined as follows:

1. जीवादीन् पदार्थान् नयन्ति प्राप्नुवन्ति कारयन्ति साधयन्ति निर्वर्तयन्ति निर्भासयन्ति उपलम्भयन्ति व्यञ्जयन्ति इति नय:।[81]
2. नीयते एकदेशविशिष्टोऽर्थः प्रतीतिविषयमाभिरिति नीतयो नया:।[82]
3. ज्ञानं प्रमाणमित्याहुरूपायो न्यास उच्यते नयो ज्ञातुरभिप्रया युक्तितोऽर्थपरिग्रह:।[83]
4. अनिराकृतप्रतिपक्षो वरस्वंशग्राही ज्ञातुरभिप्रायो नय:।[84]
5. प्रतिपत्तुराभिप्रायविशेषो नय इति।[85]
6. वस्तुन्यनेकान्तात्मन्यविरोधेन हेत्वर्पणात्साध्यविशेषस्य याथात्म्यप्रापणप्रवण: प्रयोग: नय:।[85]

It is a particular opinion or *(abhiprāya* or *abhimata)* or a viewpoint *(apekṣā)*-a viewpoint which does not rule out other different viewpoints and is, thereby, expressive of a partial truth *(vastvaṁśagrāhī)* about an object *(vastu)*- as entertained by a knowing agent *(jñātṛ). A* naya is a particular viewpoint about an object or an event, there being many other viewpoints which do not enter into the particular viewpoint under discussion.

Naya can be divided into two types: *dravyarthikanaya* or the substantive view, and *paryāyārthikanaya* or the modal (or the modification) view. The categories are also called, briefly, as *dravyanaya* and *paryāyanaya* respectively. The view of reality conceived under the division is described as the concise *(sankṣepa* or *samāsa)* one in contrast to the other (the broad) one.

By a process of further analysis the Jaina thinkers have been led to the formulation of the methodological scheme consisting of seven ways of looking at reality. They are enumerated in the following order of decreasing denotation: *naigama, saṅgraha, vyavahāra, ṛjusūtra, śabda, samabhirūḍha,* and *evambhūta.*

Naigamanaya

(The teleological or the universal-particular standpoint):

Naigamanaya relates to the purpose *(saṅkalpa)* or the end of a certain continuous series of actions, which are represented by one or a few of their number. For instance, a person carrying fuel, water, and rice, when asked "What are you doing?" says "I am cooking" instead of saying "I am carrying fuel" and so forth. This means that the general purpose of cooking controls the entire series of actions which are represented by one or more of them such as carrying the materials or drawing water enabling us thereby to grasp the purpose, which governs the individual factors relating to it. This is the aim or function of the naigama standpoint.

According to another interpretation, naigamanaya is described as the standpoint of the 'non-distinguished'. By the 'non-distinguished.' We mean the absence of distinction or discrimination between the universal or the generic and the particular or the specific elements of the object under review.

Samgrahanaya: (The class view):

This standpoint concerns itself with the general or the class character of a factual situation, unlike the naigama standpoint, which includes the specific characters as well. For instance, when, pointing to a solitary tree at some distance from you, you observe to a stranger asking for direction, "turn left near the tree there", it is not relevant to the occasion to mention whether "the tree there" is mango, banyan, or any other, although "the tree" must be one of these.

Vyavaharanaya: (The standpoint of the particular)

In contrast with the *saṅgraha* standpoint the *vyavahāra* standpoint specializes itself in being concerned with the specific feature of the object concerned, without, of course, losing sight of the fact that they cannot stand by themselves without the support of the generic properties in the larger setting of concrete reality. For example, when a person is asked to bring a mango fruit, he attempts to bring mango, but not any other fruit, although he is aware of the fact that mango is only a species in the genus of fruit.

Rjusūtra: (The standpoint of momentariness)

The ṛjusūtra standpoint relates to the momentary nature of a thing. It is narrower than the *vyavahāra* standpoint in that it looks at a particular thing as the thing appears at a particular moment. This standpoint is in operation when, for instance, we treat an actor, who is enacting the role of a king on the stage, as the king for the moment.

Śabdanaya: (the standpoint of synonyms)

The present standpoint of synonyms refers to the function of synonymous words, which despite their differences in tense, case-endings, gender, number and so forth, convey the same meanings. *kalaśa* and *ghaṭa* denote the same object *(ekārthavācakāḥ),* viz., a jar which is one of the forms taken by clay. Similarly the words *Indra, Śakra* and *Purandara* denote one and the same individual in the same manner as the words globe, orb and sphere denote, despite their several differences, the same circular entity.

A misapplication of this standpoint by treating for instance, two synonymous words as being utterly identical in their meanings is said to lead to the fallacy called *śabdanayābhāsa.*

Samabhirūḍhanaya: (The etymological standpoint)

It distinguishes the meanings of synonymous words purely on their etymological grounds. The synonyms *Indra, Śakra* and *Purandara* denote, according to the conventional approach *(ruḍhiḥ upacāraḥ)* of śabdanaya, the same individual whereas they do not do so if their difference in their etymological derivation is taken into consideration. *Indra,* for instance, signifies one who is 'all prosperous' and the other two names signify one who is 'the all-powerful' and the destroyer of the enemies' respectively.

Evambhūtanaya: (The 'such-like' standpoint)

Evambhūtanaya, or the 'such-like' standpoint, is a further specialized form of the application of the verbal method. It calls for a different designation for each of the different attitudes, which the same object assumes under different conditions. Purandara, for instance, should be, according to this naya, designated as such only when he is actually engaged in the act of destroying his enemies. Similarly the designation *Śakra* is appropriate only when he is actually manifesting his prowess. A cow ceases to be a cow when she is not in actual motion; and the onomatopoeic designation of a ghaṭa would no more denote the ghaṭa when the ghaṭa is not producing the peculiar sound ghaṭ, ghaṭ'. Consequently, because of this insistence that designations should be derived from the different functional states of what is ordinarily known as the same object, Purandara becomes as different from Śakra as a cow is different from a jar.

Nikṣepa

Nikṣepa is one more important contribution of the *Jaina* Philosophy, particularly to the theory of determining the meaning of a word. All systems of Indian Philosophy have postulated some type of *'vṛtti' (saṃbandha)* between word and meaning and the basis of that one arrives at the meaning/sense. Again in case of lexical ambiguity a specific meaning is determined following different principles.

In this context Jainas have developed the *Nekṣepa* theory, which guides in determining the desired meaning. It must be mentioned that this is one of the most important contributions of the Jainas to the Philosophy of language with regard to the problem of meaning from Indian perspective.

Yaśovijaya defines *Nikṣepa* as follows:"

''प्रकरणादिवशेन अप्रत्यादि व्यवच्छेदकयथास्थानविनियोगाय शब्दार्थरचना निक्षेपाः।''[87]

Thus, the determination of the meaning for the proper understanding, out of many possibilities is *Nikṣepa*.

Akalaṅkadeva, in his *Laghīyastraya* explains the usefulness of *Nikṣepa*. He says that *Nikṣepa* discards the unwanted meaning and the intended meaning is grasped. He writes:

अप्रस्तुतार्थापकरणात् प्रस्तुतार्थ व्याकरणाच्च निक्षेपः फलवान्।[88]

Making his observation on Nikṣepa theory, Paṇḍit Sukhalaljī Sanghavī, in his analysis of *Tattvārthasūtra,* writes "the entire behaviour and the means of verbalization of knowledge is through language. Language is formed or expressed through words. A single word on the basis of context or purpose is used in a number of meanings. Every word is capable of expressing at least four meanings. The four meanings are the four divisions of meanings in general of that word and these divisions are called *Nikṣepa* or *Nyadsas*. And knowing these *Nyāsas* it becomes convenient and easy to understand the desired meaning".

Let us take few examples for analysis:

1. King is coming: *rājā agacchati.*
2. I pray to Lord *Jagannātha: Jagannātham vande.*
3. Move the horse: *aśvaṃ cālaya.*
4. Bring the ghee pot: *ghṛta ghaṭam ānaya.*
5. Look at *Lakṣmīpati: Lakṣmīpatiṃ paśya.*

The first example, *rājā agacchati,* the word *rājā* may mean a person called *rājā* or a king. It also may refer to a rich person. In all the examples mentioned above, one has to understand the intention of the speaker and then only one can grasp the meaning of expression. The word *aśva* in the third example may refer to a horse or some other thing on which horseness is imposed. The ghee pot may mean a pot full of ghee or a pot meant for keeping ghee or a pot in which ghee was kept before and is now used for some other purpose. The word *Lakṣmīpati* may mean a person called *Lakṣmīpati,* or a person who is the husband of a lady called *Lakṣmī,* or a merely a rich person or *Bhagavāna Viṣṇu.*

To get all these possible meanings the *Jaina* philosophers have proposed the four-fold *'Nikṣepa'* theory, which would enable one to think in these lines on the basis of the *'Nikṣepa'* to approve all these meanings. The four *Nikṣepas* are *Nāma*

Nikṣepa, Sthāpanā Nikṣepa, Dravya Nikṣepa and *Bhāva Nikṣepa. Nāma Nikṣepa* would allow one to accept a word as mere name, without bothering about its meanings either from etymological or any other point of view like convention etc. Thus, some times we come across the expression like *Dhanapati* referring to a poor man or *Sundaralāl* for a ugly person or *Sunayanā* referring to a blind girl. Thus, the theory *Nāma Nikṣepa* would guide us to treat these types of expressions as mere names. Yaśovijaya defines *Nāma Nikṣepa* thus:

तत्र प्रकृतार्थ निरपेक्षानां अर्थान्तरपरिणतिः नाम निक्षेपः।[89]

Thus, the word *rājā* in the first sentence, *Jagannātha* in the second and *Lakṣmīpati* in the fifth sentence may refer to mere names of individual, on the basis of this *Nāma Nikṣepa.*

Sthāpanā Nikṣepa is that sense where a meaning is attributed or imposed on the basis of some resemblance or even in the absence of that. It is defined as :

यत्तु वस्तु तदर्थ वियुक्तं तदभिप्रायेण स्थाप्यते चित्रादौ तादृशाकारं अक्षादौ च निराकारम्।[90]

Thus, following this the word *rājā* in the first sentence or *Lakṣmīpati* in the fifth means a rich person and the word horse in the third refers to the horse in the chessboard or a horse yoked to the chariot.

Depending on its association with some future activity or past activity, to ascertain some meaning is *dravya nikṣepa.*

To ascertain the meaning on the basis of its etymology when the etymological sense and the actual activity performed by the object go together, it is *bhāva nikṣepa.* For example, the word *Sevaka* would refer to the servant when he is associated with service.

What the *Jaina* philosophers are trying to do is to show the possibilities of the meanings a speaker may intend to convey or the possible sense in which a particular expression might have been made. The *Jaina* philosopher thinks that the proper understanding of these *Nikṣepas* will guide the listener to grasp the intention of the speaker with regard to a particular meaning, from the alternative meanings presented before him.

It may be observed that *Nikṣepa* theory is the innovation of the *Jaina* philosophers and due credit may be given to them for systematically presenting this theory.

It may be further observed that the *Jainas* want that the *Nikṣepas* help in knowing the intention of the speaker, which is not fully correct. It is ultimately the context and some other factors, which helps in ascertaining the meaning and it is evident from their analysis as well. Thus, the function performed by the *Nikṣepas* is to give or suggest the various possibilities on the basis of which a word may be interpreted.

Tattvas or Categories

The term *'Tattva'* is derived from the stem *'tat'* (*i.e.* 'that' pronoun) with the suffix *'tva'* in the sense to denote the (exact sense or the real essence of that particular object *(Tattvabhāvaṃ Tattvaḥ*), But, in Indian philosophy this term is used in a very technical sense. In Vedic literature this term is used in the sense of *paramātmā* (ultimate truth) and identical with the *Bramhan.* In the *Sāṃkhya* system, it is used in the sense of the root cause of the Universe. In Indian Philosophy *Tattva, Paramārth, Sat, padārtha* are used to denote one and the same things. But in Jaina Philosophy *Tattva, Paramārthas, Dravyas, Sat, Parāpara, Dheya, Śudha, Parama* all are synonyms.[92]

Cārvāka has accepted four *Tattvas, Vaiśeṣikas* have accepted six, *Nyāya-Vaiśeṣika* system of philosophy has accepted six (later with *abhāva* seven) categories, *Shāṁkhya* system of philosophy has accepted 25 categories, and Yoga philosophers have accepted 26, *Vedāntins* have accepted only one *i.e. Bramhan,* Buddhists have accepted four *Tattvas* and *Mīmāṁsakas* have accepted Vedic sentence is the only one *Tattva* and whatever act is performed with the help of Vedic sentence is *Sat.*

Jaina philosophers have defined it following the doctrine

of *Anekāntavāda*. They have followed the middle path (*i.e. Pariṇāminityavāda),* keeping aside the two extreme systems viz. *Sarvānityavādin i.e.* the Buddhism in the one hand and the *Sarvānityavādin i.e.* the *Vedānta* system in the other. Here, one point may be noted that alike *Jainas* other systems like *Nyāya, Vaiśeṣika*, *Pātañjalayoga*, *Mīmāṁsa* systems also have accepted this *Pariṇāminityavāda* in the context of *Sat* i.e. *Dravya*, found in the Jaina system. They are as follows:

१. अपरिच्चत्तसहावेणुप्पादव्वय धुवत्तसंजुत्तं
गुणवं च सपज्जाय जं तं दव्वं वच्चति।।[93]

१. उतपादव्यध्रोव्ययुक्तं सत्।।[94]

२. सत्त सव्वपयतया सविस्सरुवा अणंतपज्जाया
भंगुप्पादधुवत्त सप्पडिवक्खा हवदि एकता।।[95]

३. दव्व सल्लकखणीयं उप्पादव्वयधुवत्संजुत्तं
गुणपज्जायासयं जं तं भण्णति सव्वण्हू।।[96]

The main essence of dravya is that, it is produced constant and it keeps changing with view of dravyārthikanaya, it is constant and with the view of paramārthikanaya, it is produced and also changed. It is also called *Matṛpadikāsiddānta* in this tradition that is *Utpādadhruvaṁ pariṇānaṁ kṣaṇe kṣaṇe dravyāṇamavirodhaśca pratyakṣādiha dṛśyate*[97]. And it can be compared with the concept of non-eternity of substance as opined by Lawoisier.

As the number of *Dravyas* are concerned, we find sometime there are two *Dravyas* viz. *Jīva* and *Ajīva*[98], and some philosopher hold their view that there are nine *Dravyas* viz. *Jīva, Ajīva, Pūṇya, Pāpa, Āśrava, Saṁbara, Nirjarā, Baṅdha* and *Mokṣa* as discussed in some *Agamic* texts[99]. Some philosophers like *Umāsvāti*[100] and Ācārya *Malayagiri*[101] also proposed seven *Dravyas*. According to them *Pāpa* and *Pūṁṇya* can be inserted under either Āśrava or *Baṅdha* or according to some, all seven *Dravyas* can be divided into three categories.

1.

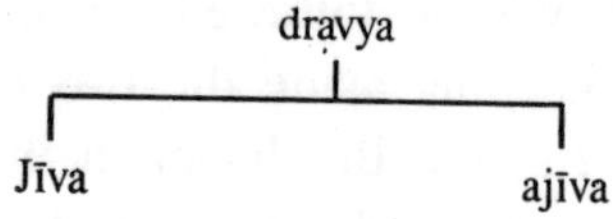

2.

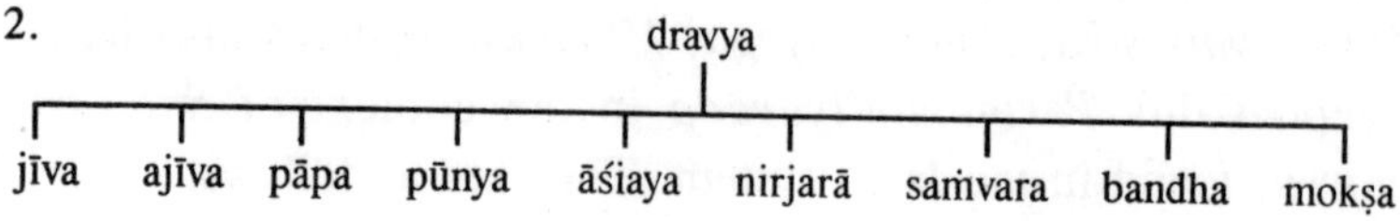

3.

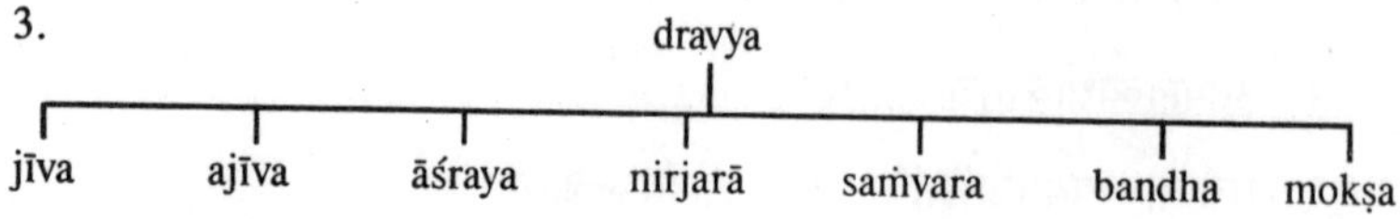

Let us discuss in some greater detail the accepted *Tattvas* of the Jainas.

Jīva (Soul) Tattva

The concept of soul and its analysis is very essential in philosophical investigation. Each system of Indian Philosophy has created enough scope for its exposition in their respective texts. Accordingly, the *Jainas* talk of soul in terms of knowledge. No soul can exist devoid of knowledge and there is no knowledge without soul. Omniscience therefore becomes the natural property of the soul and non-omniscience only adventitious or accidental owing its existence due to some external causes or objectives. *Jaina* philosophers argue unlike *Nyāya Vaiśeṣikas,* who holds that soul is devoid of all cognition *(jaḍa dravya)* and consciousness is an adventitious quality of the soul which comes temporarily as an effect of a complete cognitive machinery *i.e.* contact between sense and object, then between sense and mind and finally between mind and the soul or the *Sāṁkhya* philosophers accordingly to whom intellect or *buddhi* as unconscious being an evolute of *Pravṛtti,* or even

Vedāntins, according to whom, the quality of knowing does not constitute the nature of *Brahman,* for, *Brahman* is above these limitations. He is pure existence consciousness. The quality of knowing is the function consciousness when associated with the internal organ *(antaḥkaraṇa)*. Brahman is free from the duality of knower and known. The *Vedānta* treats all empirical knowledge as only pseudo-knowledge, or the Buddhists do not believe in the existence of any substance like soul. Cognition to them is a function of the beginningless stream of consciousness *(citta)* which takes the form of *ālaya vijñāna* and *Pravṛtti-vijñāna;* or *Bhāṭṭas* who treat consciousness as the attribute of soul and regards knowledge as not self revelatory but only inferentially cognizable by something other than itself *(parānumeya).* Thus, to the *Jainas,* knowledge is identical with the soul, just as serpent is identical with the coil of his body.

Before discussing more on this, we may see the various definitions of soul as found in the system. Following are some definitions of the soul:

1. चैतन्यस्वरूपः परिणामी कर्त्ता साक्षात् भोक्ता देहपरिमाणः पतिोत्रं भिन्नः पौदगलिकादृष्ट्वाच्चायम्।[102]
2. पाणेहिं चदुहिं जीवदि जीविस्सेदि जो हि जीविदो पुव्वं सो जीवो पाणा पुण पोग्गलदव्वेहिं णिव्वत्ता।[103]
3. दशसु प्राणेषु यथोपात्तप्राणपर्यायेण त्रिषुकालेषु जीवनानुभवात् जीवति, अजीवित जीविष्यति इति वा जीवः।[104]
4. तत्र चेतनालक्षणो जीवः।[104]
5. लक्षणमिह भणियमादाक्षेओ संभावसंगदो सोवि चेयण उवलद्धि दसण णाणं च लक्खणं तस्स।[106]
6. कर्मोपाधिासापेक्ष ज्ञान दर्शनोपयोगचैतन्यप्राणेन जीवन्ति इति जीवाः।[107]
7. अन्यासाधारणाभावाः पञ्चैपशमिकादयः स्वतत्त्वं यस्य तत्त्वस्य जीव स व्यापदिश्यते।[108]

8. जीवो त्ति हवदि चेदो उवओगविसेसिदो।[109]

9. उपओग लक्खणेगा जीवे।[110]

10. जीवो उपओगलक्खणो।[111]

11. कत्ता भोइं अमुत्तो शरीरमित्तो अणाइणिहणो य दसणणाणुवओगो णिद्दिट्ठो जिणवरिं देहिं।[112]

On the basis of the above stated definitions the main or prime characteristics of soul are:

Soul is identical with *Cetanā i.e.* consciousness *(caitanya svarūpa)*. Thus, it is the main line of demarcation between *Jīva* and *Ajīva*. And along with other general qualities of substance *(sādhāraṇadharma)* viz. existence, origination, decay, permanence etc. consciousness consists of knowledge and intuition *(Jñāna* and *Darśana Upayoga)*. *Jñāna Upayoga* is always having eight types of *Savikalpaka Jñāna* viz. *Mati, śruta, Avadhi, Manaḥparyāya* and three *viparyayas i.e.* wrong knowledge viz. *Kumati* (sensory wrong knowledge), *Kuśruta* (scriptural wrong knowledge) and *Vibhaigāvadhi* (limited direct wrong knowledge). And *Darśana Upayoga* is having the *Nirvikalpaka Jñāna i.e.* the pure knowledge that is called *kṣ āyika Jñāna,* which is produced after the complete destruction of Karma. Strictly speaking soul is that substance which possesses four infinities *(Ananta Catuṣṭayas)*. These four *Ananta Catuṣṭayas* are infinite knowledge, infinite intuition, infinite bliss and infinite power *(Jñāna, Darśana, ānanda, Sāmarthya)*. A liberated soul possesses all these infinities. The worldly soul does not possess them in their perfection because they are obstructed by the veil of four destructive karmas *(Ghātikarmas)* viz. *Jñānāvaraṇīya i.e.* covering the faculty of knowledge, *Darśanāvaraṇīya i.e.* covering the faculty of intuition, *Mohanīya i.e.* covering the faculty of bliss and *Antarāya i.e.* covering the faculty of power, hence they possess the four infinities in all perfection.

The following observation can be made on the basis of the above discussion.

1. Soul exists in present, past and future, which is beginningless and has no end and which is beyond destruction.
2. It is having a form of the body *(Dehaparimāṇa)* both smallest *(mūrta)* and highest magnitude form *(Vibhūparimāṇa)*.
3. Its form is different in each and every body *(Pratikṣ etre bhinnaḥ)*.
4. It is the means or path of knowledge *(Jñāna darśana upayoga)*.
6. It is the agent of all activities and also the enjoyer of all fruits *(kartā bhoktā* ca).
5. It is not constant in form *(Ekānta nitya)* but it has extension *(pariṇāmi)*.

The *Jaina* philosophers discuss the problem of soul in three aspects. The first aspect is known as *Jīva Samāsa i.e.* classes of souls, it divides the soul on the basis of different bodies obtained in the different kingdoms and expressed the evolution of life. The second aspect is known as *Mārgaṇā i.e.* soul quest. It comprises of other inner differences in species, sex, passion, knowledge, conation in the embodical condition of the soul. The third aspect is *Guṇasthāna i.e.* the stages of spiritual development. It discusses the inner progress of soul and describes the stages of the soul from ignorance and delusion to the state of perfection.

Ajīva Tattvas

Ajīva i.e. non-sentient means, which is not ajiva.[113] We have already seen the nature of *jīva* in the foregoing pages. Precisely it can be said that which is non-sentient conscious which can realize the pleasure and pain and which can obtain the knowledge of all the objects, that *is jīva* and opposite of that is called *ajīva,* which is completely bereft of consciousness and which can not realize sorrowness and happiness etc.[114] In *Jaina* philosophy the number of *ajīva* tattvas are five viz.

Dharma, Adharma, ākāśa, Kāla, and *Pudgala.* We can divide them into two groups viz. *rūpilmūrta i.e.* having form and *arūpilamūrta i.e.* formless. *Dharma* (medium of motion), *Adharma* (medium of rest), *ākāśa* (space), *kala* (time) are *arūpi* or *amūrta tattvas* and only *pudgala i.e.* matter is *rūpi* or *mūrta dravya.*

A brief discussion or description of these *tattvas* may be in order.

Dharma: (The medium of motion)

In *Jaina* philosophy among the six substances only *jīva* and *pudgala* are capable of moving. The rest four are devoid of motion. Hence the question is how they are moving or what makes them move. To this, *Jaina* philosophers have accepted *Dharma i.e.* the medium of motion. It can be compared with the concept of 'ether' as accepted by the scientists.[115] According to the *Jaina* philosophy *'Dharma'* is one and eternal and it is pervaded by all *'Lokas'* and it is also devoid of *varṇa* (colour), *gandha* (smell), *rasa* (taste) and *sparśa* (touch). It helps *jīva* (sentient being) and the *pudgala* (matter) to move. And due to this, *jīva* speaks, moves and does all types of developments viz. mental and physical etc. It does not compel the *jīvas* and *pudgalas* to move but when they want to move they have to depend on *Dharma.* It is the *nimitta kāraṇa* of the effect moving. *Pudgalas* and *jīvas* are the *upādāna kāraṇa* of moving. And also due to this *dharma* we can discriminate *'Loka'* from 'Aloka'.[116] Because this *Dharma* is pervaded in *loka* only and that is why it becomes discriminate factor. In the *Bhagavatisūtra*[117] Mahāviraswāmi describes the necessity of *Dharma* to *Gautama,* that if it were not there then nobody can know who comes and who goes, how the sound waves are spread, how one could see, how one could think, how one could speak and how one could move etc. Thus G. R. Jaina has rightly pointed out that science and *jaina* physics agree absolutely so far as they call *Dharma,* ether, non-material, non-atomic, non-discrete, continuous, co-extensive with space, indivisible and a necessary medium for motion and one which itself does not move.

Saṁvara (stoppage)

The obstruction of karmic influx *(āśrava) i.e.* the prevention of the inflow of karmic matter is called *saṁvara*. It always precedes liberation. Unless and until the inflow of karmic matter into the soul is stopped, the real nature of a soul *(śuddha jīva)* cannot be revealed. To obstruct this karmic matter is the main function of *saṁvara*. It is defined as follows:

1. आस्रवनिरोधः संवरः।[118]
2. कर्मागमनिमित्ता प्रादुर्भूतिरास्त्रवनिरोधः, तन्निरोधे सति तत्पूर्वकर्मादानाभावः संवरमिथ्यादर्शनादिप्रत्ययकर्मः संवरः।[119]
3. संव्रियत्ते संरुध्यते मिथ्यादर्शनादिः परिणामो येन परिणामान्तरेण सम्यग्दर्शनादिना गुप्त्यादीना वा संवरः।[120]
4. रुधियछिद्दयसहस्से जलजाणे जह जलं तु णासवदि। मिच्छत्ताइअभावे तह जीवे संवर होई।[121]
5. अभिनवकर्मादानहेतुरास्रवो तस्य निरोधः संवरइत्युच्यते।[122]

It is of two kinds viz. psychical and physical. The cessation of activities that lead to transmigration is psychical stoppage. It can be called 'yoga' in general terminology. When these activities are checked, the inflow of karmic matter is interrupted. This is physical stoppage. There are sixty-two ways to stop the karmic matter.[123] They are five *samitis* viz. *ārya-samit, Bhāṣā-samit, ādāna-samit, Nikṣepaṇā-samit, Eṣeṇā-samit* and *Pratisthāpanā-samit;* three *guptis viz. kāyā-gupti, mana-gupti* and *vāk-gupti;* five *vratas viz-Ahimsā, Satya, āstheya, Vrahmacarya* and *Aparigraha;* ten *Dharmas viz. ksamā, mṛdutā, saralatā, śauca, satya, sāṁyama, tapa, tyāga, audāsinya and brahmacarya; twelve aṇuprekṣās viz. anitya, aśaraṇa, saṃsāra, anyatva, aśuci, saṁvara, nirjarā, loka, bodhidurlabhatva, dharmānuprekud, āśrava, ekatva,* etc. twenty two *pariṣahas viz. kṣudhā, tṛṣṇā, śita, uṣṇa, daṁśamaśaka, nagnatva, arati, sthrī, caryā, nisadyā, śayyā, ākroṣa, vadha, yācanā, alābha, roga, tṛṇosparśa, mala, satkāra-pariṣkāra, prajñā, jñāna, adarśna, yathākṣāta and samāyika.*

Bahdha (Bondage)

Since time immemorial the soul and matter have been staying in the *lokākāśa*. Along with these, there are four *kaśāyas* viz. *krodha, māna, māyā* and *labha* and the impression *(saṁskāra)* of the actions performed by the soul. But the question is, if the karmic matter is non-sentient *(jaḍa)*, then how they enter into the soul. For this they have accepted the 'yoga'[124] (*i.e.* the mind, body and speech), which makes a kind of vibration *(spandana)* in the *pradeśa* of soul, and it helps the karmic matter to enter into the soul through the passage of *āśrava i.e.* influx. This process is called *baṅdha*. It is defined as follows:

1. वध्यतेऽनेन बन्धनमात्रं वा बन्धः। अथवा बन्धाति वध्यतेऽसौ, वध्यतेऽनेन बन्धनमात्रं वा बन्धः।[125]
2. अभिमनदेशगतिनिरोधहेतुबंधः।[126]
3. आत्मकर्मणोरन्योन्यप्रवेशानुप्रवेशलक्षणो बन्धः।[127]
4. दव्वस्स दव्ण भावाणं वा संजोगो समावाओ वा सो बंधो णाम।[128]

This bondage is of two kinds viz. psychical and physical[129] *i.e. bhāva baṅdha* and *dravya baṅdha*. That conscious state by which *karma* is bound with the soul is called psychical bondage. The interpenetration of the karmic particles and the soul is known as physical bondage. The cause of bondage is a particular modification of consciousness consisting of passions by which, *karmas* are tied to the soul. In other words, attachment and aversion are the cause of bondage. And also wrong belief *(mithyātva)*, negligence *(avirati), pramāda, kaṣ āya* and yoga are the causes of bondage.

Āśava/Āśrava: (Influx):

Āśava i.e. influx is a passage or way, through which the

karmic matter flows into the soul through the channel of activity done by speech, mind and body, as if water flows into the ocean through streams. It is defined in the system as follows:

1. कायवाङ्मनः कर्मयोगः स आस्रवः[130]

2. आस्रवति प्रविशति कर्म येन स प्रणतिपादिरूपः आस्रव कर्मोपादान कारणम्।[131]

3. आस्रवत्यनेन आस्रवणमात्रं वा आस्रवः पुण्यपापागमद्वारलक्षणो आस्रवः।[132]

From the above mentioned definitions it is clear that *āśrava* acts as a passage, through which the *pāpa* and *pūṇya* enter into the soul and this influx precedes bondage *i.e. baṁdha, mithyātva, avirati, pramāda* and yoga are the helping factors of *āśrava*. It is of two types[133] viz. Physical and Psychical *i.e. Dravyāśrava* and *Bhāvāśrava*. The modification of consciousness by which karma gets into the soul is known as psychical influx. The psychical influx is defined thus:

1. आस्रवत्यनेनत्यास्रवः। आस्रवत्यगच्छति जायते कर्मत्वपर्याय पुद्‌गलानां कारणभूतेनात्मपरिमाणेन स परिणामः आस्रवः।[134]

2. निरास्रवस्वसंवित्तिलक्षणशुभाशुभपरिणामेन शुभाशुभ-कर्मागमनास्रवः।[135]

In other words, psychical influx is nothing but the mental, bodily or vocal activities. It is further divided into two viz. *sāṁparāyika* and *īryāpatha.*[136] *Saṁparāyika āśrava* is defined as follows:

1. सकषायाकषायोः साम्परायिकेर्यपथयोः।[137]

2. सम्परायः संसारः तत्प्रयोजनं कर्म साम्परायिकम्।[138]

3. कर्मभिः समन्तादात्मनः पराभवोऽभिभवः सम्परायः उत्युच्यते तत्प्रयोजनं कर्म साम्परायिकमित्युच्यते यथा ऐन्द्रमहिकमिति। मिथ्यादृष्टयादीनां सूक्ष्मसाम्परायान्तानां कषायोदयपिच्छि-लपरिणामानां योगवशादानीतं कर्म भावेनपश्लिष्यमाणं आर्द्र-चर्माश्रितरेणुवत् स्थितिमापद्यमानं साम्परायिकमित्युच्यते।[139]

Īryāpatha āśrava is defined as follows:

1. त छदुमत्थवीयरायाणं सजोगिकवलीणं वातं सव्वमीरियावहकम्मं णामो। ईरणमोर्यायोगे गतिरित्यर्थः। तद्वारकं कर्म ईर्यापथम्।[140]
2. ईर्यायोगः सःपन्था मार्गः हेतुर्यस्य कर्मणः तदीर्यापथकर्म।[141]
3. लद्धूण तं णिमित्तं जोगं जं पुग्गले पदेसत्थं परिणमदि कर्मभावं तं पिहु दव्वसव वीजं।[142]
4. णाणावरणादीणं जोग्गं जं पुग्गलं समासवदि दब्वावासवो सं णेओ अणेयभेओ जिणक्खादो।[143]

The influx of *karma* is of two kinds viz. *Pūnya i.e.* virtuous and *pāpa i.e.* sinful. Meritorious activities cause the influx of virtuous *Icarmas,* while wicked actions are responsible for the inflow of sinful *karmas*. Injury, falsehood, stealing, envy etc. are wicked activities. The opposites of these are meritorious ones. How can activity be meritorious or wicked? That which is performed with good intention is meritorious. The influx of persons with passions extends transmigration and that of persons free from passions prevents or shortens it.

Pudgala: (Matter)

The concept of matter has been treated by every system of thought in its own way from the nominal and phenomenal aspects as it exists in space and continues in time with all its qualities and modes. Does matter exist? It is a very complicated problem in the sphere of philosophy. The Idealists maintain that the universe is a spiritual reality. Matter does not enjoy any separate existence independent of spirit or thought. But the realists do not agree with this view. They explicitly say that the material reality is absolutely independent of the spiritual reality. It is as real as thought itself. Jainism, being a member of the school of realism certainly believes in an independent and separate existence of matter. The *Jaina* thinkers maintain that the doubt about a non-existent object is totally unjustifiable, as in the case of sky-flower and hare-horn where non-existence is certain. The point is that our doubt is justifiable in the case of existent objects only.

The *Jaina* writers have used the term *'Pudgala'* exactly in the sense of matter. The word pudgala has two parts viz. *'pud'* and *'gala'*. The first part *'pud'* means to combine, to fill and the second part 'gala' means to dissociate, to flow. Hence, the etymological meaning of the word *pudgala* is that substance which undergoes modifications by combinations and dissociations. It is defined by the system as follows :

1. पुरणगलनान्वर्थसंज्ञात्वात् पुद्गलाः, भेदसंघाताभ्यां च पूर्यन्ते गलन्ते चेति पुरणगलनात्मिकां क्रियामन्तर्भाव्य पुद्गलशब्दोऽन्वर्थ पुद्गलनाद्वा। अथवा पुमांसो जीवाः। तैः शरीराहरविषयकरणो-पकरणदिभावेन गिल्यन्ते इति पुद्गलाः।[144]
2. गलनपुरणस्वभावसनाथः पुद्गलः।[145]
3. स्पर्शरसगंधवर्णवन्तः पुद्गलाः।[146]
4. तत्र स्वभावपुद्गलः परमाणुः विभावपुद्गलः स्कंधः। पुद्गलद्रव्यं तावत् विकल्पद्वय सनाथम्। स्वभावपुद्गलविभावपुद्गलश्चेति।[147]

Matter has four characteristics associated with it viz. touch, taste, smell and colour.[148] Each and every element of matter possesses these four characteristics. Eight types of touch are described in the *jaina* works[149] viz. soft *(mṛdu)*, hard *(kaṭ hina)*, heavy *(guru)*, light *(laghu)*, cold *(śītas)*, hot *(uṣṇa)*, smooth *(snigdha)* and rough *(ruksa)*; and five kinds of tastes viz. bitter *(takka)*. sour *(kaṭuka)*, acidic *(amla)*, sweet *(mad-hura)* and astringent *(kaṣāya)*; and two kinds of smell viz. good smell *(sbhiganūraha)* and bad smell *(asūrabhigandha)*; and five kinds of colour viz. blue *(nīla)*, yellow *(pita)*, white *(śukla)*, black *(kṛṣna)* and red *(rohita)*.[150] Along with these four *mūrtatva i.e.* having form and *acetanattva i.e.* non-sentient are the six special qualities of *pudgala*.[151] It is further mentioned that the foregoing twenty are the principal divisions. Each of these may be further sub-divided into in numerable and infinite kinds.[152]

Matter has two different forms: indivisible elementary particles and their combinations. In the technical terms of Jainism the indivisible elementary particles are called *'aṇu'* and the combinations of these particles are known as *skandhas.*[153] The last particle of matter, which cannot be further divided by any means whatever is called *'aṇu* or *paramāṇu'* [154] In the *Tattvārtharājāvārtika aṇu* is defined as the smallest material particle. There is nothing smaller than *paramāṇu*[155] According to *Pañcāsthikāyasāra,* the substance that has a single taste, a single colour, and single smell and two kinds of touch, which is the cause of sound while itself unsounding, which is different from molecules though constituting them is called atom.[156]

Since atoms are real entities, five physical attributes viz. taste, and colour, smell and two touches are always associated with them. The properties of hardness and softness, heaviness and lightness are not associated with atoms. These qualities are associated with the molecules. These properties are generated by the loose or compact aggregation of atoms and because all the atoms have the same mass there arises no question of light and heavy or hard and soft amongst the elementary particles of matter.

Skandhas i.e. molecule has been defined as an aggregate of atoms.[1"17] It possesses a gross form and undergoes process of association and dissociation. Molecules are formed in three different ways[158] viz.

(i) by division or dissociation *i.e., bheda,*

(ii) by union or association *i.e. saṅghāta,*

(iii) by the united process of dissociation and association taking place simultaneously.

Dissociation occurs on account of two causes, namely, internal and external.[159] The internal causes in the molecules themselves are the phenomenon of radioactivity and the like. External causes are the dissociation of molecules in solution, the breaking under high pressure, the breaking under artificial bombardment and the like.

Association *saṅghāta* is defined as the union of separate entities.[160] The assemblage of atoms to form molecules is an instance of association.

The united process of dissociation and association is defined as follows : by simultaneous dissociation and association molecules occupying two spatial particles etc. are produced, just when one molecule breaks the remaining part is associated by another molecules.[161]

Further, matter can be divided into classes. These classes are not different from atoms and molecules. They are in other words, their sub-divisions: [162]

(a) Solids: earth, stone and the like are the solid forms of matter. This class is known as *sthūla-sthūla*.

(b) Liquids: butter, water, oil, milk, and the like are the liquid forms of matter. They are known as *sthūla*.

(c) Energy: it manifests itself in the form of heat, light, and electricity etc. It is called *sthūla-sūkṣma*.

(d) Gases: air etc, are forms of gases. This class is known as *sūkṣma-sthūla*.

(e) Fine-matter: it is responsible for thought activities and is beyond sense perception. This type of matter is called *sūkṣma*.

(f) Extra-fine matter: the forms of single elementary particles are composed of extra fine matter. It is called *sūkṣma-sūkṣma*.

The *jaina* system admits that matter does influence the worldly soul *(sānsārika jīva)*. It forms the physical basis of the bodies, speech, mind, and respiration of the worldly soul.

According to Jainism, there are five types of bodies viz.

(a) *Audārika i.e.* the organic body of human beings, animals and vegetable kingdoms,

(b) *Baikriya i.e.* that which is possessed by the beings of heaven and hell and by human beings as well as animals possessing an extraordinary power *i.e. labdhi*. It is invisible and is capable of transformation in different shapes and sizes,

(c) *āhāraka i.e.* the subtle body, which is developed by the advanced *yogins*.

(d) *Taijas i.e.*, the electric bodies. It possesses the power of digesting the food we take,

(e) *Kārmaṇa i.e.* the inner subtle body, which is the seed of all mental and physical activities.

Thus, all these five types of bodies, speech, and mind are formulated due to the five *Vargaṇās i.e.* the kinds of molecules as accepted by the *Jaina* system. *Āhara-vargaṇā* causes the *audārika śarīra, vaikriya śarīra* and the *āhāraka śarīra. Tejo-vargand* forms the *taijasa sarlra* and speech and mind are formed by *bhdsd vargaṇā* respectively and the *karmana vargaṇā* forms the inner subtle body *i.e.* the *karmana śarīra.* And also pleasure, pain, life and death are experienced through the agency of matter. Hence, one piece of matter is capable of producing physical and chemical changes in another piece of matter.

Thus, soul is in bondage so long as it possesses the *Taijasa* and *Kārmaṇa śarīra*. According to *Tattvārtha Sūtra,*[164] the mundane soul can possess four bodies at the most at a time but not the five. Apart from the body, mind and speech there are also some other effects as the manifestation of matter. There are in the mail forms of sound, union, fineness, grossness, figure, divisibility, darkness, shade, heat and light.

Ākāśa (Space)

There are two views regarding the primary material elements *(mahābhūtas)*. One view recognized five *mahābhūtas* and the other recognized four *mahābhūtas*. Those who have accepted five elements viz. *pṛthvī, āpa, tejas, vāyu, ākāśa* and they have possessed five special qualities viz. *gandha* (smell), *rasa* (taste), *sparśa* (touch), *śabda* (sound), respectively. *Shāṁkhya-yoga, Nyāya-vaiśeṣika* and the *prabhākara mīmāmsā* have accepted this view. These *mahābhūtas* are the material causes of all the material effect-substances *i.e. bhautikakārya-dravya. Sāṁkhya* has accepted these five elements as the causes of material effect-substance. *Ākāśa* is produced from *śabda tanmātrā*[165]. But *Nyāya-vaiśeṣika* system has accepted only four elements as the causes of material effect-substance. Though, *Bhāṭṭa Mīmāṁsā* has given the status to *ākāśa* as *mahābhūta* but maintains that it is not the substratum of *śabda*. According to *Bhatta, śabda* is an independent substance.

Those who have recognized four *mahābhūtas viz. pṛthvī, āpa, tejas, vāyu* maintained that *ākāśa is* either a form of matter, produced from four *mahābhūtas* or it is non-spiritual substance. Among them, the *Theravādi* Buddhists accepted *ākāśa* as *saṁskṛta,* it is produced from the four *mahāśbhūtas,* thus, it is derived matter *i.e. upādāya-rūpa*[166]. But the *Vaibhāṣika* Buddhists recognized the four elements but they maintained that *ākāśa* is *asaṁsṛta* and it is non-material and non-spiritual or rather non-psychical.[167] *Srautrāntika* does not admit the substantial existence *of ākāśa*[168] because they believe absolute momentariness of entities. The *vedāntins* have accepted *ākāśa* as *Brahman,* since the characteristic marks are mentioned. All the prominent characteristics of Brahman are ascribed to *ākāśa.*[169]

Jainas follow this old tradition of four mahābhūtas and hence maintain that *ākāśa* is not *pudgala,* it is an independent substance. *Jaina* philosophy has conceived the space theory on the basis of the principle of space as positional quality of material objects and space as container of material objects from the stand points of its permanence, fixedness, non-corporeality, singleness, immobility or inactivity and capacity of receiving the succession of things in motion and made synthetic view of all other Indian concepts of space from the aspects of *dyavya* (substance), *kāla* (time)*kṣetra* (locus) and *bhāva* (condition)[170], they defined it as follows:

1. नित्यवस्थितान्यरूपाणि आकाशादेकद्रव्याणि च आकाशस्यावगाहः।[171]

2. सव्वेसिं जोवाणं सेसाण तह य पुग्गलाणं चाणं देदि विवरमरिवलं तं लोगे हवदि आगासं।[172]

3. जीवपुद्‌गलादीनामवगाहिनामवकाशदानमवगाहाकाशस्योपकारो वेदितव्यः।[173]

4. आकाशन्तेऽस्मिन् द्रव्याणि स्वयं चाकाशत इत्याकाशम्। अवकाश दानाद्वा।[174]

5. आगासं सपदेसं तु उडदाधो तिरिओविय। खेत्तलोगं बियाणाहि अणंतजिणन्देसिदं।[175]

6. चेयणरहियममुत्तं अवगाहणलक्खणं च सव्वगयं। तं णहदव्वं जिणुद्दिटुं।[176]

7. अवगासदाणजोग्गं जीवदीणं वियाणं आयासम्।[177]

From the above-mentioned definitions it is clear that, space is a colourless, odourless, tasteless, touchless, non-corporeal, non-living, permanent eternal and fixed substance.[178] It is that in which other substances manifest themselves or exist with their respective modes without exception or it itself gives room to them.[179] From the point of view of *dravya,* equal to the extent of the universe and non-universe *i.e. Lokākāśa,* all pervasive and infinite, from the point of view of *kṣetra i.e.* locus, it is eternal from the point of view of *kāla i.e.* time, it is colourless, odourless, tasteless and touchless, from the point of view of *bhāva i.e.* condition and it is endowed with the quality of accommodation from that of capacity or quality.[180] According to Jainism, *śabda* is not the nature of *ākāśa* nor is its quality. It is a mode of *mahubhutas* or matter *(pudgala).*[181] Aggregates *(skandhas)* of atoms strike against one another and *śabda* are produced from them. If *śabda* were its *(ākāśa)* quality, the quality *of ākāśa* being formless or non-physical it would not have been heard through the organ or hearing.[182] *Ākāśa* is one in number.[183] There is no possibility of increase or decrease in its number. It is one and will remain one for ever.[184] It is eternal in the sense that it never gives up its nature.[185] As it is present everywhere in the universe, the possibility of movement from one place to another is rejected.[186]Space is *arūpi* (formless). Here *arūpitva* means non-corporeality but not the denial of own nature, for there must be its nature. If there is not, it is not real, as the horse's horns are not proved real. The effect or conglomeration of colour, taste, smell, touch and figure is called *mūrti* (concrete-ness). Thus, there is not such *mūrti* in *ākāśa*.

Thus, if we conceive a substance infinite in extent and maintain that there is no substance more extensive than it, or not even as extensive as it, then this conception logically compels us to conceive this substance as requiring no other substance to contain it, because, there is no substance more extensive than it to contain it. *Ākāśa* is such a substance.[187] *Ākāśa* must exist in itself.[188] It is a single substance having infinite *pradeśa.*[189] *Pradeśa* means 'unit'. A primary indivisible atom of matter is the ultimate unit of matter. And the space occupied by a material atom is the ultimate unit of space. Hence, *ākāśa* is called *astikaya.* It is of two divisions viz. *Lokākāśa* and *Alokākāśa*[190] Loka is that place in which dharma, *adharma, kāla, pudgala* and *jīva* exist. That which is beyond this *lokākāśa* is *alokākāśa.*[191]

This division is not in *ākāśa* itself but it is due to its relation with the other five substances. Hence, *ākāśa* is a single substance, which has infinite *pradeśas.* When it is relatively divided into *lokākāśa* and *alokākāśa, Lokākāśa* has innumerable *pradeśas,* which *alokākāśa* from *ākāśa* is a whole; the remaining *pradeśas* of *alokākāśa* are still infinite.

Mokṣa (Liberation)

According to Jainism, liberation is nothing but the pure or true state of the soul. Injury, falsehood, stealing, envy, attachment, aversion, wrong belief etc. create influx *(āśrava).* Due to this influx the soul enters into the circle of bondage. This influx of the karmic matters are destroyed due to the *saṃbara i.e.* the stoppage and *nirjarā i.e.* the dissociation. And then slowly all karmic matters are annihilated due to the observation of penance and austerity. Then, the soul becomes omniscience *(sarvajña).* This state of soul is called *jīvanamūkti* or *bhāvamokṣa.* In this stage the four *ghātiya-karmas* viz. *jñānāvaraṇīya, darśanavarmvya, mohanīya* and *antarāya* are destroyed. It is just before the stage of liberation. And then four *aghātīyakarmas* viz. *āyu, nāma, gotra* and *vedanīya* are destroyed. And also one gets rid of the four *bhāvas* viz. *aupaśamika, kṣayopaśamika audāyika* and *bhavyatva.* Then the soul becomes liberated. The tradition has defined liberation as follows:

1. कृत्स्न कर्मवियोग लक्षणो मोक्षः।[192]
2. निरवशेनिराकृतकर्ममलकलंकस्याशरीरस्यात्मनोऽचिन्त्यस्व-भाविकज्ञानदिगुणमव्याबाधसु खामात्यन्तिकमवस्थान्तरं मोक्ष इति।[193]
3. आत्मबन्धयोद्विधाकरण मोक्षः।[194]
4. जं अप्पसहावादो मूलोत्तरपयडिसयियं मुच्चइ। तं मुक्ख अविरुद्धं।[195]
5. मोक्ष असने इत्येतस्य धञ् भावसाधानो मोक्षणं मोक्षः असनं क्षेपणमित्यर्थः स आत्यन्तिकः सर्वकर्मनिक्षेपो मोक्ष इत्युच्यते।[196]
6. मोक्ष इव मोक्षः। क उपमार्थः। यथा निगडादिद्रव्यमोक्षात् सति स्वातन्त्र्ये अभिप्रेतप्रदेशगमनादेः पुमान् सुखी भवति, तथा कृत्स्नकर्मवियोगे सति स्वाधिनात्यन्तिकज्ञान दर्शनानुपसुखआत्मा भवति।[197]

From these above-mentioned definitions the position of *Jainas* regarding the concept of soul becomes clear. They hold that the annihilation of all *karmas* is liberation. This is of two types viz. *bhāva mokṣa* and *dravya mokṣa*[198] *i.e.* psychical and physical. The modification of soul, which is the cause of the total destruction of karmas, is known as psychical liberation and the actual separation of the karmic matter is called physical liberation.[199] As it is stated as follows:

1. निरवशेषाणि कर्माणि येन परिणामेन क्षायिक ज्ञानदर्शनयथाख्यात-चरित्रसंज्ञितेन अस्यन्त स मोक्षः। विश्लेषो वा समस्तानां कर्मणा।[200]
2. कर्मनिर्मूलनसमर्थः सुद्धात्मोपलब्धिारूप जीव परिणामो भावमोक्षः, भावमोक्षनिमितेन जीवकर्मप्रदेशानां निरवशेषः पृथग्भावो द्रव्यमोक्ष इति।[201]

In the state of liberation *i.e.* the self-attainment, no new karmas flow owing to the absence of their causes. The soul exists in its pure and perfect state. It attains its natural form and possesses infinite knowledge and infinite bliss. Although, the emancipated souls have no physical forms, as they are not possessed of bodies, yet they have the psychical forms of their last bodies. The liberated soul does not expand to the extent of the universe, because, there is no cause for it. Because the expansion and contraction of the soul is determined by the physique making of *karma*. Thus, the emancipated soul maintains the form of its last physique forever.

Thus, when the soul becomes liberated it goes up to the end of the universe as it is of the nature of darting upwards. And because, there is no medium of motion *(dharma)* in the non-universe space *(alokākāśa)* so it does not go beyond the end of the universe. Though the liberated souls maintain their own forms and individualities still, in all essential qualities there is perfect equality among them and they do not obstruct one another and none of them enjoys any privilege. Thus, emancipation is the consummation of spiritual development *(guṇastana)*.

Mind

In the context of philosophical discussion the concept of mind is very important. Different systems of Indian philosophy have different opinions on this wonderful concept with reference to its ontological status like what is mind, what it is made of, where it is located, what its size is etc. With reference to its epistemological status like how to establish mind, its relation with soul, its role in the process of acquiring knowledge and finally with reference to its spiritual status like its role in spiritual development. Here we want to analyze the problem of mind from the point of view of *Jaina* philosophy. In *Jaina āgama* texts we find scattered information regarding mind. We find the discussion of mind particularly in the context of knowledge. Firstly, in the context of *matijñāna* which is derived through sense organs and mind. Secondly, the knowledge of other's mind (manaḥparyāya *jñāna)*. In first category mind is an instrument of ātman to have the knowledge and in second category manaḥparyāya *jñāna* in which the *ātman,* without the help of any other tool, have the direct knowledge of objects residing in other's mind.[202] Here, the knowledge is the modification of ātman due to cessation (kṣayopaśama) of jñānāvaraṇīya karma. The ātman is knower but the object is only mind molecules gathered in other's mind.

Specific definition of mind is rarely available in *āgama* texts. Whatever is available is in supporting of secondary literature, like Dravyasaṁgraha *bhāṣya, Gommattasāra jīvakāṇḍa, Yogośāstra, Manonuśāsanaṃ* etc. In *Dravyasaṁgraha bhāṣya,* the author states it as 'an entanglement of different thoughts[203]

1. अनिद्रियं मन: अन्त:करणमित्यनर्थान्तरतम्।[204]
2. नानाविकल्पजालरूपं मनो भण्यते।[205]

Other synonyms for mind are *anindriya, noindriya, antaṇkaraḥa* etc. It is called *anindriya* because of the absence of its external organ or manifestations like other sense organ. In *Tatvārthādhigama Sūtra* author mentions: It *(mati-jñāna)* is caused due to *indriya* and *no-indriya'.*[206]*Here no-indriya* indicates mind.

Division/Classification of Mind :

Mind is classified into two categories:

Dravyamana is the material mind (mentioned above) produced due to fruition of *aṅgopāṅga-nāma-karman*[201] whereas *bhāvamana* is the state of *ātman's* purification caused due to cessation *(kṣayopaśama)* of *vīryāntarāya* and *no-indriyāvaraṇīya karma*[20].

Bhavamana characterized with *'labdhi'* and *'upayoga'* is produced with the support of matter; thus, it is also materialistic *(paudgalika).*[209] The matters which conceive the thought process and beneficial to *ātman,* caused due to *kṣayopaśama* of *jñānāvaraṇīya* and *vīryāntarāya karma'* and fruition' of *aṅgopāṅga-nāma-karma* can only take the form of mind. Thus, they are also *pudgalika.*[210]

On the basis of mind all living beings are divided into two categories:

(1) *Samanaska* or *saṁjñī*: living beings with mind.

(2) *Amanasqja* or *Asaṁjñī*: living beings without mind.[211]

Living beings having all five senses may or may not have

mind. But rest of the living beings *i.e. jīvas* having one sense organ to *jīvas* having four sense organs are all without mind, [212] *jīvas* in hell and heaven are all with mind, but some of the animals with five senses are without mind known as *'asmjñi tiryanca pancendriya'.* Regarding human state *(maṇusya gati),* those who are born from all types of excreta of human beings are also human beings without mind known as *'asṁjñi sammūrcchima manuṣya'.*

Though *amriijnl jīva* are without mind viz. without *dravyamana,* still they have *bhāvamana* in very subtle form, as *jiidna* and *vlrya* are not completely covered. There is very minute *kasyopasama* of these two karmas. The *ātmapradeśas (rucaka-pradeśa)* are never covered by any of the karmas.[213]

This *bhāvamana* of *asmjnijīvas* is not powerful enough or rather lacks in *'labdhi',* which inspires to form *dravyamana,* in whose absence the operation of thought process cannot be conducted. Again with that subtle *bhāvamana asaṁjñī* can comprehend the knowledge of its own sense organ, whereas the *sariijfiljīvas* use their mind while operating their works with other sense organs.[214]

Some are of the opinion that mind is subtle *(aṇu-parimāna)* and others say it is *deha-parimāna.* But there is no external manifestation of mind, and again it is produced due to cessation *(kṣayopaśama)* of *jñānāvarṇīya* and *virydntardya* karmas. *Ksayopasama* like *karma bandha* and *nirjarā* happens in all *atma-pradeśa* simultaneously. These can never happen in some *ātman* points only leaving behind other points unaffected, *i.e.* all *dtma-pradeśa* will be effected simultaneously.[215] So it can be never be limited to one place, as other parts of the body cannot conduct the work of mind from those parts. So an *aṇu-parimāna* mind cannot perceive its object from the whole of universe, as mind is a beneficial of matter and matter has its own limitation.

Again it cannot be *deha-parimāna,* as there is no external manifestation of this karma (mind). It is produced out of very subtle molecules thus making it invisible. It is said that mind is an invisible quality of formless and inactive *ātman.*[216] *Svetdrhbara acdryas* agree with the point that mind is *deha-parimāna,* having more concentration near heart.

As per our observation from all these discussions, mind is *deha-parimāna,* as it is produced with all *dtmapradeśa* simultaneously. Again when we use out mind *(manoyoga)* we feel our internal sensation is more near brain.

Contact of mind with its object:

For knowledge of any object there should be a contact with that object. But mind like eyes do not need any contact with its objects, as it is *aprāpyakāri.*[211] It is said that the field of mind where it can perceive is *loka-parimāna,* because it does not have to be directly in contact with its object. That is, mind does not have *vyañjanāvagraha* in its process of knowledge.[218] It means moving out of the body or without getting in contact, mind can perceive the whole of universe. In other words, mind can create a mental screen within the body and can project anything—any matter, any place, any body, any conditions etc., on that screen. Thus, it proves that mind can perceive its object without any contact.

Do we need mind for knowledge ?

Knowledge is an inseparable characteristic of *ātman,* source of knowledge is *ātman* itself. *Ātman* in its pure state has infinite knowledge *(ananta jñāna).* But because of the karmic veil or knowledge obscuring karma (*jñānāvana karma*), *ātman* cannot perceive the knowledge directly, and has to acquire knowledge through sense organs and mind.

The living beings without mind have knowledge derived through sensory organs. They do not have logic, sense, intellect, mind, etc., to express or analyze their pain and pleasure. But they feel or experience the pain and pleasure.[219]They have *mati-jñāna* and *sruia-jñāna* from their respective sense organs. They can comprehend that much knowledge derived through sense organs. That is without mind *avagraha, īhā,* and *avāya* are possible. But in case of *dhāraṇā,* which consists of the lasting impression, which results after the object with its particulars, is definitely ascertained. It is this impression *(samskāra),* which enables us to remember the objects afterwards. There is no memory with these *asmjhljīva,* but still with the knowledge of available sense organs and drive of four basic instincts *(saṃjñā)* have desire to live and do activities for their own survival.

This is proved by the 'desire to live' by all living beings and activities towards fulfilling four basic instincts viz. *āhāra-samjña* (food), *bhaya saṃjñā* (fear), *maithuna saṃjñā* (sex) and *parigraha saṃjñā* (possession). These four *samjnas* are found in all living beings from *sūkṣma ekendriya* to *paryāpta saṃjñī pañcendriya.*

In *Bhagavatisūtra* while explaining five types of *kriyās* (the activities of *karmabandha)* which *jīvas* undergo, all living beings from pṛthvīkaya (earth body), to *asaṃjñā pahcendriya,* living beings with five senses but without mind, have bondage of karma due to all the five *kriyās.*[220] Moreover, they do not have logic, intellect, mind or speech to comprehend what they are experiencing, still they experience the feelings *(vedanā).*[221]

But the *saṃjñī jīva* has the mind to interpret all actions of other sense organs. This interpretation due to mind increases the intensity of attachment and aversion. Thus for the *saṃjñī jīva* only, the sense organs need the association with mind, whereas all other living beings *(saṃjñī)* can comprehend the knowledge derived from their respective sense organs.

Is simultaneously knowledge possible ?

Jīva, according to *Jaina* philosophy, consists of infinite *jñāna,* and *darśana,* but certain karmas viz. *jñānāvaraṇīya* karma and *darśanāvaraṇīya* karma tend to obscure these. When there is cessation *(kṣayopaśama)* of such class the respective *jñāna* or *darśana* are evolved till there is complete destruction of karma. The contact between *ātman* and object is either done partially through *ātman* directly *(pratyakṣa)* or through sense organs and mind *(parokṣa)*. But due to obscuring karma the *ātman* cannot fully utilize the power of respective knowledge or cognition *(darśana)* at a given time. The medium through which it is derived being materialistic has its own limitations.

Most important action in getting aquatinted with the knowledge of any object is *'upayoga'*. *Upayoga* is the resultant of consciousness or a sort of inclination, which arises from consciousness. In other words, the resultant of consciousness, which is inclined towards any object to accept it, is known as *upayoga*.[222]

Again, when explaining *'bhāvendriya'* it says that they *(bhāvendriya)* are due to *'labdhi'* and *'upayoga'*.[223] These terms exactly states the conditions for knowledge. *'Labdhi'* is the cessation *(kṣayopaśama)* of *jñānavaraṇīya* karma. Thus, except for the *kevalins* simultaneous knowledge is not possible for other living beings.

Sense organ

In the *Jaina* philosophy sense organ is defined as:

1. अहमिंदा जह देवा अविसेसं अहमहं त्ति मण्णंत्ता। इंसति एक्कमेक्कं इंदा इव इंदियं जाणे।[224]

2. इन्दतीति इन्द्र आत्मा। तस्य ज्ञस्वभावस्य तदावरणक्षयोपशने सति स्वयंमर्थान् गृहीतुमसमर्थस्य यदर्थोपलब्धिालिंगतदिन्द्रस्य लिंगमिन्छिद्रयमित्युच्यते। अथवा लीनमर्थं गमयतीति लिंगम्। आत्मनः सूक्ष्मस्यास्तित्वाधीगमे लिंगमिन्द्रयम्। यथा इह धूमोऽग्ने। ...अथवा इन्द्र इति नामकर्मोच्यते तेन सृष्टमिन्द्रियमिति।[225]

3. यदिन्द्रियस्यात्मनो लिंग यदि वा इन्द्रेण कर्मणा। सृष्टं सृष्टं तथा दृष्टं दत्तं वेति तदिन्द्रियः।[226]

The sense organs are five in number viz. touch, taste, smell, sight and ear having their characteristics in the capacity of apprehending touch, taste, odour, colour, shape and sound respectively and each of these are again of two kinds viz. physical *ipudgaJika)* and psychical *(ātimka)*. The physical sense is of material atoms possessed of definite shape like ear, eye etc. It is of two kinds viz. *nivrti* and *upakāraṇa*. The psychical sense is of two kinds viz. *labdhi i.e.* attainment and *upayoga i.e.* conscious activity. Attainment means acquisition of the capacity of manifestation of the sense activity. Conscious activity is a particular modification of the self due to attainment.

Omniscience

In the Jaina tradition the *kevalajñāna* is called omniscience, which is the highest type of perception that comes under the category of extra sensory or transcendental perception *i.e. pāramārthika pratyakṣa*. It is defined as follows:

It is the perfection of the cognitive faculty of the self. It is the pure manifestation of the nature of the conscious substance. The perfect manifestation of the innate nature of the self, arising on the complete destruction of all the obstructive veils *i.e.* the karmic matters is called omniscience.

The self possesses consciousness as its essence. It is luminous nature of the conscious substance. It is nothing but the self as manifested in the act of knowledge. It occurs on the complete annihilation of the obscuring veils. The annihilation is nothing more than the total destruction of all the veils of the obscuring karmas *i.e.* the *ghaṭi* and *aghāti karmas*. The person possessing the super normal faculty of omniscience perceives all the substances with all their modes. For him, nothing remains unknown. No object or any mode thereof remains unperceived. Thus, his knowledge is pure and perfect.

Karma

In Jainism *karma* is defined as:

1. कर्मशब्दस्य कत्रादिषु साधनेषु संभवत्सु इच्छातो विशेषोऽध्यवसेय। वीर्यान्तरायज्ञानावरणक्षयक्षयोपशमापेक्षेण आत्मनात्मपरिणामः पुद्‌गलेन च स्वपरिणमः व्यत्ययेन च निश्चयव्यवहारनयापेक्षया क्रियत इति कर्म। करणप्रशंसा विवक्षायां कर्तृधर्माध्यारोपे सति स परिणामः कुशलमकुशलं वा द्र द्रव्यभावरूपं करेतीति कर्म

आत्मनः प्रधान्यविवक्षायां कर्तृत्वेसति परिणामस्य करणत्वेपपत्तेः बहुलापेक्षया क्रियतेऽनेन कर्मेत्यपि भवति। साध्यसाधनं भावनभिधित्सायां स्वरूपावस्थित तत्त्वकथनात् कृतिः कर्मेत्यपि भवति। एवं शेषकारकोपपत्तिश्च योत्या।[228]

2. जीवं परतन्त्रीकुर्वन्ति, स परतन्त्री क्रियते वा यस्तानि कर्मणि, जीवेन वा मिथ्यादर्शनादिपरिणामैः क्रियन्ते इति कर्माणि।[229]

Following these definitions we can observe that in the *Jaina* tradition *'karma'* is not used in the sense of 'work' or 'deed'. According to them, *karma* is an aggregate of material particles, which are very fine and are imperceptible to the senses. It is a form of matter, which produces certain conditions in the mundane souls that are suffering from the shackles of birth and death from time immemorial. According to Jainism, the entire cosmos is full of that kind of fine matter, which can become karma. Through the action of body, mind and speech, karmic matter gets into the soul and is tied to it accordingly to the modifications of consciousness consisting of *kaśāyas i.e.* anger, pride, deceit and greed. Thus, first of all, there is influx of karmic particles and then there occur certain activities of mind, which are responsible for the actual bondage. In the state of bondage, the soul and the *karma* are more intimate than milk and water. The bondage is of four kinds according to its nature, duration, intensity and quantity. The activities of thought, speech, and body are responsible for the nature of quantity. The duration and intensity result from attachment and aversion. *Karma* may remain latent in the soul for certain period without emerging into appearance. When the moment for its enjoyment arrives, it becomes apparent and releases itself.

As we have already mentioned that the soul has been eternally affected by matter *i.e.* its association with karma has no beginning. Moreover, it is gathering new matter every moment; the liberation of soul from matter is possible by certain means. The soul must stop the influx of new karmas and eliminate the acquired ones. Through this two-fold method it can attain the highest goal *i.e.* emancipation. All obstacles, which impede the manifestation of its true nature are then automatically overcome, because, it is released from the foreign domination of *karma*. This being the situation, when liberation is attained, the soul can undisturbedly make manifest its own innate nature *i.e.* infinite knowledge.

REFERENCES

1. Tattvārthasūtra. V. No. 1. 1. 6.
2 Nyāyāvtāra. V. No. 2.
3 Āptamīmāṁsā. P. 101. *l* /4-
4 Pramāṇapariksā. P. 63.
5 Aśṭasahasrī. P. 56.
6 Prameyakamalamārtaṇda. P.7.
7 Pramāṇanayatattāloka. P. 12.
8. Pramāṇamimaṁsā. P. 2.
9 Syādvādamajñarī. P. 372.
10 Jaina Tarkabhāṣā. P. 58.
11 Bṛhatkalpa Nirukti: 4. 3. 24-25.
12 Bhagavati sūtra: 3-5-192., aṇuyogadvāra P. 211.
13 Tattvārthasūtra: I. 9-19.
14 Nandisūtra: No. 4.
15 Parikṣāmukha:II. 1., Pramāṇanaya Tattvāloka: II. 1.
16 Nyāyavatāra: 1.
17 Jñānabindu's Introduction. P. 5.
18 Pramāṇamimāṁsā. 1. 1. 8.
19. Pramāṇaparikṣā. P.68.
20. Pramāṇanayatattvālaṇkāra. I. 1. 11.
21 Pravacanasāra. . p.58.
22 Sarvārthasiddhi. 1. 12. 103.1.
23 Nyāyaviniścaya. 1.3.57.15.
24 Siddhiviniścaya. 1.16.78.16.
25 Rājavārtika.1.12.1.53.4.
26 Tattvārtha bhāṣya. 1. 15.
27 Cf. Sarvārtha siddhi. P. iii.
28 *Ibid.*
29. *ibid.*
30 cf. *Viśeṣāvaśyaka* bhāṣya: p. 333-34.
31 Cf. *Nāndisūtra*: 36.

32 Tattvārthasūtra: 1. 15. 2
33 Sarvārthasiddhi: p. iii.
34 Veśeṣāvaśyaka bhāṣya: 179.
35 Nāndisūtra: 33.
36 Tattvārthasūtra: 1.15. r :r
37 *Nāndisūtra*: 36.
38 Nyāyasūtra : 1. 1.4.
39 Laghiyastrayī. P.23.
40 Prameyakamalamārtaṇda. P.
41 Tattvārthsūtra: iv. 1.9.4.
42 Tattvārthasūtra. IV. 1.9.4.
43 Sarvārthasiddhi. 1. 13. 106.4.
44 Nyāyadīpikā. 3.8. 56. 4.
45 Parikṣāmukha. 3. 3-4.
46 Mahāpurāṇa. 21. 229.
47 Sarvārthasiddhi. 5. 31. 302. 3.
48 Syādvādamajñarī
49 Nyāyadīpikā. 3. 10.57.3.
50 Tattvārthādhigamabhāṣya. I. 18.
51 Rājavārtika. 3.1.13.119.. 168. 22.
52 Nyāyadīpikā. 3. 15-16 62. 1.
53 Syādvādamajñarī. 28. 32. 27.
54 Laghīyastrayī. P. 34.
55 Nyāyadīpikā. p.46
56 Syādvādamajñri. 20.256.13
57 Nyāyadīpikā. 3. 17.
58 Syādvādamajñarī 28.322.3.
59 Nyāyadīpikā. 3. 29.
60 Nyāyadīpikā. 3. 64.104. 2
61 Pañcādhyāyī, uttarārdha. V. 894.
62 Ratnakaraṇdaśrāvakācāra. V. 9.
63 Dhavalā.3. 122.9,11,12.
64 Rājavārtika. 1. 12. 7.54. 8.
65 Nyāyadīpikā. 3. 78. 112.
66 Syādvādamajñarī. 21. 262. 7.
67 Ratna Karaṇḍa śrāvakācāra: Verse no: 8.
68 *Ibid.*
69 Tattvasarhgraha: 3149
70 Nyāyavatāra: 56.
71 'Utpādavyayadhauvyayuktam Sat', Tattvārthasūtra. 5. 30.
72 'guṇaparyāyavaddravyam' *Ibid.* 5. 38.

73 The Jiana theory of Reality and Knowledge: p. 131.
74 Nyāyavatāra. 29.
75 Samayasāra. 519. 11.
76 *ibid.* 513. 17.
77 Svayambhustotra. 134.164.
78 Nyāyacakravṛtti. 251.
79 Rājavārtika. 1.6.5.33. 15.
80 Saptabhangītaraṇgiṇī. 16. 1.
81 Tatvārthādhigamabhāṣya. 1. 35.
82 Syādvādamajñarī. 27. 305. 28.
83. Dhavalā.1.1,1,1.11.17.
84 Prameyakamalamārtaṇda.p.676.
85 Pramāṇanayatattvālaṇkāra. 7.1.
86 Sarvārthasiddhi. 1.33. 140. 7.
87 Jiana Tarkabhāṣā. P.64.
88 Jiana Tarkabhāṣā. P.64.
89 Jaina Tarkabhāṣā. P. 65.
90 *Ibid.*
91 *Ibid.*
92 Bṛhatnayacakra. P.4.
93 Pravacanasāra. V. No. 2.3.
94 Tattvārthasūtra. 5. 2.
95 Pañcāsthikāyasāra. V. No. 18.
96 Pañcāsthikāya. V. No. 18.
97 Dravyānuyogatarkaṇā 6/2 verse, Utpāda, vyaya, dhrouvya is called Mātṛpadikā.
98 Sthānāngasūtra : Verse no: 2.251.,Bhagavatisūtra: 7/10.305.
99 Bhagavatisūtra: 7/10.305., Uttarādhayanasūtra: 2/14.
100 Tattarthasūtra: 1/4.
101 Prajñāpanāvrtti:1/4.
102 Nyāyavatāra. P.68.
103 Pravacanasāra. P. 147.
104 Rājavārtika. 1.4. 7. 25.27.
105 Sarvārthasiddhi. 1. 4. 14. 3. nhesiddhi: 6. 4. 320.
106 Nayacakravṛtti. 360.
107 Gomottasāra Jīvakāṇda. 2. 21. 8.
108 Tattvārthasāra. 2. 2.
109 Pañcasthikāya. V. No. 27.
110 Bhagavatisūtra. 13.4.480.
111 Uttarādhyayanasūtra. 28. 10.
112 Bhavapahuda. V. No. 148.
113 Sthānāngasūtra: 2. 1. 57..; ^, 454 *n.*
114 Pañcasthikāya: 2. 122.

115 Hollywood.R&T. Introduction lesson, no. 2nd. What is ether?
116 Prajñāpnā sūtra: pāda 1. Vṛtti.
117 Bhagavatisūtra: 13.4.
118 Tattvārthasūtra. 6.1.
119 Rājavārtika. 6. 1. 1,2,. 587.
120 Bhagavati ārādhanā. 36. 134. 16.
121 Nayacakravṛtti. P. 156.
122 Sarvārthasiddhi. 9.1.
123 Bhāratīya darśana of Umesh Mishra. p. 116.
124 Tattvārthasūtra: 6.1.
125 Rājavārtika. 1. 4. 10. 26. 3., 5.24.1.485.10.
126 Sarvārthasiddhi.7.25.366.2.
127 Rājavārtika. 1.4. 17. 26. 29.
128 Dhavalā. 14. 5,6,1. 2. 3.
129 Rājavārtika: 2.1O, 2.-114.
130 Tattvārthasūtra, 1.2.
131 Sarvārthasiddhi.6. 2.
132 Sūtrakṛtāṅgaśīlavṛtti. 2. 5. 17.
133 Nayacakravṛtti: 152.
134 Bhagavati ārādhanā.38. 134. 10.
135 Dravyasaṁgrahaṭīkā. 29.
136 Tattvārthasūtra: 6. 4. Sarvārthasiddhi: 6. 4. 320.
137 Tattvārthasūtra. 6. 4.
138 Sarvārthasiddhi. 6. 4. 321.
139 Rājavārtika.6. 4. 4-7.508.
140 Satkhatāgama. 13.5.4.
141 Dhavalā. 13. 5. 4, 24. 51.1.
142 Nayacakravṛtti. 153.
143 Dravyasaṁgraha. 31.
144 Rājavārtika. 5. 1. 24, 26. 434. 12.
145 Dravyasaṁgrahaṭīkā. 15. 50. 12.
146 Tattvārthasūtra. 5. 25.
147 Niyamasāratātparyavṛtti. 20.
148 Tattvārthasūtra: 5. 23.
149 Tattvārtha Rājavārtika: 5. 25. 7.
150 *Ibid*. 23. 8-10.
151 Ālāpāpadhati : 2. *i.e.* pudgalasya sparśarasagandhavarṇarh mūrtatvaṁ acetanatvamiti ṣaṭ.
152 Tattvārthasiddhi: 5. 23.
153 Tattvārtha sūtra: 5. 25.
154 Sarvārthasiddhi: 5. 25.
155 Tattvārtharājavārtika: 5. 11. 2., Jaṁbudipāpanati samgraha: 13. 17.

156 Pañcāstikāyasāra: 88.
157 Sarvārthsiddhi: 5. 25. 267. 7., Rājavārtika: 5. 25. 2. 461.16.
158 Tattvārthasūtra: v. 26.
159 Sarvārthasiddhi: v. 26.
160 *Ibid.*
161 Sarvārthasiddhi: v. 26.
162 Niyamasāra: 21.
163 Gommañasāra: Jīvakānda: 606-8.
164 Tattvārthasūtra:2. 38., 41-44.
165 Sāṁkhya pravacana bhāṣya: ch. I. 66.,Vyāsa bhāṣya on yogasūtra:II. 19., Pravacana bhāṣya: 1. 62. IV. 14., The positive science of ancient hindu: p. 24.
166 Introduction to Abhidharma dīpa: p. 90. They call it ākāśa dhātu pariccheda. It means material quality of liberation.
167 ¢ānāsrava mārgsatyaṁ trividhaṁ cāpasaṁskṛtaṁ ākāśarhdvaucirodau ca tatrākasmnāvṛtiṁ". Abhidharmakoṣa: I. 5.
168 Abhidharmakoṣa: 11.55.
169 Brahmasūtra: I. II. 22.
170 Bhagavati sūtra: 2. 1. 118.
171 Tattvārthasūtra. 5. 4,6,7,18.
172 Pancasthikaya. 60.
173 Sarvārthasiddhi. 5. 18. 284.
174 Rājavārtika.5. 1.21-22.434.
175 Dhavalā. 4. 1,3,1.4. 7.
176 Nayacakravṛtti.68.
177 Dravyasaṁgraha. 16. 57.
178 Bhagavatisūtra: 2. 10. 118., Nityāvasthitanyarupāṇi. Tattvārthahigamasūtra: v. 3
179 * Tattvārthrājāvartika: p. 434.
180 * Bhagavatisūtra: 2. 10. 118.
181 Pravacanasāra: 2. 40.
182 Pañcasthikāyatatparyavṛtti: gāthā: 76.
183 Tattvārthasūtra: 5. 6.
184 *Ibid*: 5. 4.
185 *Ibid.*
186 *Ibid*: 5. 7.
187 Sarvārthasiddhi: 5. 2., * Rājavārtika: 5. 12. 19. 456. 7.
188 Ākāśamātmapratijnaṁ: Sarvārthasiddhi: 3. 1. 204.
189 Ākāśasyāṇatmāṁ: Tattvārthasūtra: 5. 6.
190 Ākāṣaṁ dvividhaṁ lokākāṣamalokāsaṁ ceti, Sarvārthasiddhia:5. 12. 278., Rājavārtika:5. 12. 18.456. 10.
191 Pañcasthikāya: 61., Sarvārthasiddhi: 5. 12. 279. ,Rājavārtika: 5.12. 19. 456. 7.

192 Sarvārthasiddhi. 1.4.
193 Sarvārthasiddhi Uthānikā. 1.8.
194 Ātmakhyātigāthā No. 288.
195 Nayacakravṛtti. 156.
196 Rājavārtika. 1. 1. 37. 10. 15.
197 Bhagavati Ārādhanā. 38. 134. 18.
198 Nyāyacakravṛtti: 156.
199 Bhagavatiārādhanā: 38. 134. 18.
200 *Ibid.*
201 Pañcasthikāyatatparyavṛtti. P.46.
202 Sarvārthasiddhi. 1.9.64.
203 Dravyasaṁgraha. 12. 30.
204 Sarvārthasiddhi. 1. 14. 109.3.
205 Dravyasaṁgraha. 12. 30.1.
206 Tattvārthasūtra. 1. 14.
207 Sarvārthasiddhi.2. 11.282.
208 *Ibid.*
209 Sarvārthasiddhi. 5. 19. 563.
210 *Ibid.*
211 Tattvārthasūtra. 2. 12.
212 Dravyasaṁgraha. 12.
213 *Nāndisūtra*. 71.
214 Dhavalā. 1. 1.,1, 99.281.4.
215 Bhagavatisūtra. 1. 3. 113.
216 Sarvārthasiddhi. 5. 19.563.
217 Sarvārthasiddhi. 1. 19. 202.
218 Tattvārthasūtra. 1. 19.
219 Ācāraṅgasūtra. 1.
220 Bhagavatisūtra. 1. 3. 165.
221 *Ibid.*
222 Pañcasaṁgraha. Prakrit. 1. 178.
223 Tattvārthasūtra. 2. 18.
224 Pañcasaṁgraha. Prakrit. 1. 65.
225 Sarvārthasiddhi. 1. 14. 108.3.
226 Gomaṣasāra jīvakāṇda. 165.
227 Syādavādamjñarī. 28.321.8.
228 Rājavārtika. 6. 1. 7. 504. 26.
229 Āptapariksatfka. 113.269.

Chapter - 2

JAINA PHILOSOPHY AS PRESENTED IN NYĀYA AND VAIŚEṢIKA SYSTEMS

Introduction

We have already recorded in the introduction that amongst the theist schools of Indian Philosophy, it is only the *Vedāntins* and the *Naiyāyikas* who have taken the Jaina tenets for critical examination to some extent. Again out of these two, the *Vedāntins'* involvement than the *Naiyāyikas* in refuting some of the basic tenants of the Jaina is more, whereas the *Sāṁkhyas,* the *Yogas* and the *Mīmāṁsakas* have not taken the Jaina theories seriously at all except passing remarks here and there in their respective texts. Reserving the treatment of the *Vedānta* for the next chapter we present here the *nāya* treatment of the Jaina Philosophy. It must be recorded in clear terms that a very few logicians have discussed and recorded the Jaina tenants in their *pūrvapakṣa* as opponents to criticize and refute them. To be more particular, it is only Bhāsarvajñā where we get some detailed elaboration and refutation of the basic theories of the Jainas viz. *Syādvāda* etc. The number of authorities being less it was not possible to present the discussion. Hence, we have arranged the discussion on the basis of concepts or theories. All the authorities dealing with particular tenets of the Jainas are put in one place. The theories or the concepts discussed in this chapter are:

1. Sense Organ.
2. The Creation of Śarīra.
3. Sarvanityatvavāda.

4. Components of inferential cognition.
5. Prāmāṇyavāda.
6. Śabdagrahaṇaprakriyā.
7. Śabda Pramāṇa.
8. Anekāntavāda.
9. Inconsistency in the statement of the Tīrthṅkaras:
10. No distinction between Jīva and Ajīva.

Now we present the discussion following the sequence mentioned above.

Sense organ

In *Nyāyasūtra,* Gotama [2nd A.D.], the founder of Indian school logic, has recorded the view of the Jainas in connection with the sense organ, when *sūtrakāra* refutes the view of the *Sāṁkhya* philosophers viz. the sense organs are being made of matter. He records the view of the Jainas against the *Sāṁkhya* philosophers to establish their own view. In the meanwhile he has also recorded some arguments of the Jainas and finally refuted their view. Though Jaina is quoted for analysis, no reference is made to Jainas by him.

At the outset, let us see the presentation of Jainism in the *vātsyānabhāṣya*. In the context of refutation of the *Sāṁkhya* view on the material cause of sense organ: *Sūtrakāra Gotama* records the objections of the Jainas to answer the *Sāṁkhya* philosophers. The first objection is with regard to the nature or the material substance of the organs, particularly, the visual sense organ *i.e.* eye. I reproduce the texts of arguments for better understanding.

The text runs thus:

नक्तंचरनयनरश्मिदर्शनाच्च।[1]

In the nocturnal animals like the cat etc. the visual rays are actually observed. From this it is inferred that such rays also exist in the human eyes. It may be objected that just as there is a difference in species between the animals and the human beings, so also there is a difference in the nature of their visual senses; that is the visual sense of a nocturnal animal has rays whereas the visual sense of a human being has no ray. To this Vātsyāyana answers that such a difference cannot be admitted. The visual sense of all the animals are similar in nature as is evident by the fact that the visual sense of a cat is as much obstructed by a wall as that of the human being. He writes:

दृश्यन्ते हि नक्तं नयनरश्मयो नक्तंचरणां वृषदंशप्रभृतीनां तेन शेषस्यानुमानमिति। जातिभेदवदिन्द्रियभेद इति चेत्। धार्मभेदमात्रं चानुपपन्नमावनणस्य प्राप्तिप्रतिषेधार्थस्य दर्शनादिति।[2]

One of the main objections or arguments of the Jainas against the *Nyāya* view is that the visual sense cannot be made of fire, because it also reveals darkness. That which is made of fire e.g. the sun or a lamp cannot reveal darkness and that which reveals darkness cannot be made of fire. Assuming the visual sense to be made of fire, it would have been impossible for us to see darkness.

The main issue here is concerned with the nature of darkness. Like the *Mīmāṁsakas* who view darkness as substance, the *Naiyāyīkas* consider it as non-existence *(abhāva)* of the element of fire in the special form in which its colour is manifested and not subdued. The knowledge of non-existence is not possible when the "counter positive *(pratiyogī)* is present. For example, in the presence of the 'jar', there is no knowledge of the non-existence of the jar. The light of the lamp is the counter positive of darkness or the non-existence of light. Therefore, in the presence of the lamp there is no question of the knowledge of darkness. The visual rays because of the latency of their colour cannot be considered as the counter positive of darkness. Hence, it is possible to have *the* knowledge *of darkness in spite of the presence of the visual* rays. Thus, the Jainas cannot claim that nothing made of fire can reveal darkness, only that specific product of the element of fire which is the counter positive of darkness cannot reveal darkness. The products of the element of fire in other forms may reveal darkness.

The main objection is: on the process of perceptual

cognition, both the *Naiyāyikas* and the Jainas accept that in the process of perceptual cognition self or soul is connected with mind, mind with sense organ and sense organ with the object:

इन्द्रियार्थसन्निकर्षस्य ज्ञानकरण्त्वानुपपत्तिः।[3]

The Jaina objects to the last clause of the definition, namely, the sense organ is conjoined with object: To them, this may be true in case of all other sense organs minus eyes. To them, visual sense organ *i.e.* eye is *aprāpyakāri*. No cognition is accepted between sense organ *i.e.* eye and the object. Gotama has recorded the view of the Jaina as follows:

अप्राप्यग्रहणं काचाभ्रपटलस्फटिकान्तरितोपलब्धेः।[4]

The visual sense can perceive an object without actually coming in contact with it, because an object screened off by a pane of glass, a sheet of mica or a slab of crystal is also visually perceived. *Bhāsyakāra* Vātsyāyana elaborates the argument of the Jainas by giving example before refuting it. This is as follows:

तृणादिसर्पद द्रव्यं काचेऽभ्रपटले या प्रतिहतं दृष्टमव्यवहितेन सन्निकृष्यते व्याहन्यते वै प्राप्तिर्व्यवधानेनेति। यदि च रश्म्यर्थसनिकर्षो ग्रहणहेतुः स्याद् न व्यवहितस्य सिन्निकर्ष इत्यग्रहणं स्यात्। अस्ति चेयं काचाभ्रपटलस्पटि-कान्तरितोपलब्धिः सा ज्ञापयत्याप्राप्यकारीणीन्द्रियाणी। अतएवाभौतिकानि प्राप्यकारित्वं हि भैतिकधर्म इति न।[5]

It is observed that a pane of glass or a sheet of mica obstructs a blade of grass driven by wind. The contact of something is possible only with an object, which is not obstructed. The obstruction goes against the condition of contact. If the contact of the visual rays with the object is assumed to be the cause of perception, there can be no perception of an object obstructed by something because, there can be no contact with an object thus obstructed. But the fact is that an object though obstructed by a pane of glass or a sheet of mica or a slab of crystal, is actually perceived. This shows that the sense need not come in actual contact.

To this, following is the answer of the *Naiyāyikas*. Gotama notes:

न कुड्यान्तरितानुपलब्धेरप्रतिषेधः।[6]

The above argument of the Jainas does not disprove that the sense object contact is not the cause of perceptual knowledge, because an object obstructed by a wall is not perceived. Vātsyāyana makes this point very clear by saying thus:

अप्राप्यकारित्वे सतीन्द्रियाणां कुड्यान्तरितस्यानुपलब्धिर्न्न स्यात्।[7]

It means if the senses are considered as giving perceptual knowledge without coming in actual contact with the object perceived, there cannot be the absence of perception of an object obstructed by a wall.

Further, the Jainas argue that if the senses are considered as giving perceptual knowledge after actually coming in contact with the object, there cannot be the perception of what is obstructed by a pane of glass, a sheet of mice or a slab of crystal. Vātsyāyana says:

प्राप्यकारित्वेऽपि तु काचाभ्रपटलस्फटिकान्तरितोपलब्धिर्न स्यात्।[8]

The answer is given by the *sūtrakāra* as follows:

अप्रतीघातात्सान्निकर्षोपपत्तिः।[9]

It means, in the case of an object obstructed by a pane of glass etc. the sense object contact is possible because these do not obstruct the visual rays. In other words, a pane of glass or a sheet of mica does not obstruct the visual rays and hence, the visual rays being unobstructed can come in contact with the object beyond.

The next argument of the Jainas is that a material object can never be unobstructed:

न च काचेभ्रपटलं वा नयनरश्मिं विष्टभ्नाति सोऽप्रतिहन्यमानः सन्निकृष्यत इति यश्च मन्यते न भौतिकस्याप्रतिघात इति यत्र।[10]

To this the logicians say that, this is not true, because there is no obstruction in the three cases viz.

(a) the rays of the sun,

(b) what is separated by a slab of crystal

(c) the thing burned. It is stated by Gotama as follows:

आदित्यरश्मेरविघातात् स्फटिकान्तरितेऽविघाताद् दाह्येऽविघातात् अविघातादिति च पदाभिसम्बन्धभेदाद्वाक्यभेद इति। यथावाक्यं चार्थभेद इति। आदित्यरश्मिः कुम्भादिषु न प्रतिहन्यतेऽविघातात्। कुम्भस्थमुदक तपति प्राप्तै हि द्रव्यान्तरगुणस्य उष्णस्य स्पर्शस्य ग्रहणं तेन च शीतस्पर्शभिभव इति। स्फटिकान्तरितेऽपि प्रकाशनीये प्रदीपरश्मीनामप्रतिघातः अप्रतिघातात्प्राप्तस्य ग्रहणमिति। भर्जनकपालादिस्थं च द्रव्यमाग्नेयेन तेजसा दह्यते तजाविघातात्प्राप्तिः प्राप्तौ तु दाहो नाप्राप्यकारि तेज इति। अविघातादिति च केवलं पदमुपादीयते कोऽयमविघातो नाम। अव्यूह्यमानावयवेन व्यवध ाायकेन द्रव्येण सर्वतो द्रव्यस्याविष्टम्भः क्रियाहेतोरप्राप्तिबन्धः प्राप्तिरप्रतिषेध इति। दृष्टं हि कलशनिषक्तानामपां बहिःशीतस्पर्शग्रहणम्। न चैन्द्रियेणासुन्निकुष्टस्य द्रव्यस्य स्पर्शोपलाब्धिः दृष्टौ च पस्पन्दपरिस्त्रवौ। तच्च काचाभ्रपटलादिभिर्नायनरश्मेरप्रतिघाताद्विभिद्यार्थेन सह सन्निकर्षादुपपन्नं ग्रहणमिति।[11]

Vātsyāyana makes this point by saying that the word 'non-obstruction' *'avighāta'* being connected with each of the three expressions yields three different statements namely

(a) because there is no obstruction in the case of the rays of the sun

(b) because there is no obstruction in the case of what is separated by a slab of crystal and

(c) because there is no obstruction in the case of what is burned.

Thus, the rays of the sun are not obstructed by the jar etc. and being unobstructed, these produce heat in the water contained in the jar. Because of this conjunction with the rays of the sun in this water perceived the quality of a different substance viz. heat, which is a quality of fire and the cold touch *i.e.* the actual quality of water gets subdued by it.

In the case of something separated by a slab of crystal, there is obstruction between the rays of the lamp and the object to be revealed; because of this want of obstruction there can be conjunction between the two resulting in perception.

Lastly, things placed on a frying pan *(Bharjana kapāla)* the earthen frying pan get burned by the heat of fire, there is conjunction between the object placed on the pan and the fire below the pan because of the lack of any obstruction. And this conjunction causes burning in as much as the element of fire *(tejas)* does not act without getting conjoined.

The word 'non-obstruction' is being repeatedly used. Non-obstruction of an object means the absence of being totally blocked by another object, the blocking object having no space separating its parts *(avyuhyamāna avayava)*. In other words, it is the absence of any factor counteracting the cause of any action *i.e.* the want of the cancellation of conjunction. As it is observed, the cold touch of water contained within a jar is perceived on the outer side of the jar also. The touch of a substance, which is not in contact with the sense organ is not perceived. It is also observed that water oozes out *(parisravaṇa)* and comes out in droplets *(parispanda)* from a jar. Therefore, there being no obstruction separating the visual rays from an object beyond a pane of glass or a sheet of mica etc. the contact between them is possible and as such there is the perception of the object.

The Jainas further argued: "it cannot be claimed that the visual life sense is obstructed by a pane of glass etc. because it leads to the absurdity of imputing the characters of something to something else.

Gotama says:

नेतरेतरधर्मप्रसङ्गात्।[12]

To this the answer of Gotama is: An object screened off by a pane of glass etc. is perceived just as the image perceived in the mirror and water, because these are transparent by nature. He says:

आदर्शोदकयोः प्रसादस्वाभाव्याद्रूपोपलब्धिवत्तदुपलब्धिः।[13]

Vātsyāyana makes this point by saying thus:

आदर्शोदकयोः प्रसादो रूपविशेषः स्वो धर्मो नियमदर्शनात् प्रसादस्य

वा स्वो धर्मो रूपालम्यनम्। यथाऽऽदर्शप्रतिहतस्य परावृत्तस्य नयनरश्मेः स्वेन मुखेन सन्निकर्षे सति स्वमुखोपलम्भनं प्रतिबिम्बग्रहणाख्यामादर्शरूपानुग्रहात्तन्निमित्त भवति। आदर्शरूपोपघाते तदभावात् कुड्यदिषु च प्रतबिम्बग्रहणं न भवति। एवं काचाभ्रपटलादिभिरविघातश्चक्षूरश्मेः कुडयादिभिश्च प्रतिघातो द्रव्यस्वभावविनियमादिति।[14]

It means, transparency *(prasāda),* which is a special quality, is found in a mirror and water and it is a specific quality of only such things, because this is uniformly observed. It is the nature of transparency to reflect an image *(rūpaupalambhana)*. The visual rays make an impact on the mirror and being rebounded back, come in contact with one's own face, which perception is called the cognition of image. The cause of this cognition is the mirror, which is aided by its transparency; with the loss of this quality of mirror there can be no such cognition. But in the case of wall etc., there is no such cognition of an image. Thus, because of the specific nature of the different substance, a pane of glass or a sheet of mice etc. does not obstruct the visual rays while they get obstructed by the wall etc.

The Creation (Creation of śarīra)

The main objection raised against the Jaina in this topic is on the creation of *śarīra*. In *Nyāyasūtra* III. II. 68 to 72 Gotama has recorded some arguments of *Jaina* logicians regarding the process of the creation of the body *(śarīra)* immediately after refuting the view of *Sāṁkhya* and *yoga* philosophers on this issue. The question is: whether it is produced from *dharma* and *adharma* or not. Gotama presents the view of Jaina philosophers and examines it exclusively and finally refutes it as it leads to absurdity. In some five *sūtras,* the whole analysis is presented. The *sūtras* are:

तददृष्टकारितमिति चेत् पुनस्तत्प्रसङ्गोऽपवर्गे।

मनःकर्मनिमित्तत्वाच्च संयोगानुच्छेदः।

नित्यत्वप्रसङ्गश्च प्रायणानुपपत्तः।

अणुश्यामतानित्यत्ववदेतत्स्यात्।

नाकृताभ्यागमप्रसङ्गात्।[15]

Commenting on this, Vātsyāyana presents the Jaina view 'the body is produced by *adṛṣṭa* as being a quality of the atoms. In the system of Jaina philosophy, *adṛṣṭa* is only a quality of the atoms as well as the mind and produces movement in them. Being moved by it, the atoms get conjoined with one another and produce the body. The mind being moved by the *adṛṣṭa,* which is its own quality *i.e.* which is located in it, gets into such a body and the knower has the cognitions in a body as endowed with the mind.

Following Gotama, Vātsyāyana tries to refute this point of the Jainas. He has forwarded the same arguments to refute the *sāmkhya* philosophers, namely that if it is so, then there is a possibility of the body being produced even after liberation due to the absence of destruction of the quality of *adṛṣṭa.* If *adṛṣṭa* be a cause of the body as a quality of the atoms, the body may be produced even after liberation, for, *adṛṣṭa* being a quality of the atoms cannot be destroyed. Vātsyāyana says:

अदृष्टं नाम परमाणुनां गुणविशेषः क्रियाहेतुस्तेन प्रेरिताः परमाणवः सम्मूर्च्छिताः शरीरमुप्तादयन्तीति तत्र मनः समाविशति स्वगुणेनादृष्टेन प्रेरितं समनस्के शरीरे दस्टुरूपलब्धिार्भवतीति। एतस्मिव वै दर्शने गुणानुच्छेदात्पुनस्तत्प्रसङ्गोऽपवर्गे अपवर्गे शरीरोत्पत्तिः परमाणुगुण-स्यादृष्टस्यानुच्छेद्यत्वादिति।[16]

Further, Gotama says: if the conjunction of the mind with the body be due to the *adṛṣṭa* located in the mind, the conjunction can never be destroyed. Vātsyāyana makes this point clear by saying that if it is admitted that the mind gets conjoined with the body because of being moved by the *adṛṣṭa,* which is located as a quality in the mind itself the said conjunction can never be destroyed. And even if we accept the Jainas view then- what would be the cause of the mind's movement out of the body at the time of the death? If, on the other hand, *adṛṣṭa* is admitted to be the quality of self, it can be explained by saying that when some particular *adṛsta,* is destroyed through the enjoyment of its result the mind is made to move out of the body by some other particular *adṛṣṭa,* which has started yielding its results.

Then, he records some further argument of the Jainas: let it be accepted that the mind moves out of the body because of its own *adṛsṭa*. That is, let the same *adṛsṭa,* as is the cause of mind's moving into the body be also the cause of its moving out of the body. He says:

योऽदृष्टः शरीरोपसर्पणहेतुः स एवापसर्पणहेतुरपीति।[17]

To this, *Vātsyāyana* says, no, because the same *adṛsṭa* cannot be the cause of both life and death. To explain it he says: if the *Jaina's* view is accepted, it would follow that the same *adṛsṭa* is the cause of both life, when the mind moves out of the body. This, however, cannot be logically justified.

न एकस्य जीवनप्रायणहेतुत्वानुपपत्तेः। एवं च सति एकमदृष्टं जीवनप्रायणयोहेतुरिति प्राप्तं, नैतदुपपद्यते।[18]

To explain further, Gotama says: there would be the absurdity of the body being eternal, for, death cannot be explained. Death results when, due to the gradual diminution of *adṛsṭa* through the enjoyment of its result, the body falls and there is rebirth due to some other *adṛsṭa*. If the production of the body is admitted to be due to only the material elements not depending upon *adṛṣra,* what entity would there be the gradual diminution of which, may be said to be the cause of the falling of the body and death. Thus, death being logically unjustified, we would be led to the absurd conclusion that the body is eternal. And, if death is admitṭed to be merely accidental, the different kinds of death cannot be justified. That is, each person dies under some specific condition. Someone dies at an early age, someone in the mother's womb, and someone in the ripe old age and so on. This shows that death too has some specific cause and is not merely accidental.

विपाकसंवेदनात् कर्माशयक्षये शरीरपातः प्रमाणम्, कर्माशयान्तराच्चपुनर्जन्म। भूतमात्रात्तु कर्मनिरपेक्षाच्छरीरोत्पत्तौ कस्य क्षयाच्छरीरपात्तः प्रायणमिति प्रायणानुपपत्तेः खलु वै नित्यत्व प्रसंगं विद्मः यादृच्छिके तु प्रायणे प्रायणभेदानुपपत्तिरिति।[19]

Further, the Jaina philosophers argue that just as the uncaused black colour of an atom, when destroyed by conjunction with fire is never produced again, so also the body, which is produced by *adṛṣṭa,* as located in the atoms and the mind is not produced once again after its destruction. Vātsyāyana says:

यथा अणोः श्यामता नित्या अग्नि संयोगेन प्रतिविद्धा न पुनरुत्पद्यते एवमदृष्टकारितं शरीरमपवर्गे पुनर्नोत्पद्यत इति।[20]

Udyotakara, the author of *Nyāyavārtika* explains the implication of the opponent as follows. The black colour of an atom of earth, though uncaused, is destroyed by conjunction with fire. Similarly, the *adṛṣṭa* located as a quality in the atoms and the mind, though uncaused, is destroyed by 'right knowledge' *(tattva jhāna).* As such, due to the complete destruction of the *adṛṣṭa,* no further body is produced after liberation.

Gotama's answer to this objection is that, this argument does not stand to logic, because there follows the absurdity of acquiring the result of an action not performed. He says: the uncaused-ness of the black colour of an atom is not a proper instance, because of the absurdity of accepting what is not proved *(akṛtābhyagama).* The word *'akṛta'* means what is not justified by any *pramāṇa* and the word *'abhyagama'* means admitting it *i.e.* accepting it as true. Thus, one adhering to the instance of the previous *sūtra* has to admit what is not established by any *pramāṇa.* The uncaused-ness of the black colour of an atom cannot, therefore, be a proper instance. Neither perception nor inference establishing that the black colour of an atom is uncaused has been cited. Hence, the instance as stated here only is similar to the probandum of an inference. That is the black colour is actually produced by some specific cause. As such, its uncaused-ness, which is unduly accepted by the Jainas, is not yet proved and cannot be cited as an instance.

Further, Vātsyāyana makes this point more clear by giving three alternative arguments namely that, the view of the Jainas cannot be accepted because of the absurdity of the acquiring the result of an action not performed. One who tries to explain the production of the body as independent of *adṛṣṭa* with the instance of the black colour of the atom would have to face the absurdity of acquiring the result of an action not performed. That is, there arises the absurdity that the self has to feel pleasure and pain even without performing the actions, which are the causes of those particular pleasure and pain. The view of one who answers in the affirmative *i.e.* may even accept the above possibility is contradicted by perception, inference and verbal testimony. He says:

अथ वा नाकृताभ्यागमप्रसंगात् अणुश्यामतादृष्टान्तेनाकर्मनिमित्तां शरीरोत्पत्तिं समादशानस्याकृताभ्यागमप्रसङ्गः। अकृते सुखदुःखेहेतौ कर्मणि पुरुषस्य सुखं दुःखमभ्यागच्छतीति प्रसज्येत। ओमिति ब्रुवतः प्रत्यक्षानुमानागमविरोधः।[21]

Vātsyāyana further explains the contradiction with perception as follows. The different kinds of pleasure and pain of all the living beings are known perceptually, for, they are internally cognized by each self. They may be intense, mild, lasting, short-lived, of many fold types, of only one type and so on, and these are the points of difference. But following Jaina's view there are no specific cause for pleasure and pain viz. *adṛṣṭa* as located in each individual self, and a specific effect is not observed to be produced unless there is a specific cause. If on the other hand, the sensation of pleasure and pain are admitted to be due to *adṛṣṭa,* the difference in the various form of pleasure and pain can be explained to be due to the presence of intensity or mildness in the *adṛṣṭas,* virtuousness or viciousness of the actions leading to the collections of the *adṛṣṭas* and many-fold-ness or the same ness of *adṛṣṭas*. Thus, in the Jaina's view the defense in the various forms of pleasure and pain, which is an observed fact cannot be explained due to the absence of the cause and this is nothing but contradiction with perception.

He presented further to point out contradiction with inference. He says:

दृष्टं हि पुरुषगुणव्यवस्थानात्सुखदुःखव्यवस्थानम्। यः खलु चेतनावान् साधाननिर्वर्तनीयं सुखं बुद्ध्वा तज्जिहासुः साधन परिवर्जनाय यतते स च दुःखेन त्यज्यते न विपरीतः। अस्ति चेदं यत्नमन्तरेण चेतनानां

सुखदुःखव्यवस्थानं तेनापि चेतनागुणान्तरव्यवस्थाकृतेन भवितव्यमित्यनुमानम्। तदेतदकर्मनिमिते सुखदुःखयोगे विरुधयते इति। तच्च गुणान्तरमसंबेद्यत्वाद्दृष्टं विपाककालनियमाच्चाव्यवस्थितम्। बुद्ध्यादस्तु संवेद्याश्चापवर्गिणश्चेति।[22]

It means, the restriction of pleasure and pain is due to the restriction of the quality viz. the internal effort in the self of a person. That is, only a person, whose self is characterized by an internal effort for pleasure or pain experiences pleasure and pain. Only a conscious person who becomes aware that pleasure is to be produced by some particular means and being desirous of attaining the pleasure strives to get the means it can have. The sensation of pleasure and not one who is the opposite *i.e.* who does not act in the above manner will not enjoy pleasure and pain. Again, one who becomes aware that pain is to be produced by some particular means and being desirous of avoiding the pain, strives to avoid the means it does not have the sensation of pain and not one who is the opposite. But it is a fact that sometimes pleasure and pain are restricted to *i.e.* produced the different conscious persons even without such internal effort, when the cause of pleasure or pain appears suddenly and there is no scope for the person's deliberation. It is, thus, inferred that the sudden pleasure and pain, which is not due to internal effort must be due to the restriction *i.e.* presence of some other quality viz. *adrsta* of the conscious self. If the sensation of pleasure and pain are admitted to be independent of *adṛṣṭa,* the above inference becomes contradicted. The other quality of the self, established by the above inference is called *adṛṣra,* because it is imperceptible. It is also not restricted to a particular point of time, because no specific point of time for the production of its result can be cited beforehand and as such, it can be the cause of sudden pleasure and pain. Besides, the other qualities of the self like knowledge, internal efforts etc. are destroyed in the third moment after production. Thus, they cannot be the cause of sudden pleasure and pain at a later period.

Further, Vātsyāyana explains the contradiction with verbal testimony.

बहु खल्विदमार्षमृषीणामुपदेश्जातमनुष्ठानपरिवर्जनाश्रयपमुपदेशफलं च शरीरिणां वर्णाश्रमविभागेनानुष्ठानलक्षणा प्रवृत्तिः परिवर्जनलक्षणा निवृत्तिः तच्चोभयमेतस्यां दृष्टौ नास्ति कर्म सुचरितं दुश्चरितं वा कर्मनिमित्तः पुरुषाणां सुखदुःखयोग इति विरुध्यते। सेयं पापिष्टानां मिथ्यादृष्टिरकर्मनिमित्तां शरीरसृष्टिरकर्मनिमित्तः सुखदुःखयोग इति।[23]

It means, there are *śāsthras* embodying the various percepts of the *ṛṣis* concerning the performance of avoidance of different acts. The results of these percepts are the different person's caste *(Varṇa)* and stage of life *(āśrama)* as well as their being prevented from the harmful acts *i.e.* avoiding them. These two forms of activity viz. being engaged to and being prevented from ceremonies, prescribed by *śāsthras are* in contradiction with the view that there is neither virtue nor vice and the sensation of pleasure and pain of the persons are not due to *adṛṣṭa*. That is, if there is neither virtue nor vice, nobody would either perform the pious acts or refrain from the harmful ones.

In this manner, Vātsyāyana rejects the view of the Jainas by stating that the production of the body is not dependent upon *adṛṣṭa* and that the sensations of pleasure and pain are not due to *adṛṣṭa are* only some false notions of the most sinful ones.

All objects are eternal (sarvanityatvavāda)

The nature of reality as proposed by the Jainas is refuted by the *Naiyāyikas*. We have already discussed in detail the nature of reality in our introductory chapter. Still, for convenience we reproduced few points to frame the arguments of the Jainas. While making a critical analysis by Gotama in his *Nyāyasutra,* IV. I. 33, he has recorded the *Jaina* concept of object *i.e.* 'all objects are eternal' and has criticized it, by pointing out faults in it, after criticizing the *Sāṁkhya* view on the same issue. Vātyāyana presents the position of the Jaina philosophers, without naming them. In *Tātparyaṭīka,* Vācaṣpati Mishra has also mentioned that this is the view of Svayambhū [738-840 A. D], a Jaina philosopher.

Before going to the actual treatment of Svayambhū by Vātsyāyana, let us put in clear terms the position of the Jainas on the concept of *dravya*. Since, *dravya* is defined as of having three characteristics in the name of *utpāta, vyaya* and *dhrauvya,* it implies that in some sense and from the point of view of substance, all realities are eternal. For, in all changes, and destructions the .basic substance continues to exist. Thus, Jaina maintained that everything is eternal, which is known as *'Sarvanityatvavāda'* of the Jainas.

Vātsyāyana presents the position of Svayambhu that 'only some particular property of the basic material *(upādāna)* which is everlasting *(avasthita)* is destroyed and again only some particular property of the same is produced. Production and destruction are spoken of in relation to such properties only and not in relation to the basic material. The particular property, which is said to be produced, exists even before its production as latent in the basic material. And also the particular property, which is said to be destroyed, even after its destruction are latent in the basic material. Thus, all the objects are to be viewed as eternal. He asserts:

अवस्थितस्योपादानस्य धर्ममात्रं निवर्तते धर्ममात्रमुपजायते स खलूत्पत्तिविनाशयोविषयः।

यच्चोपजायते तत्प्रागप्युपजननादस्ति, यच्च निवर्तते तन्निवृत्तमप्यस्तीति।[24]

Vācaṣpati Mishra summarized it by stating that the modification undergone by substances is of three kinds viz.

(a) modification of properties

(b) modification of condition and

(c) modification of age.

For instance, the original substance 'gold' in lump becomes modified into the ear-ring and here we have the modification of the property as shape of the 'gold'. When the ear-ring is broken and made into the bracelet, we have the modification of condition *i.e.* the ear-ring has renounced its present and reverted to the past condition and the bracelet has removed its future and reverted to the present condition. In the beginning bracelet was new, young and now at this time it becomes old. So here we have the modification of age. But the original gold remains constant all the time. He says:

अपरे सर्वं नित्यमित्यन्यथा वर्णयन्ति। त्रिविधः खल्वयं धर्मिणः परिणामो धर्म-लक्षणावस्थारूपः। तद् यथा सुवर्ण धर्मि, तस्य परिणामो वर्धमानरूचकादिः धर्मस्य तु लक्षणपरिणामोऽनागतादिः। यदा खल्वयं सुवर्णकारो वर्धमानकं भङ्क्वतरूचकं रचयति तदा वर्धमानको वर्त्तमानलक्षणं हित्वा अतीतलक्षणमापद्यते, रुचकं त्वनागतलक्षणं हित्वा वर्त्तमानतामापद्यते, वर्तमानतापन्न एव तु रुचको नवपुराण भावमापद्यमानोऽवस्था परिणामवान् भवति। नवपुराणवस्थाश्च वर्त्तमानलक्षणाश्रया लक्षणपरिणामाः, सोऽयं त्रिविधः परिणामो धर्मिणः। धर्मलक्षणावस्थाश्च धर्मिणो भिन्नाश्चाभिन्नाश्च। तथा च ते धर्म्यभेदान्नितयाः भेदाच्चोत्पत्तिविनाशविषयत्वमित्युभयमुपपन्नम्। ननु यद्युपजनापायधर्मकत्वं धर्मिणां हन्तोत्पत्तेः प्राक् तेषामसत्त्वाद् विनाशाच्चोध र्वमसत्त्वात् कथं सर्वनित्यत्वसिद्धिरित्यत आह यच्चोपजायते तत् प्रागप्युपजनादस्ति धर्मिरूपेणेति शेषः।[25]

This position of the Jaina philosophers, has been refuted by ama. To him and the logicians in general, the view of the Jaina osophers cannot be accepted, because in that case, the respective erence *(vyavasthā)* in certain cases cannot be justified. He says:

'na vyavasthānupapatteḥ' **(न व्यवस्थानुपपत्तेः) [Nyāyasūtra : 4.1.33]**

While commenting on this *sūtra,* Vātsyāyana argues that if the Jainas' view is accepted, the respective difference between production and destruction as expressed by this namely 'this is the production of a property' and 'this is the destruction of a property' cannot be justified. There can also be no justification of the respective difference as expressed thus 'only this particular property produced and not any other' and 'only this particular property is destroyed and not any other'. Because there is no difference so far as the presence of the properties are concerned. That is, both the produced and the destroyed properties being equally ever present none can be spoken of as 'exclusively produced' or exclusively destroyed'.

He argues:

अयमुपजनः इयं निवृत्तिरिति व्यवस्था नोपपद्यते, उपजात निवृतयो-विद्यमानत्वात्। अयं धर्म उपजातोऽयं निवृत्त इति सद्भावाविोषादव्यवस्था।[26]

Further, he argues that the specific difference with reference to time namely 'the production of a property or the destruction of a property relates to this particular point of time and not to that particular point of time' cannot be justified. Because a property whether produced or destroyed always remains the same.

Furthermore, the specific difference between a property with production and destruction and a property without production and destruction as expressed in the form 'this particular property only has been produced and destroyed and not any other', cannot be justified, because they have no difference due to the fact that both of them always remain. He asserts:

इदानीमुपजनतिवृत्ती नेदानीमिति कालव्यवस्था नोपपद्यते सर्वदा विद्यमान त्वात् अस्य धर्मस्योपजननिवृत्ती नास्येति व्यवस्थानुपपत्तिः, उभयोरविशेषात्।[27]

Again, nor can the specific difference with reference to time such as this property existed in the past or this.property will exist in the future be justified, because existence *(sadbhāva)* is indicative of a relation in the present time only. That is, in the Jainas' view all the properties always exist. This means that they are always related to the present time and hence, they can be spoken of as related neither to the past nor to the future.

On the other hand, if it is admitted that production means the appearance of what had been previously absent and the destruction means the disappearance of what had been previously present, these charges can be avoided. Therefore, the claim made by the Jaina that property exists even before its production and that it remains even after being destroyed is illogical and hence absurd. He says:

अनागतोऽतीत इति च कालव्यवस्थानुपपत्तिः, वर्त्तमानस्य सद्भावलक्षणत्वात्। अविद्यमानस्यात्मलाभ उपजनो विद्यमानस्यात्महानिं निवृत्तिरित्येतस्मिन् सति नैते दोषः।

तस्माद्यदुक्तं प्रागप्युपजनादस्ति निवृत्तं चास्ति तदयुक्तंमिति।[28]

If we observed the whole analysis by Vātsyāyana and his followers, we noticed that the arguments is based on supposing the entire reality, the reality as a whole to be eternal, which is not the position of the Jainas, as explained elsewhere with example which clarifies that the Jainas are *anekāntavādins*. All assertions are partial from the point of view of their material substance. The substance gold continues to exist in all modes in all modification in all time and all space and hence, it is eternal. Thus, from the point of view of the continuity of this material substance the *dravya* is called eternal and hence, no contradiction and absurdity of any kind can be noticed in Jainas' position. The Jainas never said that *dravyas* or realities are eternal. On the other hand, to them, from the point of view of their changing modes, they are non-eternal. It is not surprising to note even *ātmā* is transitory from the point of view of its mode.

On avayava *i.e.* components of inferential cognition

In the context of inferential cognition *(anumiti)* the place of *Nyāya* philosophy is very high. It is generally accepted that inference is the prime issue in the *Nyāya* philosophy. That is the reason why sometimes *Nyāya* is identified with the inference. Inference is of two types viz. inference for one's own sake *(svārthānumāna)* and inference for the sake of others *(parārthānumāna)*. The second one is more complicated one owing to its involvement with dialogue between two persons *i.e. vādi* and *prativādi,* which produces the inferential cognition in the third person.

In the process of *anumiti* the components of inferential cognition *i.e. avayava* or syllogism are very much important. We have divergent views regarding the actual number of the components of inference. For instance, for the *Mimāṃasakas* the number of components are three viz. *pratijṃā, hetu* and *udāharaṇa ox hetu, adāharaṇa* and *nigamana;* for Buddhists two viz. *pratijṃā* and *hetu* or sometimes *hetu* only. However,

Jainas have postulated ten *avayavas,* though in later period some Jaina philosophers have accepted five due to the influence of *Nyāya* philosophy. *Sāṁkhya* has also the same (ten) number, but in *Nyāya* five *avayavas* are postulated implicitly in the process of inferential cognition.

In *the Nyāyasūtra* I. I. 32. Gotama has enumerated five *avayavas :*

प्रतिज्ञाहेतूदाहरणोपनयनिगमनान्यवयवाः।[29]

Bhāṣyakāra Vātyāyana, *Vārtikakāra* Udyotakara, *Tātparyaṭīkākāra* Vācaṣpati Mishra and *Vṛttikāra* Viśvanātha have commented on these sutras. While commenting upon these, they have recorded ten *avayavas* as the view of the opponent and also have rejected those and have established their own view. Unfortunately none of them have recorded the source of the reference. In the English translation of *Nyāyasūtrabhāṣya* of Deviprasad Chattopadyaya and Mrinalikanta Gangopadhyaya there is a reference to this source. From a passage in the *Yūktidīpikā,* a commentary on Iśvarakrsna's *Sdmkhyakārikā* it appears that a section of *Sāamkhya* philosophers held such a view. Phanibhusana[30] in his *'Nyāya* philosophy' however, points out that the view held by them is not exactly the same as referred by *Vātyāyana. Dhundirāja Śāsthri* in his *Hindi* commentary of *Nyāyasutrabhāṣ ya* has clearly mentioned that this view is of *Jaina* logicians, more particularly of *Bhadrabāhu,* the last *śruta kavalin* in that tradition. In his text *Daśavaikālikasūtravṛtti* he has also mentioned the same number and the same name, which is rejected by *Vātyāyana* by stating that these extra five *avayavas* are not necessary for inferential-process. He says:

दशावयवानेके नैयैयिका वाक्ये संचक्षते, जिज्ञासा संशयः शक्यप्राप्तिः प्रयोजनं संशयव्युदास इति; ते कस्मान्नोच्यते इति?[31]

The additional five *avayavas* are: *jijñāsā i.e.* inquiry, *śamsaya i.e.* doubt, *śakyaprāpti i.e.* apprehension of the potency, *prayojana i.e.* incentive and *śamsayavyudāśa i.e.* dispelling of doubt.

He, then, has defined all these additional *avayavas* and rejected nine grounds since they do not prove any object.

Then we may discuss those additional members of syllogism one by one following *Vātyāyana*'s exposition. The first one in the additional series is 'jijñāsā'. According to him, inquiry *i.e. jijñāsā* is that which provokes the desire for definite knowledge of an object.

He defines:

तत्प्रतीयमानेऽर्थे प्रत्ययार्थस्य प्रवर्तिकाजिज्ञासा।[32]

Why does one inquire about an object vaguely known?

Because after ascertaining the true nature of the object one will either seek for it, go away from it or remain indifferent to it. Thus, the result of ascertaining the true nature of the object is either the knowledge, which produces aversion, or knowledge, which produces attraction, of knowledge, which produces indifference. One is led to inquire for the sake of such knowledge.

अप्रतीयमानमर्थं कस्माज्जिज्ञासते। तं तत्त्वतो ज्ञातं हास्यामि वोपादास्य उपेक्षिष्ये वेति। ता एता हानोपानोपेक्षाबुद्धयस्तत्वज्ञानस्यार्थस्तदर्थमयं जिज्ञासते। सा खलु इयमसाधनमर्थस्योति।[33]

However, such an inquiry does not prove the existence of any object and as such is redundant as a component of inferential cognition.

The second member of syllogism rejected by the logicians is *'sakyaprāpti'* *i.e.* the apprehension of potency. The apprehension of potency *(śakyaprāpti)* is defined by him as the determination for the knower that the *pramāṇas* are capable of revealing the *prameyas*. It is not related as a component to the propositions proving a thesis *(sādhaka vyākya i.e.* inference component) as are the preliminary statement of the thesis. He says:

प्रमातुः प्रमाणानि प्रमेयाधिगमार्थानि सा शक्यप्राप्तिर्न साधकस्य भागेन युज्यते प्रतिज्ञादिवदिति।[34]

Prayojana is defined by him as, the determination of truth *(tattva)*. It is the result arrived at by the propositions providing a thesis and not a component part of this group of propositions. He asserts:

प्रयोजनं तत्त्वावधारणमर्थसाधाकस्य वाक्यस्य फलं नैकदेश इति।[35]

Similarly, *Saṁśayavyudāsa i.e.* dispelling of doubt is the demonstration of the defect in the opponent's thesis. It serves the purpose of arriving at the knowledge of truth by negating it. But it is not a component part of group of propositions proving a thesis.

संशयव्युदासः प्रतिपक्षोपवर्णनं तत्प्रतिषेधेन तत्त्वज्ञानाभ्यनुज्ञानार्थम् न त्वयं साधकवाक्यैकदेश इति।[36]

The *Nyāya* philosophers have criticized these additional member of syllogism with the ground that these additional components of inferential cognition are not required to prove the existence of any object or in other words these are not related as a component to the propositions proving a thesis *i.e. sādhaka vākya.* He observes:

वाक्यार्थं च संहत्यैते पञ्च निष्पादयन्तीत्यवयवा इत्युच्यते, न पुनर्जीसासादयः, परप्रतिपादका इत्येते न वाक्यस्यावयवा इति।[37]

Because the very definition of the inference component (*avayava*) is:

परप्रतिपादका ये ते वाक्यस्याङ्गभूता इतरेतरासंप्रत्ययितेनार्थेनार्थवन्तो वाक्यङ्गनामुपयान्ति तेऽवयवाः। वाक्यङ्गत्वमवयावार्थ।[38]

It simply means that those inference components are the part of the *sādhaka vākya* called *avayavas,* which are directly related to the *sādhaka vākya.* Therefore, *Udyotakara* explains the real utility of the inference component in the sense that these are the pre-conditions of a debate, without inquiry etc. the question of the application of *'Nyāya' (avayava)* does not arise. Thus, these five inquiries etc. are taken as the pre-conditions of the debate but not as a part of the *sādhaka vākya* by which the inferential cognition can be drawn.

The whole discussion on the member of syllogism as presented by Vātyāyana and his followers is logical. It has been rightly mentioned that the addition of five members of syllogism as included by the *Jainas* are not essential parts or do not contribute directly to the productin of inferential cognition. As a matter of fact, same is the view of the Jainas that these steps are necessary for a beginner, for, those who are not convergent with technicality of logical tradition, they also subscribe to the view that the members may be five or even less. In fact, if anything is objected to the Jainas in this regard is the non-recognition of the distinction between the essential aspects of inferential cognition and the auxiliary factors indirectly involved in it. But before branding this assertion of the Jainas as illogical, it must be remembered that the reference of ten numbered syllogism were found in the texts of the Jaina philosophers, which were composed far before the development of logic of the Jainas and the logical tradition of the Indian philosophy *in general*. That *is why, in later* logical texts like Ny*āvāvātāra, Prameyakamalamārtaṇḍa, Pramāṇanaya-tattvālaṅkāra, Pramāṇamimaṁsā and syādvādamanjarī* etc. we have the prescription of five-member syllogism, to which there cannot be any objection. In conclusion it may be mentioned that the Jaina philosophers adopted a practical approach to the problem keeping in informity with their non-absolutistic *standpoint. Thus, the number* syllogism depends on the calibre of the person to whom it is addressed. Accordingly it may be ten or five or three or two or even. None of the alternatives is to be rejected.

On Prāmāṇyavāda:

Different theories are proposed by different philosophers as to validity of one's judgement. For example, the western philosophers are provided two main theories of the test of the truth of knowledge—correspondence and coherence. In the same manner Indian philosophers have also provided two opinions viz. *svataḥprāmānya partahprāmānya.* According to the *parataḥprāmānya* theory, we have, to resort outside test-for the verification of the validity or validity of out judgement. But according to the *svataḥprāmdṇya* theory, the very condition that brings forth valid or invalid cognition *are* known as the case may be the validity or invalidity of that judgement.

Sāṁkhyas maintain that both validity and invalidity are inherent in the cognition itself. *Naiyāyikas,* on the other hand, hold that both are proved by something else, *i.e.* external causes such as inference, etc. The Buddhists are of the opinion that invalidity inheres in all cognitions, but validity is established by something else. The *Mimāmṣakas* and the *Vedāntins* believe that validity is self-evident and invalidity is determined by external causes.[39] Jaina thinkers say that "the validity is either determined intrinsically or extrinsically."[40] The determination of validity is in some cases achieved by a cognition by itself. As for instance, is the habitual cognition of one's own palm induced by a repeated course of experience or the direct achievements of results such as by the acts of bathing, drinking etc., there occurs cessation of heat, thirst etc. and this alone gives final satisfaction to the subject and a person does not feel an urge for further scrutiny of his cognition. This shows that validity is self-determined, *i.e.* intrinsic. On some occasions, the experience of validity is secured by means of an external datum. We may point out, for instance, to the primal perceptual cognition unconfirmed by repeated experience. Since such cognition has not as yet been ascertained to stand in unfailing correspondence with the object, its validity is determined by a subsequent confirmatory cognition of the same object, or by a cognition of its pragmatic consequences, or by the cognition of an object invariably concomitant with it. This establishes the fact that validity is determined by other means, *i.e.* extrinsic.

Jayantabhaṭṭa, [9th c. A. D.] of course, following the position Nyāya philosophy *i.e. parataḥprāmāṇya,* has criticized the positions of other philosophers. In this context, he has taken the position of the *Jiana* philosophers for refutation after criticizing the position of the *Mīmāṁṣakas.* At the beginning he presents the Jaina position and then refutes by showing fault in it.

According to Jaina philosophy, the truth of the knowledge of an object that has been frequently obtained when the knower has moved, for it is self evident and the truth of the knowledge of an object, which has not been frequently obtained by the knower preceeding it is extrinsically determined. Jayantabhaṭṭa presents:

अभ्यस्ते विषये स्वतः प्रामाण्यम्, अनभ्यस्ते तु परतः। तत्राभ्यासात् प्रमाणत्वं निश्चितं स्वतएव नः। अनभ्यासे तु परतः।[41]

But he holds that when an object has been frequently moved and obtained the knowledge of such an object is intrinsically true, really does not follow what he preaches though his attention has invited to his statement.

सोऽयं अभ्यस्ते विषये इति च ब्रवीति स्वतश्च प्रामाण्यं मन्यत इति स्वयमेवात्मानं वञ्चयमानं न चेतयते।[42]

Repetition literally means the doing of an act again and again. As it applies to the obtaining of an object it has a secondary sense. It signifies the frequent movement towards an object. When we very often perceive our body or the walls of our house or a post erected in house, we have an opportunity of verifying our perception and at times by an actual movement. Thus, the successful movement has established the truth of such perceptions. The truth of perception is not self-evident. The repetition, which applies to the obtaining of an object, can have no other sense. Hence, the statement of the *Jaina* philosophers is an absurdity. Therefore, the validity of knowledge is extrinsically determined. Thus, he concludes:

अभ्यासो हि नाम पुनः पुनः प्रयोगः क्रियाया अभ्यावृत्ति। विषयस्य साभ्यस्तता भूयोभूयः प्रवृत्तिः अतश्च स्वशरीरग्रहे, निजगृहकुड्यस्तम्भा-दिप्रतिभासे वा सहस्त्र कृत्यः प्रवृत्तः संवादज्ञानजन्मना प्रामाण्यनिश्चय उक्तो भवति। स्वतः अभ्यस्तत्वं चान्यथा न भवेदिति यत्किञ्चिदेतत्। तस्मात् परतः प्रामाण्यमिति सिद्धम्।[43]

On Śabda grahaṇa prakriyā (The process of hearing the sound):

In the context of the manifestation of a letter or production of a letter, sound *(sabda)* Jayantabhaṭṭa has presented the Jaina position on the process of hearing (the *grahaṇa prakriyā)* and criticized it by showing fault in it, after refuting the *Sāmkhya* view. According to Jainism, a sound is a whole and is constituted by a number of minute particles. Thus, created, it proceeds from its place of origin towards the ears of a person.

Thus it is heard. He says: each letter consists of parts. They are changing particles. They constitute the whole.[44]

सूक्ष्मैः शब्दपुद्गलैरारब्धरीरः शब्द स्वप्रभवभूमेः निष्कम्य प्रतिपुरुषं कर्णमूलमुपसर्पति इति।[45]

Then he provides some arguments against this position. He argues that these particles are never perceived. Their process of combination is consequently imperceptible. Each letter has its particular combination of parts. So which letter is constituted by which combination? He writes:

तेषांमदृश्यमानानां कीदृशो रचनाक्रमः
केन तत्सन्निवेशेन कः शब्द उपजायताम्?[46]

Further, the constituents of a letter are very tight. They have been combined by no body. They cannot frame whole in the space of a letter as a very tight and impact body. Thus, why is not the whole viz. a letter, which is very light, deflected from its path by the blowing wind? Again if it is dashed against a tree, then why is it not shattered into pieces?

लघवोऽवयवाश्चैते निवद्धा न च केनचित्।
न चैनं कठिनं कर्तुं वर्णावयविनं क्षमाः॥
कृशश्च गच्छन् स कथं न विक्षिप्येत मारुतैः।
दलशो वा न भज्येत वृक्षाद्यभिहितः कथम्॥[47]

Further, how long does such a weak letter move on to reach its destination? When it enters the ear of a person how is it also heard by other persons? If it is held that it comes out from the ear of that person and goes into the ear of another person then how will the Jaina philosophers explain the simultaneous hearing of a letter by many persons? He says :

प्रयाणकावधिः कश्च गच्छतोऽस्य तपस्विनः
एक श्रोत्रप्रविष्टो वा स श्रुयेतापरैः कथम्?
निष्कम्य कर्णादेकस्मात् प्रवेशः श्रवणान्तरे
प्रदीष्यते कथं तस्य युगपद्वहुभिः श्रुतिः।[48]

Again he has questioned that if the Jaina philosophers hold that many letters are simultaneously created by a speaker in accordance with the number of hearers, then it will be pointed out that so many letters cannot be created by the single articulation or effort of a speaker. Even if we admit that each hearer has a distinct letter to hear, then the possibility of the simultaneous hearing of a single letter by many persons is simply ruled out. He argues:

श्रोतृसंख्यानुसारेण न नानावर्णसंभवः
वक्तुस्तुल्यप्रयन्तत्वात् श्रोतृभेदतदैक्ययोः।[48]

At the end, Jayantabhaṭṭa criticized the Jaina philosophers particularly the *Digaṁbara* Jaina philosophers by simply neglecting their hypothesis with a very sarcastic expression. He comments that we shall not discuss much about the keenness of the intellect of the naked one (*Digaṁbara* Jaina) since when they display their intellect to defend their hypothesis, the critics simply laugh at their defense. He says.

तदलं परिहासस्य महतो हेतुभूतया
नग्नक्षपणकाचार्यप्रज्ञाचातुर्यचर्चया।।[50]

On Āgama or Śabda pramāṇa:

Both the *Naiyāyikas* and Jainas have accepted the authority of Śabda or āgama *pramāṇa.* In fact all the systems of Indian philosophy with the exception of *Cārvāvka* postulate *Śabda* as a valid means of proof, though there is difference of opinion on the minute details of the *pramāṇa.* For example, when most of the theists prescribe Veda etc. as authority, to the *Jainas,* only their scriptures are valid and are included under *pramāṇa,* the Veda etc. are not *pramāṇa.* Bhāṣrvajṃa in his *Nyāyabhusaṇa* has refuted the view of the Jainas.

In the context of authoritativeness of Veda, Bhāṣrvajṃa has rejected the authoritativeness of Jainas' *āgamas i.e.* scriptures, owing to its dissimilarity with the Vedas. He argues that many people have accepted the scriptures of the Jainas though there is no proof. And because it is accepted by many people, that is why it should be accepted as an authority like the Vedas, is not proper. It should be taken as otherwise. He says:

ननु जिनाद्यागमोऽपि दृष्टं प्रयोजनं विनापि बुहभिर्गृहीतस्तेन तस्यापि प्रमाण्यमेष्टव्यम् न अन्यथा तस्य ग्रहणात्।[51]

He has provided the argument as to why the scriptures of the Jainas are not considered as authority like the Vedas. He asserts that these scriptures of the Jainas are complied by Jainas who are desirous to get fame and describing the study of āgamas as the giver of more fruits *(falātiśaya),* by some ill-fated *Brāhmins* who have cheated by the advice of the Jainas as it can remove the sorrow and sufferings, who had suffered from poverty, and by the *śūdras* who have interested to learn having heard that due to learning one can get great luck and those who were prohibited to learn the Vedas. And like the Vedas these scriptures of the Jainas are not remembered by the *Vaiwstha i.e.* the pupils who are studying at the *Gurukūlas* or the *āśramas i.e.* the monastery and by the *abahisthas i.e.* the house holds. And further, like the Vedas the scriptures of the Jainas are not taught to three *varṇas* by the *Brāhmins*. Therefore, the authoritativeness of the Jaina scriptures cannot be accepted like the Vedas. He says:

अध्ययनाधयापने महाभाग्यं श्रुत्वा शूद्राः केचिदध्ययनाद्युत्सुकाः संजातास्ते चाऽनधिकारित्वेन वेदानध्येतुमलभमाना जिनादिना ख्यातिमिच्छता स्वप्रणीतागमाध्ययने फलातिशयमपवर्ण्य प्रवर्तिताः तैस्त्वन्ये तथाविधाः प्रवर्तिताः, तैरप्यन्ये ब्राह्मणादयोऽपि केचन मन्दप्रज्ञा दारिद्र्यदुःख संतप्ताश्च दुःख क्षयोपदेशेन प्रतार्य प्रवर्तिताः इत्येवं तदागमः प्रचयं गतः, न वेदवद्वनस्थैरपि सर्गागमाबाहिष्कृतैश्च कण्ठस्थ क्रियते, नापि ब्राह्मणेनैवाध याप्यमानस्त्रिभिरेव वर्णैभिधीयमानः प्रचयं गतः। तस्मान्न वेदवज्जिनाद्यागमानामपि प्रामाण्यं प्रसज्जते।[52]

Further, he argues that the Jainas have proclaimed that there are three types of Vedic sentences viz. *'pramāṇānī i.e.* authoritative sentences, *apramāṇānī i.e.* unauthoritative sentences, and *'sandigdhapramānāriī' i.e.* doubtful sentences. This is not correct; because the sentences written by *'sarvajṃa' i.e.* omniscient have to be authoritative. Similarly, the sentences written by *'asarvajṃa' i.e.* the person having limited knowledge has to be unauthoritative *(apramāṇa)*. Thus, the

Vedic sentences have to be authoritative owing to it being composed by the omniscient or *Īśvara*. Thus, he asserts:

यच्चोक्तं त्रिधा वेदवाक्यानि-प्रमाणानि-अप्रमाणानि-सन्दिग्धप्रमाणानि इति। तदनुपपन्न असर्वज्ञप्रणीतानां हि वाक्यानां कदाचिदप्रामाण्यमपि सम्भाव्यते, सर्वज्ञप्रणीतानां त्वप्रामाण्यकारणाभावात्तदनुपपत्तिः। तथा चोक्तम्

रागाज्ञानादिभिर्दोषैग्रस्तत्वादनृतं वदेत्
ते चेश्वरे न विद्यन्ते स वृयात् कथमन्यथा॥[53]

Further, he says that even the scriptures of the Jainas are not to be considered as *'pūrvapakṣārtha' i.e.* the meaning provided by the *'pūrvapakṣa,'* because its shortcomings and philosophical tenents *(siddhāntas)* are not stated; And if it is taken as *'pūrvapakṣa'* then its composer becomes *'anāpta' i.e.* not authoritative person because these scriptures of the Jainas create confusion and apprehension in the minds of the listeners. Thus, he argues:

पूर्वपक्षार्थत्वादित्यप्ययुक्तम्, तद्दूषणसिद्धान्तयोरनभिधाने ह्यागमस्य पूर्वपक्षार्थाभिधानानुपपत्तेः।

अन्यथा हि श्रोतृणां संमोहजनकत्वेन तत्प्रणेतुरनाप्तत्वप्रसंगः।[54]

He argues further that in the case of Vedas, *'pūrvapakṣa'* and *'siddhāntapakṣa'* is not possible, because these two *i.e. pūrvapakṣa* and *siddhāntapakṣa* can be possible in case of logical treatise *(nyāyaśāsthreṣu* or *yūktiśāthreṣu)*. But in the case of Veda there cannot be any *pūrvapakṣa* argument or any *siddhāntapakṣa* argument for establishing any meaning. Because the Vedic sentences are being the final preaching have to be followed as the order of the father. We cannot provide any argument to support or to oppose it. But sometimes some philosophers are engaged in discussing some Vedic sentences with some arguments, this is nothing but the meaningless talk produced from the illusion *(Bhramā),* which is created from the practice of dry argumentation *(suṣkatarkābhyāsa)*. Thus, he says:

किं च युक्तिशास्त्रेषु पूर्वपक्षोपन्यासः क्रियते। वेदस्त्वाज्ञासिद्धत्वेनोपदिष्टः पित्रादिवाक्यवत्? न ह्यय युक्ता कश्चिदर्थः प्रतिपादितस्तस्माच्छुष्क तर्काभ्यासजनितभ्रमस्याऽयमुल्लापः पूर्वपक्षार्थानि कानिचिद्वेदवाकयनिति।[55]

Let us brief the whole criticism of Bhāsarvajña on the unauthoratativeness of the Jaina scriptures. To us, it appears that whatever arguments Bhāsarvajña has provided against the Jainas can be forwarded against the *Naiyāyika* as well logically. The only assertion that the Vedas are *'apauruṣeya'* hence cannot be liable to any falsehood is mere a belief and cannot be logically established. The *Naiyāyikas* have accepted along with Vedas, the validity of *āpta nyākya,* which is the statement or expression of a trustworthy person. According to Bhāsarvajña, validity is common to all, normal, to a seer as well an ordinary person. If that is true, how then one accept the Jaina's as unauthoratative, because they are composed by human being. It must be noted that according to Jainas, the scriptures are the statements of Tirthṅkaras' who are identified with the *dptas* of the *Naiyāyikas*. From the above discussion it may be noted that the way Bhāsarvajña has presented rather criticized the authoritativeness of the scriptures of the Jainas is not adequate because without giving very sound and systematic arguments he has criticized the Jaina agamas for the sake of mere criticism.

On classification of Pramāṇa

We have already discussed in the introdūction the Jaina classification of *pramāṇa* in detail. The two-fold classification of *pramāṇa* as pratyakṣa and parokṣa[56] is being criticized by Bhāṣrvajṃa by stating that it is not experienced by any body. For example, no one says that he has knowledge through indirect means of knowing. On the contrary every one has the experience that 'I know through inference or perception or through the scriptures. He says:

प्रत्यक्षपरोक्षभेदेन द्विविधमेवेति चेत्, न, तद् वयवहाराप्रसिद्धेः। न हि परोक्षेणाहं जानामीति व्यवहारः क्वचित्पसिद्धो यथा परोक्षेणाहं जानामि अनुयानेन वाऽऽगमेन वेति।[57]

Further, there is no proof by which Jaina philosophers can maintain the indirect means of knowing *i.e. parokṣa pramāṇa,* its process, result and the validity of *pramāṇa* and its expression as in the case of perception, inference and scripture etc. And also there is no need to include inference and scripture into *parokṣa pramāṇa.* He argues:

निष्प्रयोजनत्वाच्च यया पृथक्पृथम् प्रामाण्यप्रतिपत्त्युपायप्रतिपादनं प्रत्यक्षादीनां भेदेनाभिधानप्रयोजनम्, नैवं परोक्षत्वेनानुमानागमयोः संगेहे प्रयोजनं किंचिदस्ति।[58]

Again, if at all they need to establish this two-fold division due to love on their system, by accepting indirect *pramāṇa* as very general way which comprises inference and scripture with its separate definitions then we do not have any objection. Because it does not go against of our system, as we have accepted these three means of knowing separately. Jaina philosophers also cannot say *thai pratyakṣa* and *parokṣa* means *pratyakṣa* and *anumāna* as accepted by many philosophers and agama *pramāṇa* is incorporated into inferential cognition; thus their two-fold division of means of knowing is not acceptable. But three fold division viz. *pratyakṣa, anumāna* and āgama has to be accepted. He writes:

यदि पुनरयं स्वपक्षरागेण दैविध्यमात्रसिध्यर्थं परोक्षं सामान्यं अधियाय तद्विशेषावनुमानागमौ भिन्नलक्षणौ ब्रुयात, ब्रवीतु कोऽस्त निवारयिता? न त्वेवमप्यस्मदुक्तं त्रैविध्यं निवर्त्तते, त्रयाणां परस्परतोऽसंकीर्ण-लक्षणप्रतिपादनादिति। अथ प्रत्यक्षमनुमानमिति योऽर्थः स एवार्थः प्रत्यक्षं परोक्षमिति तथापि न द्विविघं एव। ततोऽर्थान्तरस्यागमस्यापि प्रमाणत्वात्। तस्य चानुमानेऽन्तर्भावं निषेत्स्यामः ततो न प्रत्यक्षानुमानभेदनापि द्विविधम्। तस्मात् त्रिविधमेवेति।[59]

From the above discussion one thing is very clear that Bhāsarvjṃa through *Naiyāyika* accepted three-fold division of *pramāṇas* unlike other logicians who have accepted four fold divisions of *pramāṇa.* Another thing is that though Jaina philosophers have accepted two types of *pramāṇa,* they have accepted other five sub-divisions of *pramāṇa* viz., *smṛti pratyabhijñāna, tarka, anumāna,* and *āgama.*

It may be observed that the Jaina's classification *of pramāṇa* into two kinds namely *pratyakṣa* and *parokṣa,* is logical al least as they think. In one case the knowledge is quite independent, hence direct. In another, as for example, in the case of inference etc, they are dependent on perception, hence, indirect. There is nothing wrong in holding so and any opposition to this supposition can be explained away. And if it is further classified into *anumāna i.e.* inference etc. it is also all right. But the acceptance of *smṛti pratyabhijñāna, tarka* etc. as independent *pramāṇa* does not sound logical. And if the *Naiyāyikas* have to object, they may object these three suppositions. Thus, instead of opposing or objecting the two-fold classifications of *pramāṇa,* what *Bhāsarvajña* or the *Naiyāyikas* would have objected to was the independentness of these *pramāṇas,,* which they have not done. The reason for such negligence of the logicians, which is noticed through out their text is not far to seek, which we will be observing time and again.

On Anekāntavāda

Bhāsarvjña has presented the Jaina position on syādvāda in detail. He has recorded the arguments from Jaina point of view before examining them. He has quoted the argument as presented by *Samantabhadra* [600 c. A.D.] with reference to the three stages viz. *'duḥkha' i.e.* unhappiness, *'pramoda' i.e.* pleasure, and *'mādhyastha' i.e.* indifferent. It means the nature of the reality can be explained with reference to these three states viz. *'utpāda' i.e.* germination, *nyaya' i.e.* destruction and *'drauvya' i.e.* continuation. According to Jainism, the whole realities can be divided into seven types viz. *jīva i.e.* soul, *ajīva i.e.* non- soul, *āsrava i.e.* influx, *saṁvara i.e.* stoppage of the influx, *nirjarā i.e.* restraint, *bandha i.e.* bondage, *mokṣa i.e.* liberation. These seven-fold reality should be understood in the light of *syādvāda* theory. And proper understanding of these seven-fold reality leads a person to liberation.

To sum up, the whole presentation of the Jaina position can be re-arranged in the following manner.

1. In the *anekānta* theory *kuśala, akuśala, bandha* and *mokṣa* is not possible, thus, we have to accept the *anekānta* theory.
2. *Anekānta* is established due to the three stages namely *duḥkha, pramoda* and *mādhyasth* of the soul.
3. It is possible in the theory of *anekānta* and *mokṣa* is possible through the true knowledge of seven *tattvas,* which are to be understood in the light of seven fold logic *i.e. Satpabhangīnaya.*

Thus, he writes:

नित्यत्वे पुरुषस्यैकस्वभावत्वात् सुखदुःखबन्धमोक्षादिक्रमानुपपत्तिः सदैवात्मा सुखी दुःखी च स्यात्, तत्स्वभावाविनाशात्। नाप्यनित्य एवाकृताभ्यागमदिदोषः, तस्मादनेकान्तपक्ष एव निर्दुष्टाः, तदुक्तम् -

"एकान्ताग्रहरक्तानां नाथ स्वपरवैरिणाम्।
कुशलाकुशलं कर्म बन्धमौक्षौ तु न क्वचित्॥"
"कटमोलिसुवर्णार्थी नाशोत्पादव्ययेषु च।
शेकप्रमोदमाध्यस्थ्यं जनो जातित्रयात्मकम्॥"[60]

Then, Bhāsarvjna has presented the Jaina concept of seven-fold division of reality and *syādvāda* theory and finally has refuted showing contradiction with these.

Jīva i.e. soul is of the nature of consciousness defined in terms of knowledge, pleasure, sorrow and desire etc. and contrast to it is called *ajīva i.e.* non-soul *i.e.* which is different from that. He writes:

तत्र "चैतनास्वभावत्वात् तद्विकल्पलक्षणौ जीवः"। तस्याश्चेतनाया विकल्पाः पर्यायाज्ञानसुखदुःखेच्छादयः, ते लक्षणं यस्यासौ जीवः तद्विलक्षणस्त्वजीव इति।[61]

Āsrava is the door through which soul attracts *pūṇya* and *pāpa*. This is explained with an example: As the ocean is filled in continuously by the water of the river, similarly through *mithyādarśana,* the soul is uninterṛuptedly filled in by the karmic particles. Thus, the wrong vision serves the work of *āsrava*. He says:

"पुण्यपापागमद्वारलक्षण आस्त्रवः"। आस्त्रव इव आस्त्रवः। क उपमार्थः? यथा महोदधिर्नद्यादिसलिलैरहरहरापूर्यते तथा मिथ्यादर्शनादिद्वारानुप्रविष्टैः कर्मभिरनिशं प्राणी पूर्यत इति मिथ्यादर्शनादिद्वारमास्त्रवः।[62]

The obstructer of the *āsrava* is called *saṁvara*. Through this *āsrava* is obstructed. For example, the devil persons or enemies cannot enter into the house being closed by the *'kapāṭ a' i.e.* the panels of the door. Similarly the karmic matters caused from the bondage of *pāpa* and *pūṇya* are obstructed from entering the soul due to the performances of good activities *(śubhānusṭāna)*. The way of new karmic matters are being obstructed by these good activities. Thus, this is called *saṁvara*. He notes:

"आस्त्रवनिरोधालक्षणः संवरः"। संव्रियतेऽनेनेति संवरेः। यथा कपाटेन संवृते गृहे दुष्टस्य प्रवेशो नास्ति, तद्वच्छुभानुष्ठानेन संवृते पुसि पुण्यपाप-लक्षणस्य बन्धाहेतोः कर्मणः प्रवेशो नास्तीति। अभिनवकर्मागमद्वारसंवरणात् संवरः।[63]

Nirjarā is described as is in the form of destruction of the karmic particles in a particular place. It means, in this state karmic matter does not produce any result. For example, as poison does not cause any harm its power being weakened by the incantation *(mantra)* and medicine *(auṣadhi)* similarly, karma also does not produce rebirth *(saṃsāraphalapradaṃ)* its power being destructed by the hard austerity *(tapa)*. He says:

"एकदेशकर्मसंक्षयलक्षणा निर्ज्जरा"। निर्ज्जरेव निर्ज्जरा, यथा मन्त्रौषध बलादिभिर्जीर्णवीयें विषं न कोपकरम्, तथोपात्तं कर्म तपोविशेषेण निर्जीर्णरसं न संसारफलप्रदम्।[64]

Baṅdha is in the form of relation between karmic particles with the soul and vice versa. As a person is covered with chain becomes pounded or looses his freedom, so also when a soul is covered or associated with karmic particles becomes bound or looses his freedom. *Mokṣa i.e.* salvation is the from of destruction of all types of *ghāti* and *aghāti karmas*. As a person is freed from all types of bindings and becomes happy due to attainment of his desired place, so also a soul when free from all types of *karmas* becomes happy owing to attaining his desired place *i.e.* salvation. He says:

"आत्मकर्मणोरन्योन्यप्रवेशानुप्रवेशलक्षणः सम्बन्धी बन्धः" (तत्त्व. वा. 1-4-17)। बन्ध इव बन्धः। यथा निगडादिबन्धेन बद्धः पुरूषोस्वतन्त्रः, तथा कर्मबन्धेनापीति। "कृत्स्नकर्मवियोगलक्षणे मोक्षः"। निगडादिमुक्तवत् स्वातन्त्रये सति अभिप्रेतदेशगमनादेव पुमान्क सुखी भवतीत्यर्थः।[65]

After presenting the seven *tattvas* from Jaina point of view Bhāsarvajña records the nature of *syādvāda*. His presentation of *syādvādā* theory is similar and there is nothing new in it. References to be made to our introduction where we have discussed the seven *bhangas*. For convenience we reproduce the same with the text of Bhāsarvajña. The seven *bhangas* are *syādasti* etc. Bhāsarvajña comments: *ityeṣā saptabhangī syādvāda ityucyate*. Bhāsarvajña adds further that the seven realities beginning with *jīva* etc. are qualified or predicated with the above-mentioned seven *bhangas*.

"जीवाजीवौ तथान्योन्यमास्त्रवः संवरस्तथा।
निर्ज्जरा च तथा बन्धो मोक्षः सम्भ्रम इष्यते॥"
"स्याद्वादलाञ्छिताश्चैते परिज्ञेयाः समीरिताः।
तज्ज्ञानादाश्रवापेतो जीवो मोक्ष इहोदितः॥"[66]

Going further, he has reproduced the definition of *saptabhahgī* from *Tattvātharājavārtika* of *Akalanka*.

The definition runs thus:

"एकस्मिन् वस्तुनि प्रश्नवशाद् दृष्टेनेष्टेन च प्रमाणेनाविरूद्धविधि ।प्रतिषेधविकल्पना सप्तभंगी"[67]

It means the assertion or the negation in respect of a single entity or reality, guided by query without being contradicted by perception or any other means of valid knowledge is called *saptabhangī*. He elaborates further taking the example of 'jar' namely *'syād ghaṭa, syddaghaṭa, syād ghaṭa aghaṭa ca, syādavaktavya* etc. All the seven *bhangas* has to be predicated to each and every reality like *syādjīva, syādajīva,* etc.

It may be recorded here that the assertion and negation *i.e. vidhi nisedha kalpanā* with regard to *ghaṭa* can also be expressed as *syād ghaṭa asti, syād ghaṭa nāsthi* etc. He explains further, the pot exists as its own self *i.e. svātmanā ghaṭa asthi,* it does not exist as something else *i.e.* delimited by some other property. Here *svātmā* means with regard to *gahṭa* means the cause, due to which something is expressed as pot. Similarly *parātmā* means cloth etc. the cause of being expressed as *'tat'*, that different from pot. This may be anything, say a cloth or the state of pot-halves.

"तत्र स्वात्मनास्ति घटः, परात्मना नास्ति। घटबुद्ध्यभिधानानुवृत्तिलिंगः स्वात्मा। यत्र तद्बुध्द्यभिधानानुवृत्तिः। स परात्मा पटादिः। कपालाद्यवस्था च।[68]

If it is argued that the pot does not exist as delimited by its own self, then there cannot be uses of pot and if it is accepted to exist delimited by *parātmā,* then there would arise the contingency of uses of the cloth etc. in the case of pot etc, which is absurd. In other words, when there exist pot in the ground, we have the cognition *'bhūtale ghaṭo asti'* and *'bhūtale ghaṭo nāsti'*. In these cognition the pot is delimited by its own self, which means pot exists as a pot delimited by potness, which is responsible for the usage namely 'there exists pot' in a place where pot exists. Had it been the case that the pot is delimited by cloth, or any thing else then this would amount to the absurd conclusion and hence, the contingency of usage namely 'there exists cloth or the kind' in the locus of the pot.

Bhāsarvajña has quoted the whole text from Akalaṅka's *Rājavārtika* which runs thus:

तत्र स्वात्मनापि यदि नास्ति घटः, तदा घटव्यवहार एव न स्यात्। तथा परात्मनापि यद्यस्ति, तदा पटादिव्यवहारोऽपि तत्र स्यात्। तस्मात् स्वरूपेण सन् घटः पररूपेण त्वसन्निति"।[69]

A classification is given here that in this manner there would be no distinction between *'ghaṭa'* and *'aghaṭa'* and if any distinction is maintained it cannot be expressed like that due to lack of co-existence or co-referentiality. But that is not true. Therefore, the realities, say the pot, being of dual nature is called as *'ghaṭa'* and *'aghaṭa'* being expressed in a sequence.

It may be argued that the reality having the dual nature *'bidhi nisedhātmaka'* is called as *'ghaṭa'* only then this should amount to falsehood because it has not taken on account of the negative aspects of reality into consideration and if it is treated as *'aghaṭa'* alone still this will be treated as not correct, because the positive aspects or existential aspects has not taken into consideration here. To clarify: a pot is a pot and also non-pot considering the positive and negative aspects of reality thus, a pot is neither 'pot' alone nor 'non-pot' alone.

यदि तदुभयात्मकं वस्तु घट इत्येवोच्यते, तदेतरात्माऽसंग्रहादतत्त्वमेव स्यात्। अथाघट एवेत्युच्येत, तदात्मानुपादानादनृतमेव स्यात्।[70]

This gives rise to or explains the first three *bhaṅgas* namely, *syād ghaṭa or syādaghaṭa, syādasti ghaṭa or syādnāsti ghaṭa and syādasti nāsti ghaṭa.* There is no other expression to present or reveal this state of the positive and negative aspects of reality simultaneously, which amounts to the supposition of the fourth *bhaṅgas*. Since, the pot representing the positive and negative aspects of it simultaneously, it is beyond the range of any expression, thus, *iteJainas* have the fourth *bhaṅgas syāda-vyaktavya*.

न चान्यः शग्दस्तदुभयात्मावस्थानत्वाभिधायी विद्यते। ततोऽसौ घटो वचनगोचरतीत्वात् 'स्यादवक्तव्य' इत्युच्यते।[71]

By further combinations, the rest *bhaṅgas* are formulated. Following *Jainas'* philosophy *Bhāsarvajña* records that all the seven *bhaṅgas* are to be predicated to all the realities. There is nothing in this world, which is not guided by this principle of *saptabhaṅgī*.

"एवं सर्वेष्वर्थेषु सप्तभंगी योज्या"। न तथाभूतः कश्चिदर्थोऽस्ति यत्र सप्तभंगी नास्ति।[72]

Following *anekānta Bhāsarvajña* makes an interesting observations. Since *ekānta* is not accepted and invariably or universally *anekānta* is followed, this would amount to *ekānta*.

Thus, how can you say that *saptabhangī* is applied to each and every reality?

नन्वेकान्तानभ्युपगमन्नियमेनानेकान्ताभ्युपगमः प्राप्तस्ततः इति। कथं सर्वत्र सप्तभंगीति।[73]

To this, the Jainas answer in negative, stating that even in *anekānta, ekānta* view is not to be accepted. It means the *anekānta* itself is also *ekānta,* Thus, it can be phrased as: *syād ekānta, syād anekānta, syād anekānta ekānta* etc.

The whole argument or presentation of the Jaina position by Bhāsarvajña is authentic. He has quoted the texts from *Tattvārthavārtika* without much addition to it. After making a faithful presentation of *saptabhaṅgī,* Bhāsarvajña starts examining or rather refuting this position of the Jainas with argument from the point of view of *ekāntavādin* in general and *Naiyāyikas* in particular. As to the view of the Jainas that in *ekānta* theory *kuśala i.e.* good and *akuśala i.e.* bad *karmas* cannot be explained. Bhāsarvajña answers in *ekānta* theory *kuśala* and *akuśala, bandha i.e.* bondage and *mokṣa i.e.* liberation are very much explainable. There is no difficulty in explaining either *kuśala* and *akuśala* or *bandha* and *mokṣa. Bhāsarvajña* explains what is *ekāntapakṣa* or the theory of absolutism. It means whosoever be the doer or performer of any activity he would be the enjoyer of its result. In other words, a relation of causality is established between the agent and its respective effects and that in *ekānta.* And following this theory the ordinary day-to-day behaviour is explained. It is noticed that a particular individual either moves forward to act, to make an effort or to obtain something or keep himself away or runs away from it guided by the logic of *iṣṭāniṣṭa-prāptiparihāra'.* In other words, if something is *isṭa* he wants to get it, if it is *aniṣṭa* he wants to avoid it. This is possible only in theory of *ekānta.* I quote the text of Bhāsarvajña:

यतावदेकान्तगहरत्तानामित्यादि, तदयुत्तम्; एकान्तपक्ष एव कुशलाकुशलकमाद्युपपत्तेः, तथा हि - यदि य एव कर्मणाः कर्त्ता, स एव तत्फलोपभौक्तेत्ययमेकान्तः स्यात्, तदेष्टानिष्टप्राप्तिपरिहारार्थ तत्कर्मसु प्रेक्षावतः प्रवृत्तिर्घटते।[74]

Contrary to this theory of *ekānta* if one follows *anekānta-vāda* these practical verifiable human behaviours cannot be explained. Hence; *anekānta* theory of the Jaina cannot be accepted. He gives reason subscribing the view of *anekānta.* No causality between the agent and its result can be explained, for, in *ekānta* theory if the doer is different, the enjoyer will be different. There would not be any inclination towards taking food, for, it would not satisfy one's hunger. If the king is well fed the naked monk will have the satisfaction of eating. And if not, this will amount to *ekāntavāda* not *anekāntavāda.*

As can be seen, Bhāsarvajña interprets *anekānta* as lack of causality between the doer and enjoyer of any action. According to him, in *anekānta* theory the doer of an action may be different and the enjoyer of that will be different. There would not be any guiding principle if 'A' does an action he will attain its fruits for certain. And if he gets or if causality is established, that would be *ekāntavāda* to the pleasure of the *Naiyāyikas*. As a matter of fact the Jainas do not interpret *anekānta* in this way as Bhāsarvajña has interpreted. The Jainas always establish causality between the doer and the enjoyer and this does not effect that position of *ankekāntavāda.*

अनेकान्तपक्षे त्वन्यकृतमप्यन्येनोपभुज्यत इति स्यात्। तथा च भेजनादिक्रियास्वपि प्रेक्षावता न प्रवर्तितव्यम्। राजादिकृतेष्वेव भेजनादिकर्मसु नग्नश्रमणकस्यापि तृप्तिर्भविष्यति, अभवने ह्येकान्तग्रहः स्यात्।[75]

Going further *Bhāsarvajña* finds more faults with the *anekānta* theory of the Jainas. He argued that the *Jainas* finding faults with the *ekānta* theory resort to *anekānta,* For example, if some reality, say soiri is treated as absolutely eternal *i.e. 'nitya eva'* some objections or contingency will be there; similarly if something is accepted as absolutely transitory *i.e. 'anitya eva',* still some different contingency will arise. Hence, the reality should be both eternal and transitory in the mind of the Jainas. To this, Bhāsarvajña argued that by telling or treating the reality as eternal as well as transitory the Jainas will fall into the trap of inviting or involving contingencies of both the aspects *i.e.* the contingency involved in *'nityatva'* aspect as well as *anityatva'* aspect. Sarcastically criticizing the position of the Jainism Bhāsarvajña observes:

किं च नित्यानित्ययोर्दोषं दृष्टानेकान्तमभ्युगच्छता पक्षद्वयस्याप्यभ्युपगमः स्यात्। तदभ्युपगमे चोभयपक्षोक्ता अपि दोषाः प्राप्ता इति। क एवं विग्रन्थादन्यो दोषान् परिहर्तुं जानाति?[76]

Finally Bhāsarvajña concludes: the self is eternal only *(tasmāt nitya evātmā)*. Now at this state, the Jainas may argue that if the soul is eternal alone how to account for the fact that, somebody is happy at some period of time and unhappy at the other time. Soul being eternal its qualities like pleasure and pain etc. will be eternally associated with it and if somebody is happy, he will remain happy always and if some soul is unhappy, it will be unhappy forever, is the contention of the Jainas. To this, Bhāsarvajña answers that the contention of the Jainas is baseless and does not stand to logic, for, the quality of soul like pleasure and pain etc. are transitory. Pleasure and pain are produced and destroyed due to their association with soul; it is called *nitya* or *anitya. Nityatva* or *anityatva i.e.* eternality and transitoriness are not the essential qualities of soul, but of the pleasure, of the pain etc. Due to the production or destruction of these accidental properties like pleasure and pain the soul is said to be produced or destroyed. As a matter of fact, soul is always eternal. Bhāsarvajña explains this further with the examples of a staff possessor or *kundatī i.e.* one having ear ornament, *chatrī i.e.* one having umbrella, due to the association with *daṇḍa, kuṇḍala* or a *chatra.* An individual say *Caitra* is called as *daṇḍī, kuṇḍlī* or *chatrī* due to the absence of contact with these *daṇḍa* etc. the same *Caitra* is called *adaṇḍa, akuṇḍala* or *achatra:*

तस्मान्नित्य एवात्मा, तत्समवेतसुखोत्पत्तौ सुखी, दुःखोत्पत्तौ दुःखीत्युच्यते।

सुखदुःखादीनामेवोत्यत्तिविनाशौ नात्मनः स हि नित्योऽपि तेन तेन धर्मेणोत्पद्यमानेन विनश्यता च तद्वान् व्यपदिश्यते यथा दण्डादिसम्बन्धासम्बन्धभ्यां दण्डी कुण्डली छत्री वाऽदण्डोऽकुण्डलोऽच्छत्रश्चेति चेत्रो व्यपदिश्यते।[77]

Hence, the soul cannot be *nitya* and *anitya* but *nitya* alone -declares Bhāsarvajña. In this context, Bhāsarvajña took tasks Samantabhadra who advanced the logic of *'kaṭamauī* to establish the anekānta. Bhāsarvajña argued: whatever logic or arguments are forwarded by Samantabhadra in favour of establishing the *nityatva, anityatva* and *dhrauvyatva* of reality are illogical.

Samantabhadra argued that when a particular ornament *kaṭa,* made of gold is changed to *mauli,* in all the states goldness continues to exist, the *kaṭatva* is destroyed and the *maulitva* is produced. This is in fact how the Jainas defined *dravya,* which we have already recorded elsewhere.

To this, Bhāsarvajña answers: when the ornament *kaṭaka* is made to *mauli* though *kaṭaka* is not there or destroyed. The *katakatva* and *suvarṇatva* is eternal, for, *kaṭakatva* remains or continues to exist and is congnized in other individual *kaṭ akas*. The person who has attachment with *kaṭaka* becomes unhappy due to the non-existence of *kataka;* similarly when the mauli was not produced previously and now it is produced as that, a person having attachment towards that becomes happy. At the same time any one who waṇts gold remains indifferent either in the destruction of *kaṭaka* or the emergency of *mauli,* because of the fact that gold continued to exist in all states.

तत्र हि पूर्वावयविनः कटकत्वसुवर्णत्वजातियुक्तस्य विनाश एव तद्विनाशोऽपि जातिरेकापि न विनष्टा, सुवर्णत्ववत् कटकत्वस्यापि वयक्तयन्तरे प्रत्यभिज्ञानात्। उत्तरं च् द्रव्यं कटकत्वयुक्तं नोत्पादितमिति तदर्थिनः शोकः, पूर्वद्रव्यं च मौलित्वयुक्तं नासीदिदानीं तु तज्जातियुक्तमुत्पन्नमिति तदर्थिनः प्रमोदः, सुवर्णत्वेनानुयोगः पूर्वोत्तरयोरपि अवयविनोरस्तीति तदर्थिनो माध्यस्थ्यम्।[78]

Bhāsarvajña argued: the universal goldness exists in the parts and the whole of an object made of gold, hence, when the whole is destroyed the goldness is cognized in its parts and the cognition of gold continues to exist and thus, there is no knowledge of the destruction of it. Bhāsarvajña gives the example the lamp or the water of the *Gangā,* which is treated as the same water or the same light due to its similarity and continuity and individual desirous of that remain indifferent treating it as that. Bhāsarvajña writes:

सुवर्णत्वजातिस्तववयवावयर्वेष्वप्यस्ति, तेन तदवयविनाशेऽप्यवय-वेप्वनन्तर भाव्यवयव्यन्तरे च सुवर्णप्रत्ययसातत्यादविनष्टाभिमानः प्रदीपगंगोदकादिवद्वा तत्सदूषनिरन्तरभावात्तदेवेति मन्यमानः तदर्थी माध्यस्थं याति।[79]

Going further with a view to demolish the mansion built by the Jainas with the bricks of the *anekānta*. Bhāsarvajña further declares, *nityatva* and *anityatva* cannot be attributed to one and the same object or entity. *Anityatva* means destruction and *nityatva* means non-destruction. And these two are contradictory by nature and cannot be attributed to one and the same object. Not indeed there is anything, which is cognized as destroyed and non-destroyed. Samantabhadra argued:

तस्मान्नैकस्य नित्यत्वमनित्यत्वं चेति। अनित्यत्वं हि नाशित्वं प्रसिद्धं, नित्यत्वं चांनाशित्यं तच्चैतदुभयं विरूद्धत्वान्नैकन्न सम्भवति। न हि नष्टमनष्टं चेत्येकं किंचित् प्रतिभाति।[80]

At this point the Jainas argued: We noticed *utpādatva, nāśatva* and *dhrauvyatva* in one and the same object say gold, when *kaṭaka* is transferred to *mukuṭa,* where *kaṭaka* is destroyed, mukuṭa is produced and *suvarṇatva* is continude to exist.

To this, Bhāsarvajña replies: in this case, *nityatva* or *anityatva* cannot be established with regard to a single entity due to the fact that the three different forms are associated or delimited by three distinct *dharmas i.e.* properties, and not delimited by a single properties.

And if it is argued that all the three forms of *kaṭaka, mukuṭ a* and *suvarṇa* are delimited by single property, then the person who has attachment towards *mukuṭa* will be happy or remain indifferent, when *kaṭaka* is changed into *mukuṭa,* since, the three forms are distinct and not one.

कस्यचिदेकस्य नित्यानित्यत्वसिद्धिः त्रयाणामाकराणामन्योन्धर्मासंसर्गात्, संसर्गे वा कटकार्थिनः शोकवत्प्रमोदमाधयस्थ्ये अपि स्याताम्। अत एव त्रयाणामाकाराणां नैक्यम्।[81]

It may be argued that if the three forms are accepted as different, then the co-existence or co-referentiality of these three cannot be maintained.

To this, Bhāsarvajña replies pointing out that such doubts are baseless, hence coreferentiality is possible. He explains this by quoting the illustration of *daṇḍī, kuṇḍalī* etc. Even though *daṇḍa, kuṇḍala* etc. are different, there is *samānādhi-karaṇya* in their locus namely *daṇḍī, kuṇḍalī* etc.

दण्डकुण्डलादीनां भेदेपि तदाश्रये पुंसि दण्डी कुण्डलीत्यादि सामानाधि करण्यवत्।[82]

Thus, these three namely *kaṭaka, kuṇḍala* or *suvarṇa* are to be taken as distinct and different.

If it is argued that there is identity between these three, then there arise a contingency of ceasing of human day-to-day behaviour namely that when someone is asked to bring *kaṭ aka,* he may bring *buṇḍala* or any thing made up of gold and vise-versa, which is absurd.

यदि पुनरभेदः स्यात्, तदा कटकाकारग्रहणादेव मुकुटाकारदिग्रहोऽपि स्याद्।[83]

Because, the form which is known and the form which is unknown cannot be treated as one and the same. And if these are accepted as one, then there cannot be any distinction between *'khara'* and *'Jlna'*. As a matter of fact Jainas will not like that there is *abheda i.e.* identity between a donkey and *asiddha.*

गृहीताऽगृहीताकारयोरेकत्वायोगाद् एकत्वे या खरजिनादीनामपि भेदो न स्यात्।[84]

The *Jaina* may argue thus: let there be *bheda,* mutual distinction amongst the modes *i.e. paryāya,* but there is no distinction in the locus of these *'paryāyas'*. What the Jaina proposes is that the various modes may be different but the locus of these modes has to be identical.

पर्यायाणां परस्परं भेदोऽस्त्येव, न तु पर्यायपर्यायिनोरिति चेत्।[85]

To this, Samantabhadra replies: in that case also identity cannot be established, due to their cognition by mutual exclusion. To make the point clear Bhāsarvajña takes the help of the examples of *'keyūra'*, it may be cognized as in the form of gold but not in the form of *kaṭa*. Similarly what is cognized in the form of *rājatakaṭa i.e.* silver bracelet cannot be cognized in the form of gold bracelet. Therefore, due to the contradictory elements of cognition and non-cognition, there is distinction as in between a donkey and camel-concludes Bhāsarvajña.

केयूरादौ सुवर्णकारोपलम्ल्भेऽपि न कटाकारोपलम्भः, तथा राजत कटाकारोपलम्भेऽपि न सुवर्णकारोपलम्भः, तस्मादुपलम्भदिविरुद्धधर्माध्यासात् खरोष्ट्रादीनामिव भेद एवेति।[86]

Further objection is raised by the Jainas, namely that let there be difference, but to hold that there is absolute difference is not correct. Because, this *anekānta* has to be applied to each and every state. Thus, in case of difference also all the seven *bhaṅgas* are to be applied. This will amount to the seven alternatives namely *syād bheda* etc.

भेदस्तथापि भेद एवैत्ययुक्तम्: यतः स्याद्भेदः, स्याद्भेदश्चाभेदश्च, स्यादवक्तव्यः, स्याभ्देदश्चावक्तव्यश्च, स्यादभेदश्चावक्तवयश्च, स्याभ्देदश्चाभेदश्चावक्तवयश्चेति।[87]

Because according to the Jainas, the whole universe is to be interpreted in terms of *saptabhaṅgī*. And hence, there would not be any example to establish *ekānta*.

तदेवं सर्व जगत्सप्तगंग्याघ्रातं न किंचिदेकान्तसाधनेऽस्त्युदाहरणमिति।[88]

Bhāsarvajña refutes or removes such doubts that there cannot be any example for *anekānta*. Bhāsarvajña notes: how is that there is no example to establish *ekānta*. We have example of absolute difference *i.e. ekānta bhinna* between *jīna* and *khara, sūkara* etc. It means *jīna* is liberated omniscient having all excellent qualities contrary to a camel or a donkey, having low qualities, hence, they are absolutely different. The Jainas cannot argue that even the *saptabhaṅgī* or the seven *bhaṅgas* will be applied *to jīna* who is liberated and thus, one can say:

शक्नुवन्ति वक्तुम्-मुक्तावस्थो जिनः स्यान्निकृष्टतमः।[89]

i.e. Jina possessed negligible character etc. and thus, they will be similar to a camel or a donkey and hence, no difference can be maintained.

नह्येवं भवन्तः शक्नुवन्ति वक्तुम्-मुक्तावस्थो जिनः स्यान्निकृष्टतमः, स्यादनिकृष्टतमः, स्यान्निकृष्टतमश्चानिकृष्टतमः, स्यादवक्तव्यः, स्यान्निकृष्ठ तमश्चावक्तव्यश्च, स्यादनिकृष्टतमश्चावक्तव्यश्च, स्यान्निकृष्ट तमश्चानिकृष्टतमश्चावक्तव्यश्चेति। अत्राप्येवं सप्तभंगीष्यत इति।[90]

To this Bhāsarvajña say: no intelligent people will welcome or will be happy with the logic of the Jainas, because the argument given is just to defend or offend the opponents and not based on logic.

तदेतदपेतागमयुक्तिकं परस्पर्ध्दयाभिधीयमानं न विद्वन्मनः प्रीणाति।[91]

Going further, if the Jainas worship a donkey or a camel like jīna or eat stones and human excreta like milk jaggery, or curd, then only absolute difference will be established.

यदि खलु भवन्तः खरोष्ट्रसूकरादिकं जिनमिव कदाचिदुपासते, पाषाणपुरीषादिकं च गुडदधितक्रादिवभ्दक्षयन्ति, तदा न स्यादेकान्तसिद्धिः।[92]

A question may be raised here, what is the excellenceness or the speciality, which *Jīna* adorns or possesses and absent in the camel or donkey or again what is the *nikṛstabhāva i.e.* low quality possessed by a donkey or a camel, which is absent in case *of Jīna* due to which *Jīna* is worshipped and the donkey etc. are not. Still further, what is speciality that exists in jaggery etc. and lacking in stones etc. because of which people like to eat jaggery etc. not stones etc.

को हि जिनस्यातिशयो यः खरोष्ट्रदौ नास्त्येव? को वा खरोष्ट्रादेर्निकृषभावो यो नास्त्येव जिने यतः खरोष्ट्रादिपरिहारेण स एवोपास्यते? तथा पाषाण पुरीषदीनां को दोषो यो गुडादिषु नास्त्येव, गुडादीनां या कोऽतिशयो यः पाणाणदिषु नास्त्येव, यतः पाषाणादिपरिहारेण गुडादीन्येवभक्ष्यन्ते?[93]

Concluding this discussion Bhāsarvajña observes: there exists something special due to which there is *pravṛtti i.e.* inclination towards something not for everything. Thus, *anekānta* is not to be applicable to everything. Hence, the possibilities are *kaścidekānta, kaścidekānta* and in those cases, where *ekānta* will be possible, that will serve as an illustration for ekānta.

अथास्त्येव कश्चदत्रैवातिशयो यक्षशादत्रैव प्रवृत्तिरिति, न तर्हि सर्वत्रानेकान्तः। अथ क्वचिदेकान्तः क्वचिदनेकान्त इति पक्षः, एवं तर्हि यत्रैकान्तः स तावद् दृष्टान्तः।[94]

What Bhāsarvajña wants to establish here is that one can find example for *ekānta* and the argument of the Jainas that no example of *ekānta* will be available stands refuted. The difference between *jīna* and a donkey with regards to their quality is absolute, which the *Jainas* also accept- observes Bhāsarvajña.

With a view to find a fault with Jainism, Bhāsarvajña observes: as a matter of fact the Jainas do not have an example to establish anekānta.

तव त्वनेकान्तसिद्धौ न दृष्टान्तः क्वचिदस्ति।[95]

Explaining further he says, if something is different from another thing, then it will be a new thing and the difference would be like a donkey and a camel from *Jīna*. And if it is argued that there is identity from the point of view of existence, that will not stands to logic, and it will go against human behaviour. There will be dilemma with regard to distinguishing two things, due to the absence of any guiding principle with regard to something which is describable or otherwise; which is eatable or not. No *pravṛtti* will be possible. Hence, what is given, as an illustration of difference cannot again be quoted as an example of *abheda*. Thus, the *Jainas* has no example to establish *bheda* and *abheda* leading to the not-establishment *anekānta* itself.

यद्यस्माद् भिन्नं तत्तस्मादेकान्तेन भिन्नं ततोर्थान्तरत्वात् खपौष्ट्रादिभ्यो जिनादिवत्। सत्त्वाद्याकारेणाभेदोऽप्यत्रास्तीति चेत्, न; यस्याकारस्यैकान्तेन

भेद उभयोः सिद्धः;, तस्य दृष्टान्तत्वेनोपादानात् अथ न कस्याप्येकान्तेन भेदसिद्धिः;, ततः दपायस्यानुपायस्य भक्ष्याभक्ष्यादिविवेकनियमाभावान्त क्चस्यचित् क्वचित् प्रवृत्तिनियमः प्राप्नोति।[96]

Bhāsarvajña takes the view of Akalarikadeva for critical examination with regard to *syādvāda*. Akalanka in his *Laghiyasthraya* justifies the *saptabhaṅgīnayas,* Taking the example of *ghaṭa* he explains the first three *bhaṅgas* that is *ghaṭasti, ghaṭnāsti* and *ghaṭāsti nāsti ca,* justified the existence and non-existence of the one and the same pot, Aklaṅka comments that the pot exists as a pot and it does not exist as a cloth or as anything else. Thus, where it is said '*ghaṭāsti nasti ca*' what is implied that pot exists as a pot and not as a cloth.

स्वात्मानाऽस्ति घटः परात्मना तु नास्तीति।[97]

To this, Bhāsarvajña observes that if a single pot is associated with many properties and this existence and non-existence is presented taking into consideration these aspects, then the *Naiyāyikas* has no problem.

यदि तावेदकस्य घटस्यानेकधर्मयोगित्वमिति, तदा नास्ति विवादः।[98]

Because, even according to the logicians, the *vidhi* and *pratisedha* with regard to a single object is justifiable on the basis of different characteristics.

एकस्यापि धर्मिणो विधिप्रतिषेधात्मकानेकधर्मयोगित्वाभ्युपगमात्।[99]

Now as to the assertion of the Jainas that an entity is of the nature of existence and non-existence or positive and negative character, Bhāsarvajña notes: what is the meaning or the application of *ubhayātmaka.* To him, if by *ubhayātmaka* the Jaina intends *ubhayātmaka i.e.* delimited by two different properties, then the *Naiyāyikas* will welcome it. If it is intended to be by one and the same *dharma,* then there will be contradiction.

Further Bhāsarvajña notes that if the pot is to be understood as different from what is non-pot, this will amount to accepting the view of Buddhist and this will involve many faults, which he has pointed out elsewhere. As a matter of fact our concern is not to discuss the Buddhist's *'apohavāda'* to which Bhāsarvajña has made a reference here.

उभयात्मक इति कोऽर्थः? यद्युभयधर्मकः, तदा नास्ति विवाद इत्युक्तम्। अथ घट एव तदन्याभाव इति, नन्वेवं शाक्यमतं भवताभ्युपगतं भवति, व्यावृत्तदन्या नैव व्यावृत्तिरित्याभिधानात्। तत्र च दूषणंप्रपंचेनोक्तम्।[100]

The Jainas may argue that let there be the difference between *bhāva* and *abhāva* being accepted as *ubhayātmaka.* To this Bhāsarvajña objects: by mere acceptance the objects are not proved. To establish something one needs some valid means to prove and you have not given any *pramāṇa* to prove its *ubhayātmakatva.*

प्रमाणतो हि पदार्थसभ्दावसिद्धिः, प्रमाणंच त्वया नोक्तं यतस्तदुभ-यात्मकत्वसिद्धिः स्यात्।[101]

On the other hand, we have given *pramāṇa,* which proves the *ekāntabhāva i.e.* absoluteness of reality and not *ubhayātmaka* like *bhāva* and *abhāva i.e.* existence and non-existence. Explaining further, Bhāsarvajña writes: the absence of cloth is not *ghaṭa i.e.* pot, since it is the absence of pot as for example, its destruction (*i.e. paṭāāibhāva na ghaṭātmakaḥ pradhvṁsavat).* To the query asked as to how there is the expression or cognition 'the pot is not cloth' Bhāsarvajña replies: it is governed by mutual absence.

कथं तर्हि घटः पटो न भवतीति प्रतिभासः? इतरेतराभावनिबन्धनोऽयम्।[102]

To explain: the expression *'ghaṭo na paṭaḥ'* or *'paṭo na ghaṭaḥ' i.e.* 'the pot is not cloth' or ' the cloth is not pot' are based on mutual absence where the identity of one with the other is denied. Hence, there is no difficulty to explain the expression of the cognition the 'pot is not cloth', even though the absence of cloth is not in the form of pot.

Bhāsarvajña records further objection: how the *bhāva* that existence is related to *'itaretarābhāva' i.e.* mutual absence and even though a relation is established, one would have the cognition like 'there is no cloth in the pot' based on relational absence.

नन्वितरेतराभावेन सह भावस्य कः सम्बन्धः सम्बन्धेऽपि घटे पटो नास्तीति प्रतीतिः स्यादिति।[103]

To this Bhāsarvajña replies in negative and says that the answer has already been given. There is something between *bhāva* and *abhāva,* which distinguishes these two, which is responsible for that distinct cognition and it may be called by any name.

यत्तावत्कः सम्बन्धा इति, तन्न; उक्तोत्तरत्वात्-उक्तमत्र भावतदन्याभावयोः सन्निधिविशेषः कश्चितावदस्ति, यतस्तयोर्विश्लेषेण ग्रहणम्। तत्र यथेष्टं संज्ञापि क्रियताम्।[104]

Going further, Bhāsarvajña refutes the view that *bhāva* and *abhāva* are identical, as stated that even there is relation, there will be cognition like 'there is no cloth in the pot' as for example there is no pot in the ground' is not correct.

सम्बन्धेपि घटे पटो नास्तीति प्रतीतिः स्याद् भूतले घटाभावप्रतीतिवत्। तदयुक्तम्।

The distinction in cognition is based on the distinctness of the relation like the *bhāvas i.e.* the positive entities.

भाववत्सम्बन्धविशेषतः प्रतीतियैलक्षणयोपपत्तेः।[105]

The distinctness of the cognition is evidently based on the distinctness of the *bhāvasaṁbandhas*. Many examples can be quoted, 'there is blue substance in the pot' *(kuṇḍe nīlī dravyāsti)* or 'the cloth is blue' *(nīlo paṭaḥ),* similarly depending on the relation of absence, the cognition will be distinct. Hence, the cause of the difference of the cognition of absence is based on the distinction in the relation of the absence.

कुण्डेऽस्ति नीलीद्रव्यमिति, नीलः पट इति मम प्रतीतिः प्रतीतोऽर्थ इत्येवंमादि।

एवमभावसम्बन्धविशेषोऽपि प्रतीतिवैलक्षण्ये हेतुरस्तीति गम्यते।[106]

In conclusion, Bhāsarvajña notes that in all cases the distinction of cause is established from the distinction of the effect.

सर्वत्र हि कार्यविशेषेण हेतुविशेषसिद्धिरिति।[107]

Explaining further, when there is pot in the ground the pot will be the counter positive for its absence on the ground.

यस्य प्रतियोगी यथाबुद्ध्युपस्थापितस्तदभावस्य तथा।[108]

When the *pratiyogī* of something is its own self, then the counter positive of its absence would be the object itself. For example, 'this cloth is not pot.'

'यदा तु तत्प्रतियोगी तदात्मकत्येन बुद्ध्युपरथपितः, तदा तदभावोपि तदात्मैव प्रतिभात्यघटोऽयं पट इति।[109]

What Bhāsarvajña wants to explain in this line is the distinction between the two types of absence viz. relational absence and mutual absence. In the relational absence the relation of the counter positive with its counter correlative is denied where as in mutual absence the identity is denied. Finally Bhāsarvajña concludes that the bhāva and *abhāva* cannot be identical. Further, as is argued *ghaṭa* and *aghaṭa* are not different from one another is not correct, because this is contradicted by all experiences. If the negation is interpreted as either *prasajya pratiṣedha* or *paryudāsa* then also the identity between *bheda* and *abheda* cannot be justified. In the case of *prasajya abhāva* the absence of 'sarpa' snake) will be *'asarpa'* ('non-snake) because the same cannot be identical with its absence. Now if *sarpa* is identical with *asarpa* then we should be afraid of the absence of *sarpa i.e. asarpa* as in the case of the presence of *sarpa.* Because, both are identical, which is not logical, hence, *prasajya* is not *tenable.* In the case *of paryudāsa* also the *aghaṭa* means *ghaṭatva anya i.e.* paṭatva. And a cloth obviously is different from pot, which needs no proof. And if one accepts identity between *ghaṭa* and *aghaṭa* in the sense of *paryudāsa,* then one has to meet with the contingency of cognition 'pot' in the case of 'cloth' or vice-versa. Thus, resorting to either *prasajya pratiṣedha* or *paryudāsa* identity cannot be established between *bhāva* or *abhāva* and *ghaṭa* or *aghaṭa i.e.* negative and positive aspects of the same reality.

प्रसज्यपर्युदासपक्षेऽप्यभेदानुपपत्तेश्च-प्रसज्यपक्षे तावद् घटत्वभाव एवाघटत्वम्, न च तदेव तदभावः। सर्पाभावोऽसर्प एव स्यात्ततश्च

सर्पवत्तदभावादपि भयं स्यात्, तद्विविक्ताविविक्तप्रदेशयोस्तुल्योपलम्भश्च स्यात्। पर्युदासपक्षेपि घटत्वादन्यदघटत्वं पटत्वादिकमुच्यते, तच्च भिन्नमेय अभेदे हि घटादिष्वपि पटबुद्ध्यभिधानानुवृत्तिः स्यात्पटेऽपि घटादिबुद्धिः स्यात्।[110]

Bhāsarvajña finds fault with the assertion of the Jainas' view that a pot is known as a pot by its own self and not as some other self, *ghaṭatvena ghaṭa na paṭatvena.* To him, this view of the *Jainas* is illogical. To explain, when a pot exists, can the cognition of *aghaṭa i.e.* absence of pot would arise or known like that delimited by *paṭatva. (paṭātmanā hi kim jñāpyate iti)*? There is no proof to establish this. When the pot is produced from the clay, it is cognized of the pot delimited by potness. It is not that the *'aghaṭa'* is being produced by some other properties. When the pot is destroyed, if it is *aghaṭa,* then it is not a pot. Therefore, it is not that the *ghaṭa* is cognized as *aghaṭa,* delimited by cloth ness.

विनष्टो हि यद्यघटः स्यात्, तदा चासौ न घटः, तस्मान्न पटात्मना घट एवाघटः क्रियते।[111]

It is also not cognized like the knowledge of silver on non-silver. Further objection is raised: the pot is not known as delimited by clothness, hence, this is called *aghaṭa.*

अथ पटात्मना न घटः प्रतिभातीत्यघटोप्यसावुच्यते।[112]

To this Bhāsarvajña replies in negative stating that this is contradictory. The pot is known as pot only not as cloth but pot alone.

Further, where it is intended to be of dual characteristics due to the existence of both the *dharmas,* there also it is not dependent on one's own self and other than that. For example, 'the lotus that is blue', is not intended it as blue lotus as accepted as by other self, but by its own form. Similarly the *sadāsadātmaka* is to be accepted by its own form and not by *svātmanā* or *parātmanā.*

यत्राप्युभयधर्माधिकरणत्वेनोभयात्मकत्वमुच्यते, तत्रापि न स्वात्मपरात्मापेक्षया तदुभयात्मकं यथा नीलं च तदुप्पलं चेति। न हि परात्मना वन्नीलमुत्पलं चेत्युच्यते, किं तु स्वरूपेणैव तथा सदसदात्मकत्वमपि स्वरूपेणैव वाच्यम्।[113]

The *satva* and *asatva* cannot be primary by some other form. It cannot be argued that the 'gold' etc. exists in the form of 'mṛt' etc. not also the *asatva* or non-existence of sky-flower etc. in the form of pole etc. because they are non-existence by their very form.

नान्यरूपेण सत्त्वमसत्त्वं वा मुख्यम्, न हि सुवर्णादेर्मृदादिरूपेण सत्त्वम्, नापि खपुष्पादेः स्तम्भदिरूपेणाऽसत्त्वम्, स्वरूपेणैवासत्त्वादिति।[114]

If the positive entities are of *ubhayātmaka* namely *satva* and *asatvātmaka,* then by its own form only there would be the cognition of *ghaṭa* and *aghaṭa.*

तद्यदि भावानामुभयात्मकत्वं स्यात्, तदा स्वरूपेणैव घटश्चाघटश्च स्यात्।[115]

If it is taken as *aghaṭa* by some other form that *aghaṭatva* will be secondary. Thus, the dual characteristics of object by *svātmā* and *parātmā* is secondary and primarily, an object is known as that by its own form. If it is argued that let the *ubhayātmaka i.e.* the dual character of the reality be its own form that will be not accepted, because *iṣṭa* and *aniṣṭasvabhāva i.e.* desired and non-desired objects cannot go together in case of living beings. And this will amount to cessation of human behaviour.

स्वरूपेणैवोभयात्मकं वस्त्विति चेत्, न; इष्टानिष्टस्वभावाव्यवस्थितेः प्राणिव्यवहाराभावप्रसंगात्।[116]

For example, the pleasure etc. in case of living beings is *iṣṭa i.e.* desirable; similarly the absence of that is *aniṣṭa.*

And further the presence of *duḥkha* etc. is *aniṣta* and its absence is *iṣṭa i.e.* desirable. If by its own form an entity is *ubhayātmaka i.e. sadāsadātmaka,* that being both *sukhaduḥkhātmaka* as *iṣṭāniśtātmaka,* no *pravṛtti* or *nivṛtti* will take place.

प्राणिनां सुश्वादिसत्त्वमिष्टम्। तथा तदसत्त्वमनिषृम्। यथा च दुःखादिसत्त्वमनिष्टम् तथा तदसत्त्वमिष्टम् ततश्च स्वरुपेणैव सदसदात्मकत्वं सुखदुःखादिसाधनानामिष्टानिष्टत्वेन व्यवस्थानात् तत्प्राप्तिपरिवतर्जनाथें प्रवृत्तिनिवृत्ती न स्याताम्।[117]

Further, knowing that something is the cause of pleasure, if some one is inclined to do some work, it will not be possible for him to do it because of the absence of it. And by non-performing that he will not attain liberation being dragged by this presence and absence of pleasure, which states one would attain. Criticizing the Jainas, Bhāsarvajña says: to what a pitiable condition and unavoidable difficulties, which the human beings are fallen by the bad logic of the naked Jaina.

अपि चायं सुखादि हेतुः सत्त्वात्स्वकार्यकरणप्रवृत्तोऽप्यस्त्वान्न शक्नोति कर्तुम, अकुर्वतोऽप्यस्य मोक्षो नास्ति सत्त्वात्तदयं सत्त्वासत्त्वाभ्यामाकृष्य माणः कामवस्थां च तत्प्राप्नोतु? दुस्तरे हि व्यसने नग्नश्रमणक दुर्बुध्दिनायं वराकः पतित इति।[118]

What Bhāsarvajña wants to express is that in the Jainas theory, no activities will be possible due to lack of concrete direction. One should know for certain that by performing something, one will get pleasure and by not performing something one will avoid pain. But in case of Jainas as Bhāsarvajña understand in each and everything *ubhayātmaka* by its own form *i.e. sukhāduhkhātmaka*.

Inconsistency in the statement of the Tīrthaṅkaras:

Even maintaining the position of the Jainas a doubt is being raised about the validity of their very scripture. Bhāsarvajña asked: is there any truth in the statement of the *Tīrthaṅkaras*? It cannot be argued that their statements are true, because it would amount to postulate *ekāntavāda,* which the Jainas would not like to accept. Here also Jainas want *saptabhaṅgī* to employ, then result will be 'it may be true', 'it may be false', 'it may be true and untrue' etc. Then there would arise doubt about the validity and non-validity, because *Syādvāda* has to be employed everywhere. If *syādvāda* is employed to all the doctrines of the Jainas then there would be *oxwasthā i.e.* inconsistency with regard to *āsrava, saṁbara, sinrjarā* and *mokṣa* as well. This will amount to inconsistency in all cases of the Jaina philoscphy.

अपि च त्वत्तीर्थेंकरवचनं किं सत्यम्? आहोस्विदसत्यमिति? सत्य मेवेति न युक्तम्, एकान्तवादप्रसंगात्। अथात्रापि सप्तभंगीष्टा-स्यात्, सत्यम्, स्यादसत्यम्, स्यादुभयम्, स्यादवक्तव्यमित्येवमादिका, तदा प्रमाणाप्रमाणव्यवस्थानुपपत्तिः, स्याद्वादस्य सर्वत्राविशेषात्।[119]

To explain, Bhāsarvajña notes: the Jainas have prescribed the process of attaining *saṁvara, nirjarā* and *mokṣa* and also the avoidance *of āsrava* and *bandha.* Those who follow or perform some specific observances prescribed by the Jainas attain the state of *saṁara, nirjarā* and *mokṣa* gradually and those not performing these specific observances incur *āsrava* and *bandha* gradually. By employing *syādvāda* or *saptabhaṅgī* to this, no consistency will be maintained with regard to the performance and non-performance of the prescribed observation, because by employing *saptabhaṅgī* the prescription will be *syād viśiṣṭa, syādaviśiṣṭa* etc. for both the cases viz. in case of *mokṣa* as well *bandha.* This means that no distinction can be maintained between *saṁvara, nirjarā,* and *mokṣa* or *āsrava* and *bandha.*

तथा त्वत्तीर्थकराणामप्यनुष्ठानं स्यात्कुत्सितम्, स्यादकुत्सिसम्, स्यादुभयम्। चौरादीनामपि तथैवेति ने कश्चिद्विशेषः। तथा चाश्रवादिव्य-वस्थानुपपत्तिः किल, विशिष्टानुष्ठानवतामेव संवरनिर्ज्जरामोक्षा भवन्त्य-विशिष्टानुष्ठानवतां त्वास्त्रवबन्धावेत्यभ्युपगमः। तच्चोभयमप्युनुष्ठानं यदा स्याद्विशिष्टं स्यादविशिष्टमित्यव्यवस्थितम्, तदा कथमास्त्रवादि- व्यवस्था?[120]

No distinction between jīva and ajīva:

Not only that, the acceptance of the *syādvāda* theory of the Jainas will go against their very doctrine of the classification of the reality viz. *jīva* and *ajīva* etc. Bhāsarvajña says: how to maintain a distinction between *jīva* and *ajīva* etc. because following *syādvāda jīva* will be *ajīva, ajīva* will *be jīva.*

तथा जीवाजीवव्यवस्थाऽप्ययुक्ता। स्याद्वादे हि जीवोऽप्यजीवः स्यादजीवोऽपि जीवः स्यादिति कुतस्तयोर्व्यवस्था?[121]

And if the *Jainas* say for argument sake that let there be inconsistency then is that inconsistency absolute from ultimate point of view or is it only to confuse us ? To this, *Bhāsarvajña* argues without resorting to *ekānta,* no consistency can be maintained by which some consistency of principle with regard to objects can be established or proved.

अथाव्यवस्थाप्यस्ति; सा किं परमार्थतः? किं वाऽस्मानेवमेव प्रतारयसि? न ह्येकान्तपक्षानभ्युपगमे क्वचिद् व्यवस्थोपपद्यते। येन च प्रकारेणार्थानां व्यवस्थोच्येते।[122]

Finally Bhāsarvaijṃa concludes that the reality cannot be of both *i.e. 'sat'* and *'asat'* तस्मान्न वस्तुतः सदसदात्मकं वस्तु।[123]

The view of the Jainas that the object is both eternal and transitory is also refuted by Bhāsarvajña. He says *'nāpi nityānityātmaka'*. The reality is not transitory and eternal simultaneously. He further explains this thus: when the soul etc. are eternal in the form of its own *paryāyī* then they are eternal in reality; in that case the supposition that they are transitory from the point of view of their *paryāyas* are secondary; primarily they are eternal as stated.

यद्यात्मादि वस्तु स्वेन पर्यायिरूपेण नित्यम्, तदा वस्तुतस्तन्नित्यमेव, तत्र पर्यायनित्यत्वेनानित्यत्वं कल्प्यमानं गौणमेव स्यात्।[124]

It may be argued: by its own form the soul is treated as destroyed and not destroyed. स्वरुपेणैव च तन्नष्टमनष्टं चेत्युपपद्यते। [125] Bhāsarvajña replied that in that case the human behaviour will cease because by knowing a soul to be destroyed for certain one makes such usages स्वरूपेणैव च तन्नष्टमनष्टं चेत्युपपद्यते। नष्टमेवेति निश्चयपूर्वकः सर्वप्राणिव्यवहारश्च दृश्यते, साऽपि न स्यात्।[126] The Jainas may further argue that the soul is treated as eternal and transitory due to the association with pleasure and pain etc. To this, Bhāsarvajña replies that this cannot be accepted because the pleasure etc. are different from the soul and how pleasure etc. are different from soul have been established elsewhere, while finding faults with the Buddhists.

अथात्मनः सुखादिरूपेणानित्यत्वमप्यस्ति, न; सुखादेस्तोऽन्यत्वात्तदन्यत्वं च शाक्यमतदूषणप्रस्तावे समर्थितम्।[127]

To the argument namely that "there is *ananyatva i.e. anyatva bhinna* between soul and pleasure then Bhāsarvajña replies in negative. When *anyatva* is definite as in the case of moon and sun, the *ananyatva* can be accepted and if the *ananyatva* is real, then the *anyatva i.e.* difference will be unreal like the knowledge of another moon by a diseased person who is affected by the *'tīmira'*.

अनन्यत्वमप्यस्तीति चेत्, न; अन्यत्वनिश्चयनैवाऽनन्यत्वस्य बाधितत्वाच्चन्द्रादित्ययर्योरिव। अनन्यत्वस्य वास्तवत्वे चान्यत्वमवास्तवं तैमिरिकोपलब्धचन्द्रान्तरवत्।[128]

What Bhāsarvajña wants to establish is that the pleasures etc. are to be distinguished from soul. A clear distinction between the two has to be maintained on the basis of the destruction and emergence of pleasure and pain etc. the soul is not treated as transitory, which is already elaborated by him elsewhere.

As to the argument namely that in some form soul is eternal, by other it is transitory Bhāsarvajña asks: are these two forms different from the soul or identical with it ? If they are different then the *nityatva* and *anityatva* of the soul cannot be established on the basis of their *anityatva* and *nityatva,* these being different. And if they are identical, this will amount to the fact that delimited by which form they are nitya, they will be *anitya* delimited by some property or form. And this will involve many faults, which we have already explained.

अथ ते रूपे पुरुषात्परस्परं च किं भिन्ने? उताभिन्ने चेति? भेदपक्षे तावन्न तयोर्नित्यानित्यत्वेन पुरूषस्य नित्यानित्यत्वम्, अतिप्रसंगात्। अभेदपक्षे तु येनैव रूपेण नित्यत्वं तेनैववनित्यत्वमिति प्राप्तम्, तत्रोक्तोमेव दूषणम्।[129]

And if it is argued that they are *bhinna* and *abhinna* they are treated as identity-cum-difference or identity in difference, then in the difference and identity is by one and the same form or property or by different form or property. If by one and the same form then the same fault will arise by different names, which would amount to the fault of infinite regress.

अथ भिन्नाभिन्ने, तत्रापि किं येनैव रूपेण भेदस्तेनैवाभेदः अथ रूपान्तरेणोति? यदि तेनैव, तदा पुनस्तदेव दुषणमथ रूपान्तरेण, ततोऽनवस्थाप्रसंग।[130]

In conclusion, refuting the position of the Jainism, Bhāsarvajña observes that in Jainas' view there cannot be any definite knowledge with regard to any object namely 'this is this'. And the absence of a definite cognition there cannot be any inclination towards the final *i.e. purusārtha.* It is seen that intelligent people by their activities through predeterminate definite knowledge attains *'puruṣārtha'* and not in the absence of that. Thus, there should not be inconsistency with regard to the distinction between *'nitya-anityatva'; 'bhinna-abhinnatva'* etc- concludes Bhāsarvajña.

REFERENCE

1. Nyāyasūtra. III. 1. 44.
2. Nyāyasūtrabhāṣya on III. . 44.
3. *Ibid.*
4. Nyāyasūtra. III. 1. 45.
5. *Ibid.*
6. Nyāyasūtra. III. 1.46.
7. Nyāyasūtrabhāṣya on III. 1. 46.
8. *Ibid.*
9. Nyāyasūtra. III. 1. 47.
10. Nyāyasūtrabhāṣya on III. 1. 47.
11. *Ibid.* III. 1.48.
12. Nyāyasūtra. III. 1. 49.
13. *Ibid.* III. 1.50.
14. Nyāyasūtrabhāṣya on III. 1. 50.
15. Nyāyasūtra. III. 2. 68-72.
16. Nyāyasūtrabhāṣya on III. 2. 68.
17. *Ibid.* III. 2. 69.

18. *Ibid*.
19. *Ibid*. III. 2. 70.
20. *Ibid*.m.2.7i.
21. *Ibid*. III. 2. 72.
22. *Ibid*.
23. *Ibid*.
24. Nyāyabhāṣya on IV. 1. 33.
25. *Ibid*.
26. Nyāyavārtikatātparyatīka on IV. 1. 33.
27. *Ibid*.
28. *Ibid*.
29. Nyāyasūtra. I. 1. 32.
30. Nyāya Philosophy. Part. I. p. 107.
31. Nyāyasūtrabhāṣa on I. 1.
32. *Ibid*.
33. *Ibid*.
34. *Ibid*.
35. *Ibid*.
36. *Ibid*.
37. *Ibid*.
38. Nyāyavārtikatātparyatīka on I. 1. 32.
39. Sarvadarsanasamgraha. P. 557
40. Pramāṇamīmāmsa. I. 1. 8.
41. Nyāyamajṃarī. P. 450.
    cf. Tattvāthavārtika. I. 10. 125.
42. *Ibid*. p. 451.
43. *Ibid*.
44. cf. (a) सहो सो पुग्गलो चिता Pravacanasāra. 2. 40.
    (b) शब्दस्यचिन्द्रियग्राह्यत्वाद् गुणत्वं न खल्वाशङ्कनीयम्, तस्य वैचित्र्यप्रपञ्चित-वैश्वरूपस्याप्यनेकद्रव्यात्मकपुद्गलपर्यायत्वेनाभ्युपगम्यमानत्वात्। गुणत्वे वा न तावदमूर्त्तद्रव्यगुणः शब्दः गुणगुणिनोरविभक्तप्रदेशत्वेनैकवेदनवेद्य-त्वादमूर्तद्रव्यस्यापि श्रवणेन्द्रियविषयत्वापत्तेः। पर्यायलक्षणेनोत्खात गुणलक्षणत्वान्मूर्त-द्रव्यगुणोऽपि न भवति। पर्यायलक्षणं हि कादाचित्कत्वं गुण लक्षणं तु नित्यत्वम्। ...... ततोऽस्तु शब्दः पुद्गलपर्याय एवेति। pravacanasāratattvadīpikā on 2. 40.

45. Nyāyamajṃarī. P. 536
46. *Ibid.*
47. *Ibid.*
48. *Ibid.* p. 537.
49. *Ibid.*
50. *Ibid.*
51. Nyāyabhūṣaṇa. P. 393.
52. *Ibid.*
53. *Ibid.*
54. *Ibid.*
55. *Ibid.*
56. Nyāyāvatāra. 1.1.
57. Nyāyabhūṣaṇa. P. 80.
58. *Ibid.*
59. *Ibid.*p. 81.
60. Nyāyabhūṣaṇa. P. 552-53.
    cf. Aptamīmāmśā. 59.
61. Nyāyabhūṣaṇa. P. 553.
    cf. Tattvārtharājavārtika. 1.4. 14.
62. Nyāyabhūṣaṇa. P. 553.
    cf Tattvārtharājavārtika. 1.4. 16.
63. Nyāyabhūṣaṇa. P. 553.
    Tattvārtharājavārtika. 1.4. 18.
64. Nyāyabhūṣaṇa. P. 554.
    cf. Tattvārtharājavārtika. 1.4. 19.
65. Nyāyabhūṣaṇa. P. 554.
    cf. Tattvārtharājavārtika. 1.
66. Nyāyabhūṣaṇa. P. 554.
    cf. Tatrvārthsūtra. 1.4.
    cf. saddravyasamuccaya. 47.
67. Nyāyabhūṣaṇa. P. 554.
    cf. Tattvārtharājavārtika. 1. 6. 5.
68. Nyāyabhūṣaṇa. P. 554.

69. Nyāyabhūṣaṇa. P. 554.
    cf.Tattvārtharājavārtika. P.33.
70. Nyāyabhūṣaṇa. P. 555.
71. Nyāyabhūṣaṇa. P. 555.
72. Nyāyabhūṣaṇa. P. 555.
    cf. Tattvārtharājavārtika. P.34.
73. Nyāyabhūṣaṇa. P. 555.
74. Nyāyabhūṣaṇa. P. 555.
75. Nyāyabhūṣaṇa. P. 555.
76. Nyāyabhūṣaṇa. P. 555.
77. Nyāyabhūṣaṇa. P. 556.
78. Nyāyabhūṣaṇa. P. 556.
79. Nyāyabhūṣaṇa.. P. 556.
80. Nyāyabhūṣaṇa. P. 556.
81. Nyāyabhūṣaṇa. P. 556.
82. Nyāyabhūṣaṇa. P. 556.
83. Nyāyabhūṣaṇa. P. 556.
84. Nyāyabhūṣaṇa. P. 556.
85. Nyāyabhusana. P. 556.
86. Nyāyabhūṣaṇa. P. 556.
87. Nyāyabhūṣaṇa. P. 556.
88. Nyāyabhūṣaṇa. P. 557.
89. Nyāyabhūṣaṇa. P. 557.
90. Nyāyabhūṣaṇa. P. 557.
91. Nyāyabhūṣaṇa. P. 557.
92. Nyāyabhūṣaṇa. P. 557.
93. Nyāyabhūṣaṇa. P. 557.
94. Nyāyabhūṣaṇa. P. 557.
95. Nyāyabhūṣaṇa. P. 557.
96. Nyāyabhūṣaṇa. P. 557
97. Nyāyabhūṣaṇa. P. 557.
98. Nyāyabhūṣaṇa. P. 557.
99. Nyāyabhūṣaṇa. P. 557.

100. Nyāyabhūṣaṇa. P. 558.
101. Nyāyabhūṣaṇa. P. 553.
102. Nyāyabhūṣaṇa. P. 558.
103. Nyāyabhūṣaṇa. P. 553
104. Nyāyabhūṣaṇa. P. 558
105. Nyāyabhūṣaṇa. P. 558
106. Nyāyabhūṣaṇa. P. 553.
107. Nyāyabhūṣaṇa. P. 553.
108. Nyāyabhūṣaṇa. P. 558
109. Nyāyabhūṣaṇa. P. 558
110. Nyāyabhūṣaṇa. P. 559
111. Nyāyabhūṣaṇa. P. 559.
112. Nyāyabhūṣaṇa. P. 559.
113. Nyāyabhūṣaṇa. P. 559.
114. Nyāyabhūṣaṇa. P. 559.
115. Nyāyabhūṣaṇa. P. 559.
116. Nyāyabhūṣaṇa. P. 559.
117. Nyāyabhūṣaṇa. P. 559.
118. Nyāyabhūṣaṇa. P. 560.
119. Nyāyabhūṣaṇa. P. 560.
120. Nyāyabhūṣaṇa. P. 560.
121. Nyāyabhūṣaṇa. P. 560.
122. Nyāyabhūṣaṇa. P. 560.
123. Nyāyabhūṣaṇa. P. 560.
124. Nyāyabhūṣaṇa. P. 560.
125. Nyāyabhūṣaṇa. P. 560.
126. Nyāyabhūṣaṇa. P. 560.
127 Nyāyabhūṣaṇa. P. 560.
128. Nyāyabhūṣaṇa. P. 561.
129. Nyāyabhūṣaṇa. P. 561.
130. Nyāyabhūṣaṇa. P. 561.

Chapter - 3

JAINA PHILOSOPHY AS PRESENTED IN VEDĀNTA SYSTEMS

Introduction

In this chapter the *Jaina* Philosophy as presented in the *Vedānta* Philosophy is critically analyzed and examined. At the out set it may be recorded that amongst the theist school of Indian Philosophy, it is the *Vedāntins* who have given due importance and considerable space for the treatment of the basic tenants of *Jaina* philosophy *i.e. Anekāntavāda.* The other tenants of the Jainas, which are also analyzed by Vedāntins, are:

1. The concept of soul.
2. Theory of creation.
3. Concept of God *(Īśvara).*
4. Causes of salvation.

Of the *Vedānta* systems we have taken into consideration five important schools for discussion viz. *Advaita Vedānta, Dvaita, Dvaitādvaita, Viśiṣṭādvaita* and *Śuddhādvaita Vedānta.* The most important ground and arguments that are common to all systems of *Vedānta* criticizing Jaina doctrine of *Anekānta,* is contradiction. All have pointed out absurdity and contradictions in the tenants of the Jainas' arguments, which are primarily similar, though differ in expression. All have presented *Jaina* doctrines with regard to the above concepts in the beginning followed by their argument to refute the *Jaina* tenants are also identical though vary in details. We now present the treatment of Jaina Philosophy by *kāvaitins* following the order.

Jainism As Presented in Advaita Vedānta Philosophy

Adviata vedantins have also presented the Jaina theory of *Anekānta* and finally have criticized it by showing contradiction in it, which we have already recorded.

In *Brahmasūtra Śaṅkarabhāṣya* II.2.33-36, *Śankarācārya* has recorded the *Anekānta* theory and allied problems related to it, on the context of analyzing the nature and type of reality after refuting the position of Buddhist.

Śankarācārya has criticized two basic theories to the *Jainas* namely

(a) the theory of *Anekānta* on which the whole philosophy of *Jainism* stands

(b) the concept and nature of soul of the *Jainas*.

For convenience we can organize our whole discussion into four parts:

(A) *Jainism* as presented by *Śankarācārya*..

(B) The arguments forwarded by *Śankarācārya* against the *Jaina* theory of *Anekānta* and the doctrine of soul.

(C) An analysis of *Śankarācārya's* criticism.

(D) Observations.

Now let us proceed to discuss following the above-mentioned arrangements.

In the presentation of *Jainism* and framing objections against the *Jaina* doctrine, my source have been the *Bhāmti* of *Vācaśpati Mishra* on *Śaṅkarabhāṣya* and *Kalpataru* of *Appaya Dixita* on it, along with the *Śaṅkarabhāṣya* itself.

The whole discussion from the point of view of *Jainism* as recorded by *Śaṅkara* may be reorganized in the following manner.

The *Jaina* postulates seven categories or *Tattvas,* viz. soul *(jīva),* non-soul *(ajīva),* the issuing outward *(āsrava),* restraint *(saṁbara),* destruction *(nirjarā),* bondage *(bandha)* and release *(mokṣa)*. In short these can be divided into two main categories, viz. *Jīva* and *Ajīva.*

सप्तचैषां पदार्थासमता जीवाजीवसंवरनिर्जरबंधमोक्षा नाम, संक्षेपतस्तु द्वावेवपदार्थों जीवाजीवाखौ।[1]

To make this point clear *Bhāmatikāra* stated that there are two constituents, which forms the reality, viz. sentient and non- sentient *i.e. jīva* and *ajīva* respectively. *Kalpatarukāra* has given the description of *jīva* beautifully. The very nature of *the jīva* is going up as like a bird that goes up being freed from the cage; or as the sprout getting up from the seed being socked with the water being dissolved in the mud which was pasted on it and which was kept on the bottom of the water. It means it goes up being freed from the state of bondage in which it was associated for a long time. He says:

ऊर्धगमनं जीवस्य स्वभावः केचितु चिरकालशरीरावस्तितप्रयुक्तबन्ध ामुक्तावूध्वगमनं, यथा पञ्जरमुक्तशूकस्य यथा वा वारिनिर्भिन्नपरिण-तैरण्डबीजस्य यथा वा दृढपङ्कलिप्तजलनिम्ज्जनप्रक्षीणपङ्कलेप शुष्कालम्बुफलस्य, इह त्वनानादिकालप्रवृत्त बन्धविगमात् सततोर्ध्वगमनमिति।[2]

Further, the *Jainas* hold the view that there are five *samakāys* viz. *jīva* (soul), *ajīva* (non-soul), *pudgala* (matter), *dharam* (the medium of motion), *adharma* (the medium of rest) and *ākāsa* (space)[3]. He asserts:

तरोरिमपरं प्रपञ्चमाचक्षते पञ्चास्तिकायाः नाम, जीवास्तिकायो पुद्गलास्तिकायो धर्मसितकायोऽधर्मस्तिकायोआकाशास्तिकायश्चेति।

These issues are further discussed by *Bhāmatikāra* and Parimalalkāra as follows:

Jīvāstikāya is of three kinds viz. bonded soul or mundane soul *(baddha),* liberated soul *(mukta)* and ever liberated soul *(nitya siddha)*[4]. *Pudgalāsthikāya* is of six kinds viz. four *mahābhūtas i.e.* earth, water, fire, air, and immovable substances *(shtāvaras)* and the mobile things *(jaṅgamas)*[5]. *Dharamāsthikaya* is that which is understood from the principle of motion and *adharmāthikāya* is from`the principle of rest. In other words, *dharamāsthikāya* is the principle of motion and *aharmāsthikāya* is the principle of rest[6]. *Akāsāthikāya* is of two types viz. *lokākāśa* and *alokāśa*. *Lokākāśa* is that *ākāsa* which remains inside the two *lokas,* which exist in an ascending order or in other words, *lokākāśa* exists in the space between the two *lokas* and above this is *alokāśa* in which there is no *lokas,* and it is the place of salvation[7].

After this description of reality" *Bhāmatikāra* and *Kalpatarukāra* have given the ethical division of the reality viz. *āśrava, nirjarā, sambara* and *mokṣa.*

According to *Bhāmati āśrava, nirjarā* and *sambara* are in the form of efforts and efforts are of two folds viz. true and false. *Āśrava* is the false effort and *sambara* and *nirjarā* are the true efforts. *Āśrava* pursues the senses to relate or connect with objects. It means the soul gets connected with objects through the senses and is transformed into various knowledge like tactual etc. According to some other *Jaina* philosophers *āśrava* is nothing but the karmic matter only. It is treated as false effort, for, being the ground of the wrong object *i.e.* the other than *mokṣa. Sambara* and *nirjarā* are treated as true effort because it leads to salvation. Thus, *sambara* is that effort which is in the form of self-restraint *(dama)* and mental quietness *(śama)* and it stops or obstructs the out coming flows *of āśrava. Gupti i.e.* control over body, speech and mind and *Samiti i.e.* without giving pain to other creatures and to travel and to eat as per the minimum requirement being observed the sun's movement. *Nirjarā* is the cause of vanquishing of efforts which has been associated with the *kaṣāyas i.e.* the attachment of worldly objects, *kaluṣa i.e.* the sinful acts and *pūṇya i.e.* virtuous acts since the infinite time and also it causes the soul to mount on the hot-rock *(siddhaśilā)*. And ultimately it destroys completely the enjoyment, pain and pleasure, good and evil etc.

आस्त्रवसंवरनिर्जरास्त्रयः पदार्थाः प्रवृत्तलक्षणाः प्रपञ्जन्ते। द्विधा प्रृवृत्ति सम्यग् मिथ्या च। तत्र मिथ्याप्रवृत्तिराास्त्रवः सम्यग्प्रतृत्तिः तु सम्बरनिर्जरौ। आस्त्रवयन्तिपुरूषं विषयेष्वितीन्द्रियप्रवृत्तिरास्त्रवः। इन्द्रियद्वारा है पौरूषं ज्योतिर्विषयान् स्पृषद्रूपादि ज्ञानरूपेण परिणमत इति। अन्ये तु कर्माण्यास्त्रवमाहुः। तानि हि कर्तारमभिव्याप्य स्त्रवन्ति कर्तारमनुगच्छन्ति इति आस्त्रवः। सेयं मिथ्याप्रवृत्तिरनर्थहेतुत्वात्। तत्र शमदमादिरूपा प्रवृत्तिसम्बर। सा ह्यास्त्रवस्त्रोतयों द्वारं संम्बृणोतीति संवर उच्यते कायवाङ्मनोतिग्रहो गुप्तिः। भूमिगतजंतु

हिंसापरिहारायाः प्रहतेमार्गे सम्यगादित्यरश्मिप्रकाशते निरीक्ष्य संचारणं नियताहारनिषेवणमित्यादिकं समितिरिति। निर्जरस्त्वनादिकाल प्रवृत्तकषाय कलुषपुण्यप्रहाणहेतु तप्तशीलारोहणादि। स हि निशेषपुण्यापुण्यं सुखदुखोपभोगेन जरतीति निर्जरः।[8]

Bandha is that which binds soul with the *karmas*. Thus, the bondage is in the form of eight *karmas*. These eight fold *karmas* can be divided into two viz. *ghātikarma* and *aghātikarma*. *Ghātikarma* is of four kinds viz. *jñānavaraṇīya, darśanāvaraṇīya, mohanīya* and *aṅtarīya*. *Aghātikarma* is also of four kinds viz. *vedanīya, nāmaka, gotrika* and *āyuṣka*. *Jñānāvaraṇīya karmas* are in the form of illusion *(viparyaya)* *i.e.* that knowledge which neither causes salvation nor makes known the true nature of object. *Darśānāvaranīya* karma is in the form of that salvation which cannot be obtained through the practice of *Arhatadarśana*. Many *Tirthṅkaras* in *Jaina* philosophy have advised many ways and failing to comprehend the most special path out of these, for salvation is *mohanīya* karma. The person who wants to get salvation in having the knowledge of the obstacles of the salvation is *aṅtarīya* karma[9]. These four *karmas* are called *ghātikarma,* because of these *karmas* the real intention *(sreya)* is destroyed.

घातिकर्म चतुर्विघम् तद्यथा ज्ञानावरणीयं दर्शनावरणीयं मोहनीयमन्तरायमिति। तथा चत्वार्यघातिकर्माणि तद्यथा वेदनीयं नामिकं गोत्रिकमायुष्कम् चेति। तत्र सम्यग्ज्ञानं न मोक्षसाधनम्, न हि ज्ञानाद्वस्तुसिद्धिरतिप्रसंगादिति विपर्ययौ ज्ञानावरणीयं कर्मोच्यते। अहर्त्तदर्शनाभ्यासान्न मोक्ष इति ज्ञानं दर्शनावरणीयं कर्म। बहुषुविप्रतिविद्धाषु तीर्थंकरैरूपदर्शिनेषु विशेषानवधारणं मोहनीयं कर्मा मोक्षमार्गप्रवृतानां तद्विघ्नकरं विज्ञानं अन्तरायं कर्म। तानीमानि श्रेयो हन्तृत्वाद्घाति कर्मोच्यते।[10]

Mokṣa is the up word movement of the soul being detached liberate from the principle of the motion *(dharma)* and the Principe of rest *(adharma)*. But according to some *Jaina* philosopher when soul exists in the highest state only in the stage of bliss of knowledge, which is not covered by any impression *i.e.* the complete destruction of all miseries or sorrows is called liberation.

ऊर्ध्वगमनशील हि जीवो धर्माधर्मस्तिकायेन बद्धस्तद्विमोक्षादूर्ध्वं गच्छेत्येव स मोक्षः इति। विगलित समस्त क्लेशस्याद वासना स्यानावराणज्ञा-नस्यसुखैकतानस्यात्मन उपरिदेशावस्थानं मोक्षः इत्येके।[11]

The prime objection of *Śaṅkara* is against the postulation of *Anekānta* theory, called *syādvāda* which are as follows:

(a) In certain sense it is *(syādasti)*

(b) In certain sense it is not *(syādnāsti)*

(c) In certain sense it is and it is not *(syādasti nāsthi ca)*

(d) In certain sense it inexpressible *(syādavaktavya)*

(e) In certain sense it is and it is inexpressible *(syādasti avyaktavyaśca)*

(f) In certain sense it is not and it is inexpressible *(syādnāsthi avaktavyaśca)*

(g) In certain sense it is, it is not and it is inexpressible *(syādasti nāsti avaktavyaśca)*[12].

The other objections of *Śaṅkara* is about the size of the soul:

Unlike the other systems of Indian philosophy, the *Jainas* postulate that size of the soul is as equal as the size of the body, it occupies and it has infinite parts or limbs and therefore it could expand and contract[13]. The soul has no definite size. Thus, when it animates the body of an infant or youth it has that size, when it occupies the bodies of horses of elephants it gets the respective sizes by successive expansion and dilation like gas, it fully occupies the entire body, which animates for the time being[14]. Though the size of a particular soul changes form depending on the size of its locus still it is eternal. It simply means that the permanence of the final size of the soul is that which it has at the time of release[15].

In this way *Śaṅkara* has presented the *Jaina* position. Before going to see the objections and arguments of *Śaṅkara* against the *Jaina* doctrine, a remark on their presentation or their faithfulness or otherwise is in order. As can be seen, *Śaṅkara, Vācaśpatimishra* and *Appaya Dixit* putting together have presented the *Jaina* doctrines faithfully without any bias. It can even be said in appreciation of their presentation that one can read *Jainism* on the basis of their presentation, which we have shown, by drawing comparison of the *Vedāntins'* presentation with some original texts of *Jainas*.

Let me now record the objection of *Śaṅkara* against the *Jainas*. Following are the prime objections raised by *Śaṅkara:*

Objection: 1.

In one substance it is not possible that contradictory qualities should exist simultaneously *i.e.* the very expression of *'syādasti nāstica'* is contradictory in nature. *Śaṅkara* makes this point clear by giving some example. An object cannot be hot or cold at the same time or light and darkness cannot reside in one place at the same time.

न ह्यकस्मिन् धर्मिणि युगपत्सदसत्वादि विरुद्धधर्मसमावेशः सम्भवति। शीतोष्णवत्।[16]

Objection: 2.

Following the theory of *Anekānta* no judgement can be made for certain and all our assertions would be probable. Thus making room for ambiguity and doubt and if everything is probable, then what about the doctrine of the *Jaina*? Are they probable or definite? If they are not definite, how are the followers going to accept those?

नन्वनेकात्मकं वस्त्विति निर्धारित रूपमेव ज्ञानं शंशयज्ञानवन्नप्रमाणं भवितुमर्हति।[17]

Objection: 3.

The term *'avyaktavya* in the fourth of the seven bhaṅgas is meaningless by its nature. Because if the nature of object is inexpressible, how do the *Jainas* talk about the reality itself?

एवं सति कथं प्रमाणभूत संस्तीर्थकंर प्रमाण प्रमेय प्रमातृ प्रमितिष्वनिर्धारिताषु पदेषु शक्नुयात्।[18]

Objection: 4.

On the nature and size of soul *Śaṅkara* has formulated the following objections:

(a) Since the soul is of limited size and subject to change hence, it could not be eternal and it cannot be omnipresent. To clarify, the bodies of the different classes of creatures are of different sizes. The soul of a man taking the body of an elephant on account of its past deeds will not able to fill up the body of an elephant. Similarly the soul of an elephant will not have sufficient space in the body of an ant or the soul of a child or youth being smaller in size will not be able fill completely the body of a grown up man unless they change their sizes. Thus the soul has to be *'anitya'*.

शरीरपरिमाणतायां च सत्यामकृत्स्नऽसर्वगतः परिच्छिन्न आत्येत्यतो घटादिवत् नित्यत्वात्मनः प्रसज्येत।[19]

(b) To the classification by *Jainas* that the soul is having infinite parts and therefore it could expand or contract, the *advaitins* argued: could these infinite parts be in the same place or not? If they could, then all the parts must be in the same place and could not expand into a big body. Therefore, *Jainas* have no right to assume that a soul has infinite limbs. What is the proof to justify the view that a body of limited size contains an infinite number of particles?

अनन्तावयवो जीवस्तस्य न एवावयवा अल्पेशरीरे संकुच्चेयुर्महति च विकसेयुरिति.......

अपि च शरीरमात्रपरिच्छिन्नाः जीवावयवानामानन्त्यं नोत्प्रक्षितुमपि शक्यम्।[20]

(c) *Jains'* clarification that the soul is really of indefinite size means that whenever the soul enters into a body having bigger size some particles accede to it and some withdraw from it when it enters into a body having smaller size. Therefore by successive expansion and dilation, like the air or the light, it fully occupies the entire body which animates for the time being. To this, *Śaṅkara* would say that even in this case *Jaina* philosophers cannot get over the objection and the soul would be liable to change and consequently would not be eternal. Since the soul is not eternal, there is no question of liberation and rebirth.

पर्यायेणाप्यवयवोपगमापगमाभ्यामेतद्देहपरिमाणत्वं जीवस्याविरोधेन उपपादयितुं शक्यते।[21]

(d) If the limbs of the soul can be increased or decreased depending on the respective locus, then how could it be different in nature from the body. So one of the limbs can only be the soul, how do they determine where do the limbs of the soul come? Where do they take rest etc? They cannot spring from the material elements and re-enter because the soul is eternal.

अवयवोपागमाभ्यां ह्यनिसमापूर्यमाणस्यापक्षीयमाणस्य च जावस्य विक्रियावत्वं तावदपरिहार्यम्।[22]

(e) From their thesis that soul has a definite and eternal size at the state of release it follows that its initial size and its intervening size must be permanent. Therefore, there is no difference between the size of soul in different states or stages. There is no peculiarity or difference according to the *Jainas* between the state of release and the mundane state.

तद्वत् पूर्वयोरप्याद्यमध्यमयोः जीवपरिमाणयोः नित्यत्व प्रसंगः स्यात्। एक शरीर परिमाणतैव स्यान्नोपचितापचितशरीरान्तरप्राप्तिः। अथवा अन्त्यस्यजीवपरिमास्य अवस्थितत्वात् पूर्वयोरप्यवस्थयोरवस्थितिपरिमाण एव जीव स्यात्।[23]

Thus, the soul must be regarded as being always of the same size whether minute or infinite and not of the varying size of the body. Therefore, the Jaina doctrine of the soul and *anekānta* theory is untenable and inadmissible and hence stands refuted.

We have formulated in the foregoing pages the arguments and the objections of *Śaṅkara,* which are basically grounded on two major aspects. One is contradiction, second is absurdity. Let us now see to what extent those arguments stand justified on the light of *anekānta* theory of *Jainas*.

Now the main contention of *Śaṅkara* is contradiction arising from the expression in the third of the alternatives viz. *'syādasti nasti ca'* which is just quoted. To clarify, *Śaṅkara* thinks: if something 'is' *i.e.* exist how it 'is not' *i.e.* non-existence. Thus assertion of the *Jainas* is nothing but absurd leading to contradiction. The *Jainas'* answer to this objection of contradiction is simple which will be clear from the analysis of third assertion itself.

The classification proposed in the *syādvāda* theory is dialectical and not ontological. It simply suggests that the reality can be verbalized in seven different ways viewing it from different angles or different aspects of reality. At one and the same moment all aspects of reality cannot be expressed, for, the reality is so dynamic to be brought under one and encompassed by one.

Individual intention only presents one-sided view of reality, which served a single aspect of reality. Hence, there is no contradiction in the *Jaina* theory of relativity of manifoldness. On the basis of the expression given by the speaker, the listener uses on a particular aspect of reality. When it is said 'the pot is' in the sense of existence, the user wants to emphasize on the *'dravyatva' i.e.* the continual aspects of a pot and when it is said 'the pot is not', he emphasizes on the *paryāya'* aspect of reality. Further, on the basis of spatio-temporal limitation the expressions 'the pot is and 'the pot is' not' are also valid. There is no contradiction, whatsoever can be pointed out in the *Jaina* theory of relativity. In no point of time the *Jainas* say that a reality delimited by the spacio-temporal relation and delimited by one and same aspect *i.e.* 'a thing is' and 'is not' in the third alternative expression, the expression of the reality is delimited by two different entities.

The *Brahmasutra* reads *"naikasminasaṁbhavāt"* to mean it is not possible to predicate positivity and negativity *i.e.* *'astittva'* and *'nāstittva'* to one and the same object due to impossibility and non-applicability. The *Jainas* also favour the same idea that contradictory characteristics cannot be attributed to one and the same reality delimited by the quality of continuation which is one

I aspect of the reality and 'is not' *i.e.* non-existent is qualified by the quality of change which is also the essential aspect of reality. And making a singular assertion of the reality in the form of either 'it is' r it is not' would amount to concealing or suppressing the real nature of reality. Thus, there is no contingency of any kind in the *Jaina* theory or relativity is the conclusion of *Jainas*.

As regards the objection to the fourth alternative viz. *"syādavaktavya"* it may be pointed out that the concept of inexpressibility should be differentiated from *'avyapadesya'* concept as elaborated by *Nyāyasūtrabhāṣya* (1.1.4) or from the *'avaktavya'* of the *Vedāntins* with regard to the nature of *Brahman*. The *Jainas* do not propose that the reality cannot be verbalized. In fact such a view will go against the supposition of the theory of relativity, which is dialectical and verbalizes the experiences of the reality. What the *Jainas* propose in this *'bhaṅgas'* is that the attribution of two or more contradictory properties or aspects in a single expression is not possible. In other words, *'syādavaktavya'* means the inexpressibility of an expression of experience of existence and the non-existence of a reality in a particular place and time delimited by one and the same property. For example, it is not possible to verbalize the cognition of a pot as being present and absent in a particular space and time as delimited either the aspects of continuity or the aspect of change alone. Thus, one cannot have an expression like 'pot exist delimited by this place and that time delimited further by substanceness, (looking from the point of view of *dravyattva* of reality) and the pot does not exist being delimited by the above mentioned delimiters like the same place, the same time and the same properties. This is the meaning of the term *'avaktavya'*. Thus, the objection that nothing can be verbalized or the realities are inexpressible as posed by the *Vedāntins* is misleading and based on the wrong interpretation of the concept *'avaktavya'* which is not intended by the *Jainas*.

As to the objection regarding the size of the soul, the *Jainas* have a practical and empirical approach to it. They feel that it is convenient to assume the size of the soul as limited pervaded by the individual, occupied in a given time. The objection that due to the identical size of the various sizes of soul in various states like the stages of the bondage and the liberation the distinction between bondage and liberation cannot be maintained is not true. The *Jainas* argue that it is not the size that is responsible or in the cause of bondage or liberation but the qualities that soul possesses. When the soul is devoid of *karmas,* it is liberated and when associated with *karmas,* it is bounded. Size has no role to play in this regard.

Further, the objection regarding the soul that it will be transitory or subject to destruction it being of limited size does not sound logical to the *Jaina* logicians. To them eternality or transitoriness or a reality is not dependent on its size but its nature. The *Jainas* are true followers of the rebirth theory. To them the soul is eternal irrespective of its size. It is the presupposition of the *Vedāntins* or the logicians that if some reality is on limited size, it is subject to destruction, which is not acceptable to the *Jainas*. The *Sainas* argued that a thing is eternal judging from the point of view of its continuity and transitoriness from the aspect of its change. For *Jainas 'dhrauvya' i.e.* the continuity and *'vyaya' i.e.* change and *'utpāta' i.e.* emergence are the real nature of each and every reality. When soul takes or fits into different bodies having different sizes like the body of elephant or the body of an ant what happens is that the size and the shape are changed but not the essential nature of the soul. Thus, it is illogical to argue that the soul will be transitory *i.e. unity* if it is accepted to be the size of body it resides.

In conclusion it can be observed that the *Jaina* approach towards the reality is more practical. The *Jainas' 'anekānta'* theory is grounded on the prime supposition that realities are so dynamic and it is very difficult to encompass of its absolute nature in a single judgement. Hence, all the assertions in the form of judgement are partial truth, which reveal a single aspect of reality where the other aspects are suppressed for the present time. *Jainas'* classifications of seven *'bhahgas'* are dialectical and are not to be confused with ontological classifications. The *Jain* concept of *'avaktavya'* should be differentiated from *'avapadesya'* of logicians and *'avaktavya'* concept of *Vedāntins*. The concept of *'nityatva'* is relative as is understood differently by the *Jainas* from the others. The dialectical analysis of relativity is more practical and nearer to reality to reveal the real nature to it.

Dvaitādvaitas' presentation on Jaina Philosophy

Nimbārkācāry is the founder of *Dvaitādvaita* school of Vedānta philosophy. In *Brahma Sūtra Bhāṣya* of *Nimbārkācārya i.e. Veāānta Pārijāta Saurabha* II. 2.33 to 36, *Nimbārkācārya,* the founder of dvaitādvaita school of *Vedānta* has recorded the theory of *Anekānta* and allied problems related to it, on the context of analyzing the nature and type of reality after refuting the Buddhist.

Nimbārkācāya has criticized four basic theories of the *Jainas,* viz.

(i) the theory of *Anekāntavāda* on which the whole philosophy of *Jianism* stands,

(ii) the theory of creation and

(iii) the causes of salvation

(iv) the concept and nature of soul of the *Jainas.*

We can organize the whole discussion in four heads:

(a) Jainism as presented by the *Dvaitādvaita* philosophers

(b) The arguments forwarded by the *Dvaitādvaita* philosophers against the *Jaina* philosophy.

(c) An analysis of their criticism against the *Jaina* philosophy.

(d) Observation.

Let us now proceed to discuss the aforesaid problems following the above-mentioned arrangements.

In the presentation of Jainism and framing the objections against the Jaina doctrine, our source have been the *Vedānta Pārijāta Saurabha,* the *Bhāṣya* of *Nimbārkācārya, Śrinivāsa's Vedānta Kaustubha* and the *Vedānta Kaustubha Prabhā* of *Kesava Kasmira Bhatta.*

The whole discussion from the point of view of Jainism as recorded by the *Dvaitādvaita* philosophers may be reorganized in the following manner.

The *Jaina* philosophers hold that the universe comprises souls *(jīva)* and non-souls *(ajīva),* and is without a lord. They also maintain that atoms are the causes of the world.

ते हि जीवाजीतात्मकं निरीश्वीरं जगदाहूः। परमाणूनाञ्जगत्का-णत्वाञ्चाहूः।

अस्तित्वनास्तित्वादि विरूध्दधर्मव्दयं पदार्थेषु कल्पयन्ति।[24]

They imagine couple of contradictory attributes like existence and non-existence, in all the categories. Thus according to them, there are seven categories, summing up all the scriptural teachings, viz. soul, its stoppage, freedom from decay, bondage and release.

सप्तचैषां निरीश्वरवादीनां पदार्थाः शास्त्रसंग्रहभूताः। जीवाजीवा-श्रवसंवरनिर्जरबन्दमोक्षा इति।[25]

Among these, the souls are sentient, and endowed with the attributes of knowledge, perception, happiness and strength. Thus, knowledge means the apprehension of the real nature of objects through the right discrimination between the soul and the non-soul. Perception means cognizing objects, being free from attachment and detachment. The souls in bondage have worldly happiness, while the freed souls have the happiness, which inheres in them. Likewise strength means proper endurance. The souls are assessed of parts and are the size of the body. Among them, some are souls in bondage some are freed souls, some are ever perfect. The freed souls are omniscient and possessed of unsurpassed happiness.

तत्र जीवाश्चेतनाः ज्ञानदर्शनसुखवीर्यगुणैयुक्ताः। तत्र जीवाजीवविवेकेन पदार्थवगमों ज्ञानम्। रागव्देषशून्यतया पदार्थावलोकनं दर्शनम्। वध्दानां वैषयिकं मुक्तानां स्वात्मभूतं सुखम्। एवं वीर्यञ्च यथायथगूह्यम्। ते च जीवाः सावयवाः देहपरिमाणाः, तत्र केचिद्वध्दात्मनः, केचिन्मुक्तात्मनः, केचिन्नित्यसिध्दाः। ये मुक्तात्मनस्ते सर्वज्ञाः निरतिशयं सुखाश्चासते।[26]

The non-soul is the group of objects to be enjoyed by the souls. It is divided into merit, demerit, matter, time and space. Thus, merit *(dharma)* is special kind of substance, inferable from proper actions. Demerit *(adharma)* is the cause of the existence of the non-freed souls.[27]Matter is a substance possessed of colour, smell, taste and touch. It is of two kinds viz. atoms and their aggregates. The atoms are the causes of the earth and the rest. And they are not of four kinds as hold by the logicians, but identical in nature. The distinctions of the earth and the rest are due to the modifications of these atoms. The four-fold elements beginning with the earth as well as the body, the worlds and so on, are their aggregates.

पृथिव्यादि हेतवः परमाणवस्ते च न तार्किकादीनामिव चतुर्धा, किन्तुएकस्वभावाः।

पृतिव्यादि भेदस्तु परिणामकृतः। पृथिव्यादिचतुष्टयं तनुभूवनादिक्रञ्च तत्संघतः।[28]

Time, on the other hand, is a special kind of substance, which is the cause of the conventional distinctions of long, quick and fast and so on and is atomic in form.[29] Space is the absence of covering. It is of two kinds, viz. worldly space, which is mundane and non-worldly space, which is the abode of freed soul.[30] Influx means the activity of the sense organs, which causes a person to know sense objects. Or else, influx means Karma that compiles to *i.e.* follows after, pervading the agent *i.e.* pertains to him. Stoppage means that which stops, the activities of the sense organs, *i.e.* the stoppage of the sense organs, consisting in a deep meditation.

Freedom from decay means that which destroys the prior accumulated sins *i.e.* austerities known from the teaching of the *arhatas,* consisting in non-bathing, non-speaking, squatting on the things with the lower legs crossed over each other, eating what is spit out from the mouth, mounting on heated stone, plucking out the hairs on the head and so on.

आश्रवयति पुरुषं विशयेष्वितीन्द्रियप्रवृत्तिराश्रवः॥ कर्तारभिव्याप्यास्रवत्यनुगच्छतीत्याश्रवं कर्मेति वा। इन्दियवृत्तीः संवृणोतीति संवरमिन्द्रियनिरोः समाधिरूपः। पूर्वसंचितं कल्मषं निर्जरयतीति निर्जरो नामो। अस्नानमौन वीरासन निष्ठ्यूतभोजन तप्तशीलारोहण केशोपलुञ्चनादिलक्षणमर्हदुपदेशावगतं तपः।[31]

Bondage means *Karma* and is of eight kinds. Among these, there are four destructive *Karmas,* viz. relating to the obscuration of knowledge, relating to the mental blindness of perception, relating to delusion and relating to what hinders, which obstruct the attributes of the souls, viz. knowledge, perception, happiness and strength. And there are four non-destructive *Karmas* viz. relating to the knowable, relating to the name, relating to family descent and relating to life, which are the causes of the body, its sense of igoity, regard and disregard for the happiness and the rest due there to. On the cessation of bondage, there is salvation the manifestation of the natural and real nature of the soul through the grace of the ever-perfect *Arhatas*.

बन्धस्त्वष्टविधः कर्मलक्षणः। तत्र ज्ञानावरणीयं, दर्शनावरिणीयं, मोहनीयमन्तरीयमिति चत्वारि घातिकर्माणि। वेदनीय, नामिकं गौत्रिकमायुष्कमिति चत्वार्यघाति कर्माणि। बन्धनिवृतौ नित्यसिद्धार्हदनुग्रहात् स्वाभाविकात्मरूपाविर्भावो मोक्ष भवतीति।[32]

They have also a set of different categories, consisting of five ontological categories *(astikāyas)* viz. the category of soul, the category of matter, the category of merit, the category of demerit and the category of space. The term ontological category is denotative of conventional objects occupying many places.[33]

To all these, they apply the system of seven parallelisms *i.e. saptabhangī-nayas*.

The aggregate of the seven dialectical formulas is *saptabhangi,* its reasoning *i.e. saptabhangīnaya*. The word 'may' *(syād)* is an indeclinable represented by a verbal ending and should be understood to have the meaning of littleness. Thus, it is to be construed, as it exists partly and does not exist partly and so on. The sense is this, the whole mass of object consisting of substances and modifications are variable. The form of the substance being one, permanent and conceivable as existent, existence, oneness, permanence and the rest are justifiable in reference to it. The modifications are the particular states of the substance having the form of pots, pieces of cloth and the rest and they being many non-permanent and conceivable as non-existent, non-existence, non-permanence and the rest are justifiable in reference to them.

सर्वत्र योजयन्ति-स्यादस्ति, स्यान्नास्तिइमञ्च सप्तभङ्गीनयं सादस्ति स्यान्नास्ति स्यादवक्तव्यः, स्यादस्ति च नास्ति च, सादस्तिचावक्तव्यश्च, स्यान्नास्तिचावक्तव्यश्च, स्यादस्तिच नास्तिचावक्तव्यश्चेति। अस्तित्वादिसप्तभ्ंगानां समाहारः सप्तभ्ंगी तन्नयो युक्तिः। स्यादितितिङ्गी तन्नयो युक्तिः। स्यादितितिङ्गन्तप्रतिरुपकमव्ययम्। किञ्चिदर्थे वर्त्तमानं वाच्यम्। किञ्चिन्नास्तीत्येवं योजनीयम्। अयं भावः। सर्वं वस्तुजातं द्रव्यपर्यायात्मकमनेकान्तिकं द्रव्यरूपस्यचैकत्वात् स्थिरत्वात् सद्बुद्धि वोद्ध्यत्वात्तदात्मना सत्वैकत्वनित्वादुपपद्येत। पर्यायश्च द्रव्यस्यावस्थाविशेषाः। घटत्वपटत्वादिरूपास्तेषां धानेकत्वादिस्तिरत्वादसद्धुवोध्यत्वात्तदात्मना हि असत्वानित्यत्वादिकमुपपद्येतेति।[34]

On this contention of the *Jainas,* the *Dvaitādvaita* philosophers maintain: this is not correct. The sevenfold reasoning, like partly existent, partly non-existent and the rest, is not possible in one object. The simultaneous co-existence of darkness and light is never seen or heard. In the same manner, couples of contradictory attributes like existence and non-existence and so on are indeed impossible in the same place.

अत्र ब्रुमः, नैवं वाच्यम्। एकस्मिन् पदार्थे किञ्चिदस्ति किञ्चिन्नास्ति इत्यादि सप्तभङ्गयुक्तेरसंभवात्। न हि तमप्रकाशयोर्युगपदेकान्तोपलभ्यो दृष्टः श्रुतो वा। एवमेन्नास्तित्वनास्तित्वादिविरुद्धर्मद्वयस्यासम्भव एव।[35]

The *Dvaitādvaita* philosophers forward further argument to support their position: If the *Jainas* say that a thing exists by its own form, *i.e.* a pot exists by its own form but it does not exist in the form of cloth, then no knowledge will be possible. Since, there is no speciality with regard to seven-fold logic in each and every entity. Simply we have to accept that things exist by their own form. If we do not accept it, then no knowledge will arise and you will be always in doubt.[36]

They provide a further argument thus: *Jainas* hold that 'everything exists with regards to *Anekāntavāda'* is a definite knowledge. Now, whether this definite knowledge is definite or probable? If everything is probable, your *mokṣa* will be probable. And if it is not definite, then no one will be persuaded to follow your philosophy, where, nothing is definite, including the sole objective namely, *mokṣa*. In the absense of definite knowlede where will the *pravrtis* come towards it. This will lead to the fact that whatever scriptures are written by your *Tīrthaṅkaras* will be meaningless or nonsensical talk.[37]

Further, he provides a couple of arguments to refute the *jaina's* argument that 'atoms are the causes of the creation[1].

First of all, whether atoms are possessed of part or not? If they were possessed of parts, this would amount to the fault of an infinite regress, and conversely if without parts then it will be impossible for them (atoms) to be the producer of other evolutes. Thus, there is inconsistency in the origin of the binary compounds from the atoms. And there is all the more inconsistency in the origin of ternary compounds from these binary compounds. Like this, everything admitted by the exponents of the atomic view is inconsistent.

सावयवत्वेऽनवस्थाप्रसङ्गान्निरवयवत्वे परिमाणान्तरोत्पादकत्वासम्भ-वात् परमाणुभ्यां द्व्यणुकोत्पत्तेरसामञ्जस्यम् तेभ्यस्त्र्यणुकोत्पत्तेश्च सुतरामसामञ्जस्यम्, तद्धत् परमाणुकारणवाद्यभ्युपगतं सर्वमसामञ्जस भवति।[38]

In addition to it, he further says, because it is impossible for the unseen principle *(adṛṣṭa)* to inhere in the atoms, as well as because it is impossible for it being connected with the soul, to be the instigator of the motion of the atoms. Thus, even in both ways, the first motion of the atoms is not possible. Hence, there will be absence of the creation of the world through the successive order of binary compounds and the rest, due to conjunction, which again is due to the motion of the atoms.

अदृष्टस्य परमाणुवृत्तित्वासमभवादात्मसम्बन्धिानस्तस्य परमाणुगत कर्मप्रेरकत्वासम्भवाचेत्येवमुभयथाप्यद्यं कर्म परमाणुगतं नसम्भवत्यातः कर्मनिबन्धन संयोगपूर्वकद्व्यणुकादिक्रमेण जगदुद्भवस्याभावः।[39]

To complement it further the *dvaitādvaitins* say, on account of the admission of the relation of inherence also, the doctrine of atoms is not possible, since just as a binary compound is connected with its own cause by the relation of inherence, being absolutely different therefrom, so the relation of inherence itself, too, is to be connected with the two related objects, by another relation of inherence, absolute difference from the two related objects, being the same, that too, by another relation and so on, creating an occasion for the fault of an infinite regress.

समवायाभ्युपगमाच्च परमाणुकारणपक्षासम्भवः यथाद्व्यणुकं समवायसम्बन्धेन स्वकारणे समवैत्यत्यन्तभिन्नत्वात् तथा समवायोऽपि समवायिभ्यः समवायसम्बन्धान्तरेण सम्बध्येतात्यन्तभेदसाम्यात् सोऽपि सम्भन्धान्तरेणेत्यनवस्थानात्।[340]

Further, he provides another argument that, if the atoms are admitted to be active by nature, then there being eternal activity alone, there cannot be dissolution. If they are admitted to be inactive by nature, there being eternal inactivity alone, the absence of creation will necessarily result. Thus, the atomic theory is untenable.[41]

Then he gives final argument by asserting that since the effects are possessed of colour etc. the atoms, too, are admitted to be possessed of colour and so on. Thus, the four kinds of atoms are possessed of colour, taste,smell and touch, non-eternity results, as pot and the rest, possessed of colour and so on are found to be non-eternal. If they are not admitted to be possessed of colour and the like, then the fact that the effects are possessed of colour and so on will come to be contradicted and the initial proposition that 'possessed of parts and eternal too will come to be contradicted. For this reason too, there is the absence of creation. The sense is that an unseen object cannot be determined in accordance with what is seen. Hence the cause of the world is to be understood in accordance with scripture.

कार्यस्य रूपादिमत्वात् परमाणवोऽपि रूपादिमन्तोऽभ्युपगम्यन्ते, तथा चतुर्विधानां परमाणुनां रूपादिमत्वात् रूपरसगन्धस्पर्शवत्यान्नित्य-त्वादिविपर्ययोऽनित्वत्वादि प्रसज्येत। रूपादिमतां घटादीनामनित्यन्यादिदर्शनात्। तेषां रूपादिमत्वानङ्गीकारे कार्यस्यरुपादिमत्वं विरुद्धमापद्येत, रुपादिमन्तो नित्याश्चेतिप्रतिज्ञाहानिश्च प्रसज्येत। अतोऽपि तदभाव एवेति चकारार्थः। नहि दृष्टानुसारेणादृष्टार्थो निर्णेतुं शक्यः। अतो यथाश्रुति जगत्कारणं प्रतिपत्तव्यमिति भावः।[42]

To complement it, he says: if the atoms are possessed of more numerous qualities, then the earth, water, fire and air will become similar. If they be possessed of less numerous qualities *i.e.* each are possessed of its peculiar quality then, too, all the different kinds of atoms being connected with one quality each, the earth and the rest too, having qualities corresponding to their causes, must be connected with one quality each.

यद्युपचितगुणाः परमाणवस्तदा पृथिव्यप्तेजोवायूनां तुल्यतापत्तिः। अपचितगुण इत्यत्रापि सर्वेषां परमाणुनां प्रत्येकमेकैकगुणयोगेन पृथिव्यादीनामपिकारणगुणानुगुण्येन प्रत्येकमेकैकगुणयोगः स्यादित्युभयथाऽपि दोषात्तदभाव एव।[43]

In this way they have refuted the views of the *Jaina* philosophers on theory of creation, that the 'atoms are the causes of the creation. In the same manner, they have pointed out further that if the Jainas accept *anekāntavāda,* then their hypothesis of five ontological categories *i.e. paṃcāstikāya* stands invalid, because the number 'five' is not definite. It may be increased or decreased.

The *Jainas* may find the same fault with the *dvaitādvaitins* by pointing out contradictions in their theory. The *Veda* or *Vedānta* itself, too, admits couples of contradictory attributes in one and the same substratum. For example, in the text *'sarvaṃkhalvidaṃ Brahmaṃ i.e.* all this verily is *Brahama* (cha.Upa.3. 14. 1.) unitary is established. While in the texts *pradhāna kṣetrajna patirguṇesah' i.e.* the lord of matter and soul, the controller of the *guṇas* (śve.Upa. 6. 16.), *dvā suvarṇā sayujā śākhāyāḥ* two birds are seated in a golden branch (mun.Upa. 3. 1. 1./sve.Upa. 4. 6.) plurality is established.

The answer of the *dvaitādvaitins* is that those statements are based on scripture; hence, their validity cannot be doubted. Thus, it being impossible for the entire universe, consisting of the sentient I and the non-sentient, to be non-different from Brahman by nature, it is non-different from Him only as having its existence and activity under His control and not by nature as indicated by the phrase *'sarvaṃkhalvidaṃ Brahmaṃ', 'tajjalān'* Cha.Upa. 3. 14. 1.) *i.e.* emanating from him and so on. But there is indeed a difference of nature between the categories viz. the sentient, the non-sentient and Brahman. Because the texts designated duality, too, are no less authoritative, just as leaves, flowers and the rest are different by nature from the tree and are not different from it on account of having no separate existence. And just as in spite of the difference of the sense organs from the vital-breath by nature, their non-difference from it, as being under its control, similar is the case with the statements showing contradictins. In the same manner the difference and non-difference between the universe and Brahman are natural and established in scripture and *smṛti*. There is no contradiction between them. In the very same manner, the complementary passage confirms the relation of difference non-difference between the universe and Brahman. The phrase emanating from Him *(tajjalān)* is denotative of the reason, because it emanated from that supreme cause *(tajjalān,* disappears in Him and breathes *i.e.* acts in Him *(tadena)*. The elision of the parts is in accordance with *Vedic* use.

ननु भवन्मतेपि एकस्मिन्धर्मिणि विरुद्धर्मव्दयाङ्गीकारोऽस्ति, तथा सर्व खल्विदम्ब्रह्मोतयादिषु एकत्वम्प्रतिपाद्यते प्रधान क्षेत्रज्ञपतिर्गुणेश द्वा सुवर्णोतयादावनेकत्वञ्च प्रतिपाद्यत इति चेन्न। अस्यार्थस्य युक्तिमुलत्वाभावत्, श्रुतिभिरेव परस्पराविरोधोन यथार्थ निर्णीतत्वात्। तथा सर्वस्य चिदाचिदात्मकस्य जगतः स्वरूपतो ब्रह्माभिन्नत्वासम्भवात्ततज्जत्वादिना, तदधीनस्थितिप्रवृत्तिमत्तयैव खलु ब्रह्माभिन्नत्वम् स्वरूपतस्तु चिदचित् ब्रह्मपदार्थानां भेद एव, द्वैतश्रुतिप्रामाण्यात्। यथा पत्रपुष्यादीनां स्वरुपतो भिन्नानां पृथक् प्रवृत्याद्यभावात् वृक्षाभिन्नत्वम् यथा चेन्द्रियाणां स्वरूपतः प्रणभिन्नानामपि प्राणयत्ततया प्राणाभिन्नत्वमविरुद्धम्। इत्थं जगत्ब्रह्मणोर्भेदाभेदौ स्वाभाविकौ श्रुतिस्मृतिसूत्रसाधितौ भवतः, कोऽत्रविरोधः। एवमेव भिन्नाभिन्नलक्षणं जगद्ब्रह्मसम्बन्धं वाक्यशेषो द्रढयति। तज्जलानितीति इति शब्दो हेतुवचनः, यतस्तस्मात् परमकारणाज्जायत इति तज्जम्, तस्मिंल्लीयत इति तल्लं तस्मिन्ननिति चेष्टत इति तदनं, तज्जञ्च तल्लञ्च तदनञ्च तज्जलान्। अवयवलोप श्छान्दसः।[44]

Thus, a single cause of the world being established by correct evidence, the causality of a plurality of atoms doesn't stand to reason, because that would involve unnecessary combrousness and also because causality is impossible on their parts, adding to their non-sentience.[45] Further they criticized the *Jainas'* argument namely that one can attain salvation by the grace of the perfect souls (*i.e. Siddhas)*. They say: How, the one reality, known from the *Veda,* being the giver of salvation to result from the grace of the perfect souls, that being impossible. Does the grace of the perfect souls depend on meditation or not? It the first then, salvation cannot arise through the meditation on one perfect soul among many perfect souls of the same nature, for there will be the fault of disregarding many other equally perfect souls. It there is Citation on all that would involve unnecessary complication. If it is argued that there is one great soul higher than the others, then you fall in with a theistic view. On the second alternative, the consequence would be a universal release. Moreover, there being no evidence of direct perception and the rest for the existence of perfects, it is impossible that salvation can result from their grace.[46] Further, *dvaitādvaita* philosophers criticize the Jaina view regarding the soul that the size of the soul is equal to the size of the body. They say that as their *(Jainas')* view is open to the objection that contradictory attributes are impossible on the part of one and the same substratum, similarly, their view that the soul is of the size of body, too, is open to serious objections. When the soul, which is of the size of the body of an ant, attains the body of an elephant through the influence of its *karmas,* then there must be 'non-entirity' on its part *i.e.* it would not be able to fill up the whole of the elephant's body. And when the soul comes out of the body of the elephant and enters into a small body, it would fail to be small like it.

तन्मते यथैकस्मिन्धर्मिणि विरुद्धर्मासंभवरूपो दोषः, एवं तदभिमते देहपरिमाणे जीवेपि दोषास्ति। देहपरिमाण आत्मा कर्मवशात्पिपीलिकाशरीरं विहाय गजशरीरं यदाप्नेति तदा तस्याकास्यान्त्यं स्यात्। गजाकारदेहाद्देहनिर्गतस्य चात्मनः सूक्ष्मशीरी प्रविषटस्य तदनुरूपं सूक्षमत्वञ्च न स्यादित्यर्थः।[47]

They provide a further argument against the *Jainas'* view on the same context, that 'the soul is possessed of parts'. There is an increment of its parts in the body of an elephant and decrement in a small body. Thus, on account of modification there is no contradiction. They say that 'this cannot be maintained'. Because, on account of change and the rest *i.e.* because it will then result in faults like change and the rest. If the body were possessed of parts, on your view, then it must be mutable like the body and the rest and also non-eternal. Such other faults also would arise.

न च वाच्यं सावयवो हि खल्वस्माकमात्मा, तस्यावयवानं गजशरीरे उपचयः सूक्ष्मशरीरे उपचयश्चेत्येव पर्यायादविरोध इति। विकारादिभ्यः। विकारादिदोषप्रसंगात्। यदि भवन्मते आत्मा सावयवस्तर्हि देहादिवच्छिका-रीस्यादनित्यश्च स्यात्। एवमादयो दोषाः स्यूः।[48]

Again they criticize the argument of the *Jaina* philosophers on the same issue that 'the size as well as the real nature which the soul attains during its state of salvation, after the destruction of the final body, are eternal. At that time there is no assumption of a subtle or gross body by the soul. So there is no contraction or expansion of its. Thus, on account of permanence of the final size as well as of the real nature of the soul, the permanence of both the initial and intervening size, too, must be so. Then, there must be non-distinction everywhere. In short, the soul must have a permanent and constant size in a gross body as well as in a subtle body, in its bondage as well as in its state of release. And the doctrine that, it is of size of body must be but a childish prattle. Thus, this notion of the soul cannot be accepted.

चरमदेहविनाशानान्तरं यन्मोक्षदशायां परिमाणं स्वरूपञ्च तद्धि नित्यम्भवति। तदा सूक्ष्मस्थूलशरीरपरिग्रहाभावात्तस्य संकोचविकाशाभावो भवति। एवम्भूतस्यान्त्यस्य परिमाणस्य स्वरूपस्य चावस्तितेरुभ-योराद्यमध्ययोरवस्थयोरपि नित्यत्वमिष्यते आर्हतैस्तस्माश्च सर्वत्राविशेषः स्यादित्यर्थः। स्थूलशरीरे सूक्ष्मशरीरे बद्धावस्थायां मोक्षवस्थायाञ्च नित्यनियतपरिमाण आत्मा स्यात्। शरीरपरिमाणप्रतिज्ञा बालभाषिता स्यादिति संक्षेपः। अतो भ्रान्तिमूलेन दिगम्बरपक्षेणमपि नस्मत्सिद्धान्तस्य विरोध इति सिद्धम।[49]

In this way the *dvaitādvaita* philosophers have presented the *Jaina* position. Before going to see the objections and arguments of *dvaitādvaita* philosophers against the *Jaina* doctrine, a remark on their presentation or their faithfulness or otherwise is in order. As can be seen, *Nimbārkācārya, Śrinivāsācārya* and *Keśavakāsmirabhaṭṭa* putting together have presented the *Jaina* doctrines faithfully without any bias. It can even be said in appreciation of their presentation that one can read Jainism on the basis of their presentation, which we have shown by drawing comparison to the *Vedāntins'* presentation with some original texts of the *Jainas* by putting them side by side in the foot notes.

Let me now summarize again the objections of the *dvaitādvaita* philosophers against the *Jainas*. Their arguments are mainly concerned with four major issues viz. on the reality *i.e.* regarding *Anekāntavāda,* on the creation *i.e.* the causes of the creation, on the soul *i.e.* its nature and size, and finally on salvation *i.e.* cause of the salvation. Following are the prime objections raised by the *dvaitādvaita Vedāntins* against the *Jaina* philosophy:

Objection on the reality and Anekāntavāda:

Objection 1:

In one substratum it is not possible that contradictory qualities should exist simultaneously, *i.e.* the very expression of *'syādasti nāsti ca'* in the third alternative of the sevenfold logic is contradictory in nature. They make this point clear by giving an example that light and darkness cannot reside in one place at the same time.

Objection 1. ii.

Following the theory of *anekānta,* no judgement can be made for certain and all our assertions would be probable, thus, making room for ambiguity and doubt. If everything is probable, then what about the doctrine of the *Jainas?* Are they probable or definite? They cannot be definite, if they are probable, then the scriptures written by the *Tirthaṇkaras* will be meaningless talk *(unmāda pralāpa)* and no one will go to attain the salvation.

Objections regarding the creation

Objection 2

Atoms are not the causes of the creation because, if you accept it, then the problem will arise whether atoms are possessed of part or not? If they are possessed of parts, then there will result an infinite regress and if without parts, then it will be impossible for them to be the producer of other evolutes. Thus, there is inconsistency in the origin of the binary compounds from the atoms. And there is all the more inconsistency in the origin of ternary compounds from these binary compounds. Like this the atomic view is inconsistency.

Objection 2. ii.:

It is impossible for the unseen principle (adṛṣṭa) to inhere in the atoms, so also it is impossible for it, connected with the soul, to be the instigator of the motion of the atoms. Thus, resorting to either of the alterrnatives the first motion of the atoms is not possible. Hence, there will be absence of the creation of the world through the successive order of binary compound and the rest.

Objection 2. iii.

On account of the admission of the relation of inherence *(samavāya)* the doctrine of atoms is not possible. Since, just as the relation of inherence connects a binary compound with its own cause, being absolutely different therefrom, so the relation of inherence itself, too, is to be connected with the two related objects by another relation of inherence. Its absolute difference from the two related objects, being the same that, too, by another relation and so on. Thus, there will be an infinite regress.

Objection 2. iv.

If the atoms are admitted to be active by nature, then there being eternal activity alone, there cannot be dissolution. If they are admitted to be inactive by nature, there being eternal inactive alone, the absence of creation will necessarily result. Thus, the atomic theory is untenable.

Objection 2. v.

Since the effects are possessed of colour etc. the atoms, too, are admitted to be possessed of colour and so on. Thus, the four kinds of atoms are possessed of colour and so on *i.e.* possessed of colour, taste, smell, and touch, non-eternity results, as pot and the rest, possessed of colour and so on are found to be non-eternal. If they are not admitted to be possessed of colour and the like, then the fact that the effects are possessed of colour and so on will come to be contradicted and the initial proposition *i.e.* 'though the atoms are possessed of parts still eternal' will come to be contradicted. For this reason, there is the absence of creation. This means an unseen object cannot be determined in accordance with what is seen. Hence, the cause of the world is to be understood in accordance with scripture.

Objection 2. vi.

If the atoms are possessed of more numerous qualities, then the earth, water, fire, and air will become similar. If they are possessed of less numerous qualities *i.e.* each are possessed of its peculiar quality then, too, all the different kinds of atoms being connected with one quality each, the earth and the rest, too, having qualities corresponding to their causes, must be connected with one quality each.

Objection regarding the Salvation

Objection 3

Grace of the perfect souls (*i.e. siddhas*) results the salvation is not possible. Because, does the grace of the perfect souls depend on meditation or not? If yes, then salvation cannot arise through the meditation on one perfect soul among many perfect souls of the same nature. For there will be fault of disregarding many other equally perfect souls. If it is said that there is one great soul higher than the other, then you fall in with a theist view. If no, the consequence would be a universal release. Moreover, there being no evidence of direct perception and the rest for the existence of perfect souls, it is impossible that salvation can result from their grace.

Objection regarding the soul

Objection 4

If the size of the soul is equal to the size of the body, then it leads us to a contingency namely 'non-entirety'. If the body of an ant attains the body of an elephant through the influence of its *karmas,* then there must be 'non-entirety' on its part *i.e.* it would not be able to fill up the whole of the elephant's body. And when the soul comes out of the body of the elephant and enters into a small body, it would fail to be small like it.

Objection 4. ii.

'Soul is possessed of parts and it takes some modification when it goes from one body to another cannot be possible. Because if the soul is possessed of parts and it takes some modification, then it must be mutable like the body and the rest and also non-eternal and other such faults would arise.

Objection 4. iii.

The size of the soul and its real nature which the soul attains during the state of salvation, after the destruction of the final body are eternal. At that time there is no assumption of a subtle or gross body by the soul, is not possible. Because, if it is so, then you cannot distinct or discriminate between the soul of bondage state and the soul of released state. In short, the soul must have a permanent and constant size in a gross body as well as in a subtle body in its bondage as wall as in its state of release. And the doctrine that it is of the size of body must be a childish prattle.

We have formulated in the foregoing pages the arguments and objections of the *dvaitādvaita* philosophers against the *Jaina* philosophy. Let us now see to what extent those arguments stand justified on the light of *Jainas'* theory and doctrine.

The answer to most of the objections recorded here can be found in our discussion/presentation of the Jaina Philosophy in the Advaita Vedānta, where we have tried to answer their objection of the Jaina point of view.

As to the objection "grace of the perfect souls *(i.e. siddhas)* results the salvation is not possible", our answer is that this is not the exact position of the *Jainas,* as quoted by the *dvaitādvaita* philosophers. Though the Jaina philosophers hold that the grace of the perfect souls may helpful to attain salvation, but it is not the sole cause to get it. On the contrary, for salvation the *Jaina* philosophers have prescribed fifteen *guṇastānas* along with severe penance, in mind, body and action. Through these *guṇastānas* one can destroy the *bandhahetus i.e.* the causes of the bondage and the *nirgarās.* Thus after complete destruction of the *jnānāvaranlya karma, darśanāvaraṇīya karma, antarāya* and *mohanīya karmas,* a soul can be in his real state what is called salvation in Jainism. Thus, the argument of the *dvaitādvaita* philosophers on the grace of the perfect souls is the cause in attaining salvation is not sound.

To the objection that atoms are the causes of the creation is not tenable, because it creates a contingency called infinite regress and so on also is baseless. As we have quoted, just before, the arguments of the *dvaitādvaita* philosophers against the *Jaina* philosophers on atoms are the causes of the creation and the allied arguments related to it, it is not the exact proposition of the *Jainas*. Though the *Jaina* philosophers maintain that atoms are the cause of the creation, yet they do not persuade any unseen principle *(adṛṣṭa)* to create the first motion in the atoms as pointed out by the *dvaitādvaita* philosophers. According to Jainism, it's the very nature of the atoms *i.e.* 'the nature of conjunction' and 'the nature of subtraction', which creates the first motion in it. Then they combine with each other to create *skandhas*. In this way the whole creation is created. Not only this, they say that these atoms are having twenty attributes in it and they are eternal. But as the *dvaitādvaita* philosophers have pointed out that they accept that atoms are the causes of the creation then they have to accept that atoms are also having form *(rūpa)*, taste *(rasa)*, smell *(gandha)* and touch *(sparśa)*, which amounts to say that they (atoms) are non-eternal. Because it is not true, it is the presupposition of the *Vedāntins* or the *Nyāya* philosophers that if something is having forms and touches etc. are subject to non-eternality. For the *Jaina* philosophy it makes no problem. Thus, the arguments of the dvaitādvaita philosophers against the Jaina philosophy are not justified in the philosophical framework of Jainism.

In addition to our observation made earlier regarding the Jaina theory the following may be added from the point of view of the *Dvaitādvaita Vedānta* Philosophy.

(a) *Jainas'* approach on salvation is very much practical and it depends on the practice of severe penance and good activities of the Jīvas, it does not depend only on the grace of the god or the perfect souls *(siddhas)* as held by many systems.

(b) The arguments of the *Jainas* on atoms as the causes of the creation look more scientific than others.

Jainism as presented in Dvaita Vedānta system of Indian philosophy

Madhvācārya (1228 AD.), the founder of *dvaita vedānta* system of philosophy, recorded the *Jaina* view regarding the reality and the soul. While commenting upon the *Brahmasutra* II.2.33-36, he has recorded various arguments of the *Jainas,* particularly the arguments of non-absolutism *(anekāntavāda)* and the soul, its size and nature etc.

Here, we have taken into consideration the whole system of dvaita *vedānta* philosophy starting from Madvācārya's *Pūrṇaprajṃā bhāṣya* along with Padmanābhatīrtha's *Sattarakadīpāvali, Tattvaprakāśikā* of Jayatīrtha, *Tattvapradīpikā* of *Trivikrama, Gurvarthadīpikā* of *Vādirājatīrtha,* Raghuttom- atīrtha's *Bhāvabodha, Rāghavendratīrtha's Bhāvaālpa, Vākyārthamuktāvali* of Tāmrapāṇi Śrinivāsa, pāṇdurangi Śrinivāsa's *Tattvabodhini,* Śrinivāsatīrtha's *Vākyārthavivaraṇaṁ* and *Vākyārthamaṃjarī* of *Śrisarkarā Śrinivāsa.*

For convenience, we organized the whole discussion of the *Dvaita* philosophers into four parts.

(a) Jainism as presented in the *Dvaita* system of philosophy.
(b) The arguments forwarded by the *Dvaita* philosophers against the *Jaina's* view.
(c) An analysis of their arguments or Criticism.
(d) Observation.

The *dvaita* Philosophers, firstly, have presented the *Jainas'* view followed by its criticism and refutation by showing some defects in it, in the context of creation *(sṛṣtitattva)* of this world.

According to the *Jaina* Philosophy, there is no need to accept *Īśvara* (*i.e. viṣṇu)* as a creator of the universe. The universe *(Jagat),* is in the form of *'sat'* and *'asat'* etc. Seven fold is created due to the *adṛṣṭa* of the *Jīva* (soul) and some other visible instruments, but not due to *Īśvara*. And size or dimension of the *Jīva* (soul) is equal to the body *(śarira-parimāṇa).* Thus, there is no need of accepting *Īśvara* as a creator. Jayatīrthācārya says.

सदसदुभयमुभयविलक्षणं नैतत्सर्वचेति सप्तभंगि जगंदात्मादृष्टात्परिदृष्ट-साधनैश्च भविष्यति। स च कायपरिमाणः। अतः किमीश्वरेणेति।[50]

Thus, *dvaita* Philosophers have recorded the view of the *Jainas*. Before presenting the criticism on the *Jaina* view, let us have a very short discussion about he *dvaita* position regarding the creation of the universe. *Dvaita* Philosophers hold that the universe is created attribute-less by the Supreme *Brahman i.e. Viṣṇu,* which is not *nirguṇa* as *Śaṅkara* says. He is *ananta-guṇa-paripūrṇa i.e.* filled with countless attributes. It is stated in the Brahma Sūtra I.I.2. *(Janmādyasya yataḥ)* Thus the view of the *Jainas* is opposed to this idea of the *Vedāntins*. Not only this, but it is also opposed to the Veda[51]. Thus the cause of those things stand to criticize the *Jaina's* view.

They have presented the *Jaina* position in the following manner. *Jaina* Philosophy have accepted a theory called *saptabhangīnaya* related to the reality. They are as follows:

तत्र सदित्येकः प्रकारः असदिति द्वितीयः उभयं सदसदात्मकमिति तृतीयः उभयविलक्षणं सदसद्धिलक्षणमिति चतुर्थः एतावतः सत्स्यादि भाष्यं यथाश्रुति व्याख्यातं भवति। सदसदुभयविलक्षणमिति पञ्चमषष्टौ। तत्र सत्वे सति सद्विलक्षणमिति पञ्चमः। असत्वे सत्यसद्विलक्षणामिति षष्ठः। सर्वं सदसदात्मकं नैतत्सर्व सदसत्वे सति सदसद्विलक्षणमिति सप्तम उक्तमिति दृष्टव्यम् ।[52]

We can re-arrange it in the following manner:

1. *syādasti i.e.* in certain sense it is
2. *syādnāsti i.e.* in certain sense it is not,
3. *syādasthināsti ca i.e.* in certain sense it is and it is not,
4. *syādavaktavya i.e.* in certain sense it is not expressible,
5. *syādasti avaktavya sea i.e.* in certain sense it is and it is not expressible,
6. *syādnāsti avaktaya sea i.e.* in certain sense it is not and it is not expressible
7. *syādasti nāsti avaktavya śca i.e.* in certain sense it is it is not and it is not expressible.

It means, according Jainism, the reality is in the form of these seven-fold or in other words the reality can be expressed or known by these seven ways. And this reality is produced from the *adṛsta* of the soul or some visible causes, but not by the *Iśvara,* and the size of the soul is *kāyaparimāṇa,* equal to the body.

From their presentation of Jainism it is clear that they have presented the *Jaina* view very precisely. Their whole argument can be formulated under two heads. Viz. (1) argument regarding the reality, *i.e.* the arguments against the *anekānta* they (2) Argument regarding the soul and its dimension or size etc.

About the first argument *Madhvācārya* has rejected it by pointing out that one and the same object cannot have such contradictory attributes. He says:

सत्स्यादसस्यात्सदसत्स्यात्ततोऽन्यच्च स्यादित्येतन्नैकस्मिन्युज्यते अदृष्टत्वेन असम्भवात्।[53]

Jayatīrtha records that according to Jainism, the whole universe can be expressed through seven *bhaṅgas i.e.* called *Syādvāda,* which is not correct. Because, these two viz. *sat* 'to be' or 'to exist' and *asat* 'to be not' are sufficient to explain and there is no proof in establishing any further varieties. The Jainas may argue that resorting to any particular type of the above mentioned two *bhaṅgas* there will be contingency. Hence, all the seven bhaṅgas are to be accepted. To this, *Jayatīrtha* argues: if due to the fear of *'dosa' i.e.* contingency the two fold theory of *'sat'* and *'asat'* are to be discarded, then the Jainas have to give up the whole theory of *Syādvāda,* because many a contingency can be pointed out in the seven theory of *Jainas*. Thus, there is no fault in the two-fold classification of universe in terms of *'sat'* and *'asat.' Jayatīrtha* concludes

जैनैर्जगत्सप्तभंगीति न तद्युक्तम्। व्यवस्थितसदसत्प्रकार द्वयातिरिक्त प्रकारस्याप्रमाणिकत्वेनासंभवात्। एकैकप्रकाराभयुपगमे दोषदर्शनादेतदुपेयत इति न वाच्यम्। तथा सति दोषभीरुणा सर्वमपि परित्याज्यं स्यात्। सदसत्प्रकारद्वये च न कोऽपि दोष इति भाव:।[54]

On the argument that the dimension or size of the soul is equal to the body, *Jayatīrtha* asks: why do you accept so.

यदपि जीवस्य शरीरपरिमितत्वमभयुपेयते तत्प्रष्टव्यम्। किं तत्सर्वशरीरगतचेष्टोपपत्त्यर्थमभ्युपेयत शरीरावच्छेदमन्तरेणात्मनः परिमाण-भावप्रसंगभयाद्वा।[55]

There are main two arguments of the *Jainas* as presented by Jayatīrtha regarding the dimension or size of the soul.

(1) The size of the soul is equal to the body size because the bodily activities are taking place all over the body.

(2) The size of the soul is equal to the body size because without accepting it contingency may arise that 'soul has no size', which is not admissible.

It means that if we do not accept soul as equal to the body, then we have to accept soul as size less. To avoid this inadmissible contingency we accept it.

To the first argument, Madhvācārya says that the *Jainas'* theory that the dimension of the soul is equal to the body does not work. If such a position is accepted, then a *Jīva* that was not an ant in one birth if born as an elephant in the next birth due to the good karmas, will not be able to occupy the whole body. He says:

जीवस्य शरीरपरमितऽण्वाङ्गीकारेत्वादिशरीरस्थस्य हस्त्यादिशरीरेऽकात्स्न्यं स्यात्।[56]

Jayatīrtha also thinks in that direction and makes this point by stating that the soul of an ant can not occupy the whole body of an elephant or a donkey if due to the good *karma* he gets the birth of an elephant or a donkey etc. in the next birth and vice-versa also. Thus, the theory that the soul is equal to the body size will not stand to logic. He says:

यद्यात्मा सर्वशरीरचेष्टोपपत्त्यर्थं शरीरपरिमाणोङ्गीऽक्रियते वं तर्हि पिपीलिकादिशरीरस्थत्परिरस्थस्तत्परिमाण एव स्यात् तथा च तस्यैव कर्मवशाद्गजगर्दभादिशरीरप्राप्तौ तत्रापूर्णता स्यात्। ततश्च न सर्वशरीरचेष्टेति

भावः। गाजदिशरीरस्थस्याणुशरीरप्राप्तावतिरेकः स्यात् तथा च शरीरपरिमाणत्वभगं इत्यपि द्रष्टव्यम्।[57]

To this argument Jaina logicians may think that the size of the body is equal to the respective body in which it enters in each birth. To this argument of the *Jainas' Madhvācārya* says, in this case also it will have to undergo modification and consequently it will not be eternal. He says :

नत्तच्छशीरस्थस्य तत्तत्परिमाणत्वमिति न मन्तव्यम्। विकारित्वादनित्यत्व प्रसक्तेः।[58]

Jayatīrtha also thinks in the same line as Madhvācārya thinks. In addition to it he says : if the soul undergoes modification, then it will be subject to decay and hence will be called non-eternal (*anitya*). And if it is *anitya,* then it cannot be emancipated. This will go against the whole scripture, which is not proper. Thus, the theory that "soul is equal to respective body in which it enters in each birth" will not be acceptable to us. He says :

न चात्मनस्तत्तच्छरीरस्थस्य तत्तत्परिमाणत्वमिति युक्तम्। तथा सति विकारित्वापत्तेः। ततश्चनित्यत्वप्रसक्तेस्तेन चानिर्मोक्षप्रसंगात्तथा च शास्त्रव्यैर्थ्यापातादिति भावः।[59]

Further, he shows the defect on the second reason provided by the *Jaina* logician for accepting the size of the soul as equal to the size of the body that "without body the soul has no dimension" (*i.e.* Śarīrāvacchedamantareṇātma-naḥ svataḥ parimāṇābhāvāt). On this argument of the Jainas, a question is raised : whether in the liberated state the soul has the dimension or not ? It cannot be stated that it has no dimension, because no entity can exist without dimension. Therefore, the dimension of the soul has to be accepted even in the liberated state. And since the size of the soul depends upon the size of the body, and then a body also has to be accepted in the liberated state.

To this, another question may be asked, whether this body is eternal or perishable? It cannot be perishable. In that case there will not be any difference between the liberated state and the *Saṁsāra* state. And if the body is also accepted as eternal in the liberated state, then further question may be asked why not accept the body as eternal even during the *saṁsāra* state because there is no difference between these two bodies. If you accept it, then you have to accept both soul and the body are eternal, which is not admissible. Thus, your theory that 'without body the soul has no size or dimension' is not proper. He says:

शरीरावच्छेदमन्तेरणात्मनः स्वतः परिमाणाभावात् शरीरपरिमाणत्वं वदन् प्रष्टव्यः। किं मोक्षे जीवस्य परिमाणमस्ति न वेति। न तावद् द्वितीयः। परिमाणभावे स्वरूपाभावप्राप्तेः। न हि परिमाणशून्यं द्रव्यमस्ति। अतो मोक्षे परिमाणभभ्युपगन्तव्यमेव। किं चातः। तथा सति तस्य शरीरमन्तरेणानुपपत्तेः। मोक्षेऽपि शरीरमुरीकरणीयं प्रसज्येत। अंगीक्रियत एवातो नानिष्टमिति चेत्तहींदं भवान्पृष्टो व्याचष्टाम्। तच्छरीरमनित्यं नित्यं वा। नाद्यः। संसारसमानधर्मतापातात्। न द्वितीयः यद्यात्मा देहश्चेत्युभयं नित्यं तर्हीदानीतनसर्वशरीरैः किमपराद्धम्। तेषामपि नित्यत्वं स्यात्। शरीरत्वाविशेषदिति भावः। तस्माज्जैनमतस्यानुपपन्नत्वेनाविरोधकत्वाद्युक्तं जगत्कारणत्वलक्षणं विष्णोरिति सिद्धम्।[60]

In this way the *Dvaita* philosophers have rejected the view of *Jaina* philosophers that 'one and the same object cannot have contradictory attributes' and ' the dimension of the soul is equal to the body'. And hence, this creation is not created by some visible *i.e.* external causes that are in the form of *kāla* (time), *ākāśa* (space) and *pudgala* (atoms) of the soul, but it is created by the *Viṣṇu*.

In this way the *dvaita* philosophers have presented the *Jaina* position. Before going to see the arguments of the *dvaita* philosophers against the *Jaina* doctrine and analyzing it, a remark on their presentation or their faithfulness may be made. As can be seen that starting from *Madhvācārya* to *Jayatlrth* and *Śri Śarkarā Śrinivāsa* etc. putting together have presented the *Jaina* doctrine faithfully without any bias. But one thing is that in their presentation of *syādvāda* or *saptabhahgīnaya* they have not presented it in the same wording as *Jainas* have done, but with some other words, for instance, for *'avyaktavya'* they have used *'vilakṣaṇa'*in the same sense.

From the foregoing presentation following are the prime objections of the *dvaita* philosophers against the *Jaina* doctrine:

Objection 1

In one substance it is not possible that contradictory qualities should exist simultaneously *i.e.* the very expression *sadasadca"* is contradictory in nature.

Objection 2

Since the size of the soul is equal to the size of the body and subject to change hence, it could not be eternal and it cannot be omniscient. To clarify, the bodies of the different classes of creatures are of different sizes. The soul of an ant taking the body of an elephant on account of its past deeds will not able to fill up the body of an elephant. Similarly the soul of an elephant will not have sufficient space in the body of an ant. Thus, the soul has to be *anitya*.

Objection 3

If the size of the soul is equal to the respective body into which it enters in each birth, then in this case also it will have to undergo modification and consequently it will be subject to destruction. Thus, it has to be *anitya*.

Objection 4

Against the *Jainas'* argument that "without body the soul has no dimension or size", they argue: whether in the liberated state the soul has body or not? as no entity can exist without body or form. Therefore, they have to accept the dimension of the soul even in the liberated state. And since the size of the soul is dependent upon the size of the body, then they have to accept a body of the soul in the liberated state.

In addition to it, they further argue that whether that body is perishable or eternal. If it is perishable, then what is the difference between liberated state and an ordinary state? If it is eternal, then why do they say so, as both the body at the ordinary state and the liberated state are same? Thus, they have to accept the body as eternal like soul. Therefore, the theory of *anekānta* and the doctrine of soul of the *Jaina* philosophers is untenable and inadmissible and hence, stands refuted.

The whole argument of the *dvaita* philosophers start with the problem that the *Jagat i.e.* universe is created by omnipotent *Viṣṇu,* which is objected by the *Jaina* philosophy, as they have accepted some eternal causes like 'dharma' and *'adharma'* and some external causes like *kāla, ākāśa* and *pudgala* as the causes for the creation of the universe. In this context they have rejected the nature of the universe as postulated by *Jaina* philosophers and the concept of the cause *i.e.* soul holds by the *Jiana* philosophers.

Jainism As presented in Viśiṣṭādvaita Vedānta system of Indian philosophy:

Like the other schools of *Vedānta, Viśiṣṭādvaita* philosophers have also recorded the *Jaina* view when they commented upon the *Brahamasūtra* II. 2. 31-34, after refuting the view of the Buddhist philosophers. The present discussin is based on the *Śribhāṣya* of *Rāmānujācārya, Śribhāṣyavṛtti* of *Vāsudevashatri* and *Śribhāṣyaprakāsikā* of *Śrinivāsa dash.* While commenting upon the above-mentioned aphorism, *Viśiṣ ṭādvaita* philosophers have recorded some arguments of the *Jainas* regarding the *Anekāntavāda* and the nature of reality, arguments on creation and arguments on the soul.

The presentation is organized under four heads: viz.

(a) their presentation of the *Jaina* doctrine in their respective texts,

(b) the arguments forwarded by the Viśiṣṭādvaita philosophers against the *Jaina* philosophy,

(c) an analysis of their arguments or criticism and

(d) observation.

The whole discussion from the point of view of Jainism as recorded by the *Viśiṣṭāāvdita* philosophers may be reorganized in the following manner

According to the *Jaina* philosophy, the world consists of selves and non-selves and is without a lord. And it is made up of six substances viz. *Jīvas* (selves), *ajīvas* (non-selves), dharma (the cause of motion), *adharma* (the cause of rest), *pudgala* (matter), *kāla* (time) and *ākāśa* (space)[61]. Of these, the *Jīvas* are of three kinds viz. the bound *(vaddha),* those who have obtained perfection through yoga *(yogasiddha)* and those who have obtained final release *(mukta)*[62].

जीवाजीवात्मकं जगदेतत्, निरीश्वरम्। तच्च षड्द्रव्यात्मकम्। तानि च द्रव्याणिजीव धर्माधर्मपुदगलकालाकाशख्यानि। तत्र जीवाः बद्धाः मुक्तश्चेतित्रिविधाः।

Dharma (the cause of motion) is known to be that particular substance which in regard to things possessing motion forms the cause of motion and which pervades the whole world. And *adharma* forms the cause of inertia and is all-pervasive[63].

धर्मो नाम गतिमतां गतिहेतुभूतः द्रव्यविशेषो जगद्व्यापी, अधर्मश्च स्थितिहेतुभूतः व्यापी।

The matter *(pudgala)* is that substance which possesses colour, smell, taste and touch. And it is also of two kinds viz. that which consists of atoms and that which has the nature of their aggregates. And it consists of air, fire, water, earth, the body, the world etc. *Kāla* (time) is a particular atomic substance, which forms the cause of the practical realization of the present, the past and the future. The *ākāśa* (space) is also one and consists of infinite special divisions.

पुद्गलोनाम वर्णगंधरसस्पर्शवत् द्रव्यम् तच्च द्विविधम् परमाणुरूपम् तत्संघातरूपं च पवन-ज्वलन-सलिल धरणी-तनु-भूवनादिकम् कालस्तु अभूत, अस्ति, भविष्यति इति व्यवहार हेतुः अणुरूपो द्रव्यविशेशः। आकाशेऽपि एकः अनंतप्रदेशश्च।[64]

Out of these, again five substances are abstracted, which are other than atoms and are known as *astikāyas i.e.* groups viz. *jīvāstikāya, dharmāstikāya, adharmāstikāya, pudgalāstikāya* and *ākāsāstikāya,* which are used to denote a substance which exists in more places.

तेषु च अणुव्यतिरिक्तानि द्रव्याणि पञ्च अस्तिकायाः इतिच संगृह्यन्तें जीवास्तकायः, धर्मास्तिकायः अधर्मास्तिकायः पुद्भलास्तिकायः आकाश-स्तिकाय इति।[65]

The *Jaina* philosophers also make another list of things, which are helpful for the *jīvas* in the attainment of final release. These are the self *(jīva),* the non-self *(ajīva),* the influx of sense impressions *(āśrava),* bondage *(bandha),* austerities *(nirjarā),* meditation *(saṁbara)* and final release *(mokṣa).* They also have prescribed the means for attaining final release; such means consists of perfect knowledge *(samyakjñāna),* perfect vision *(samyakdarśana)* and perfect conduct *(samyakcaritra).*

जीवानां मोक्षोपयोगिनम्, अपरमपि संग्रहं कुर्वन्ति, जीवाजीवास्रवबन्ध निर्जरसंवरमोक्षाः इति। मोक्षसंग्रहेण मोक्षोपोयश्च गृहीतः। स च सम्यग्ज्ञान-दर्शन-चरित्ररूपः।[66]

Perfect knowledge is that which is devoid of illusion, and which emerges by its own through the deep study and listening and meditating on it after the complete destruction of the *pramāda,* which is in the form of not encouraging the good deeds *puṇyakarma)* or false knowledge *(mithyājñāna),* which is in the form of doubt of the true nature of the object, which always covers the knowledge, which is in the form of un-controlled sense organs, as if the autumnal sun shines after the complete destruction of the clouds. In short, knowledge is produced by itself. Further to have faith on the advice given by the *arhatas* is called *samyakdarśana i.e.* the perfect vision. And, to have a desire to get salvation being bereft of the sinful deeds *(pāpa karma)* is called perfect conduct *(samyakcaritra).* These three are called three jewels[1] *(triratna)* in Jainism.

मोह रहितं ज्ञानं सम्यग्ज्ञानम्। तच्च श्रवणमननाद्यभ्यासपाटवेनेन्द्रिया-संयमरूपा अविरतेज्ञानावरकस्य वस्तुतत्वनिश्चयरूपमिथ्यादर्शन्स्य पुण्यकर्मामुत्साह रूपप्रमादस्य चोपशमे सति स्वयंमेव समुदेति। शरदि मेध गापाये भानुवत्। अत एव ज्ञानं स्वप्रकाशमिति व्यवह्रियते। आहतोपदिष्टेर्थे विश्वासः सम्यग्दर्शनम्। मुमुक्षोः पाकर्मेभ्योः विरतिः सम्यक्चरित्रम्। एतानि समुदितानि मोक्षकारणं न प्रत्येकम्। सम्यग्ज्ञज्ञनादित्रयमस्मिन् शास्त्रे रन्तशब्देनोच्यते।[67]

Of those things, the *jīva,* however, is that which possesses the qualities of knowleāge, vision, pleasure and power. The non-self consists of all those things, which are fit for the enjoyment of the *jīva.* The *āśrava* is the sensory organs etc. that forms the instruments of enjoyment of those *jīvas*. Bondage also is of eight kinds viz. the four-fold *ghātikarmas* and the four-fold *aghātikarmas*. *Ghātikarmas* are that which injuriously affects the knowledge, vision, power and pleasure, which are all the natural qualities of *the. jīvas*. These are four in number viz. *jñānāvaraṇīya, āarśanāvaraṇīya, moharīya* and *antarāya*. *Jñānāvaraṇīya karma* is that obstructs the perfect knowledge and which is in the form of that 'one cannot know the true nature of the object *(vastu)* through knowledge[1]. *Darśanāvaraṇīya* karma is that which obstructs the perfect vision and which is in the form of the knowledge that 'one cannot attain salvation with the help of the ways prescribed by the *arhatas'*. *Moharīiya karmå* is that which affects the *vīrya i.e.* powers, which is in the form of apprehension that 'one unable to chose the perfect or the best way as there are a lot of ways for salvation'. *Antarāya karma* is that which affects the pleasure of the salvation and which creates difficulties in the person, who is engaged in attaining the salvation. Thus, these four karmas being the obstructer or slayer of *sreya i.e.* salvation are called *ghātikarmas*.

जीवस्तु ज्ञान-दर्शन-सुख वीर्यगुणः। अजीवश्च जीवभोग्यवस्तु जातम्। आस्रवः तदुपभोगोपकरणभूतम् इन्द्रियादिकम्। बन्धश्च अष्टविधः घातिकर्मचतुष्टयम् अघातिकर्मचतुष्टयं चेति। जीवगुणानां स्वाभाविकानां ज्ञानदर्शनवीर्यसुखानां प्रतिघातकरम्। ज्ञानावरणीयं दर्शनावरणीयं

मोहनीयमन्तरायमिति घातिकर्मचतुष्टमयम्। तत्र सम्यग्ज्ञानं न मोक्षसाधनम्। न हि ज्ञाना द्वस्तुसिद्धिरतिप्रसंगादिति विपर्ययो ज्ञानावरणीयं कर्मोच्यते। इदं सम्यग्ज्ञानस्य प्रतिघातकरम्। आर्हतमताभ्यासात्र मोक्षो इति ज्ञानं दर्शनावरणीयं कर्म। इदं सम्यग्दर्शनस्य प्रतिघातकरम्। वहूषु परस्परविरुद्धेषु मोक्षमार्गेषु विशेषानवधारणं मोहनीयं कर्म। इदं वीर्यस्य प्रतिघातकरम्। मोहजाते सदपि वीर्यं अकिंचत्करं भवति। मोक्षप्रवृत्तानां तद्विघ्नकरं विज्ञानमन्तरायं कर्म। इदं मोक्षसुखप्रतिधारकम् इमानि श्रेयोहन्तृत्वाद्धातिकर्मण्युच्यन्ते।[68]

Aghātikarmas form the cause of the bodily configuration, its personality, its preservation and its consequences of pleasure, pain and indifference.

शरीरसंस्थानतदभिमान-तत्स्थिति-तत्प्रयुक्तसुखदुखोपेक्षा हेतुभूतम्।[69]

They are four in number viz. *vedaīya, nāmika, gotrika* and *āyuṣka*.

Nirjarā is the *tapas* which is the means of attaining final release, and which is learnt from the teaching of an *arhata*. *Sambara* is known to be that restraint of the sensory organs, which has the nature of mental concentration. *Mokṣa,* on the other hand, is the manifestation in its natural and true form, of the self of the person, whose sins beginning with attachment have all been removed.

निर्जरं मोक्षसाधनम्, अर्हदुपदेशावगतं तपः। संवरो नामो इन्द्रियनिरोः समाधिरूपः। संवरो नामो इन्द्रियनिरोधः समाधिरूपः। मोक्षस्तु निवृत्तरागादिक्लेशस्य स्वभाविकात्मस्वरूपाविर्भावः।[70]

The atoms which also form the cause of the earth etc. are not of four kinds as in the theory of *Vaiśeṣikas* and Buddhists, but are all of one nature. The distinctions among them such as the earth etc. are the results of their transformations.

पृथिव्यादिहेतुभूताश्च आवः वैषेषिकादीनामिव न चतुर्विधाः। अपि तु एकस्वभावः पृथिव्यादिभेदस्तु परिणामकृतः।[71]

They also say that the whole of the totality of things has a varied character in that it is differentiated into existence and non-existence, the eternal and the non-eternal, the identical and the different etc. This is because universally the sevenfold doctrine comes into operation thus, 'a thing is', 'a thing is not', 'a thing is indefinable', and 'a thing is, is not and is indefinable'. Because the whole of the totality of things is made up of modified states of substances, they hold that existence, oneness, eternity etc. are appropriate and as consisting of modified states, it is made up of opposites of those. Modified states are also particular conditions of substances and these conditions have also a positive as well as negative form and hence existence and non-existence and all else will be appropriate.

सर्वं च वस्तुजातं सत्त्वासत्त्व, नित्यत्वानित्यत्व, भिन्नत्वाभिन्नत्वादिभिः अनैकान्तिकमिच्छन्ति। स्यादस्ति, स्यन्नास्ति, स्यादस्ति च नास्ति च स्यादवक्तव्यम्, स्यादस्तिचावक्तव्यं च, स्यान्नास्ति चावक्तव्यं च, स्यादस्ति च नास्ति चावक्तव्यं च। सर्वं वस्तुजातं द्रव्यपर्यायात्मकमिति, द्रव्यात्मना सत्त्वैकत्व नित्यत्वादि उपपादयन्ति, पर्यायात्मना च तद्विपरीतम्। पर्यायाश्च द्रव्यस्य अवस्थाविशेषाः तेषां च भावाभावरूपत्वात्, सत्त्वासत्त्वादिकं सर्वमुपपन्नम् इति।[72]

The theory of the *Jainas* is not true, because of the impossibility of the existence of contradictory qualities in one thing *i.e.* in one and the same thing; it is impossible for contradictories such as existence and non-existence to be found together as in the case with shadow and light.

एकस्मिन् वस्तुनि, अस्तित्व-नास्तित्वादेः विरूद्धस्य छायातपवत् युगपदसम्भवात्।[73]

It is further explained, as a substance and its characteristic, which is a particular condition denoted by the word 'modification' *(paryāya),* form distinct categories, it is not possible for contradictory attributes to meet in one and the same thing. Thus, a thing, which is qualified by particular modification such as existence, cannot possibly be, at the very same time, associated with non-existence, which is the opposite of existence. The impermanence of a substance is it is the abode of the particular modifications known as birth and destruction. The opposite of this is also permanence and how can this co-exist in that substance? To be different from a thing is also to be the seat of a contradictory attribute in relation to that thing. Its opposite also is to be identical and how indeed can co-exist in that substance? For instance, it is not possible for the generic properties of the horse and the buffalo to co-exist in one and the same thing at one and the same time.

द्रव्यस्य तत्तद्विशेषणभूतपर्यायशब्दाभिधेयावस्थाविशेषस्य च पृथक्पदार्थत्त्वात् न एकस्मिन् विरूद्धधर्मसमावेशः सम्भवति-इति। एकेन अस्तित्वादिना अवस्थाविशेषेण विशिष्टस्य, तदानीमेव न तद्विपरीतनास्तिलादि-विशिष्टत्वं सम्भवति। उत्पत्तिविनाशारव्यपरिणाम-विशेषास्पदत्वं च द्रव्यस्य अनित्यत्वम्। तद्विपरीतं च नित्यत्वं तस्मिन् कथं समवैति? विरोधिधर्माश्रयत्वं च भिन्नत्वम्, तद्विपरीतं च अभिन्नत्वं, कथं वा तस्मिन् समवैति? यथा अश्वत्व-महिषत्वेयोः युगपत् एकस्मिन् असम्भवः।[74]

In as much as time is perceived to be merely an attribute of things, it cannot be predicated that it has separate existence or non-existence, nor are these required to be disproved here. To those who practically realize things, the practical realization that 'time is or is not' resembles the practical realization relating to the existence or non-existence of the universal etc. It has already been stated that universal etc. are perceived merely as adjuncts of substances.

कालस्पदार्थविशेणतयैव प्रतीतेः, तस्य पृथगस्तित्व-नास्तित्वादयो न वक्तव्याः, न च परिहर्तव्याः। कालः अस्ति, नास्ति इति व्यवहार व्यवहर्तुणां जात्यद्यस्तित्व-नास्तित्व व्यवहारतुल्यः। जात्यादयो हि द्रव्यविशेषणतयैव प्रतीयन्त इति पूर्वमेवोक्तम्।[75]

It may however be asked how it is declared by those who are learned in the Veda that one and the same *Brahman* constitutes all things. The reply has been given that it is because the highest person, who is omniscient and omnipotent and who wills the truth, has also been already stated that the difference is complete between the body and the embodied being on the one hand and their several attributes on the other.

कथंपुनः एकमेव ब्रहम सर्वात्मकमिति श्रौत्रियेरूच्यते? सर्वचेतनाचेतन शरीरत्वान् सर्वज्ञस्य सर्वशक्तेः सत्यसंकल्पस्य पुरूषोत्तमस्येत्युकम्। शरीरशरीरिणोः तद्धमीणां च अत्यन्तवैलक्षण्यमप्युक्तम्। शरीरत्वात् सर्वतस्य सर्वशक्तेः सत्यसंकल्पस्य पुरुषोत्तमरयेत्युकाम् शरीरशरोरिणो तद्धमीणां च अत्यन्तवैलक्षण्यमय्युक्तम् कथं पुनः एकमेव ब्रह्म सर्वात्मंकमिति श्रौत्रियैरुच्यते? सर्वचेतनाचेतन।[76]

Moreover, the six substances beginning with the *jīvas* do not possess the character of being the modifications of one substance and therefore in relation to them, it can hardly be predicated, among others that they are one or many, either because, they consist of one substance or because they consist of modifications. It may be said that these six substances are many or one, either through their own modifications or through their selves individually. In this case also there results contradiction of the admitted theory that all things vary in character from one another, because there is no mutual identity among them. Therefore, this view held by the *Jainas* is improper.

जीवादीना षण्णां, एकद्रव्यपर्यायत्वाभावात्, तेषु द्रव्यैकत्वेन पर्यायात्मना च एकत्वानेकत्वादयो दुरूपपादाः। अथोच्यते-षडेतानि द्रव्याणि, स्वकीयैः पर्यायैः स्वेन स्वेन चाऽऽत्मना तथा भवन्ति इति। एवमपि 'सर्वमनैकान्तिकम्' इत्यभ्युपगमविरोधः अन्योन्यतादात्म्याभावात्। अतः न युक्तमिदं जैनमतम्।[77]

The Jainas' position is this that the *jīva*, which has no definite dimensions in space, has also the dimensions of the body it occupies. It being so, in as much as the self, which occupies the bodies of elephants and the like, has to occupy a smaller space when it enters the bodies of ants etc. which occupy a smaller space than those bodies of elephants etc. the character of being a whole does not result to it. The meaning is that it amounts incompleteness.

भवदभ्युपगमे सति, आत्मनश्च आकात्स्न्र्यं प्रसज्यते। जीवः अंरण्यातप्रदेश, देह परिमाणः इतिहि। भवतां स्थितिः। तत्र हस्त्यादिशरीरे अवस्थितस्य आत्मनः, ततो न्यूनपरिमाणे पिपीलिकादिशरीरे प्रवशितः, अल्पदेश व्यापित्वेन आकात्स्न्र्यं प्रसंज्यते-अपरिपूर्णता इत्यर्यः।[78]

Again it may be said that the self, owing to its possessing the properties of countraction and expansion attain the different states, that means owing to its modifications (*paryāyas*), it attains the different states and that thereby the above contradiction is negated. To this, they say that it is impossible to set aside the above contradiction by reason of the self-acquiring different conditions consisting of contraction and expansion, because the resulting evil, such as other modifications and impermanence etc. due to those modifications, will lead to the assumption by the self of a character exactly equivalent to that of a pot.

न च संकोच-विकासरुपावस्थान्तरापत्त्याऽपि, विरोधः परिहर्तु शक्यते, विकारतत्प्रयुक्तानित्यत्वादिदोषप्रसक्तेः घटादि तुल्यत्व प्रसंगात्।[79]

Further, the Jaina philosopher may say that the final dimension of the self is found in association with the condition of final release. This gets established owing to the self not taking up any other body thereafter. Hence, the self and its dimensions in association with the condition of final release are both eternal. And therefore, that final dimension is the natural dimension of the self. And so there can be no difference with the prior state. Consequently the self cannot possess the dimension of the body. Thus, this view of the *Jainas* is indeed full of inconsistencies.

जीवस्य यत् अन्त्यं परिमाणं मोक्षावस्थागतं, तय पश्चाद्देहान्तरपरिग्रहाभावात् अवस्थितत्वात्, आत्मनश्च मोक्षावस्थस्यतत्परिमाणस्य च उभयोर्नित्यत्वात्, तदेव आत्मनः स्वाभाविकं परिमाणमिति, पूर्वमपि तस्मादविशेषः स्यात्। अतः देहपरिमाणत्वम् आत्मनो न स्यादिति, असंगतमेवेदम् आर्हतमतम्।[80]

Further, they have objected the view of the *Jaina* philosophers on the issue that the infinitesimal atom is the cause of the world. They say that there is inconsistency in the view of the *Jainas*. They argue: as *Jainas* maintain that from *'hrasva'* *i.e.* the short one and the from *'parimaṇdala' i.e.* the secondary particle *(dvaṇuka)* and the infinitesimal atom, likewise the *'mahādīrgha' i.e.* very big and long is produced inconsistent. Likewise, all others that is accepted by them *(Jainas)* are also inconsistent.

ह्रस्व-परिमण्डलाभ्यं द्वयणुकपरिमाणुभ्यां महद्दीर्घवत्-त्र्यणुकोत्पत्तिवादवत्, अन्यञ्च तदभ्युपगतं सर्वम्, असमञ्जसम्। परमाणुभ्यः द्वत्यणुकादिक्रमेण जग दुत्पत्तिवादवत्, अन्यदपि असमञ्जसमित्यर्थः।[81]

Threads and other divisible parts produce the whole cloth, when they are conjoined on six sides forming their own parts. The infinitesimal atoms can become the producer of the secondary and other particles when they are conjoined together on all their six sides. Otherwise, as infinitesimal atoms have no distinct and particular locutions in space, although thousands of infinitesimal atoms are conjoined together, the resultant dimension will not exceed that of one infinitesimal atom. And consequently atomicity and minuteness, which are the qualities of the secondary particles and magnitude and length, which belong to the tertiary particle and other qualities, will not result from the infinitesimal atom. If distinct locations in space is admitted, the infinitesimal atoms become divisible into parts and made up of their own parts and they *i.e.* the parts of the atom are made up of their own parts and so on, thus, resulting in a regresses as infinitum.

तंतुप्रभतयो हि अवयावाः, स्वांशैः पार्श्वैः संयुज्यमानः अवयविनमुत्पादयति। परमाणवोऽपिस्वकीयैः षडभिः पार्श्वैः संयुज्यमाना एव, द्वयणुकादीनामुत्पदका भवेयुः। अन्यथापरमाणुनां प्रदेशभेदाभावे सति सहस्रपरमाणुसंयोगेपि, एकस्मात्परमाणोः अनतिरिक्तपरिमाणतया अणुत्व-ह्रस्वत्व- महत्वदीर्घत्वाद्यसिद्धिः स्यात्। प्रदेशभेदाभ्युपगमे परमाणवोऽपिसांशाः स्वकीयैरंशैः, ते च स्वकीयैरंशैरिति अनवस्था।[82]

It should not be urged that the inequality between a mustard seed and a mountain arises solely out of the smallness or largeness in the number of the constituent parts arises between the mustard and the mountain and there is thus, no inequality between them. And that, therefore, it has necessarily to be accepted that the ultimate constituent part has a limit, because, if the infinitesimal atoms have no location in space, then any size exceeding the magnitude of a single infinitesimal atom cannot come to existence. And therefore, the mustard and the mountain will themselves not be established. If it is asked what then we are to do, it is replied that the view based upon the *Veda* may be accepted.

न च वाच्यम् अवयवाल्पत्व-महत्त्वाभ्यां हि। सर्षप-महीधरयौर्वैषम्यम्, परमाणोरपि अनन्तावयवत्वे, अवयावानन्त्यसाम्यात् सर्षप-महीधरयोः वैषम्यासिद्धेः, अवयवापकर्षकाष्ठा अवश्याभ्युपगमनीया इति, परमाणुनां प्रदेश भेदाभावे सति, एकपरमाणुपरिमाणा तिरेकी प्रथिमा न जायेततेति, सर्षप-महोधरयोरेव असिद्धेः। किं कुर्मः? इति चेत्। वैदिकः पक्षः परिगृह्यताम्।[83]

In short, the production of the tertiary particle and the secondary particle out of the secondary particle and infinitesimal atom respectively is inconsistent.

Furthermore, according to he *Jainas'* view that the infinitesimal atom is the cause, the origin of the world is thought to take place in the order which begins with the production of the secondary particle, which is based on the conjunction of the infinitesimal atoms, which results out of the motion resident in them. It being so, the earliest motion, which is found in the infinitesimal atoms and forms, the cause of the origin of the whole world, is held to be produced by the *adṛṣta* or the unseen result of work.

परमणुकारणवादे हि परमाणुगतकर्मजनिततत्संयोगपूर्वकद्वयणुकादिक्रमेण, जगदुत्पत्तिरिष्यते। तत्र निरिवलजगदुप्तत्तिकारणभूतपरमाणुगतम् आद्यं कर्म अदृष्ट कारितम्।[84]

The above-mentioned motion found in the infinitesimal atom is either produced by its own *adṛṣṭa* or by the *adṛṣṭa* found in association with the individual self. In both the cases also, it cannot be possible for the *adṛṣṭa,* which is produced by the working out of the merit and demerit of individual souls to be found resident in the infinitesimal atom. If it were so found, it is not possible for the *adṛṣṭa* found resident in always. Moreover, it is not possible for the *adṛṣṭa* found resident in the individual self to be cause of the production of the motion resident in the infinitesimal atom. Again it may be said that the motion is originated in atoms through the association of the individual self-possessing the *adṛṣṭa*. Under such circumstance, the unceasing flow of the *adṛṣṭa* being eternal, it follows that creation would be eternal.

तदिदं परमाणुगतं कर्म, स्वगतादृष्टकारितम्? आत्मगतादृढकारितं वा? उभयथाऽपि न संभवति, क्षेत्रज्ञपूण्यपापानुष्ठानजनितस्य अदृष्टस्य, परमाणुगतात्वासम्भवात्। संभवे च, सदोत्पादकत्वप्रसंगः। आत्मगतस्य च अदृष्टस्य, परमाणुगतकर्मोत्पत्तिहेतुत्वं न संभवति। अथ अदृष्टवदात्मसंयोगात् अणुषु कर्मोत्पत्तिः। तदा तस्य अदृष्टप्रवाहस्य नित्यत्वेन नित्यसर्गप्रसंग।[85]

It may further be said that the *adṛṣṭa* is capable of giving fruits, provided it is ripe. Therefore, some *adṛṣṭa* then and there assume the condition of yielding fruits, while others do so in other future births and others again in other future period of time known as the *kalpas*. And that, therefore, because of dependence on the ripening of the *adṛṣṭa,* its capability to produce it is not established by any authoritative means of knowledge that the *adṛṣṭas* which are produced by many kinds of karmas, performed not simultaneously and out previous understanding among one another by the infinite individual selves, can all at one time attain one and the same time ripening yields fruits.

ननु अदृष्टं विपाकापेक्षं ग्लायाऽलम्। कानिचित् अहष्टानि तदानीमेव विपच्यन्ते। कानिचित् जन्मांतरे। कानिचित् कल्पांतरे। अतः विपाकापेक्षत्वात् न सर्वदात्पादकत्वप्रसंगः इति। नैतत् अनन्तैः आत्मभिः, असंकेत पूर्वकम् अयुगपदनुष्ठितानेकविधाकर्मजनितानाम् अदृष्टानाम् एकस्मिन्काले एकरुपविपाकस्य, अप्रमाणिकत्वात्।[86]

For this very reason the simultaneous absorption of all things and their existence in a condition unripe for yielding fruits *i.e. pralaya,* do not come to pass during *parārdhas i.e.* period of time each equal to half the life of *Brahmā*[87].

Again, motion does not exist in the atoms in consequence of the association with them of the individual souls possessing the particular *adṛṣṭa* assigned to them at the will of the lord because under the *sūtra* "that the Brahman is the cause of the creation etc, of the universe follows altogether from the scriptures because scriptures form the source of the knowledge relating to Him[88]. It has been already explained how such a lord as is arrived at by the logical process of inference is disproved. Therefore, the origination of the world has not for its basis the motion associated with atoms.

न च ईश्वरेच्छहितविशेषादृष्टसंयोगात् अणुषु कर्म, आनुमानिके-श्वरासिद्धेः,

शास्त्रयोनित्वात् इत्यत्र उपपादितत्वात्। अतः जगदुत्पत्तेः अणुगतकर्मपूर्व-कत्माभावः।[89]

If the *Jaina* philosophers accept relation of inherence to explain it, there also arises inconsistency. Because the relation of inherence also requires by parity of reasoning some other thing to explain it, like an organic whole, a genus and a quality respectively to explain them, that other thing to explain it and so on. Thus, there results the fallacy of regresses and infinitum.

समवायाभ्युपगमाच्च असमञ्जसम्। कुतः? साम्यादनवस्थितेः। समवायस्याऽपि अवयवि जातिगुणवत् उपपादकान्तारापेक्षासाम्यात्, उपपादकान्तरस्याऽपि तथेति अनवस्थितेः असमञ्जसमेव।[90]

Samavāya possesses the character of a relation. Therefore, if this relation is accepted to be eternal, then one which possesses this relation will undoubtedly acquire permanent existence. Thus, there arises inconsistency. It means if *Samavāya* is eternal, the postulation by the *Jainas* of eternal atoms and God is unnecessary.

समवायस्य सम्बन्धत्वात्, सम्बन्धास्य नित्यत्वे सम्बन्धितो जगतश्च नित्यमेव भावात्, असमञ्जसम्।[91]

Further, the four kinds of infinitesimal atoms of the elements of earth, water, fire and air are admitted by them to possess the qualities of colour, taste, smell and touch and therefore is contradiction of the conditions of subtlety, indivisibility etc. which are accepted by them as characterizing infinitesimal atoms which amounts to the atoms having non-eternity, grossness, divisibility etc. For a pot that possesses colour etc. are seen to be non-eternal and to be produced out of other causes of a similar kind having colour etc. Thus, an unseen thing assumed in accordance with what is seen is not capable of definitely establishing one's accepted particular conclusion. 'It is assumed by you only in accordance with what is seen that infinitesimal atoms possess colour etc. Therefore, the atomic theory is inconsistent'.

परमाणुनां पार्थिवाप्यतैजसवायवीयानां चतुर्विधानां रूपरसगंध-स्पर्शवत्त्वाभ्युपगमान् अभिमतनित्यत्व-सूक्ष्मत्व निरवयवत्वादिविपर्य- येण अनित्यत्व-स्थूलत्व सावयवत्वादि प्रसज्यते। रूपादिपानां घटादीनां अनित्यत्व-तथाविधकारणान्तरब्धत्वादि दर्शनात्। न हि दर्शनानुगुण्येन अदृष्टोऽर्थः कल्प्यामानः स्वाभिमान विशेषे व्यवस्थापयितुं शक्यः दर्शनानुगुण्येन हि परामाणुनां रूपादिमत्वं त्वया कल्पयते। अतोऽपि असमञ्जसम्। समवायस्य सम्बन्धत्वात्, सम्बन्धास्य नित्यत्वे सम्बन्धिातो जगतश्च नित्यमेव भावात्, असमञ्जसम्। समवायाभ्युपगमाच्च असमञ्जसम्। कुतः? साम्यादनवस्थितेः। समवायस्याऽपि अवयवि जातिगुणवत् उपपादकान्तारापे- क्षासाम्यात्, उपपादकान्तरस्याऽपि तथेति अनवस्थितेः असमञ्जसमेव।[92]

Again it is not merely the admission alone that the infinitesimal atoms possess colour etc. is erroneous. Even though they are admitted to be devoid of colour etc. in as much as the qualities of the effect are based upon the qualities of the cause, the earth and other things, which are effects, will have to be devoid of colour etc. If with the object of avoiding this difficulty, the atoms are admitted to possess colour etc. then the error mentioned above comes into existence. Thus error arising in either case has inconsistency.

न केवलं परमाणुनां रूपादिमत्त्वाभ्युपगम एव दोषः। रूपादिविरहेऽपि कारणगुापूर्वकत्वात् कार्यगुणानां, पृथिव्यादयो रूपादिशून्याः स्युः। तत्परिजिहीर्षया रूपादिमत्त्वाभ्युपगमे, पूर्वोक्तदोष इति, उभयथा च दोषात्, असमञ्जतसम्।[93]

In this way the *viśiṣṭādvaita* philosophers have presented the position of the *Jaina* philosophers. As can be seen, *Rāmānujācārya, Vásudevashastri* and *Śrinivāsācārya* putting together have presented the *Jaina* doctrines faithfully without any bias.

Let me now again record the objections of the *Viśiṣṭādvaita* philosophers against the *Jaina* philosophy. Their arguments are mainly concerned with three major issues viz:

(i) objections on the nature of reality

(ii) objections on the nature and size of the soul and

(iii) objections on the theory of creation.

Following are the prime objections of *viśiṣṭādvaita* philosophers against the *Jaina* philosophy.

Objection 1

The *Jaina* theories postulate that in one and the same object the contradictory qualities are not possible to put simultaneously, because in one and the same thing, it is impossible for contradictories such as existence and non-existence to be found together, as in the case with shadow and light. Or it is not possible for the generic properties of the horse and the buffalo to co-exist in one and the same thing at one and the same time.

Objection 2 (i)

The *Jainas'* position on soul is that it has no definite dimensions in space, has also the dimension of the body it occupies. It creates contingency called 'incompleteness' *i.e. aparipurṇatā*. They clear this point by giving an example that a soul of and elephant while enters into a body of an ant and vice-versa, due to good and bad deeds, then the soul cannot occupy the entire body, sometimes less and sometimes more. Thus, this position of the *Jainas* on soul cannot be admissible.

Objection 2 (ii)

The *Jaina* philosophers may argue that owing to its (soul's) contractions and expansions, in other words owing to its modifications *i.e. paryāyas*, it attains various different states or bodies. Then, it will be resulting a contingency called 'non-eternal' *i.e. anityatva* in it which will go against the very concept of the soul.

Objection 2 (iii)

The *Jaina* philosophers maintain that the final dimension of the soul is found in association with the condition of final release. This gets established owing to the soul not taking up any other body thereafter. Hence, the soul and its dimensions in association with the condition of final release are both eternal. And therefore, that final dimension is the natural dimension of the soul. So, there can be no difference with the prior state. Consequently the soul cannot possess the dimension of the body.

Objection 3 (i)

The infinitesimal atoms are not the causes of the creation, because if they accept this, it creates a further problem namely, whether the atoms are possessed of parts of not? If yes, then it leads to a contingency called infinite regress and if no, then it would be impossible for the atoms to produce other evolutes. Thus, there is inconsistency in the origination of both binary and ternary compounds from infinitesimal atoms and binary compounds respectively. Thus, the atomic view is inconsistent.

Objection 3 (ii)

It is impossible for the unseen principle *adṛṣṭa* to inhere in the atoms as well as connected with the soul to be the instigator of the motion of the atoms to produce the creation. Even in both the cases, it cannot be possible for the *adṛṣṭa,* which is produced by the working out of the merit and demerit of individual souls, to be found resident in the atom. If it is so found, then it will be always capable of production. And it is not possible for the *adṛṣṭa* found resident in the individual self to be cause of the production of the motion resident in the infinitesimal atom. Or if it is said that the motion is originated in atoms through the association of the individual self, possessing *adṛṣṭa*, then the unceasing flow of the *adṛṣṭa* being eternal follows that creation is eternal.

Objection 3 (iii)

In acceptance of the relation inherence to explain it there

also arises inconsistency. Because, the inherence also requires by parity of reasoning some other thing to explain it, like an organic whole, a genus and a quality which requires the part, the species and the substratum of the quality respectively to explain them. That other thing which explains inherence also similarly requires some other thing to explain it and so on. Thus, there results the fallacy of regress ad infinitum. Not only this but *samavāya* possesses the character of a relation. Therefore, if this relation is accepted to be eternal, then the one which possesses this relation will also undoubtedly acquire permanent existence. It means if *samavāya* is eternal, the postulation by the *Jainas* of eternal atoms and god is unnecessary.

Objection 3 (iv).

The four kinds of infinitesimal atoms of the elements of earth, water, fire and air are admitted by them to possess the qualities of colour, taste, smell and touch and therefore, in contradiction of the conditions of subtlety, indivisibility etc. which are accepted by the *Jainas* as characterizing infinitesimal atoms, amounts to the atoms having non-eternity, grossness divisibility etc.

We have formulated in the foregoing pages the arguments and objections of the *viśiṣṭādvaita* philosophers against the *Jaina* philosophy. The answers to the objection raised by the *Visistddvaita* Philosophers against the *Jainas* are more or less same as formulated by us earlier[94], hence, need not be repeated here.

Śuddhādvaitas'presentation on Jaina philosophy

The Philosophers of *Śuddhādvaita* school of *Vedānta* have also criticized some of the doctrines of Jaina Philosophy. *Vallbhācārya* the main *ācārya* of the *Śudhhādvaita* School has recorded the *Jaina* position while commenting upon the *Brahmasūtra* II. 2. 33-36. of Bādurāyana. They have criticized mainly the *Jaina* doctrine of *anekāntavāda* and the allied problems related to it, the theory of creation and the nature of soul.

First of all they have presented the *Jaina* position and then pointed out some inconvenience in their system by showing some contingency in their framework of understanding and then refuted their position with suitable arguments.

In the presentation of Jainism and framing argument against the *Jaina* philosophy our sources have been the *Anubhāṣya* of *Vallabhācārya, Bhāvaprakāśikā* of *Gośwāmi Śripurusottaṁajee, Balabodhiriī* of *Śripurusottamajee Śridharasarmā* and *anubhāṣya pradīpa* of *Śri īchhārāma bhaṭ ṭajee*

There is no novelty in their presentation of *Jaina* Philosophy or any addition to it by the *Śuddhādvaitins*. As a matter of fact the text quoted by earlier authorities of *Vedānta* like *Viśiṣṭddvaita* etc. are identical. The reason for such sameness in the treatment of presentation is not far to seek *Śuddhādvaita* as a system is later development and the original texts of the *Jainas* and the texts quoted by *Dvaitins* and *Viśiṣṭ ādvaitins* are earlier to them. And hence, they have made good use of those by merely drawing the text from them. Thus, in the presentation of the realities like the concept of *Jīva* and *Ajīva* etc. the seven *bhaṅgas,* and in their arguments as well they have reproduced the text as it is not making any change whatsoever.

REFERENCES

1. (a) cf. Tattvārthasūtra. 1.4, Tattvārthasāra. 1.6, Jñārarṇava. 4.9.
   (b) Śaṅkarabhāṣya on BS.II.2.33.
2. Kalpataru on BS bhāṣya. II.2.33.
3. (a.) cf.Jīva samāsā prakaraṇa. 85.
   (b) Śaṅkarabhāṣya on BS. II.2.33.
4. जीवास्तिकायस्त्रिधाा बद्धो मुक्तो नित्यसिद्धश्चेति। Bhāmati on BS. II.2.33.
5. पुद्गलास्तिकाय: षोढा पृथिव्यादिनी चत्वारिभूतानि स्थावरं जङ्गमश्चेति। *ibid.*
6. धर्मास्तिकाय: प्रवृत्तेरनुमेयोऽधर्मस्तिकाय: स्तित्यनुमेय। *Ibid.*
7. आकाशास्तिकायो द्विधा लोकाकाशोऽलोकाकाशश्चेति। तत्रोपर्युपरि स्तितानां लोकामं अन्तर्वती लोकाकाशऽस्तोषामुपरि मोक्षस्थानमलोकाकाश:। तत्र न लोकासन्ति। *Ibid.*

8. *Ibid.*
9. *Ibid.*
10. ऊर्ध्वगमनशील हि जीवो धर्माधर्मस्तिकायेन बद्धस्तद्विमोक्षादूर्ध्वं गच्छेत्येव स मोक्षः इति। *Ibid.*
11. विगलित समस्त क्लेशस्याद् वासनास्यानावराणज्ञानस्यसुखैकतानस्यात्मन उपरिदेशावस्थानं मोक्षः इत्येके। *ibid.*
12. Śaṅikarabhāṣya on BS. II.2.34.
13. (a) cf. Syādvādamañjarī. 9; Dravyasaṁgraha. 2; Jñānārṇava. 6.17; Tattvārthavṛtti on Pañcāsthikāya. v.no. 31.
    (b) *Ibid.*
14. (a) *Ibid.*
    (b) cf. Brahmadeva on Dravyasaṁgraha. V. no. 10; Tattvārtharājavārtika. P. 202.
15. *Ibid.*
16. Śaṅikarabhāṣya on BS. II.2.33.
17. *Ibid.*
18. *Ibid.*
19. Śaṅkarabhāṣya on BS. II.2.34
20. *Ibid.*
21. Śaṅkarabhāṣya on BS. II.2.35
22. Śaṅkarabhāṣya on BS. II.2.35
23. Śaṅkarabhāṣya on BS. II.2.36
24. Vedānta Kaustubha on BS. II.2.33
25. Vedānta Kaustubha Prabhā on BS. II.2.33
26. Vedānta Kaustubha on BS. II.2.33
27. जीवभोग्यं वस्तुजातमजीवं स च धर्माधर्मपुदगलकालाकाशभेदभिन्नः। सम्यक पवृत्यनुमेयो द्रव्यविशेषो धर्मः। अमुक्तानां स्तितिहेतुरधर्मः। Vedānta Kaustubha on BS. II.2.33
28. Vedānta Kaustubha on BS. II.2.33
29. कालस्तु चिरक्षिप्रभूतादिव्यवहारहेतुरणुरूपो द्रव्यबिशेषः। *Ibid.*
30. आवरणाभाव आकाशो द्विधा, लोकाकाशः सांसारिकः, अलोकाकाशो मुक्ताश्रयः। Vedānta Kaustubha Prabhā on BS. II.2.33
31. *Ibid.*
32. *Ibid.*
33. तेषमेवापरः प्रपञ्च पंचस्तिकायो नाम। जीवास्तिकायः पुदगलास्तिकायः धर्मास्तिकायः अधर्मास्तिकायः आकास्तिकायश्चेति। अनकदेशवर्ती सांकेतिकपदार्थनाञ्च, अस्तिकायशब्द जीवश्चासावस्तिकायश्चेत्येवं सर्वत्र कर्मधारयः। *Ibid.*

34. Vedānta Kaustubha on BS. II.2.33
35. *Ibid.*
36. ननु पटरुपेण घटनोनास्ति, स्वेनरूपेणास्तीति न विरुद्ध इति चेन्न, स्वरूपेऽपिसप्तभङ्गीयस्या-विशेषात् स्वरूपमस्तीत्यपि तत्रानध्यवसानमेव स्यात्। किञ्च ये सप्तपदार्थास्ते तथैव स्युः। अन्यथा वेत्यनिश्चितज्ञानमाप्रमाणमेव स्यात्। Vedānta Kaustubha on BS. II.2.33
37. ननु सर्वमनैकान्तिकमित्यवधारण्ज्ञानं निश्चितमेवेति चेन्न, अवधारणमप्यनैकान्तिकमेव स्यात्। अवधारणं स्यान्नास्ति चावधाारणमिति न क्वचिन्निश्चयः स्यात्। मोक्षोस्ति, नास्तीत्यवधाणादप्रवृत्तिरेव स्यात्। तत्रैवं शास्त्रं प्रयन्नुन्मत्ततुल्यतीर्थंकरः स्यात् ।*Ibid.*
38. Vedānta Pārijāta Saurabha on BS. II. 11.
39. *Ibid.*
40. *Ibid.*
41. परमाणुनां प्रवृत्तिस्वभावत्वे प्रवृत्तेर्भावान्नित्यसृष्टिप्रसङ्गादन्यथा नित्यप्रलयप्रसङ्गात्तदभावः। Vedānta Pārijāta Saurabha on BS. II. 14.
42. Vedānta Kaustubha on BS. II. 2. 15.
43. यद्युपचितगुणाः परमाणवस्तदा पृथिव्यप्तेजोवायूनां तुल्यतापत्तिः। अपचितगुण इत्यत्रापि सर्वेषां परमाणुनां प्रत्येकमेकैकगुणयोगेन पृथिव्यादीनामपिकारणगुणानुगुण्येन प्रत्येकमेकैकगुण-योगः स्यादित्युभयथाऽपि दोषात्तभाव एव। Vedanta Pārijāta Saurabha on BS. II. 16.
44. Vedānta Kaustubha on BS. II. 2. 33.
45. किञ्च एकस्मिन् जगत्कारणे प्रमाण प्राप्ते बहूनां परमाणुनां कारणत्वं नोपद्यते गौरवात्तेषां जडत्वेन कारणत्वातासंभवाच्च। *Ibid.*
46. एकस्मिन्वेदवेद्ये मोक्षप्रदे सति सिद्धानुग्रहान्मोक्षो दुर्घटः, असम्भवात्। सिद्धानुग्रहः आराधनासापेक्षादोषत्सर्वेषामाराधने गौरवं स्यात्, असति चेदेको महान् तर्हि सर्वपक्षे प्रविष्टो भवान्। द्वितीये, सर्वमोक्षप्रसंगः। किञ्च सिद्धसत्वे प्रत्यक्षदिप्रमाणभावात्सिद्धानुग्रहान्मोक्षो दुर्घटः। *Ibid.*
47. Vedānta Kaustubha on BS. II. 2. 34.
48. Vedānta Kaustubha on BS. II. 2.35.
49. Vedānta Kaustubha on BS. II. 2. 36.
50. Tattvaprakāśikā on Brahmasūtra II. 2. 33.
51. Bhāvabodha on BS. II. 2. 33.
52. Tattvabodhiī on BS. II. 2. 33.
53. Púrṇaprajṃābhāṣya on BS. II. 2. 33.
54. Tattvaprakāśikā on Brahmasūtra II. 2. 33.
55. Tattvaprakāśikā on Brahmasūtra II. 2. 34.
56. Pūmaprajṃābhasya on BS. II. 2. 34.
57. Tattvaprakāśikā on Brahmasūtra II. 2. 34.

58. Pūmaprajṃābhāṣya on BS. II. 2. 34.
59. Tattvaprakāśikā on Brahmasūtra II. 2. 34.
60. Tattvaprakāśikā on Brahmasūtra II. 2. 34.
61. Śribhāṣya on BS.II. 2. 31.
62. *Ibid.*
63. *Ibid.*
64. *Ibid.*
65. *Ibid.*
66. *Ibid.*
67. Vṛtti of Śribhāṣya. P. 254.
68. *Ibid.*
69. *Ibid.*
70. *Ibid.*
71. *Ibid.*
72. *Ibid.*
73. *Ibid.*
74. *Ibid.*
75 *Ibid.*
76. *Ibid.*
77. *Ibid.*
78. Śrībhāṣya on II. 2. 32.
79. Śrībhāṣya on II. 2. 33.
80. Śrībhāṣya on II. 2. 34.
81. Śrībhāṣya on II. 2. 10.
82. *Ibid.*
83. *ibid.*
84. Śrībhāṣya on II. 2. 11.
85. *Ibid.*
86. *Ibid.*
87. *Ibid.*
88. Vedāntasūtra. I. 1.3.
89. Śrībhāṣya on BS. II. 2. 11.
90. Śrībhāṣya on BS. II. 2. 12
91. Śrībhāṣya on BS. II. 2. 13.
92. Śrībhāṣya on BS. II. 2. 14.
93. Śrībhāṣya on BS. II. 2. 15.

Chapter - 4

JAINA PHILOSOPHY AS PRESENTED IN BUDDHIST LITERATURE

Buddhists' Criticism on *Jaina* concept of Reality

Unlike other systems of Indian philosophy it is the Buddhists who have singularly taken the *Jaina* philosophy seriously for analysis and critical examination. It is noticed that amongst the Brahminical schools of Indian philosophy the *Naiyāyikas,* the *Vedāntins,* have, to some extent, considered the view of *Jaina* philosophy which we have discussed separately. In comparison to them we found that Buddhist philosophers particularly Dharmakīrti, Śanatarakṣita, Nāgārjuna and Dignāga have taken or cared to consider the *Jaina* doctrines and have refuted some of the basic assumptions of the *Jainas*. In this chapter we will critically evaluate the presentation or the treatment of Buddhist philosophers. We have selected some most important doctrines or philosophical concepts of the *Jainas* and have analyzed those in the light of Buddhist philosophy. The concepts taken for analysis in the present chapter are:

1. Concept of Reality.
2. Concept of Soul
3. Omniscience.
4. Perception and its object.
5. Determinate perception.
6. *Śmṛti* as *pramāṇa.*
7. *Pratyabhijṃā pramāṇa.*

8. *Anumāna pramāṇa.*
9. *Anekāntavāda.*
10. *Syādvāda.*
    (a) Dharmakīrti's presentation.
    (b) Prañākaragupta's presentation.
    (c) Karṇakogomin's presentation.
    (d) Nāgārjuna's Presentation.
    (e) Chandrakīrti's presentation.
    (f) Arcata's presentation.

To understand or analyze the reality is the beginning point of all philosophical investigations. In the context of Indian philosophy some systems of thought accept only the universal character *(sāmānya dharma)* of reality as the ultimate.

Advaitavedāntins and the *Sāṁkhya* philosophers are the representatives of this view. Some other schools led by the Buddhists recognize only particular character *(yiśeṣadharma)* of reality.

The third school of thought belongs to *Nyāya-Vaiśeṣikas,* who treats universal and particular as absolutely distinctive entities. The Jainas, singularly however subscribe to the theory of universal-cum-particular nature of reality where the reality is a composition of universal and particular.

In this context, Śantarakṣita presents the view of *Jainas* and after critical examination refuted that by showing fault in it. According to Jainism, each and every reality is of the nature of universal-cum-particular *(sāmānya veśeṣātmaka)* along with substance with modes *(dravyaparyāyātmaka)*. *Śāntarakṣita* presents the view of *Jainas* that every entity has more than one aspect viz. the general *(sāmānya)* and the particular *(veśeṣ a),* just like the lustrous gem, which appears to be of variegated colour. Why then should there be any contradiction or incompatibility between existence and non-existence, in view of which it is said that the two couldnot co-exist in the same substratum ? Kamalaśila states:

सर्वमेव वस्तु सामान्यविशेषात्मकत्वेनानेकात्मकम् यथा शबलाभासं रत्नम् तत् कथं सदादीनां विरोधः येनोच्यते समावेशो नचैकत्र इति ।[1]

To prove the general and particular character of things, *Jaina* philosophers have primarily formulated the following arguments. If an entity were not equal to entirely different entities in essence, then it would not differ from the fictitious entities like sky-flower etc. On the other hand, if it were entirely devoid of non-equality/difference, then it could not be regarded as anything different from those things. Thus, Śāntarakṣita says:

भावो भावान्तरातुल्यः खपुष्यान्न विशिष्यते
अतुल्यत्वविहीन्श्च तेम्यो भिन्नो न सिध्यति।[2]

Kamalaśila explains it by stating that if a certain thing say a 'jar', for instance, were not equal to *i.e.* different from all other things, such as the cloth; and the like and if it were always excluded or differentiated from these, then there would be no difference between the jar and the sky-flower. And if it were always differentiated from all other things, it can have no other state save that of the sky-flower. Consequently, one who is not willing to admit the equality of that thing with the sky-flower must admit that it is equal or similar to other entities, as being an entity. Hence, this general character *i.e.* universality, in the shape of the universal 'entity' has to be admitted. Thus, he says:

भाव इति किञ्चित् विवक्षितं वस्तु घटादि, स यदि घटादिर्भावः पटादि भावान्तरेणातुल्यः स्यात् ततो यदि व्यावृत्ताः स्यात् तदा खपुष्यान्न तस्य विशेषः स्यात्सर्वथा वस्त्वन्तराद्व्यावृत्तत्वात्। न च वस्त्वन्तराद् व्यावृत्तस्यान्या गतिः संभवति खपुष्पान्मुक्त्वा। तस्मात् तस्य वस्तुनः खपुष्पातुल्यत्वमभ्युपगच्छता भावान्तरतुल्यात्वं वस्तुत्वं नासामान्यमभ्युपगन्तव्यमिति सिद्धं सामान्यत्मकत्वम्।[3]

If it were entirely devoid of non-equality, then it could not be regarded as different from those things. If that same entity, jar were devoid of non-equality to other things like the cloth *i.e.* if it were non-equal to them, then the jar could not be regarded as anything different from the cloth etc., in the form "this is a jar" I "that is a cloth", just like the specific individuality of things. And, yet as a matter of fact, it does differ from other things. Hence, it gets established that it has the particular character also. He says:

स एव घटादिर्भावो यदि घटादिना भावेन यदतुल्यत्वं तेन विहीनः स्यात् तेन घटादिना

यद्यतुल्यो न भवेदिति यावत् तदा अयं घटः, अयं च पटः इति पटादिभ्य घटादिर्भिन्नो

न सिध्यते् स्वस्वरूपवत्। भिद्यते च, तस्माद् विशेषात्मकत्वमपि सिद्धम्।[4]

It means, if the intended entity is entirely non-equal to other things, then it ceases to be an entity. For that which is excluded from all other entity, where could there be any other position, except non-existence as in the case of the sky-flower. Thus, in that case, one who wishes the entity to be not equal to the sky-flower must accept the universal entity as the character common to all entities. He says:

सर्वथापि ह्यतुल्यवादभिप्रेतेऽस्य वस्तुनः
वस्त्वन्तरेण नियतं वस्तुत्वमवदीयते॥
वस्तुनो हि निवृत्तस्य कान्या सम्भाविनी गतिः
लक्ष्यते नास्तितानां मुक्त्वा तारापथसरोजवत्॥
तस्मात् खपुष्पातुल्यत्वमिच्छता तस्य वस्तुनः
वस्तुत्वं नाम सामान्यमेष्टाव्यं तत्समानता॥[5]

Further, Śantarakṣita gives another argument in favour of the view that every entity has universality, a general character. If it were not as asserted, then, to what would this fact be due to that the common notion of entity does not appear in connection with the crow's teeth, while it always appears as restricted is due to similarity. Then, the answer is that the same similarity is what we call universality. This same remark also applies to the view that the said restriction is due to a certain capacity in the nature of things. Absolute difference from other entities, therefore, is not possible for any entities because, entities do not differ from each other, on the point of being entities. He asserts:

अन्यथा हि ना सा बुद्धिर्वलिभुग्दशनादिषु
वर्त्तते नियता त्वेषा भावेष्वेवेति कि कृतम्।
सारुप्यानियमोऽयं चेत् सामान्यं च तदेव नः
स्वाभावानुगत शक्तिरनेनैवोपवर्णिता।
अत्यन्त भिन्नता तस्माद् घटते नैव कस्यति्
सर्व च वस्तुरूपेण भिद्यते न परस्मरम्।[6]

Kamalaśila explains it by asserting that if an entity were not equal, to differ from every other entity, then how is it that the common idea of 'being an entity is found to appear only in connection with the jar and such things and not in connection with the crow's teeth and other non-entities? It might be urged that the basis for this is similarity amongst the entities. Then, it becomes established that, same similarity is the universality, the common character. It might be explained that the said comprehensive potency subsists in the jar and other entities only and not in the crow's teeth and such non-entities. Hence, the capacity of the nature of things is what forms the basis of the notion in question. This view is also dispensed with by what has been explained; in other words the answer to this is the same as that to the view regarding similarity; because, the said capacity may be regarded as the required universality[8].

From this discussion it follows that in the form of entities, all things -the jar and the rest,- are not different from one another.

Further, Śāntarakṣita presents the *Jainas'* argument, which provides reason for accepting the difference *i.e.* particular character of things from one another. He quotes:

अवधीकृष्तवस्तुम्यो वैरुप्यरहितं यदि
तद्वस्तु न भवेद् भिन्नं तेभ्योऽभेदस्तदात्मवत्।।
तेभ्यः स्वरूपं भिन्नं हि वैरूप्यमभिधीयते
वैरूप्यं न च भिन्नं चेत्येतदन्योऽन्यबाधितम्।।
तस्माद् भिन्नत्वमर्थानां कथञ्चिदुपगच्छता
वैरूप्यमुपगन्तव्य विशेषात्मकताऽप्यतः।।[9]

It means, if the said entity were entirely devoid of dissimilarity from the other standard entities, then that entity would not be different from these. There would be complete non-difference, as from their own-selves. What is called 'dissimilarity' is only a form different from those. Hence, the idea that 'there is no dissimilarity and yet the thing is different would involve a self-contradiction. Consequently, one has to accept dissimilarity also and hence, also the particular of things.

Kamalaśila makes this point very clear by stating an example that, the cloth and the rest, *i.e.* to which the jar is being compared as being different. If the jar were entirely devoid of dissimilarity to these other things cloth etc., then, there being no difference between them, the jar could not be anything different from those things, as it would be non-different from it, like the form of its own self. For instance, what is called dissimilarity is only that form of the jar, which is different from the cloth and nothing apart from that form. Hence, to say that, there is dissimilarity in the cloth etc. and yet there is no difference from the jar would involve self-contradiction, as difference and dissimilarity are synonymous terms.

पटादिभ्योऽर्थान्तरेभ्यो यदि घटादि वैरूप्येण रहितं भवेत् तदाऽभेदात् तेभ्यः पटादिभ्यस्तद् घटादि भिन्नं न भवेद्। आत्मस्वरूपवदभिन्नत्वप्रसङ्गात। तथा हि तेभ्यः पटादिभ्यो यद्विभिन्नं स्वरूपं घटादिनां तदेव खुल वैरूप्यमुच्यते, नान्यत्। ततश्च सत्यपि वैरूप्ये पटादिनां न च घटादिभ्यो भेदोऽस्ति इति स्ववचन व्याहितः, भेदवैरूप्ययोः पर्यायत्वात्।[10]

Thus, having established the fact that every entity has two fold characteristics viz. the general and the particular, the *Jainas* have shown that these two aspects serve as the basis of usage.

वस्त्वेकात्मकमेवेदमनेकाकारमिष्यते
ते चानुवृत्तिव्यावृति बुद्धिग्राह्यतया स्थितिः॥
आद्या एतेऽनुवृत्तिव्यावृत्ति सामान्यमिति कीर्तिताः
विशेषास्त्वभिधीयन्ते व्यावृत्तत्वात् ततोऽपरे॥[11]

It means, the entity itself is only one in essence, but is regarded as having several aspects. And these aspects are there in the form of being apprehended by inclusive and exclusive cognition. The former one being inclusive is spoken of, as commons *i.e.* universal or general, while the latter, being exclusive are called particular.

Kamalaśila makes it very clear by stating that, the real truth of the matter is as follows: like the gleaming sapphire, every entity, while being one, has several aspects. Of these aspects, some are apprehended by inclusive notions and others by exclusive notions. Those, that are apprehended by exclusive notions are exclusive and hence said to be particular. The inclusive notion appears in the one non-distinctive form of entity, while the exclusive notion appears in the distinct form 'this is jar not cloth'. Thus, he says:

अयमत्र परमार्थः मेचकरत्नवदेकमेव वस्त्वनेकाकारम्, ते चाकाराः केचिदनुवृत्तिबुद्धिग्राह्यः, केचिद् व्यावृत्तिबुद्धिग्राह्याः। तत्र ये अनुवृत्तिबुद्धिग्राह्याः, तेऽनुवृत्तया 'सामान्यम्' इति कीर्त्यन्ते। ये तु ततोऽपरे व्यावृत्तिबुद्धिग्राह्याः, ते व्यावृत्तत्वाद् विशेषाः इति कल्प्यन्ते। तत्रानुवृत्तिबुद्धि 'भावो भावः' इत्याद्यभेदाकारा व्यावृत्तिबुद्धि–'घटोऽयं' न पट इत्येवमादिभेदाकारा।[12]

After presenting the arguments of the *Jaina* philosophers regarding the nature of reality, Śāntarakṣita has refuted the aforesaid arguments by finding faults in such assertions and arguments. First of all, Śāntarakṣita says if the general and the particular were of the nature of each other, commingling and confusion would be inevitable. Hence, it cannot be possible that every entity has two aspects. If they are not of the nature of each other, then they are diverse two distinct things, and hence, it does not follow that there are two aspects of a single entity. Thus, he says:

परस्परस्भावत्वे स्यात् सामान्य विशेषयोः
साङ्कर्यं तत्वतो नेदं द्वैरूप्यमुपपद्यते॥
परस्परास्भावत्वेऽप्यनयोरनुषज्यते
नान्यत्वमेवम्भावेऽपि द्वैरूप्यं नोपद्यते॥[13]

Kamalaśila argues that, there are two alternatives possible viz. (1) the 'general' is the same as the 'particular' (2) the 'general' is something different from the 'particular'; this would imply that no distinction between universal and particular could be maintained. In the former case, the particular and the general being of the nature of one another or one and the same, there would be commingling and confusion, the result of which would be that it could not be discerned that 'this is general and that is particular'. This amounts to the fact that, there cannot be two aspects of the same entity[14].

If in order to avoid the confusion, the later alternative is accepted even then, the two being regarded, as not of the nature of each other, there would be diversity or difference of nature between the general and the particular. Thus, there would be no confusion between the two only if the two were entirely different. And in that case the universal and the particular would be two different independent things and not two aspects of one thing[15].

It may be argued that even when there has come about a difference in the nature of general and the particular, the entity that exists in the form of general and the particular, is one and the same[16]. This however will be a contradiction. For instance, if the general and the particular are regarded as non-different and one and the same thing, how could there be any difference in the nature of those two? Being non-different from one and the same thing, they must be non-different from one another, like the nature of any single entity. When, however the difference between the nature of the general and that of the particular is accepted there could not be non-different between those two. Because, being non-different what is meant is one would have to be regarded as two, like the form of the general and the form of the particular. He says:

यदि नाम सामान्यविशेषयोः परस्परं स्वभावविवेको जातः तथापि सामान्य विशेषात्मकं वस्त्वभिन्नमेवेति? तदेतत्तु परस्पर विरुद्धम्। तथा हि एकस्माद्वस्तुनः सामान्यविशेषयोरभेदेऽङ्िगक्रियमाणे कथमनयोः परस्परं स्वभावविवेकः सिध्येत्ः एकस्मादभेद तयोरप्यभेदप्रसङ्गाद्, एकवस्तुस्वभाववत्। सामान्य- विशेषयोश्च परस्परं स्वभाव विवेकेऽङ्गीक्रियमाणे ताभ्यामभिन्नमेकं वस्तु न सिध्येत्ः

ताभ्याभिन्नत्वात् तस्याप्येकत्वेनाभिमतस्य द्वित्वप्रसङ्गात् सामान्यविशेषे-स्वरूपवत्। तस्माद् एकमुभयात्मकम् इति परस्परव्याहतमेतत्।[17]

Then, Śāntarakṣita presents the arguments of the *Digambara Jaina* philosophers particularly of Sumati against the aforesaid arguments of the Buddhist.

According to Sumati, though the entity may be of one nature only, yet it can have different properties. There could be no incongruity in the presence of different states in one and the same thing, which is found, for example, in the case of the potencies of the active agencies. Nor can there be any incongruity in what is actually seen. And it is noticed that even though the general and the particular are aspects of one and the same object, yet, in actual practical life there is difference between them. He says:

सत्यप्येकस्भावत्वे धर्मभेदोऽत्र सिध्यति
भेदसंस्थाऽनिरोधश्च यथा कारकशक्तिषु॥
न दृष्टेऽनुपपन्नं च तत्सामान्यविशेषयोः
ऐकात्म्येऽपीक्ष्यते भेदलोकयात्रानुवर्त्तनम्॥[18]

Sumati has given some explanation in connection with the objection against the *Jaina* doctrines, namely 'if the general and the particular were not regarded as different, there would be confusion'. This does not affect the case at all. Though by reason of their being of the same nature, there can be difference in their properties, as is found to be the case with the potencies of active agencies. For instance, there are such expressions as *'balāhako vidvotote'* the cloud flashes, where the cloud appears as the active agent, and *balāhakādviyotate* 'flashes from the clouds, where the cloud appears as the source. In such cases we find the potencies of the active agencies varying through the diversity of their effects. Even though they being all of the nature of 'substance' there is a certain amount of confusion. If this were not admitted, that would be quite contrary to common experience as well as scientific or grammatical principles. He says:

तत्सामन्यविशेषयोः परस्परस्वभाव विरहानभ्युपगमे संकीर्णता प्राप्नोति? नैष दोषः, तयोरेकस्वभावतया सत्यामपि संकीर्णतायां धर्मभेदः प्रसिध्यति,

कारकशक्तिवत्। तथा हि बलाहको विद्योतते, बलाहकाद् विद्योतते इत्यादिकार्य-भेदाद् विद्यमानात्मानः कारणशक्तयः समुपलभ्यन्ते द्रव्यस्वभावव्यतिरिक्ततया संकीर्णतायामपि सत्यां तदनभ्युपगमे लोकशास्त्रविरोधोऽवस्यम्भावी।[19]

Further, he says that there can be non-incongruity urged against what is actually seen. For instance, in the case of general and particular, though they are aspects of one and the same thing, and are quite distinct and never confounded, yet, all practical business is actually found to be carried on, on the basis of their difference. And this is carried on though the entity is one only embracing both the aspects. The argument may be formulated thus: when a thing is treated as diverse, it is on the basis of the diversity of its properties, as in the case of the potencies of active agencies. The idea of the general and the particular is being aspects of one and the same thing involves treatment of the thing as diverse. This is the reason based on the nature of thing.

सामान्यविशेषयोरेकवस्तुस्वभावत्वेऽप्यसंकीर्णताया भेदेन लोकयात्रानुव-र्तनमुपलभ्यत एवं। एकस्य वस्तुनो यो भेदव्यवहारः स धर्मभेदनिबन्धनः, यथा कारकशक्तिषु। भेदव्यवहारश्चयमेकस्मिन् सामान्यविशेषलक्षण इति स्वभाव हेतु।[20]

To this argument of Sumati, Śāntarakṣita provides some rejoined arguments to answer it. He says "in fact if the thing has only one form, it cannot have diverse properties. A diversity that is not a creation of fancy is what is called plurality".

ननु सत्येकरूपत्वे धर्मभेद न सिध्यति
अकल्पितो विभेदो हि नानात्वमभिधीयते।।[21]

Kamalaśila clearly refuted the view or the clarification of Sumati, by stating that 'this shows the reason adduced by the *Jaina* is contradictory, in as much as it proves the contrary of what is intended to be proved. For instance, what the *Jaina* intends to prove is real diversity of properties, but no such diversity of properties, which is not a creation of fancy, is proved by the reason adduced. As 'one-ness' of the thing itself is admitted and what is one entity cannot be compatible with diversity, as diversity is what is called plurality. And how can a thing that is plural be one or vice versa? He says:

अनेन हेतोर्विरुद्धतामाह, इष्टविपरीतसाधनात्। तथा हि पारमार्थिको धर्मभेदोऽत्र वादिनः साधयितुमिष्टः। स चाकल्पितो धर्मभेदो न सिध्यति। वस्तुन एकत्वाभ्युपगमात्, तस्य चैकस्य वस्तुनो भेदविरोधात् यतो भेद इतिनानात्वमभिधीयते, यच्च नाना तत् कथमेकं स्यात् [22]

Śāntarakṣita presents the corroborative instance which has been cited by the *Jaina* philosophers. 'Devoid of the probandum and the probans also is one that is concomitant with the contrary of the probandum. He says: as regards the pretences, their diversity is merely a creation of the 'speaker's desire to speak'. Here also no diversity can be reasonable in what is essentially one.

नानात्मत्वं शक्तिनां विवक्षामात्रनिर्मितम्
एकवस्त्वात्मकत्वे हि न भेदोऽत्रपि युक्तिमान।[23]

Even though diversity is what is called plurality, why should such real plurality of a single entity be incompatible by virtue of which the reason is said to be contradictory, as proving the contrary of the desired conclusion.

To this Śāntarakṣita provides an answer that things are said to be one when it is said 'this is that' whereas they are said to be diverse when it is said 'this is not that'. Being that and not being that, thus, being mutually contradictory, cannot, in any way be attributed to any one entity. He maintains:

एकमित्युच्यते तद्धि यत् तदेवेति गीयते
नानात्मकं तु तन्नाम न तद् भवति यत् पुनः।
तद्भावश्चाप्यतद्भावः परस्परविरोधतः
एक वस्तूनि नैवायं कथञ्चिदवकल्प्यते।[24]

When it is stated categorically that 'this is that', then the things are said to be one, as in the case of consciousness and spirit. On the other hand, when the identity between things is denied, they are said to be diverse, different, as in the case of matter and consciousness. As it is impossible for both affirmation and denial to pertain to any one thing, there is clear contradiction between unity and plurality, which are based respectively upon the said identity and difference. Hence, any diversity of properties of a single entity can only be a creation of fancy[25]. To give an answer to the argument that 'there may not be contradiction between identity and difference *i.e.* affirmation and denial'. Śāntarakṣita argues:

विधानप्रतिषधौ हि परस्परविरोधिनौ
शक्यावेकत्र नो कर्तुं केनचित् स्वस्थचेतसा।।[26]

It means: affirmation and denial are mutually contradictory, and they cannot be made by any sensible person, with regard to one and the same thing. It might be urged that what is the basis of the assumption of the diversity of properties? There must be distinct basis for it. Otherwise there would be confusion among things.Hence it follows that which would be that distinct basis would be the real 'diversity of properties' for us[27]. Answering this, he remarks:

सजातीयविजातीयानेकव्यावृत्तवस्तुनः
ततस्ततः परावृत्तेधर्मभेदस्तु कथ्यते
एकस्यापि ततो युक्ता कल्पितासङ्ख्यरूपता
वास्तवं नैकभावस्य द्वैरूप्यमपि सङ्गतम्।।[28]

It means that when an entity excluded from several like and unlike objects, is differentiated from this and that is called the diversity of properties. In this way even a single thing may be assumed to have innumerable diverse forms. But in reality, no single thing can reasonably have two forms.

Further, it can be argued that, the argument urged by Buddhist is inclusive, in view of entities like *Narasimha* and others. Though these beings are of a single nature, yet the real presence of the dual character *i.e.* half man and half lion is not found to be incompatible. To answer this he says:

नरसिंहादयो ये हि द्वैरूप्येणोपवर्णिताः
तेषामपि द्विरूपत्वं भाविकं नैव विद्यते।।

स ह्यनेकाणुसन्दोहस्वभावो नैकरूपवान्
यच्चित्रं तदेकं हि नानाजातीयरत्नवत्॥
एक्ये स्यान्न द्विरूपत्वान्ननाकारावभासनम्
मक्षिकापदमात्रेपि पिहितेऽनावृतिश्च न॥[29]

It means, such entities as *Narasimha* and others, which has been described, as having dual characters is not tenable. In that case also the dual character is not real. As a matter of fact, *Narasimha* is of the nature of an aggregate of many atoms and is not endowed with any one uniform form. What is variegated cannot be one as is found in the case of the collection of several kinds of gems. If there were one form, there could not be a dual character and the consequent appearance of several shapes. And even if the smallest part of the body that could be covered by the leg of a fly were hidden, the body could not be said to be non-hidden.

Kamalaśila makes this point further clear by stating that, what is variegated cannot be one, for instance a collection of several kinds of gems. And *Narasimha* has a variegated form, so that the *Jaina* reasoning involves an idea contrary to the nature of things.

The fact that 'if it were one, it could not have a dual character and consequently there would be appearance of several forms', provides an argument against the said unity. This argument being grounded on the idea of diversity is based entirely upon the appearance of diverse forms.

If any one part of the body were hidden, the whole might become hidden under the *Jaina's* idea. This provides another argument against the conclusion of the *Jainas*. Because it cannot be right that one and the same thing should have the contradictory character of being hidden and being non-hidden at one and the same time. He asserts:

यच्चित्रं न तदेकम् यथा नानाजातीय रत्नसमूहः। चित्रश्च नरसिंह इति स्वभावविरुद्धोपलम्भः व्यापकविरुद्धस्य वा। एक्ये सति द्विरूपत्वनिमित्तनाना-कारावभासानुपपतित्तर्बन्धकं प्रमाणम्। प्रतिभासभेदनिबन्धनत्वाद् भेदव्यव-

स्थायाः। एकदेशावरणे सर्वावरणप्रसङ्गश्च बाधकं प्रमाणम्। न ह्येकस्यावृत्ततत्वमनावृतत्वं चेति युगपद्विरुद्धधर्मसंसर्गो युक्तः।[30]

Further, Śāntarakṣita presents another argument from the Jaina point of view regarding the same issue that if *Narasimha* is only one and aggregate of many atoms, then how is it that there is an idea regarding him as being a single entity with a dual character?

To this Śāntarakṣita states thus:

नृसिंहभागानुस्यूतप्रत्यभिज्ञानहेतवः
ते चाणवः प्रकृत्यैव विशिष्टप्रत्योद्भवात्।।
एतेनेव प्रकारेण चित्ररत्नादयो गताः
नानात्मना हि वैचित्र्यमेकत्वेन विरुध्यते।।[31]

It means that by their very nature, the said atoms are the basis of the recognition that envisages the salient features of the man and the lion, as is clear from the fact of its arising from a particular idea. In the same way the variegated gems and other cases are answer to dispose off. The variegated character, based upon the presence of several forms, is certainly incompatible with unity.

Kamalaśila asserts that, the recognition that envisages the features of the body of the man and the lion in the body of *Narasimha* is that of the atoms composing those features. What then would be the use of assuming the composite whole body?

And what is the nature of atoms? The answer to this is that it proceeds from a particular cause. The particular idea in this case is in the shape of the past deed leading up to the particular state of existence and also the factors and other parts of the body peculiar to the particular animal species. The same idea can be applicable to refute the example namely the "glittering gems" as well.

नृसिंहयोर्ये भागास्तैरनुस्यूतम्–निर्भासीकृतं यत् प्रत्यभिज्ञानं तत्तथोक्तम्। एवम्भूतस्य प्रत्यभिज्ञानस्य यदा प्रकृत्यैव त एवाणवे हेतवो भवन्ति, तदा किमपरमवयविना कल्पितेन। सा च तादृशी प्रकृतिः कुतस्तेषामिति चेद्?

आह-विशिष्टप्रत्ययोद्भवात्-विशिष्टात् करणादुत्पतेः। तत्र विशिष्टः प्रत्ययो गतिविशेषसंवर्त्तनीयं कर्म, स्वजातिसमुद्भूतः कललादिश्च। अनेनैव नरसिंहविचारेण मेचकरत्नादयो गताः-व्याख्याताः।[32]

Further, Śāntarakṣita provides an answer to the *Jaina* argument which we have already quoted namely "in the form of entities all things are not different from one another. Śāntarakṣita says:

अर्थक्रियासमर्थत्वं वस्तुत्वमभिधीयते
यदि तस्यानुगामित्वं सर्वं स्यात् सर्वकार्यकृत्॥
एकोऽपि जनकस्तस्य भावः सामर्थ्ययोगतः
तच्चाविशिष्टमन्यस्मिन्नित्यनुत्पादकः कथम्॥
नीलाद्येव च वस्तुत्वमनुगामि यदीष्यते
सितपीताद्यपि प्राप्तं नीलसंसाध्यकार्यकृत्॥
एकमेव ततो जातं द्वितीयात्मविवर्जितम्
सर्वविश्वमतो नैकमनेकाकारमसित वः॥
तदेव चेन्न वस्तुत्वं कणाशिमतसत्ववत्
नैकस्यानेकरूपत्वमेव वः स्याद् विभेदतः॥
विरुद्धधर्मसङ्गश्च वस्तूनां भेदलक्षणम्
कथञ्चिदन्यथेष्टोऽपि न भेदो नीलपीतयोः॥
अनुगाम्यन्यथाभावात् स च सामान्यभेदयोः
विद्यते तत कथं नास्ति तयोर्भेदः परिस्फुटम्॥[33]

It means being an entity is said to consist in the capacity for successful action. If this were all pervasive, then every thing would be capable of doing everything. Generally, one thing is held to be productive of another, only by reason of the presence in it, of the capacity for that action. If then that capacity is equally present in another thing or every thing, why should not this be productive of the same? If the 'blue' and other objects themselves were held to constitute the all-embracing character of entity, then the white and yellow things also would do what is done by the blue one. And in that case, the whole universe would become a single entity, devoid of a second.

And thus, it would not be true that a single thing has several aspects. If the blue etc., themselves do not constitute entity, and this is like the 'being' *'sattva'* posited by Kanada, then it cannot be as the Jainas hold that one thing cannot have several aspects as there would be clear difference. Further, what constitutes difference among things is the presence of contrary properties and no other kind of difference is held to lie between blue and yellow. The same condition is present between the general and the particular; because, while the former is inclusive the later is other wise. Why then should not difference be admitted as clearly lying between them?

Kamalaśila clearly refuted this argument of the *Jaina* by stating thus:

अर्थक्रियाकरि यद्रूपं तद् वस्तुत्वमुच्यते, नान्यत्। तच्चेत सर्वत्रानुगामि सर्व सर्वार्थक्रियाकारि प्राप्नोति। तेनैव हि रूपेण सर्वे जनका इष्यन्ते। तस्य च सर्वत्राविशिष्टत्वादिति यत्किञ्चित् यतः कुतश्चिदुत्पद्येत। किञ्च-यदेतन्नीलपीतादि, तदेव किं वस्तुत्वम् आहोस्विदन्यत्? यदि तदेव, तदा तस्यानुगामित्वात् सितपीतद्यपि नीलसाध्ववस्त्ररञ्जनाद्यर्थक्रियाकारि प्राप्नोति। अपि च द्वितीयस्य स्वभावस्याभावात् एकस्यैव च भावे सर्व जगदेकमेव वस्तुजातमिति 'एकमनेकाकारम्' इति प्रतिज्ञानार्थहानिः स्यात्। अथान्यदेव वस्तुत्वं नीलादिभ्यः कणादाभिमतस्त्ववत् यथा कणादस्य अभिमतं सत्ताख्यं व्यतिरिक्तं वस्तुत्वं नामेति, एवमपि सुतरामेकस्यानेकत्वमयुक्तम् एकान्तेनैव भेदात्। किञ्च यौ विरुद्धधर्मसंसर्गिणौ तौ भिन्नौ, यथा शीतोष्णौ। विरुद्धधर्मसंसर्गश्च सामान्यविशेषयोर्विद्यते, अनुगाम्यन्यथाभावादिति स्पष्ट एव तयोर्भेदः। अन्यथाभावः अननुगामित्वम्। यदि च विरुद्धधर्मसंसर्गेऽपि भेदो नेष्यते, तदा नीलपीतोर्योऽप्ययं कथञ्चिदविशेषरूपेण भेद इष्टः स न स्यात् बुद्धिर्भेदान्न चैकत्वं रूपादीनां प्रसज्यते इति वचनात् कुमारिलेन नीलादीनां भेदस्योपवर्णितत्वात्।[34]

The whole arguments are based on the following assumptions. The entity is said to be that which is capable of effective action and nothing else. If this capacity were present in all things, then every thing would be capable of doing every thing. It is only in this sense that things are held to be productive. This capacity then being equally present in all cases, every thing might be produced out of anything[35].

Further, is the 'entity' the same as the blue, the yellow and other things? Or is it something different? If it is the same, then, as it would be all-pervasive, even the white, the yellow, could bring about the colouring in the cloth that is brought about by blue. Then again, there being no other character or nature possible, the entire universe would become a single conglomeration of things and this would upset the proposition that a single entity has several aspects. If on the other hand, the 'entity' is something different from the blue etc. like the 'Being' posited by Kaṇāda, *i.e.* just as Kaṇāda has postulated the 'entity' called Being, as something different from the particular things, then it becomes all the more unreasonable to attribute plurality to any single entity, and in that case there would be clear and absolute different[36].

Then again, any two things are different only when they have contrary properties, e.g. hot and cold. The general and the particular are found to have contrary properties, because while the former is inclusive, the latter is otherwise, *i.e.* non-inclusive or exclusive. If even on the presence of contrary properties, difference were not admitted, then there would be no difference even between the blue and the yellow, which is admitted in some way, by the other party. Kumārila himself has declared in *Ślokavārtika* that as their cognitions are different, colour etc. cannot be one and the same in the context, where it has been declared that there is difference among the blue and other things[37].

In this context Śāntarakṣita presents the argument of Kumārila Bhaṭṭa against the Buddhist philosophers and finally has refuted his view by showing contradiction in it.

Then, Śāntarakṣita gives an argument to refute the view of Jainism, which we have already pointed out. That which has been excluded from 'entity' where could there be any other position *i.e.* वस्तुनो हि निवृत्तस्य काऽन्या सम्भाविनी गतिः।[38]

To this argument he says:

एकस्माद् वस्तुनोऽन्यत्वे तादात्म्यविकलं भवेत्
नाकाशपुष्पसङ्काशं तद्ध्यप्यर्थक्रियाक्षमम्।।[39]

If a certain thing were excluded from one 'entity' it would be devoid of sameness only with that entity. It would not become fictitious like the sky flower, as it would still be capable of one efficient action. Kamalaśila makes it clear by asserting that if what is cited as the reason is exclusion of all entities and similarity to the 'sky-flower' is meant to be proved by it, then the reason is 'inadmissible'; because, the exclusion of jar from all entities cannot be admitted. All that can be admitted is that it is excluded or differentiated from things other than itself[40].

If on the other hand, the reason meant to be adduced is exclusion from something, then it is inconclusive. For instance, the jar, excluded or differentiated from the cloth and other things, could be recognized as absolutely devoid of essence *i.e.* existence as even as thus, excluded, it would be capable of efficient action[41]. He says:

यदि हि वस्तुमात्रात् परावृत्तिर्हेतुत्वेन क्रियते खपुष्प विशेषत्वे साध्ये तदा हेतुरसिद्धि।

न हि घटस्य वस्तुमात्रात् व्यावृति सिद्धाः किं तर्हि? स्वस्वभावामुक्तवाऽन्यस्माद् वस्तुविशेषात्। अथ वस्तुविंशेषाद् व्यावृत्तिर्हेतुत्वेनोपादीयते, तदाऽनैकान्तिाको हेतुः।

तथा हि एकस्माद् घटादेर्वस्तुनो व्यावृतं घटादिकं वस्तु यदि पर तादात्म्यविकलं सिध्यत् न तु सर्वथा निःस्वभावम्, तस्याप्यर्थिक्रियाकारित्वात्।[42]

As a matter of fact, the capable (potent) form of one entity does not reside in other entities. Because the effect produced and the form of the apprehension are found to be different and so forth. This has been explained before, that a certain entity is not the same as the other, this alone can follow from the exclusion or differentiation there from, and not the fact of its being a non-entity devoid of all properties. Śāntarakṣita says:

शक्तं रूपं न चैकस्य वस्तुष्वन्येषु वर्त्तते

कार्योपलम्भनिर्भासभेदादेरिति वर्णितम्।
अतद्वस्त्वात्मकत्वं तु तदश्लेषेण युज्यते
नाविशेषमवस्तुत्व वस्तुलक्षणभावतः।।[43]

If the character of 'entity', consisting of capacity for effective action, were something embracing all entities collectively, then alone could be the thing differentiated from others be said to be featureless or non-existent, the 'entity' being something that is characterized by capacity for effective action. As a matter of fact however, the capable or potent form of one entity, the blue for instance, cannot subsist in other things like the white and the rest[44].

It may be asked: why can't it subsist in other things? Because, the effect produced is different and the form of apprehension or idea is different. For these reasons, all that non-contact or differentiation from another entity can be proved in only that 'the entity in question is not the same as this latter. It cannot prove it to be devoid of properties, a mere- entity, because, the capacity for effective action, which constitutes the essence of 'entity' present in it[45].

Further, Śāntarakṣita presents another argument of the *Jainas* in this context and finally refuted it. If there is absolute difference among entities, how can there be such all-embracing notions as 'this is entity', 'this is an entity' with regard to all things? How too can there be any difference between the entity and the sky-flower etc. if, there were no similarities [46]? To this Śāntarakṣita has given the following answer:

तदप्यर्थक्रियायोग्यमिति वस्त्विति कल्पने
असमर्थपरावृत्तिः सादृश्यं तद्विकल्पितम्।।
ततश्चात्यन्तभेदेऽपि तुल्याताऽस्ति विकल्पिता
भावो भावान्तरैस्तुल्यः खपुष्पात् तद्विशिष्यते।[47]

It means, the conception being there that 'that also is capable of effective action'. There would be this idea that 'it is an entity, thus, would be subjective similarity consisting in differentiation from what is incapable. Thus, even though there is absolute difference, there is a subjective similarity. And thus, an entity being equal to other entities, becomes distinguished from the sky-flower.

Again, Śāntarakṣita presents the arguments of Sumati, against the Buddhist philosophy and finally refuted his view by showing fault in it. He first framed the objection raised by Sumati as follows:

> ननु येनात्मना वस्तु समानापरावस्तुनः
> व्यावृत्तं तत्सजातीयैस्तेनैव सदृशं यदि॥
> विज्ञायेत विजातीयैरपि तुल्यतया तदा
> तस्यात्मनोऽविशिष्टत्वान्न च तज्ज्ञायते तथा॥
> सजातीयासमानोऽपि तस्माद् येन भवत्ययम्
> आत्मना तत्समानश्च तयोर्भेदः स्भावयोः॥[48]

Kamalaśila makes it clear by asserting that, that form in which a certain thing is differentiated from homogeneous and heterogeneous things, if in the same form, it were similar to the homogeneous things, then it should be recognized as similar to the heterogeneous things also as the form would be the same in both cases. And yet as a matter of fact, it is not so recognized. Hence, it follows that form in which it is similar to these things *i.e.* between these two forms there must be difference. It might be asked 'when it is homogeneous to them, how can it be dissimilar? If it is dissimilar to them, how can it be homogeneous to them? These two are contradictory. This however does not affect our position because the *Jainas* regard everything as having two aspects, the general and the particular. Hence, in the general aspect all things are said to be 'homogeneous' to that thing, while in its 'particular' aspect, it is held to be 'heterogeneous'. And in this latter sense, it is said to be dissimilar. So, the objection urged does not affect the position. He says:

येनात्मना सजातीयविजातीयभ्यां व्यावृत्तं वस्तु तेनैवात्मना तद्वस्तुयदि सजातीयैः सदृशं भवेत् तदा विजातीयैरपि तुल्यतया विज्ञायेत, तस्यान्मनोऽविशिष्टत्वात्। न च ज्ञायते, तस्माद्येन स्वभावेन सजातीयासमानोऽपि भवति, येन च स्वभावेन तत्सदृशो भवति। तयोः स्वभावयोर्भेदोऽभि-

वाञ्छितव्यः। ननु स यदि सजातीय कथं तेनासमानो भवति, अथ तेनासमानो भवति कथं सजातीयः इति परस्परव्याहतमेतत्? नैष दोषः यतः परेण सर्वमेव वस्तु सामान्यविशेषात्मकमिष्टम्, तस्माद वस्तुत्वादिना सामान्येन सर्वमेव सजातीयमित्युच्यते, विशेषरूपेण तदेव विजातीयमिष्टमिति, तदपेक्षया पुनरसमान इत्यभिधीयत इत्यदोषः[49]

To answer it Śāntarakṣita says that, it is in that same form that it is understood to be similar, because the cause of understanding is present in the shape of being the cause of one and the same conception, as differentiating these from other things. He answers:

तेनैवासौ स्वभावेन समान इति गम्यते
एक प्रत्यवमर्शस्य हेतुन्वेनान्यभेदतः।[50]

It means, it is the same forms that it is said to be similar, because they form the basis of the same conception. What is meant is that those that do not form the basis of the same conception are treated as similar, while those that so serve as that basis are regarded as similar[51].

Then Sumati argued: why do not all things become the basis of the same conception, the difference being equally present in all?

To this Śāntarakṣita says that it is only certain thing that can serve as the basis of one and the same conception. The restriction being due to the capacity of the form of things, even where there is difference, as is found in the case of the sense-organs and the *amṛtā* and the like. He asserts:

एकप्रत्ययवमर्शस्य हेतवः केचिदेव हि
समर्थरूपनियमाद् भेदऽप्यक्षामृतादिवत्।[52]

Śāntarakṣita makes this point clear by asserting that no question can be raised regarding the nature of things, such as, 'why should fire and not water burn or be hot? All that can be reasonably asked is: as to what is this nature due? For, if the nature of things were not due to any cause, there could be no restriction, which could lead to incongruities. Hence, it should be said that, it is due to its own cause. But then the question would be, to what is that due? And so on and on it would go on to a beginningless series of causes. He then clarified with the example namely, *akṣa* and *amṛtā*. Here *akṣa* means sense organ, *amṛtā* means *guduchi*. It means that, it is only the *guduchi* and other herbs that have the capacity to allay fever and other diseases not other things. And it is the sense organs, the object, the light and attention that have the capacity to produce particular cognition. In the same way, it is only certain things to which belongs the capacity to bring about a single conception. He writes:

न हि स्वभावाः पर्यनुयोमर्हन्ति कस्मादग्निर्दहत्युष्णो वा नोदकमिति। एवं तु युक्तं वक्तुंम्-कुतोऽस्यायं स्वभाव इति। निर्हेतुकत्वे त्वेनपेक्षस्य नियमायोगेनाति-प्रसङ्गात्॥ तस्मात्सवहेतोरिति वक्तव्यम्, तस्यापि कुत इत्यनादिहेतुपरम्परा। अक्षम्-इन्द्रियम्, अमृताः गुडूची। यथा गुडूच्यादीनामेव ज्वरादिशमेनशक्तिः, नान्येषाम्; इन्द्रियविषयालोकमनस्कारादीनां च विशिष्टज्ञानोत्पादने, तथैकप्रत्यवमर्शेऽपि केषाञ्चिदेव शक्तिनियम इति।[53]

Śāntarakṣita shows the Jaina objection that the corroborative instance cited by the Buddhist cannot be admitted. He says: how can the eye be productive of the cognition of the blue and others, if it is held to have that form alone which is differentiated from the blue and others? In fact, just as the ear is not regarded as productive of the cognition of blue etc. on account of its being different from the blue etc. which are productive of the cognition of blue etc, so also the eye should not be regarded as the cause of that cognition. How could any other thing, which is different from the productive cause, be productive of it? From all this follows the conclusion that there must be inclusiveness also among things. He observes:

ननु नीलादिविज्ञानजननं लोचनं कथम्
व्यावृत्तरूपभागेव नीलादिभ्यो यदीष्यते॥
नीलादि ज्ञानजनकानीलादेर्भेदवद् यथा
श्रोत्र च तस्य जनकं तथा चक्षुरपीष्यताम्॥

जनकाद्धि परावृत्तः कोऽपर जनको भवेत्
भावस्तस्मात् पदार्थानामन्वयोऽपीति निश्चय।। [54]

If the eye were held to be that which has a form exclusive of the blue etc. and not any, that is inclusive. This is what is meant by the particle *'eva'* alone. In that case the eye cannot be the cause of the perception of the blue etc. Because, it has been differentiated or excluded from what is productive of that perception. When a thing has been excluded from the cause of a certain thing, it cannot be cause of that thing. For example, the ear, which is differentiated from the blue etc., which is the cause of the perception of the blue etc., is not the cause of the perception of the blue etc. The eye is also differentiated from the blue etc., which is the cause of the perception of blue etc. Hence, there is the possibility of an apprehension contrary to a universal truth.

As a matter of fact, however, it is not so. *The eye is not non-productive* of the perception of blue etc. Hence, the truth should be otherwise than this, which is when one thing is productive of another, it cannot be excluded from the nature of being so productive. For example, the blue, which is the productive of the perception of blue, cannot be excluded from its own nature, and the eye actually productive of the perception of the blue etc. This is a reason based upon the nature of things.

From all these, it follows that there is inclusiveness among things. Thus, through the contrary of the reductio-ad-absurdum, it has been shown that the example cited is not admissible. He says:

रूपभागेव लोचनमिप्यते, नानुवृत्तिभागित्वभागित्यवधारणेनाह। तदा नीलादिविज्ञानजनक लोचनं न प्राप्नोति, तज्जनकस्वभावात् परावृत्तत्वात्। योहि यज्जनकस्वभावात् परावृत्तः स तज्जनको न भवति। यथा नीलादिज्ञानजनकानीलादेर्व्यावृत्तं चक्षुरिति व्यापकविरुद्धडोपलब्धिाप्रसङ्ग। न चैवं भवति, तस्माद्विपर्ययः। योहि यज्जनकः स तज्जनकास्वभावापरावृत्तः। यथा नीलज्ञानजनकं नीलं स्वस्मात्। नीलज्ञानजनकं च चक्षुरिति स्वभावहेतु। तस्माद् अस्ति भावनामन्वयः इति प्रसङ्गविपर्ययेण दृष्टन्तासिद्धिमाह। [55]

It may be further argued that[1] the thing could be excluded from the other things and yet to be productive of the cognition, so that the reductio-ad-absurdum is inclusive.

To this argument an answer is given by Śāntarakṣita from the point of view of *Jainas*. If it were not as above then, differentiation being the same in both cases why isn't the ear also regarded as productive of the cognition of blue etc. just like the eye, which is also different from the colours. He writes:

अन्यथा निर्विशिष्टत्वाद् भेदेन श्रवणाद्यपि
जनकं तस्य किं नेष्टं चक्षु रूपादिभेदवत्।[56]

The possibility of the ear being regarded as the cause of the cognition of blue etc., is a proof of the contrary of the conclusion arrived by the Buddhist. But the difference is the same in both the cases. The difference between the eye and the blue is the same as the difference between the ears and blue *i.e.* the ear is different from the blue etc. as the eye is[57].

To this argument of the opponent Śāntarakṣita further argued: The exclusion *i.e.* differentiation of the eye is not admitted, without qualification, because the nature of the eye etc. is also regarded as the cause. And it is not possible for anything to be excluded from its own nature. If there were exclusion of a thing from its own nature, the thing would become devoid of all character. When exclusion'is spoken of, what is meant is exclusion from another cause. Thus, what is productive of the cognition is described precisely as it exists. In fact all cognitions proceed from their own specific causes. If on the ground of their being of the same nature, they were regarded as a single productive cause, then as the said nature itself is there as the cause, what would be the use of other auxiliaries? If it were held that on account of defects in other particulars the one nature is not productive of the cognition, then the answer is that, those causes are incapable of bringing about the cognition in question, by reason of difference. If there were no difference, how could they be defective, just as, even when there is difference as among particular things, everything is not the cause of every other thing. In the same way even though there would be no difference in particular, yet there would be restriction of only some causes bringing about some effects. Even when there is difference it is only a certain thing that would be productive of the particular effect by reason of its nature. In the case of inclusiveness, how could one thing be productive and non-productive of the same one thing? If there is difference, in this case also the difference may be there. But is that difference from that thing only? There can be no difference apart from the 'inclusive' productive cause. And this is non-productive. In fact, that alone is a real entity, which is capable of effective action. And this entity is non-inclusive. And what is inclusive, that is not produced. In fact, difference and non-difference cannot be imaginary *i.e.* real only in relation to that form or nature with reference to which the man has recourse to activate. Otherwise the difference is there by its very nature and the general character is also there due to exclusion. The thing itself is not inclusive *i.e.* comprehensive. As in that case there must be incongruous activities. Thus he says:

व्यावृत्तिश्चक्षुरादीनां न सिद्धाजनकादियम्
अविशेषण यत् तेषामात्मापि जनको मतः॥
स्वभावान्न च भावानां व्यावृत्तिरूपपद्यते
स्वभावाद्धि परावृत्तौः नैःस्वाभाव्यं प्रसज्येत॥
अन्यस्माज्जनकात् तेषां व्यावृत्तिरूपवर्ण्यते
अतज्जनकरूपत्वं वाच्यं तच्चेष्टमेव नः॥
न ह्यप्युत्पादकं तस्य स्वरूपेणैव वर्ण्यते
नियतास्तत्र ते सर्वे स्वहेतुभ्यः समुत्थितः॥
एकात्मानुगतत्वात् नु यद्येकजनका इमे
आत्मैकत्रापि सोऽसिति किमन्यैः सहकारिभिः॥
विशेषान्तरवैकल्यादेके न जनकं यदि
ननु भेदादसत्क्तास्तेऽभेदे वा विकलाः कथम्॥
यथा त्वयं विशेषेऽपि न सर्व सर्वकारणं
नानात्वस्याविशेषऽपि तथैव नियमो भवेत्॥

अन्वये त्वेक एकस्य जनकोऽजनकश्च किम्॥
भेदोऽप्यत्रास्ति चेदस्तु स किं तस्यैव वस्तुनः
न हि तस्यान्ययादन्यो ननु भेदादकारकः॥
स एव भाविकश्चार्थो यो नामार्थक्रियाक्षमः
स च नान्वेति। योऽन्वेति कार्य तस्मान्न जायते॥
यं चात्मानमभिप्रेत्य पुमानेष प्रवर्त्तते
चिन्त्यते तद्गतावेव भेदाभेदावकल्पितौ॥
अन्यथा ह्यात्मना भेदो व्यावृत्या च समानता
अस्त्येव वस्तु नान्येति प्रवृत्त्यादिप्रसङ्गतः॥[58]

Kamalaśila makes it clear by asserting that if mere differentiation from the character of the productive is put forward without any qualification, as the probans, then it cannot be admitted. Because, as a matter of fact it is not admitted that there is unqualified 'differentiation' of the eye etc. from the character of being productive. For, the nature of the eye etc. is also regarded as productive. Why should then there be any such restriction as that the effect must always be produced by this cause, not by another? This cause may produce it, and the other may produce it. We see no incongruity in this. Under the circumstances, if the differentiation of the eye etc., were meant without reservation of any kind, then there would be their differentiation from their own nature, which would mean that they are devoid of nature or character and would be featureless. It is for this reason that there can be no differentiation of things from their own nature. He comments:

अविशेषण तज्जनकस्वभावात् परावृत्तिमात्रं यदि हेतुत्वेन वर्ण्यते तदा न सिद्धो हेतुः। न ही चक्षुरादीनां नीलादिज्ञानजनकात् स्वभावादिविशेषेण व्यावृत्तिः सिद्धाः यतस्तेषामपि चक्षुरादीनां यः स्वभावः सोऽपि जनकः इष्टः। को ह्यत्र नियमः तेनैव तत्कार्य पुनरविशेषेण व्यावृत्तिः स्यात् तदा स्वस्वभावादपि स्यात् ततश्च निःस्वभावताप्रसङ्ग स्यात् तस्मान्न अस्वभावाद् भावानां व्यावृत्तियुक्त।[59]

If the differentiation of the eye etc. meant to be probans is that from other productive causes of cognition than their own nature, then the probans is inconclusive. As in that case what is differentiated from the other nature may not be of that nature, but it need not cease to be productive of the cognition, because everything is productive, in its own form, not in the form of something else, and from that nature of itself in which it is held to be productive, so that the probans put up is found to be inclusive. He says:

स्व स्वभावं मुक्तवाऽन्यस्माजनकाद्वा व्यावृत्तिश्चक्षुरादीनां सा हेतुत्वेनाभिमता, तदाऽनैकान्तिकता हेतोः। तदा ह्यन्यस्मात् स्वभावाद् व्यावृत्तस्तत्सवभावो मा भूत्, न तु तदजनकः यतः सर्वं एव स्वरूपेणैव जनको न पररूपेण। येन चात्मियेन स्वभावेनासौ जनक इष्येत, तसमाचच न व्यावृत्त इति कथमजनकः स्यादित्यनैकान्तिका हेतोः। अथातत्ज्ञस्वभावता पर्युदासवृत्त्या साद्यते, तदा सिद्ध साध्यता, परस्परं भावानां स्वभावविवेकस्येष्टत्वात्।[60]

If what is meant by not having the nature or character of a certain thing is exclusion by way of 'contradiction', then the argument is superfluous because 'differentiation of character' among things mutually is what is admitted by both parties. One may ask a question, namely, that in bringing about certain effect, why should the independent or unmixed productive character be attributed to the eye etc. themselves, by virtue of which these alone could be restricted to that effect?

Kamalaśila gives an answer to the objection that the nature of things being restricted even when there is difference, it is only one thing that is productive not the other. There is nothing incongruous in this. He says:

अथैकस्मिन् कार्ये कर्तव्ये स एव तेषां चक्षुरादीनां परस्परासंकीर्णो जनकः स्वभावः कुत आयातः, येन त एव तु कार्ये नियताः स्यु इत्यनशङ्क्याहः यदुक्तम् 'भेदेन विर्विष्टत्वाच्छ्रवणाद्यिपि जनकं तस्य किं नेष्टम् इति तदनेने परिहृतम् तस्मात् स्वभावनियमाद्भेदेपि कश्चिज्जनको भवेन्नपर इति न किञ्चिद्विरुद्धम्।[61]

If the eye etc. were regarded as productive, on the ground of their having a common character, though different, then that one nature of them would be productive and hence the only cause, which would mean that the effect proceeds from that alone. And in that case, the other contributory causes would have to be regarded as superfluous. Some one may argue that "one cause cannot produce the effect, on account of defects in other particulars", then those particulars those are regarded as 'defective' would be incapable *i.e.* 'impotent'. Because by reason of difference *i.e.* since they are different from the comprehensive nature, which has been regarded as capable of producing the effect, they cannot produce it. And if what is incapable happen to be defective, then that cannot hamper the production of the effect. As in that case anything might cease to be produced at all. He comments:

यदि तु पुनरेकस्वभावानुगतत्वेन भिन्ना अपि चक्षुरादय जनकाः स्युः, तदैकस्तेषां स्वभावो शेषसहकारिकारणवैयर्थ्यप्रसङ्गः स्यात्। अथ विशेषान्तरवैकल्यानैकस्मात् कार्योत्पत्तिरिति चेत् ये ते विशेषा विकला इष्यनते तेषामशक्तत्वात्। कस्मात्? भेदात् समर्थाभिमतादनुयायिनः स्वभावाद्, अन्यत्वादिति यावत्। न चाशक्तस्य कार्यानुत्पत्तियुक्ता, कस्यचिद- नुत्पत्तिप्रसङ्गत।[62]

It might be argued: "we do not regard the general and particular aspects of things to be absolutely distinct, and hence the reason put forward by reason of difference becomes inadmissible. He provides an answer to this: 'if there were no difference, how could they be defective? That is if the particulars are non-different from the general, then it should not be said that one thing is not productive by reason of the defective character of particulars. Hence, when the general is there in its perfect form, those particulars that are non-different from that general cannot be defective. When between two things, one does not always share the fate of the others, they cannot be of the same nature. He observes:

न ह्यसमाभिः सामान्यविशेषणां परस्परमत्यन्तं भेद इष्टः ततश्च 'भेदात्' इत्यसिद्धो हेतुः? इत्याह–अभेदा वा विकलाः कथमिति। सामान्याद्विशेषाण-मभेदेङ्गीक्रियामाणे न तर्हि वक्तव्यम्- विशेषान्तर- वैकल्यादेके न जनकम् इति। अतस्तस्मिन् सामान्ये तिष्टत्यविकले सति तदव्यतिरिकिणा विशेषणामपि वैकल्यासिद्धि। न हि यो यदेकयोगक्षेमो न भवति, स तत्सवभाव युक्तः।[63]

Then he proceeds to show incongruity in the *Jainas* view also. He says: 'in your case also presence or inclusion being the same in all things, why does not every thing produce every thing'?

Just as in your case, though the presence or inclusion is there in all cases, every thing does not produce everything, same may be true in our position. Thus, there is no force in the arguments of the *Jainas*. And further, even when the difference is equally present in several things, it is one thing, not others, that produce certain effect. And this might be due to the restriction on the productiveness of things, on the principle that the nature of one thing is not the nature of the other and there can be no incongruity in this.

अपि च समान एवायं भवतामपि, अन्यस्याविशिष्टत्वात् किमिति सर्वः न जनयेत्? यथा भवतामन्वयस्याविशेषेऽपि सर्वं सर्वस्य जनक न भवति, तथाऽस्माकमपीति यत्किञ्चिदेतत्। किं च भेदाविशेषेऽपि कश्चित् जनयति नापर इति जनकस्वभावप्रतिनियमादेवं भवेत् एकस्य यः स्वभावो नासौ परस्येति कृत्वा, न चैवं सति किञ्चिद् विरुध्यते।[64]

However, if the productiveness belongs to one comprehensive entity, then one and the same entity would be productive as well as non-productive. How could these two mutually contradictory affirmations and denial subsist in the same entity? There could be no incongruity if they subsisted in different entities. This is what is meant by *'ekasya yaḥ svabhāva'etc*. How could the one thing be both productive and non-productive?

It might be argued that we do not regard anything to be absolutely comprehensive *i.e.* inclusive, on account of which there would be the incongruity of the same thing being both productive and non-productive of an effect. What we hold is that there is difference also, so that non-productiveness would not be incongruous. To this, Kamalaśila argues that there may be difference but it has to be explained whether this difference from the productive nature is meant to belong to same comprehensive productive nature as to another. It cannot belong to that same, because there can be no exclusion/

difference of a thing from its own nature. As in that case it would become nature-less *i.e.* devoid of its own peculial character; nor can it belong to another. If it is different, then it would be of the productive nature and not imperfect and it could not be regarded as non-productive.

It may be granted that same thing may be different from its own nature. Even so, the incongruity of one and the same thing being both productive and non-productive remains unanswered.

For instance, even when the difference is there, it could not be effective in bringing about the effect in question. There can be no difference apart from its inclusion or comprehensiveness. In fact, it would amount to the incongruity of the same thing being both productive and non-productive would still be there. He records:

नास्माभिरेकान्तेनान्वय एवेष्टः, येनैकस्यैकत्र जनकत्वाजनकत्व विरोधः स्यात्, किं तर्हि? भेदोऽप्यत्रास्ति, तेनाजनकत्वं न विरुद्धमिति? अस्तु भेदः, स किं जनकस्वभावाद् भेदस्तस्यैवानुगतस्य जनकात्मनोऽभीष्टः, आहोस्विदन्यस्येति वक्तव्यम्? न तावत्तस्यैव न हि स्वभावाद् भावस्य परावृत्तिर्युक्ताः, निस्वभावत्व-प्रसङ्गात् नाप्यन्यस्य भेदे तस्य जनकस्वभावस्याविकलस्याजनकत्वं युक्तम, अतिप्रसङ्गात्। भवतु वा तस्यैव स्वस्वभावाद् भेदः। तथाप्येकस्य जनकत्वाजनकत्वविरोधो न पराहृत एव। तथाहि भेदादपि तस्यैकस्याकारको भवेत्।[65]

Further, it is found from positive and negative concomitance that the effect is produced from particulars only. Hence, these particulars themselves should be regarded as associated with specific individualities, which latter therefore, do not necessarily indicate the universal or general aspect of things, because the character of the entity consists in capacity for effective action. Under the circumstances, whether the general is different from the specific individuality or non-different from it does not concern the man who seeks only for effective action and who is not concerned with the said difference or non-difference. As a matter of fact when a person seeks for effective action, he has recourse to that which he considers fit for that action. And he ponders over the difference or non-difference of only that thing. And he does not ponder over them simply because he likes to do it. If difference or exclusiveness and non-difference or inclusiveness were not regarded as real, then of the thing capable of effective action, there would be real difference or exclusiveness in its own form. And the general or inclusive character would be there, through the exclusion of all other things, which would be determined by the conceptual content, so that there would be no dispute on this point. It is only to this extent that a man seeking for activity has recourse to the consideration of difference in general. And where would there be any need for his considering any such general entity as is not capable of effective action? He says:

अन्वयव्यतिरेकाभ्यां विशेषेभ्यो एव कार्यसिद्धस्त एवं वस्तुलक्षण युक्ताः, न सामान्यर्थम्; क्रियाकारिलक्षणत्वात् वस्तुत्वस्य, ततश्च किं सामान्यं स्वलक्षणाद्भिन्नम्, आहोस्विदभिन्नमिति किमर्थं क्रियार्थिनस्तत्र भदाभेदचिन्तया। यस्माद् यमेव स्वभावमर्थक्रियार्थिभिः न व्यसनितया। अन्यथा हि यद्यकल्पितौ भेदाभेदौ नेष्येते, तदा तस्यार्थक्रियायोग्य स्यात्मना स्वेन रूपेण भेदाः पारमार्थिकोऽस्त्येव इत्यविवाद एव। इयतैवार्थक्रियार्थिनो भेदसामान्य चिन्ता समाप्तेति किमनर्थक्रियाकारिणः सामान्यस्य भेदाभेदचिन्तया।[66]

It might be argued that 'the thing itself may be the general *i.e.* the comprehensive factor, then why assume exclusion at all? To this, Kamalaśila gives an answer namely that if the form of the cloth were present in the jar, then the man seeking to carry honey or water might take up the cloth. And there would be other such incongruous activities. The other likely incongruities meant are all things being produced and destroyed at the same time and so forth.

Buddhists' Presentation on the *Jaina* concept of Soul

Soul, according to Jainism, is in the form of consciousness or in other words it is identical with knowledge. We have already discussed the *Jaina* concept of soul elsewhere. Here, a presentation is made on the basis of arguments provided by the Śāntarakṣita and Kamalaśīla regarding the notion of soul of the *Jaina* philosophy, particularly of *Digambara Jaina* philosophers. Śāntarakṣita, firstly presents the view *of Jaina* philosophers about soul and refuted that idea of the Jainas showing fault in it.

Śāntarakṣita says: the *Jainas* like *Mīmāṁsakas* assert that the soul is characterized by sentience, that in the successive factors, it is exclusive. He says:

जैमिनीया इव प्राहजैंनाश्चिल्लक्षणं नरम्।
द्रव्यपर्यायरूपेण व्यावृत्त्यानुगमात्मकम्॥ [67]

The *Jainas* assert that 'the soul is characterized by sentience only. And in the form of substance, it remains the same under all states and as such is inclusive *i.e.* comprehensive in its nature. While in the form of successive factors, being distinct with each state, it is exclusive in its nature. The two fold character of the soul is recognized by direct perception and hence does not stand in need of being proved by any other proofs. Thus, the sentience, which is found to continue to exist through all the states, even though these states are diverse in the forms of pleasure and the rest, is substance, while the successive factors consist of the diverse states which appear one after the other and all these are distinctly perceived. Kamalaśīla says:

जैना इति दिगम्बराः। त एवं प्राहुः चिलक्षण एमात्मा, स च द्रव्यरूपेण सर्वावस्थासवभिन्नत्वादनुगमात्मकः, पर्यायरूपेण तु प्रत्यवस्थं भिन्नत्वाद्व्या-वृत्त्यात्मकः। एवाच्च प्रत्यक्षत एव सिद्धमात्मनो द्वैरूप्यमिति न प्रमाणंतरतः प्रसाध्यम्। तथा हि-सुखाद्यवस्थाभेदेऽपि यदवस्थातृ सर्वावस्थासु चैतन्यमुपलभ्यते तद् द्रव्यम्। पर्यायास्तु क्रमभाविनः सुखाद्यवस्था भेदः ते च प्रत्यक्षत एवं सिद्धा इति परस्य भावः। [68]

Śāntarakṣita refutes this view of the *Jaina* philosophers by saying that 'under this view also, if the unmodified substance is connected with the successive factors, then there is no difference or change in it. And in that case it could not be liable to modification. He says:

तत्राप्यविकृतं द्रव्यं पर्यायैर्यदि सङ्गतम्
न विशेषोऽस्ति तस्येति परिणामि न तद्भवेत्॥[69]

Kamalaśīla makes this clear by arguing that there are two opinions possible viz. (a) the substance that exists in the form of sentience may be connected with the successive factors in its modified form *i.e.* without renouncing its previous character of sentience or (b) it is connected with the successive factors in its modified form *i.e.* in a form in which the previous character has been abandoned. If this latter view is accepted, then there is disappearance of the eternality of the soul. As under this view, there would be no single entity existing throughout the series of successive factors. If the former view is accepted that it is connected in its unmodified form, then there is no difference *i.e.* change, as between the preceding and succeeding states, so that the sentience would not be liable to modification *i.e.* it has to be regarded as unmodifiable, as modification is of the nature of change, becoming something else. And yet it is held to be modifiable. The argument may be formulated by in this way namely 'when a thing cannot be differentiated between its preceding and succeeding states, it cannot be regarded as modifiable. For example, the *ākāśa*, sentience is not differentiated at all in any state, so that the wider character being absent, the narrower one must be denied.

अत्र पक्षद्वयम् यत्तच्चैतन्यात्मकं द्रव्यं तत्पर्यायैः सम्बध्यमानं कदाचिदविकृतमत्यक्तपैरस्त्यचैतन्यादिरूपं सत् सम्भध्यते, यद्वा परित्यक्त-पूर्वरूपम्। तत्र यद्यनन्तरः पक्षः तदा नित्यत्वहानिप्रसङ्गः अवस्थातुः कस्यचिदपयभावात्। अथाविकृतमिति प्रथमपक्षः तदा पूर्वोत्तरयोरवस्थायोर्न विशेषः अन्यथात्वम् अस्तीति परिणामि तच्चैतन्यं न भवेत्ः न प्राप्नोति अन्यथालक्षणत्वात् परिणामस्य। इष्टं च परिणामि। प्रयोगः यत्पूर्वोत्तरावस्थासु न विशिष्यते तत्परिणामि न भवति, यथा आकाशम्। न विशिष्यते च चैतन्यं सर्वावस्थास्विति व्यापकनुपलब्धः।[70]

Further *Jaina* philosophers have argued that the reason just put forward is unproven, that is why it will not be admitted. They say that when sentience is spoken of as one, it is with reference to space, time and nature. When it is spoken of as difference, it is with reference to number, characteristic, name and function. When we speak of the jar' (singular) and its colour and the rest (plural), there is difference of number and name. There is also difference of nature in as much as inclusiveness *i.e.* comprehensiveness, *is the* nature of the substance jar, while exclusiveness *i.e.* distributiveness is the nature of the successive factors in the form of colour and the rest. And there is difference also of function in as much as the purposes served by the two are different. Thus, substance is not absolutely undifferentiated, as it is differentiated in the form of the successive factors. Śāntarakṣita says:

देशकालस्वभावानरमभेदादेकतोच्यते
सङ्ख्यालक्षणसञ्ज्ञार्थभेदात् भेदस्तु वर्ण्यते॥
रूपादयो घटश्चेति संख्यासंज्ञाविभेदिता
कार्यानुवृत्तिव्यावृत्ती लक्षणार्थविभेदिता॥
द्रव्यपर्याययोरेवं नैकान्तेनाऽविशेषवत्
द्रव्यं पर्यायरूपेण विशेषं याति चेत् स्वयम्॥ [71]

It means, if the substance was absolutely different from the successive factors, then no differentiation in it would be possible; because, on the ground of their non-difference regarding place, time, and nature the two are held to be one and the same. As a matter of fact, however, the two are different as regard numbers and other factors. For instance, the difference regarding number is that while the substance is one, the successive factors are many. That is, the substance is characterized by the number one, while the successive factors are distributive (exclusive). It has been stated that between the qualified and the qualification, there is non-difference, due to non-difference in their place, time, nature and function as is found between the jar and its colour and other properties. That is, between the jar and its colour etc. there is non-difference regarding place etc. For example, while the jar is different from colour etc. regarding number etc. e.g. the jar is one while its properties, colour and the rest are many, there is difference in their name also. While the one is named 'jar', the other is named colour and the rest. There is difference regarding their nature also. While the substance, in the shape of the jar etc. is comprehensive in its nature, the successive factors colour etc. are distributive. There is difference in their function also. The jar serves the purpose of containing water, while colour and the rest serve the purpose of lending colour to the cloth and so forth.

It has been said above regarding the jar and colour etc. that it should be understood to hold respecting the substance 'soul' which is the nature of sentience and the successive factors, pleasure, pain and the rest. In this case, the difference of function should be understood, as the function performed by sentience as the apprehension of things, while that is performed by pleasure, pain etc, is happiness, unhappiness and the like. Thus, the arguments of Buddhists suffer from the fallacy of being 'unproven' in the reason put forward by the Buddhist as against the *Jainas*. What is meant is that, as shown above, the substance is not absolutely undifferentiated. As a matter of fact it becomes differentiated through the diversity in the forms of the successive factors. We reproduce the whole arguments of Śāntarakṣita:

यद्येकान्तेन पर्यायेभ्यो द्रव्यं व्यतिरेकि भवेत् तदा स्यात्तस्या विशेषः यावता देशकालस्वभावाभेदाद् द्रव्यपर्याययोरैक्यमिष्टम्। संख्यादिभेदात्तु भेदः। तत्र संख्या एकत्वबहुत्वादि। तथा हि द्रव्यमेकसंख्यायुक्तम्, पर्यायास्तु सुखादयोऽनेकसंख्याविशिष्टाः लक्षणमपि भिन्नम्, यतोऽनुवृत्तिलक्षणं द्रव्यम् पर्यायास्तु व्यावृत्तिलक्षणः, संज्ञा-नाम, अर्थ-कार्यम्। तथा चोक्तम् देशकालस्वभावाभेदादभेदो धर्मधर्मिणोः, संख्ययासंज्ञालक्षणकार्य भेदात्तु भेदः। तद्यथा घटस्य रूपादीनां च इति। तथा हि- एको घटो बहवस्तु रूपादय इति संख्याभेदः। घटो रूपादयः इति च संज्ञाभेदः अनुवृत्तिलक्षणंघटादिद्रव्यम् व्यावृत्तिलक्षणास्तु रूपादयः पर्याया इति लभणभेदाः। घटेनोदकाहरणं कार्यं क्रियते, रूपादिभिस्तु वस्त्ररागादिति कार्यभेदः। एवमात्मद्रव्येऽपि चैतन्यात्मके सुखदुःखादिषु पर्यायेषु चोह्यम्। कार्यभेदस्तु तत्रैवं बोद्धव्यं -चैतन्येनार्थानुभवः क्रियते, सुखादिभिस्तु पीडानुग्रहादीति। द्रव्यपर्याययों इति वक्षमाणं सम्बध्यते। कार्यानुवृत्ति व्यावृत्ती लक्षणार्थविभेदितेति यथायोगं संबन्धः। कार्यभेदोऽर्थविभेदिता, अनुवृत्तिव्यावृत्ती लक्षणविभेदतितिसम्बन्धः। द्रव्यपर्यायोरित्यत्र छेदः। एवमित्यादिना हेतोरसिद्धिमुपसंहरति। एवं च कृत्वा द्रव्यमेकान्तेन नाविशिष्टम्। किन्तु पर्यायरूपभेदेन पर्यायरूपविभागेन विशेषं प्रतिपद्यते। तेनपर्यायेभ्यो द्रव्यस्यैकान्तेन भेदाभावादित्यसिद्धो हेतुः। [72]

To this argument of the Jainas, Śāntarakṣita gives an answer that if one-ness *i.e.* sameness or identity, consists in non- difference nature of this one-ness between two things, then difference between them would be hard to prove in any away, as in the case of the forms of the successive factors themselves. He says:

स्वभावाभेद एकत्वं तस्मिन् सति च भिन्नता
कथञ्चिदपि दुःसाधा पर्यायत्मस्वरूपवत्।। [73]

Kamalaśīla makes it clear by asserting that even admitting that there is non-difference between the substance and the successive factors, such being the case, the non-difference should be absolute. How could then there be difference between them, which is the contradictory of non-difference? It cannot be right to affirm and deny a theory, affirmation and denial being mutually contradictory. For instance, when two things are spoken of, as one what is meant is that there is non-difference in their nature or character, this non-difference being inseparable from negation of non-difference? This argument may be formulated thus: as in a case where there is non-difference between two things; there can be no room for difference, which is the contradictory of non-difference. For example, as is found in the case of the same 'successive factors' and 'the substance' with regard to the specific individuality of each, where the non-difference is clearly present. Hence, there is perception of what is contrary to the probandum *i.e.* difference.

यदि हि द्रव्यपर्याययोरभेदोऽप्यङ्गीक्रियते, तदा सर्वात्मनैवाभेदोऽयं भवेत्। भेदश्च तद्विपरीतः कथं भवेत्। न ह्यकस्यैकदा विधिप्रतिषेधौ परस्परविरुद्धौ युक्तौ। तथा हि – एकमित्येन भेदनिषेधनान्तरीयकः स्वभावाभेद उच्यते; तस्मिश्च स्वभावाभेदे सति कथं तदानीमेव भेदस्तत्प्रतिषेधात्मा भवेत्। प्रयोगः यत्राभेदस्तत्र तद्विपरीतो न भेदोऽवकाशं लभते, यथा तेषामेव पर्यायाणां द्रव्यस्य च यत्प्रतिनियतमसाधारणमात्मरूपं तस्य न स्वभावाद्भेदः। अभेदश्च द्रव्यपर्याययोरवस्थित इति विरुद्धोपलब्धेः। [74]

Thus, in reality there being non-difference between substance and the successive factors, there cannot be any difference between them, as regard their characteristics also. Śāntarakṣita says that the one-ness thus, between substance and the successive factors being not figurative *i.e.* real, the substance should also be distributive like the forms of the successive factors themselves and should be comprehensive in their character like the substance, because the one-ness of these with substance is duly established.

अगौणे चैवमेकत्वे द्रव्यपर्याययोः स्थिते
व्यावृत्तिमद् भवेद् द्रव्यं पर्यायाणां स्वरूपवत्॥
यदि वा तेऽपि पर्यायाः सर्वेऽप्यनुगतात्मकाः
द्रव्यवत् प्राप्नुवत्येषां द्रव्येणैकात्मता स्थितेः॥[75]

It means, when a thing is non-different from another thing, which is exclusive in its nature, the former also, must be exclusive. As for example, the form the successive factors, which are exclusive, so there is a natural reason for the substance also being exclusive. The same argument may be formulated differently. When a thing is non-different from another, which is inclusive in character, the former must also be inclusive. For example, the form of the substance and the successive factors in the form of pleasure etc. are non-different from the substance that is inclusive. Hence, this is a natural reason regarding these as inclusive. If there were not so, then as the fate befalling them would be different, the two would have regarded Malaśīla says:

यद्व्यावृत्तिमद्रूपाभिन्नस्वभावं तद् व्यावृत्तिमत् यथा - पर्यायाणां स्वरूपम्। व्यावृत्तिमद्रूपाव्यतिरिक्तं च द्रव्यमिति स्वभावहेतुः। अथ वा तदानुगतात्म-रूपाव्यतिरिक्तं तदनुगातात्मकमेव, यथा - द्रव्यरूपम्। अनुगतात्मरूपाविभिन्न स्वभावाश्च सुखादयः पर्याया इति स्वभावहेतुरेव। अन्यथा विभिन्नयोग-क्षेमत्वाद्भेद एव भवेत। विरुद्धधर्मध्यासितस्याप्येकत्वे भेदव्यवहारोच्छेद एव स्यादिति विपर्यये बाधकं प्रमाणम्। [76]

There is also an argument, which proves the contrary to the conclusion, in the form that 'if things possessed of contradictory properties would be regarded as one, there would be an end to all behaviour of day-to-day life'.

From all this, if follows that there is no such lasting substance as the 'soul' and the like, because they are not different from the successive factors themselves. *Śāntarakṣita* concludes:

ततो नावस्थितं किञ्चिद् द्रव्यामात्मादि विद्यते
पर्यायाव्यतिरिक्तत्वात् पर्यायाणां स्वरूपवत्॥ [77]

Further, he shows another proof for it, namely none of successive factors can also be beset with appearance and disappearance, because they are non-different from substance like the permanent form of the substance. He says:

न चोदयव्ययाक्रान्ताः पर्याया अपि केचन
द्रव्यादव्यतिरिक्तत्वात्तद् द्रव्यनियमात्मवत्॥[78]

For this reason it should be admitted either that there is absolute destruction of all or that all is permanent or eternal. Exclusiveness and inclusiveness could not exist in any single thing. He says:

ततो निरन्वयो ध्वंसः स्थिरं वा सर्वमिष्यताम्
एकात्मनि तु नैव स्तो व्यावृत्त्यनुगमाविमौ॥[79]

It means that any such comprehensive entity, as substance cannot be accepted, because, it is non-different in nature from the successive factors. It is not perceived apart from the successive factors even when the conditions of its perception are present and hence it should be treated as non-existent[80].

As a matter of fact, there is no perception of substance, which should be perceptible, as something permeating through and comprehensive of the successive factors. Hence, it cannot be regarded as existing like the sky-flower. *Śāntarakṣita* says:

न चोपलभ्यरूपस्य पर्यायानुगतात्मनः
द्रव्यस्य प्रतिभासोऽस्ति तन्नास्ति गगनाब्जवत्॥[81]

This shows that the statement that the soul in the form of substance, is permeating through the successive factors is apprehended by perception of self is not true. Because, as a matter of fact no such substance as soul is perceived to appear in that comprehensive or all embracing form, in any such cognition as is admitted by all philosophies to be sense perception. Kamalaśīla asserts:

प्रत्यक्षतः एवानुगतो द्रव्यात्मा सिद्धः इति तदसिद्धम्, न हि पर्यायव्यतिरिचयमानशरीरः क्वचिदपि विज्ञाने प्रत्यक्षसम्मेत प्रतिभासमानोऽनुगतैकरूपो द्रव्यात्मा लक्ष्यते। [82]

It may be asked that if it is so *i.e.* if there is no such substance as soul apart from the successive factors, then how do the distinctions of number etc. come about? To this Śāntarakṣiata has given an answer: in fact, things are capable of diverse fruitful actions. They are causes of the notion of similarity etc. and they are amendable to conventional verbal expressions connecting such things: He answers:

विविधार्थक्रियायोग्यास्तुल्यादिज्ञान हेतवः
तथा विधार्थसंकेतशब्द प्रत्ययगोचराः।। [83]

Kamalaśila makes it clear by asserting that the fruitful actions of the successive factors, colours are of various kinds distinguished as similar and dissimilar. The similar actions are the holding of water etc. and the similar actions are the colouring of cloth, the bringing about the visual perception etc. of these actions, the successive factors are capable. As regards the similar action, all the successive factors are used simultaneously. Hence, in order to indicate their common causal efficiency, even though there is no common identical substance permeating through them and even though they are different from each other yet, they are spoken of by means of the single turn, 'jar' as being one in number. And when it is intended to indicate the dissimilar specific actions of ' each of the successive factors, they are spoken of by means of words expressive of the plural number. It is in this way that the diversity in number, as also diversity in action or purpose is explained.

One may further ask how then is there diversity of characteristics? To this Kamalaśila says: they are causes of notions etc. the thing, jar for example, become causes of notions of similarity, when under all conditions, of baked, unbaked etc. that are conceived of as jar and the jar only, being apprehended as objects of indeterminate cognitions. As even though they are destroyed every moment, they are produced at each succeeding moment as particular things but of similar shape. But when they are produced in the different colours of dark, red and the like, they become causes of notions of dissimilarity. Thus, even in the absence of any simple comprehensive entity permeating through them, the things became the causes or basis of notions of similarity and dissimilarity and thereby come to be regarded as comprehensive and exclusive in character. And thus, the diversity of character becomes established. He asserts:

विविधाः-नानाप्रकाराः-रूपादीनां पर्यायाणां समानासमानभेदात् तत्र समाना जलसन्धारणादिलक्षणाः, असमाना वस्त्ररागलोचनादिज्ञानोत्पादलक्षणाः, तत्र योग्याः समर्था सति विग्रहः। तत्र साधारणे कार्ये सर्वेषामेव यौगपद्येनोपयोग इति समस्तानां हेतुत्वज्ञापनार्थमभिन्नद्रव्यरूपाभावेऽपि एव भेदिनोऽपि घटः इत्यादिना शब्देनैकसंख्याविशिष्टा उच्यन्ते। असाधारणकार्यो पयोगित्वाविवक्षायां तु नानासंख्यास्त इति संख्याभेदः, कार्यभेदश्च तेषु व्यवस्थाप्यते। लक्षणभेदस्तर्हि कथम्? इत्याह तुल्यादिज्ञानहेतव इति। आमपक्वाद्यवस्थासु प्रतिक्षणध्वसिनोऽपि सदृशसन्निवेशा विशेषा एवोत्पद्यमाना निर्वीकल्पानुभवविषया अनुभूयमानाः सर्वावस्थासु घटो घट इत्यादि शदृशप्रत्ययहेतवो भवन्ति। श्यामलोहितादि वर्णवैलक्षण्येन जायमाना अतुल्यप्रत्ययहेतवः इत्येवमेकरूपानुगममन्तरेणाऽपि तुल्यातुल्यज्ञान हेतवो भवान्तोऽनुवृत्ति व्यावृत्तिरूपेण व्यवस्थाप्यन्त इति लक्षणभेदो व्यवस्थाप्यते। तुल्यादि इत्यादिग्रहणेनातुल्यं ज्ञानं गृह्यते। कथं तर्हि संज्ञा भेदः -इत्याह - तथाविधः विविधार्थक्रियायोग्यस्तुल्यादि ज्ञान हेतुश्च पदार्थो रूपादिः, अथ्रः विषयो यस्यः घटः इति रूपादय इति च संकेतस्य स तथोक्तः, तथाविध ार्थः संकेतो येषां शब्दप्रत्ययानां ते तथोक्तः, तेषां गोचरा इति विग्रह।[84]

Thus, what is proved by perception is the fact that things are without soul; this is what pointed out by the Śāntarakṣita that it is only the successive factors that are designated as characterized by appearance and disappearance. Hence, pure soullessness becomes clearly established. He says:

उदयव्ययधर्माणः पर्याया एव केवलाः
संवेद्यन्ते ततः स्पष्टं नैरात्म्यं चातिनिर्मलम्।।[85]

It means successive factors *i.e.* colour etc. as felt in their own nature only, *i.e.* without any one substance, non-different from them because of an eternal entity, any fruitful action, either simultaneous or consecutive, is incompatible. In fact, fruitful action in the case of things is possible only when they are liable to appearance and disappearance. Thus, through inference also, it becomes established that those things, which are capable of fruitful action are without soul, this being indicated by their more existence. Kamalaśila says:

पर्याया इति रूपादयः स्वसंविदितस्वभावाश्च दुःखादय। अभिनैकद्रव्य-रूपविरहिणः। नित्यस्य च क्रमयोगपद्यीयामर्थक्रियाविरोधात्। अर्थक्रियाका-रित्वमेषा-मुदयव्ययधर्मित्व एव सति युज्यत इत्यनुमानतोऽप्येषामर्थक्रियाकारिणां सत्त्वलिंगानैरात्म्यं प्रसिद्धम्।[86]

Further, Śāntarakṣita presents another argument of the *Jaina* philosophers regarding the same issue *i.e.* the soul. He presents the *Jaina* view that something exists in the mixed form of the substance and the successive factors, because it is held to be dual in form, but impartite like *Narasimha*. He writes:

अथ सम्मूर्च्छितं रूपं द्रव्यपर्याययोः स्थितम्
तद् द्विरूपं हि निर्भागं नरसिंहवदिष्यते?[87]

Jaina philosophers have argued that the form of the substance, though existent, is not perceived due to its mixed character. Because the soul and other things, though dual in form are held to be impartite like *Narasimha*. And because the soul is impartite, therefore, it exists in the joint dual form, and hence, is not perceived separately. Kamalaśila argues:

आत्मदिकं वस्तु, यस्मात्तद् द्विरूपमपि सन्निर्भागमिष्यते, यथा नरसिंह, तस्मान्निर्भागत्वात् सम्मूर्च्छितोभयरूपं तदिति न पृथगुपलभ्यते।[88]

To this argument of the Jainism Śāntarakṣita gives an answer that the assertion that a certain thing is of dual forms can be based on existence of several things. He argues:

ननु द्वैरूप्यमित्येष नानार्थविनिबन्धनः
निर्देशो रूपशब्देन स्वभावस्याभिधानतः॥[89]

It means, if the things are impartite, then to speak of it as of dual form is a contradiction in terms, because such an assertion can be based only upon the existence of several things. Because when a thing is spoken of as *dvirūpa* or dual form, what is meant is that it has two forms or two natures. And one and the same thing cannot have two natures. As what would deprive it of its one-ness? What the Jainas have proved is only that there are two forms or characters and not that there is a single entity with two forms; and that for the simple reason that the character of being one and being many are mutually contradictory and preclusive. Kamalaśila asserts:

यदि हि निर्भागम्, तदा द्विरूपमित्येतद् व्याहतम्। नानार्थविनिबन्धनत्वादस्य व्यपदेशस्य। कस्मात्? रूपशब्देन स्वभावस्याभिधानात्। तथा हि द्वे रूपो, द्वौ स्वभावौ यस्य स द्विरूप उच्यते। न चैकस्य स्वभावद्वयं युक्तम्; एकत्वहानिप्रसङ्गात्। केवलं द्वावेव स्वभावो भवता प्रतिपादितौ, न पुनरेकं वस्तु द्विरूपम्; परस्परपरिहारस्थितलक्षणत्वादेकत्वानेकत्वयोः।[90]

And as regards *Narasimha,* he is one and why is not regarded as of dual form? Thus, Śāntarakṣita pointed out that *Narasimha* also cannot be one and also of dual nature; as he is perceived as such because he is an aggregate of many atoms. He writes:

नरसिंहोऽपि नैवैको द्रव्यात्मश्चोपपद्यते
अनेकाणुसमुहात्मा स तथा हि प्रतीयते॥[91]

So what is meant is that it is not only the thing under dispute that cannot be 'of dual form', *Narasimha* through the diverse character of the parts of the body and also through his occupying large space. Otherwise he would not appear as he does. Even a small part of the fly's leg of his body were concealed, he would be hidden to that extent.

Buddhists' presentation on Omniscience

In the Buddhist text the *Jaina* concept of Omniscient and its process to attain is criticized and refuted. In most of the text of the *Jainas,* the concept of omniscient has been discussed and in fact it is one of the most important doctrines of the *Jainas*. The concept omniscient is discussed in the context of knowledge.

The *Pāramārthika pratyakṣa* is the outcome of the destruction of *jṃānāvaraṇa karma i.e.* knowledge-obscuring karma. It comes forth from the purified soul itself without the assistence of the sense organs or any other external or internal instruments. It is of two kinds: *sakala pratyakṣa* (complete direct knowledge) and *vikala pratyakṣa* (incomplete direct knowledge). Thus, *kevala jñāna* comes under the *sakala pratyakṣa* whereas *avadhi* and *manaḥparyāya jñāna* comes under the *vikala pratyakṣa.*

These three types of knowledge we have discussed elsewhere. According to Jainism, no one can become *Tirthaṅkara,* without being omniscient. This perfect knowledge can be obtained by the purified soul, which has consciousness *i.e. cetanā* or *upayoga* as its sole characteristics[93]. The term *'upayoga'* is used for both *jñāna* and *'darśana'*. Akalaṅka says that when the soul cognizes the object it is called jñāna and when the soul perceives itself, it is called *darśana* [94]. It is apparent that at the destruction of *jñānavaraṇna, darśanāvaraṇa, mohanīya* and antarāya karmas the soul obtains inner illumination and becomes omniscient, as the soul has infinite capacity to know all the objects. When one obtains such power, he knows all the objects[95] and severe penance with right vision, right knowledge and right conduct and is required to attain such purified stage of soul.

The Buddhist philosophers criticize this concept of omniscient of the *Jainas*. The early *pāli* cannon as well as the later Buddhist philosophical literature have presented the concept of omniscient and then refuted it.

In the early *pāli* cannon like *Majjhimanikāya* and *Dhammapada aṭṭhakathā,* there are some references to omniscient. In *Majjhimanikāya* it is stated:

इद्ध सण्डक ओकच्चो सत्थ सव्वण्णु कव्वदैसावीअपरिसोसं पटिजानाति चरोत च में तिटठातो च सुत्तस्स च जाग्रस्स च सेततं समितं णानदस्सनं पक्कुप आटि्ठतं ति, सो अहुनाझंपि अगरंपि पविसति, पिण्डं पि नलभति, कुक्कुरो पि

दसति, चण्डेन पि हत्थिना समागच्दति, चण्डेन पि अस्सेन समागच्छति, चण्डेन पि गोणेन समागच्छति, इत्थिया पि पुरिससा पि नानं गोत्तं पि पुच्छति, गामस्स पि निगमस्स पि नानं पि मग्गं पि पुच्छति।[96]

Here Buddha says to Saṇḍaka Paribrājaka: "some teachers are all knowing *(sabbṃmā),* all seeing *(sabbadassāri)* claims all embarrassing knowledge and vision *(apparisesam ṃānadassanaṃ),* Buddha says whether I am walking or standing still, sleep or awake. Knowledge and vision are constantly and perpetually *(satataṃ samitaṃ)* before me". Further, Buddha says "he enters an empty place and he does not receive alms and dogs bite him and he encounters a fierce elephant, he encounters a fierce horse and he encounters a fierce bullock and he asks a woman and man their name and clan and he asks the name of a village or market town and the way Being asked why he needs or asks question in this manner if he is omniscient he replies this "I had to enter in an empty place, therefore, I asked.

In another place in that book Buddha says to Mahānāma that he had seen *Niganṭhas* performing severe penance at *Rajagṛha* on the *Isigili kālasilā.* He then asked them, "Why do you people do so?" They replied that the Nigaṇṭanātaputta was omniscient and he had said that by severe penance all past deeds will be destroyed and the new deeds would be prevented. In this way they will attain salvation. Then the Buddha asked them, "Do all of you know the past and the future of yourselves and your deeds. He went on to say, "You do not know whether you did an evil deed like this or that, you do not know the getting rid of unskilled states of mind, the uprising of skilled states". Getting the reply "no" from them Buddha remarked these beings revered *Nigaṇṭthas,* do those who are born again among man in the world and are wrathful *(luddha),* blood-handed *(lohitapāṇino),* dealing in cruelty *(krūrakammāntā)* do these go forth among the *Nigaṇāhas*. He says:

एकमिहां महानाम समयं राजगहे विहरामि गिझकुटे पव्वते। तेन खोपन समयेन निगण .... कतुका वेदना वेदयंति ..... निगण्ठो नातपुत्तो सव्वण्णु

सव्वदस्सावी किं पन तुम्हें। ना हिंद। एवं सन्ते आवुसो निगण्ठा, ये लोके लुब्धा, लुहितपाणिनो, कुरुरकम्मंता मनुस्सेसु पच्चाजाता ते निगण्ठेषु पव्वजंति इति।[97]

In the same way also *Uddyi Paribrdjāka* says to Gotama in the same book:

पुरिमानि, भंते, दिवसानि पुरिमतरानि, सव्वण्णु, सव्वदस्सावी ... सो मया पुव्वंत आरीा पण्हं पुटो समानो, अण्णेनाण्णम् पटिचरि, वहिरद्ध कथं अपनमेसि, रोपां च दोसं च अपच्छयं च पात्वाकाशि।[98]

He says that the all-knowing omniscient (Nigaṇṭha Nātaputta) was asked a question by me concerning the past, shelved the question by asking another answered off the point and evinced temper and ill will and sulkiness.

Dhammapada Aṭṭhakathā also presents a strong argument regarding the omniscient. It is in the form of a dialogue between Sirigutta and Garahadinna, the followers of the Buddha and the Nigaṇṭhas Nātaputta respectively. Garahdinna said to Sirigutta that the *Nigaṇṭhas* were omniscient. They know the past, present and future. Afterwards, Sirigutta, the follower of the Buddha decided to try the boastful claim of the naked ascetics *(Nigaṇṭ has)*. He got a ditch-dug between two houses and had it covered. *Nigaṇṭhas* were then invited to alms. When the *Nigaṇṭ has* came, they fell into the pit and their bodies were covered with mud and filth. Then it is said that he had beaten them with sticks and brought humiliation upon them. After similar trial he proved that Buddhist monks were omniscient.[99]

It may be noted here that all the *Nigaṇṭhas* are not said to be omniscient, but only a very few who could attain the perfect knowledge after performing the required duties. This story, however, refers to the *Jaina* tradition that its *Tirthaṅkaras* and some prominent monks were omniscient.

In the logical literature also there are references to the *Jaina* conception of omniscience or *Kevala Jñāna*. Dharmakīrti, in his *Pramāna Vārtika,* points out the superfluity of *Jainas* view of omniscience, in the course of establishing the *Dharmajṇatva* in the *Buddha*. He says *Anuṣṭānagata* jñāna *i.e.* a knowledge that has bearing on life or practice is more important than having a knowledge of the number of bacteria (*i.e. kiṭasaṁkyā),* which is of no use at all for human beings. The real *tattvadrasta i.e.* knower of scripture, in the opinion of Dharmakīrti is one who knows what is to be abandoned and what is to be accepted and not everything. It is immaterial whether one knows everything or not but what matters is whether he knows the essential thing that is what he ought to know. If the mere range of knowledge was valuable in itself without its bearing on life, why not worship vultures who soar into the atmosphere and thereby get a long range of sight. He says:

तस्मादनुष्ठेयगतं ज्ञानमस्य विचार्यताम्
कीटसंख्यापरिज्ञातं तस्य नः क्वोपयुज्यते।।
हेयोपादेयतत्त्वस्य साभ्युपायस्य वेदकः
यः प्रमाणमसविष्टो न तु सर्वस्य वेदकः।।
दुरं पश्यतु वा मा तत्त्वमिष्टं तु पश्यतु
प्रमाणं दुरदर्शी चेदेत गृघ्रानुपास्महे।।[101]

Thus, he asserts the view that an absolute purity in life and not unlimited knowledge is the essential characteristic of a teacher.

Prajñākaragupta, the commentator of Dharmakīrti also supports Dharmakīrti's view, but he goes one step further and establishes the omniscience of the Buddha. He also says that any spiritual aspirant, who masters the art of subduing passion, can attain it. He says:

ततोऽस्य वीतरागात्वे सर्वार्थज्ञान संभवः
समहितस्य सकलं चकास्तीति विनिश्चितम्।।
सर्वेषां वीतरागाणामेतत् कस्मान्नविद्यते
रागादिकणयमात्रे हि तैर्यन्तस्य प्रवर्तनात्।।
पुनः कालान्तरे तेषां सर्वत्र गुणरागिणां
अल्प यत्नेन सर्वज्ञत्वसिद्धिरवारिता।। [102]

The *Jaina* philosophers did not emphasize *Dharmajñatva* like Dharmakīrti, but they endeavoured to point out that a person is omniscient when he is both *Dharmajṃa* and *sarvjña,* because *Dharmajñatva* depends on *Sarvajñatva.*

Dharmakīrti and his Prajñākaragupta think that the *Jaina* concept of omniscience cannot be accepted for want of *Sāhaka-badhaka Pramāṇa i.e.* supporting and contradicting evidence. In answer to this criticism of the Buddhists, Akalaṅka replies: one cannot establish the non-existence of omniscience without being omniscient. He further says that, there is no *Bādhaka Pramāṇa* to refute omniscience of Jainism and the absence of *Bādhaka Pramāṇa* itself can serve as *Sāhaka Pramāṇa.* He says:

प्रत्यक्षस्य भिदा किं स्यादेकरूपे स्वलक्षेण
नानारूपं न तत्कस्मादाद्येऽवभासते॥
यदनुष्ठानवैयर्थ्यं न स्यात्? नाप्यवभासनम्
असमग्रस्य भावस्य सौगतैरनुमन्यते॥
तन्न स्वलक्षेणप्येष विशेषोऽयक्षगोचरः
अन्यत्र चेत्; तथाप्यस्य कैमर्थक्येन कल्पनम्?
तत्त्वस्वलक्षणं यस्माद्विना तेनापि गृह्यते।
विशेषणोत्तरणेति नानुष्ठानस्य तत्फलम्॥[103]

As regards *Anuṣṭānagata jñāna* urged by Dharmakīrti, Vādirājasuri, and commentator of Akalaṅka questions: which *Pramāṇa* does the Buddha perceive the *Anuṣṭheyagatavastul?* Neither can *Pratyakṣa Pramāṇa* be helpful in this respect, otherwise that will be the use of *Anuṣṭhāna.* Nor will be the *Anumāna Pramāṇa* solves our Problem, because it depends on the *pratyakṣa.* Thus, the *Anuṣṭheyagata* jñāna in itself has no importance.

As regards the *Kiṭsaṁkhyā-pariñāna* and its *puruāthopayoga* are concerned, he says that it is essential to include *Kiṭasaṁkhyā-pariñāna* as an integral part of omniscience as *Caturāyasatya* implies the *Dukhasatya* of creatures living around. If the Buddha has not grasped *Caturāyavedanattva,* how could he preach to his disciples convincingly? He then remarks that if the *Kiṭasaṁkhyā-pariñāna* serves no useful purpose, what then is the use of *Bhikṣu-Samkhyā-pariñāna* in Buddhism[104]

From the aforesaid discussion it is clear that the whole *Jaina* tradition seeks to establish the fact that *Jaina Tirthaṅkaras* are omniscient, whereas Buddhist refuted it. But in Buddhism also, Buddha is made an omniscient.[105]

As may be noticed in the early literature of Buddhist no proof is given to refute the Jaina concept of omniscience. The stories narrated have no historical value and they also do not provide any proof or argument atainst the Jaina concept of omniscience. They only show that some Jaina saints were not omniscient. Even in the late logical period there is no development. Neither Dharmakīrti nor any other Buddhist logicans provide the arguments against the Jaina concept of omniscience. As can be seen that Dharmakīrti argues that it is not important to be omniscient *i.e.* to know every thing but what matters is whether you know the essential things *i.e.* truth. It is interesting to note that the Buddhists want to establish the omniscience of Buddha as the commentaor Prajñākaragupta has done. Thus, it appears to us that there is no point in denying the omniscientness of Jaina monks and accepting Buddha as omniscient. In any case logical arguments must be provided to refute the existence of omniscience by the Buddhists.

Object of Perception

It has already been discussed that in Jainism *Pramāṇa* is identical with knowledge and it has been classified into two ways viz. canonical *i.e. agamika* and logical or philosophical *i.e. darsanika* ways. From this one thing is very clear that in agamika period knowledge is divided into five types viz. *sruta jñāna* (scriptural knowledge), *mati jñāna* (sensitive knowledge), *avadhi jñāna* (visual knowledge), *manaḥparyāya jñāna* (mental knowledge) and *kevala jñāna* (perfect knowledge).

Out of these five, *manaḥparyāya jñāna, avadhi jñāna* and *kevala jñāna* are treated as *pratyakṣa pramāṇa* in logical period or rather to be more particular called *pdramdrthika pratyakṣa*. Another five types of knowledge viz. *smarana, pratyabhijñāna, tarka anumāna* are accepted as the synonymous to *matijhdna*. Thus, along with the *sruta jñāna i.e. āgama* there are five types of *Paroksa Pramāṇa*. And this *mati jñāna* is also treated *sdriivyavahdrika Pratyakṣa* in the logical period.

Now we will take for discussion the object of perception to which the Buddhists have objected to.

In *Tattvāsaṁgraha,* Śāntarakṣita has depicted the *Jaina's* view regarding the object of perception and nature of *Savikalpaka Pratyakṣa,* which is the real perception of the *Jainas* and finally refuted their view.

In Jainism the object of perception is related to both types of perception viz. *sāṁvyavahārika Pratyakṣa* and *Pāramdrthika Pratyakṣa*. The validity of *Pramāṇa* in Jalina philosophy is based on the nature of things. It asserts that a reality is a multitude of atoms and possesses a characteristic of being substance-cum-mode *(dradyaparyāyātmakam)*. The permanence in change is its common nature. Each atom or reality, in its conception is quite indestructible and independent and always changes into different modes. This system is natural as well as eternal. The whole universe continues in this way. Thus, there is no need to postulate a creator God to explain the origin and evolution of the universe.

Śāntarakṣita refers the view of Sumati, in the context of the examination of external world. He says:

तुल्यं रूपं ग्राह्यमतुल्यं नैव गृह्यते
अणुनां द्वयरूपत्वे तदा किं नोपपद्यते॥
तत्सामान्यविशेषात्मरूपत्वात् द्विरूपा अणवः स्मृताः॥
समानं तत्र तद्रूपं तदक्षज्ञानगोचरम्
एकाकारमतो ज्ञानमणुष्वेवोपपद्यते॥
असमानं तु तद्रूपं योगिप्रत्यक्षमिष्यते
इति दुर्मतय केचित् कल्पयति समाकुलम्॥[106]

To explain this Kamalaśila in his commentary called *TattvasaṁgrahaPañjikā* states that:

सामान्यविशेषात्मत्वात् सर्वपदार्थानां तुल्यातुल्यरूपेण द्विरूपाः परमाणवः तत्र समानं यद्रूपं तदिनिद्रयैर्गुह्यते, नासमानम्। ततश्चैककारं विज्ञानमणुष्व-विरुद्धमिति प्रत्यक्षसिद्धाः परमाणवः इति।[107]

Sumati has argued that all things have two aspects viz. universal and particular. Consequently atoms exist in two forms viz. the universal and the particular. The objects perceived by sense organs possess the universal character. These objects are conglomerations of atoms, which appear as an entity with a shape and size. Only the emancipated one, who attained the *Pdrmarthika pratyakṣa* or *Yogi Pratyakṣa,* can know the true duality of atoms. In this way there is nothing incongruous in their view being one uniform cognition apprehending all atoms and thus, it is by perception that atoms get established.

This point is made clear in the *Syādvādamanjari* of Mallisena.[108] It is said that atoms, which were correlated, generate *paryayas.* They have infinite and continuous changes, which depend on the type of contact or relation with others. Pot, for instance, is produced when the atoms of the soil come into contact with each other and they become compact. This process does not come about due to external pressure but it is the result of an internal connection with each other. Therefore, *Jaina* philosophers have not accepted the extra *avayavidravyas.* As regards the external existence of atoms we have both *pratyakṣ a* and *Anumāna.* We see the mass of atoms wherein they get combined in the form of Pot. The atoms that cannot be perceived by ordinary men due to their minuteness are perceived by the *Yogins.*[109]

This idea of the *Jainas* has been criticized by the Buddhist philosophers, particularly by the *Vijndnvddins,* an extreme form of idealism, which is pronounced by the Śāntarakṣita *and Yogdcdra* Schools. It asserts that there is no causal *(yaddkdrm-jñānam)* world of external reality. According to them, reality is only the *vijhdnai.e.* idea.

It is obvious that the *Vijñānavddins* should criticize the *Jaina* position. Acarya Śāntarakṣita also denies the existence of atom by saying:

द्वे हि रूपे कथं नाम युक्ते एकंस्य वस्तुनः
द्वे तदा वस्तूनी प्राप्ते अपरस्पररूपतः
परस्परात्मतायां तु तद् द्वैरूप्यं विरुध्यते
विशेषश्चोपलभ्यते चक्षुरादिभिरिन्द्रियैः॥[110]

It means, how can it be right to say that a single thing has two forms? In fact, there would be two things, each differing from the other in form. If they were of the same form as one another, the duality of forms would be annulled. And it would be the uncommon form that would be apprehended by the eye and other sense members.

Following to Śāntarakṣita, Kamalaśila argues thus:

द्वाभ्यां रूपाभ्यां वस्तुतोऽन्यान्यत्वाद् द्वे एव वस्तूनी प्राप्ते, रूपद्वयस्यैव केवलस्यापरापरस्य भावात्, ततश्च नैकस्य द्विरूपत्वमुक्तम्। एकसमाद्व वस्तुनो रूपद्वयस्याव्यतिरेकादेकवस्तुस्वरूपवद् रूपद्वयस्य परस्परात्मकतैवेति कथकेक द्विरूपं स्यात् किञ्च सामान्यरूपव्यतिरेकाद् विशेषरूपस्योपलम्भप्रसंगः। ततश्चेयमसंकीर्ण व्यवस्था न प्राप्नोति -समानं रूपमक्षज्ञानगोचरोऽसमानं तु योगिप्रत्यक्षमिष्यते।[111]

To him, if there are two forms of thing different from each other, then there are two things, as the two forms, being different from one another, would be two different things. And it would not be right to say that a single thing has two forms.

Again he says, the two forms being not different from the thing itself, would be identical, both being like the form of a single thing. How then could it be a single thing having two forms?

Further, he explains it by asserting that, as the particular form of a thing is not entirely different from the universal form, there would be a possibility of the former being apprehended by the senses and in that case there could not be the clear cut distinction that the common form is amenable to sense cognition and the uncommon form is amenable to mystic cognition.

Further, the assertion that 'one thing has two forms' involves not only a self contradiction but it also implies what is more damaging that is one thing, having two mutually contradictory forms. Śāntarakṣita says :

परस्परविरुद्धात्मनैक रूपं कथं भवेत्।[112]

How could one and the same thing have two mutually contradictory forms and characters, because the forms common and uncommon are such that the absence of one implies the presence of the other and vice versa? That is why any single thing cannot have these two forms, comments *Śāntarakṣita.*

The above criticism is based on *Vijñānavāda* as stated before, which holds the view that there is no existence of external world. We see it only owing to the hypothesis of *Vāsanā.*[113]

In later *Jaina* literature we find an answer to this criticism. Hemacandra tries to reply that the existence of the world cannot be refused since knowledge is the action *i.e. kārya* in which the object is supposed to be directed. Without the external object there can be no perception. Therefore Jainism admits the existence of both atoms and the body. As regards the criticism that the atoms of the body would be conflicting with one another, *Jaina* philosophy admits this fact but it tries to solve this problem through *Anekāntavāda.* As he says: criticism of atoms, therefore, cannot affect those who believe in *syādvāda* according to which a body is one and manifold.[114]

On determinate perception *(Savikalpaka Pratyakṣa)*

In the *Jaina* philosophy, it is accepted that knowledge *(jsdna)* and vision *(darśana)* are the two main characteristics of the soul, which we have already discussed, in the previous chapter. The *Darsanopayoga i.e.* indeterminate cognition and *Jnanaopayoga i.e.* determinate cognition are called *Nirvikalpaka* and *Savikalpaka Pratyakṣa* respectively in the *Jaina* tradition.[115]

In the agamic tradition both *Nirvikalpaka and Savikalpaka* were valid due to spiritual considerations. From the relative standpoint both *Nirvikalpaka and Savikalpaka* were valid because from the practical point of view both are valid as a man obtains right knowledge is right in his cognition and a man who holds a wrong view *(mithyddrsti)* is wrong in his cognition. That is why Umasvati divided knowledge into two—right and wrong ones. The *Avadhidarśana and kevaladarśanas* are indeterminate transcendental perception, while *Avadijhdna, Manahparyāya jñāna and kevala jñāna* are determinate transcendental perception.[116]

But in the logical tradition the validity of *Pramāṇa* has been changed. To refute the opponents' view specially those of Buddhists the *Jaina* philosophers have used some words like *nirnaya* (determination) or even *jñāna* (determinate cognition) in the definition of *Pratyakṣa*.

Acarya Sumati holds his view that both *nirvikalpaka* and *savikalpaka Pratyakṣa* should be recognized as valid as the first reflects the general form of a thing (*i.e.* in the form of *idarh kincit)* or in other words its existence as an indefinite thing while the *savikalpaka Pratyakṣa* reflects the special characteristic of an entity thus perceived (it is in the form of *idarh purusa)*.[117]

Abhayadeva, the commentator of the *Sanmatitarka* also maintains the same position.[118] And we have discussed elsewhere that in the process of general perception commencing from *avagraha i.e.* more apprehension and ending with *dhdrand i.e.* retention passes from the indeterminate *(nirvikalpaka)* state of knowledge to determinate *(savikalpaka)*. Hence, in Jainism particularly in logical tradition *savikalpaka* perception is the real perception.

Before going to discuss the Buddhist refutation on *savikalpaka* perception, let us have an idea of Buddhists' theory of perception. According to Buddhism, only *nirvikalpaka jñāna* comes under the purview of perception. And determination perception cannot come under the purview of perception, *i.e.* indeterminate perception as valid knowledge. As per as the definition of perception is concerned, there are two schools or traditions in Buddhist literature. One is headed by Dignāga who does not accept the non-illusory *(abhranta)* nature of perception and the other is headed by Dharmakīrti who does so. Śāntarakṣita and his followers support the later, stating that sense perception is free from conceptual contexts and hence not erroneous as he says:

प्रत्यक्षं कल्पनापोढमभ्रान्तम् अभिलापिनी
प्रीतिः कल्पना क्लृप्तिहेतुत्वाद्यात्मिका न तु।[119]

We see a thing first and then realize its name etc. Thus, the determinate knowledge *(savikalpaka jñāna)* depends on indeterminate knowledge *(nirvikalpaka jñāna)* and therefore only indeterminate knowledge is perception.[120]

In the context of *pratyakṣa lakṣana pariksd,* Śāntarakṣita has presented the view of ācārya Sumati's view on perception, particularly on determinate perception and his argument against the Buddhist notion *of nirvikalpaka pratyakṣa.* He also presents the view of Kumarillas, the founder of Bhaṭṭa School of *Purva Mimdmsd,* and Sumati's argument against his view. At the end, Śāntarakṣita refutes the idea of Sumati on *savikalpaka pratyakṣ a* (*i.e.* determinate perception).

Firstly, Śāntarakṣita presents the arguments of *Sumati* on perception, which is as follows: Kamalaśila explains it by stating the following:

ननु नामादिकं मा भूत् तस्य ग्राह्यं विशेषणम्
तथाप्यसिद्धता हेतोर्नैव व्यावर्त्तते यतः॥[121]

Kamalaśila explains it by stating the following :

सा हि सामान्यविशेषात्मकत्वेनोभयरूपं सर्वं वस्तु वर्णयति। सामान्यं च द्विरूपम् १. विशेषेणावच्छिन्नं यथा गोत्वादि. २. अनवच्छिन्नं यथा सत्तावस्तुत्त्वादि। तत्र यदनवच्छिन्नमकेरूपं तदालोचनामत्रस्य निर्विकल्पक प्रत्यक्षस्य गोचरः; इतरन् पुनः सविकल्पकस्य इत्येषा तस्य प्रक्रिया।[122]

Sumati describes all things as existing in two forms, the universal and the particular. The universal again is of two kinds, one is determined by the particular e.g. the cow and that not so determined (conceptual), e.g. 'being', 'entity'. That universal which exists only in the undetermined (non-conceptual) form is of only one form and is amenable to non-conceptual perception *i.e.* perception free from conceptual context, in the form of mere observation, purely subjective ideation, while the other *i.e.* the universal determined by particulars is amenable to conceptual perception. But the *Jaina* philosophy does not accept it. Jainism asserts that, a thing is perceived by *darśana* or cognition, not by *alocana* or observation.[123] The *Visesdvasyakabhdsya* criticizes the view viz. 'कैदिहलोयण पुव्वामोग्गाह्म वेंति' which means a thing can be apprehended by a purely subjective ideation. Thus, it seems that Kamalaśila has misunderstood the view of Sumati.[124]

Kumarilla has asserted two types of sense perception. According to him, non conceptual perception *(nirvikalpaka pratyakṣa)* is purely subjective ideation as apprehending the specific individuality of the particular 'आलोचनाज्ञानं निर्विकल्पकं व्यक्तिःस्वलक्षणविषयम्'[125] and the conceptual perception *(savikalpaka pratyakṣa)* is the apprehension of universal 'सामान्यविषयं तु सविकल्पकं प्रत्यक्षम्'[126]

Ācarya Sumati does not agree with the idea of Kumarilla. Therefore he questions:

अर्थांतरव्यवच्छिन्नरूपेणाग्रहणं यदि
अर्थमात्रग्रहो वा स्यादग्रहो वा घटे यथा।।
घटांतरव्यवच्छिन्नरूपेणाग्रहणं यदि
घटमात्रग्रहो वा स्यादग्रहो वा घटस्य वै।।[127]

Kumārilla explains it further by making the following comments:

किं तदिन्द्रियस्य पुरःस्थितमर्थमात्रं स्वेन रूपेणार्थान्तराऽसम्भविना विशिष्ठं गृह्यते? उत नेति। यद्यसौ ब्रुयात-नेति, अत्रोच्यते-अर्थातंरव्यवच्छिन्नरूपेणाग्रहणं यदि विवक्षितादर्थाद् यदर्थान्तरम् ततो व्यवच्छिन्नं तत्राविद्यमानं विवक्षितार्थस्थं रूपम् स्वभावः, तेन विशिष्टस्य यदि तस्याथस्याग्रहणभिष्ते, तदा तदर्थमात्रग्रहो वा स्यात्, यत्तदर्थमात्रमर्थानतरासम्भवि स्वभावरहितं तस्यैव ग्रहणं स्यात्। अथ तदपि न गृह्यते तदा अग्रहो वा अग्रहणमेव स्यात्। घटे यथेति निदर्शनमुक्तम्, तच्श्लोकांतरेण व्याचष्ठे। अवधीकृतघटासम्भविना। रूपेण यदि तस्य घटस्याग्रहणम्, तच्श्लोकांतरेण व्याचष्ठे। अवधीकृतघटासम्भविना रूपेण यदि तस्य घटस्याग्रहणम्, तदा घटमात्रग्रहो वा स्यात् केनचिद्रजतताम्रादिना विशेषणाविशिष्ठस्य घटमात्रस्य ग्रहणं सादित्योग्रहो वा घटस्य वै। एवमत्रापि दार्ष्टान्तिके विशेषाग्रहणेऽर्थमात्रग्रहणं न ग्रहणं वा स्यादित्येकान्तः।[128]

The idea of Kumārilla is based on the definition of perception given by *Jaimini* is his *Sūtra.*[129] All philosophers, Vedic as well as Buddhist except the *Mimaṁsakas* have refuted them and Sumati appears to be the first Jaina *ācārya* to join with them in refuting this view.[130]

Sumati says that is the thing before the eyes of the observer apprehended purely by itself as characterized by its own form which is impossible anywhere else? Or is it not so apprehended? If Kumarilla answers that there is non-apprehension of the thing in a form distinguished from other things, then Sumati states that in this position either there would be apprehension of the thing itself only or there would be no perception of the thing at all. He illustrated his theory by reference to the perception of a 'Jar'. The Jar should be either apprehended without having the form of others or it should not be apprehended. There could be no escape from these two alternatives.

Śāntarakṣita was the follower of Dharmakīrti, thus he defines perception as knowledge, which is free from conceptual contents and not erroneous. He tries to prove his theory by means of inference and establishes that the *nirvikalpaka pratyakṣa i.e.* the indeterminate perception is the only real perception. To clarify this, he cites an example that, in case of a thing that has no particular form cannot be accepted as a particular thing. For instance, a white house owing to different characteristics cannot be mistaken for a cow. It is the same case with the perception.[131]

Here *Kalpana* is defined by Śāntarakṣita as विशिष्टयावबोध:। *i.e.* knowledge of qualified object. Thus, Sumati argues against this view. He says:

विशेषणानविच्छिन्नं परैः सामान्यमिष्यते
निर्विकलपकविज्ञानग्राह्यं तत्राप्यतः समम्॥
विशेषाद्धि तत् सामान्यमवगम्यते
तद्ग्राहकतः प्राप्तं विज्ञानं सविकल्पकम्॥
निर्विशेषं गृहीतश्चेद् भेदः सामान्यमुच्यते
ततो विशेषात् सामान्यविशिष्टत्वं न युज्यते॥ [132]

Kamalaśila explains this argument by stating thus:

न हि दण्डसम्बन्धमन्तरेण तद्वान भवति, तद्वद्विशिष्टोऽपि विशेषसम्बन्ध मन्तरेण न युक्त इति भावः। तस्माद् तद्विशेषण सम्बन्धग्रहणम्, तत्

सविकलपकमिति। प्रयोग विवादास्पदी भूतं विशिष्टविषयं ज्ञानं सविकल्पकम् विशिष्टविषयत्वात् पटोऽयमित्यादिज्ञानवदिति।[133]

Sumati argues that a thing cannot be qualified without having a connection with the qualifications, as in the case of a stick *(daṇḍa)* and the stick-holder *(daṇḍin)*. Hence, the cognition, which apprehended the qualifications *(viśeṣatā)*, is conceptual *(savikalpaka)*.

Again he says that, if there is always the apprehension of the things as distinguished from homogeneous *(sajātīya)* and heterogeneous *(vijātīya)* things, then the apprehension would become determinate *(savikalpaka)* for it can be conveyed 'this is different. Otherwise how does it apprehend the difference between things? He says:

सजातीयविजातीयव्यावृत्तार्थग्रहान्मतः

विशिष्टविषयो बोध न विशेषणसंङ्गतेः॥[134]

यत्र यदि व्यतिरिक्तिविशेषणसम्बान्धात्, विशिष्टविषयत्वात् इति हेत्वर्थः तदा न सिद्ध हेतुः। तथा-हि-न बौद्धस्य विशेषणं नाम किञ्चिदस्ति, येन तत्सम्बनधग्रहणाद् विशिष्टविषयो बोधः स्यात् किं तर्हि? सजातीयविजातीयेभ्ये व्यावृत्तस्यार्थमात्रस्य गृहात् ग्रहणान्मत इष्टः, विषयो बोधः।[135]

Further, he points out another defects of the Santarakuita's arguments: The argument runs thus:

ग्राह्यन्तरव्यवच्छिन्नं भावेन ग्राहि चेन्मतम्

सविकल्पविज्ञानं भवेद् वृक्षादिबोधवत्।[136]

If perception is regarded as apprehending the thing as distinguished from other apprehensible things, then this cognition would be conceptual (detenninate) just like the cognition of the tree and other things.

He asserts that there is no particular *(viśeṣa)* without a touch of the universal *(sāmānya)*. It cannot be argued in his opinion that the universal or 'being' is not touched at all by the sense perception at all time of apprehension. Because in this position the particular would be devoid of existence and thus it could become characterless and as such could not be apprehended by sense perception, because it would be devoid of 'being' and become like the sky flower *(ākāśa kuṣuma)*. Thus, Sumati is of the view that the particular is perceived with the character of the universal. Thus he says:

विशेषोऽस्पृष्टसामान्यो न च कश्चन विद्यते
ग्रहणे चेत् तदस्पष्टं विभावत्वान्न गृह्यते।[137]

Elaborating on this Kamalaśila observes:

अत्र मात्रं नाम सामान्यमुच्यते यत्तत् सत्तेत्याख्यायते, तन्निरपेक्षो न कश्चिद् विशेषो विद्यते, यो गृह्यते तत्र। एतत् स्यात् त्वन्मत्या यद्यपि तदस्ति सामान्यम् ग्रहणकाले तु तन्न स्पृश्यते। ग्रहण काले यदि तत् सामान्यं सत्ताख्यम् इन्द्रियज्ञानेन न स्पृश्यते, विशेषमात्रमेव गृह्यते, तदा तद्विशेषमात्रं गृह्यमाणं भवरहितं सत्ताख्यस्वभावविकलं निःस्वभावं प्राप्तमिति नेन्द्रियज्ञानग्राह्यं स्यात्, विभावत्वात् विगत भावत्वात्, वियत्पुष्पवदिति॥[138]

Not only Sumati, other *Jaina* logicians have also tried to refute the Buddhist theory of sense perception following the footsteps of Sumati. In this regard Akalanka has added the adjectives viz. *anadhigatārthagrāhin, avisaṁvādin and viṣada* to the definition of perception and established that the *nirvikalpaka pratyakṣa* gets transformed into the *savikalpaka* is the *pramāṇa.*[139] Later *Jaina* logicians such as Prabhacandra[140], Anantavirya[141], Vidyānanda following his idea have refuted this view.

Śāntarakṣita, after presenting the arguments of Sumati against the Buddhist philosophy, has refuted the conception of determinate perception of the *Jaina* philosophers, particularly of Sumati.

Śāntarakṣita has criticized the view of Sumati on the ground that an entity does not have any particular qualities by which it can be differentiated at the moment of apprehension. Thus, there cannot be possible any particular thing at all, but the particular characteristic of a thing is implicit in his classification of the universal *(sāmānya)* into two types viz. distinguished by qualification and not distinguished by qualifications. The first cognition or awareness is *nirvikalpaka*;

the next, which is followed by is *savikalpaka pratyakṣa* (conceptual perception). The former is the real *pratyakṣa* while the later is practical. Thus, *Kamalaśila* says:

द्विरूपंहि सामान्यम् विशेषणावच्छिन्नरूपम्, अवच्छिन्नरूपं च। तत्र यदनविच्दिन्नरूपं तन्निर्विकल्पकविज्ञानं ग्राह्यमिष्टम्। तत्रापिः सामान्ये। अत। एकद्विकल्पकविज्ञानग्राह्यत्वं तुल्यम्।[142]

Śāntarakṣita presents two arguments to refute Sumati's theory. The first is that an entity does not possess any characters by which it can be differentiated. We see a thing at first and then realize it as a pot or any particular thing. When the thing is apprehended, the negation of all other things comes forth naturally. Hence the non-conceptual perception *(nirvikalpaka pratyakṣa)* in the specific form and shape etc. appears and then, there follows the conceptual content *(vikalpatmaka jñāna)* associated with the words which is different. Thus he says:

स्वभावापरनिशेष पदार्थव्यतिरेकिणि
गृहिते सति तस्मिस्तु विकल्पो जायते तथा।[143]

Kamalaśila explains this point by stating thus:

सत्यसाधारनीलाद्यकारप्रतिभासनात् पश्चाद् भेदाध्यवसायी शब्दाकारानुस्मृतो भिन्नमित्यभिलपन्नुत्पद्यते विकल्पः। न चेदस्त्वभिलापस्वभावं तत्संसृष्टात्मतत्त्वं वा, येन 'भिन्नम' इति 'अभिन्नम्' इति नाम्ना संयोज्यग्रहणे सत्यगृहीतं स्यात्। तस्मादसिद्ध एव हेतुः॥[144]

Here the words do not lead to cognition. The reason behind this is that the specific individuality *(svalakṣaṇavastutva)* itself is independent of the words. The perception generated by them should also be deprived of the words. The words do not have any relation with the meaning. In the absence of a thing we use the words, which are dependent on gestures and intentions. There is, therefore, no possibility of words in the *nirvikalpaka pratyakṣa*.

The second argument that Śāntarakṣita puts forth is that in particular thing there should be no other characteristics except that of the particular. He says:

विशेषात्मतिरेकेण नापरं भेदलक्षणम् तद्रूपास्पर्शने तेषु ग्रहणं कथमुच्यते॥
तद्रूपस्पर्शने चापि भेदान्तरविभेदिनः
गृहीता इति विज्ञानं प्राप्तमेषु विकल्पकम्॥[145]

Commenting on this Kamalaśila explains:

भेदेभ्यो हि नान्यो विशेषः तस्य च विशेषस्य सामान्यग्राहिणा ज्ञानेनासंस्पर्शे कथं भेदास्तेन गृहीता भवेयुः, अगृहीतस्वीाावाव्यतिरेकात्तेऽप्य-गृहीता एवेति भावः। अथ गृहीता इति मतम्? तदा तद्रूपसंस्पर्शने भेदरूपसंस्पर्शने ग्रहणे, गृहीताव्यतिरेकाद् गृहीतास्वभाववद् विशेषोऽपि गृहीता एवेति। एषु भेदेषु, यद् सामान्यविषयत्वेनाभिमतं ज्ञानं तद्विकल्पकं प्राप्तम्।[146]

Thus, whatever cognition appears with regard to the specific individuality of things, it is beyond the range of words and is hence, non-conceptual. In his opinion, the lucidity and determination in the *savikalpaka pratyakṣa* is not its own characteristic but it really comes from *nirvikalpaka pratyakṣ a*. After a moment of *nirvikalpaka pratyakṣa* the *savikalpaka pratyakṣa* is generated and the ascertainment and lucidity of a thing, which comes from *nirvikalpaka pratyakṣa,* appears to be *savikalpaka pratyakṣa*. In this manner *savikalpaka pratyakṣ a* also determinates a thing and is called perception from a practical viewpoint *(vyavahāra),* but the real perception is only the non-conceptual *(nirvikalpaka)* perception.

The whole discussion of Śāntarakṣita can be summed up that his main arguments are that the *nirvikalpaka pratyakṣa* is the real *pratyakṣa* and thing cannot be both universal and particular. Both these arguments are met by the later *Jaina ācārya*. They say that the *nirvikalpaka jñāna* of the Buddhist is the formless perception, which is not capable of determining the nature of a thing. Therefore, it is determinate *(sākāra)* and lucid *(viṣada)* and could be accepted as *a pramāṇa*.

To sum up the Buddhist in general and Santarasita in particular object to the basic assumption of the *Jainas* that a reality is of dual nature consisting of universal-cum-particular.

On parokṣa pramāṇa

Jaina philosophers have accepted five types of *Paroksa pramāṇa* viz. *smaraṇa, pratyabhijñā, tarka, anumāna* and *āgama,* because these *pramāṇas* are dependent on other *pramāṇa,* which is defined in the system as *'aviṣada parokṣaṃ' i.e.* non-distinct knowledge is *parokṣa.* We have presented a detailed account of *parokṣa pramāṇa* from Jaina point of view with elsewhere. We shall give a brief account about these *pramāṇas.*

Anumana Pramāṇa (*i.e.* inferential cognition)

In Jainism *anumāna pramāṇa* is included in the *parokṣa pramāṇa,* owing to its dependence on other cognition *i.e.* perceptual cognition *(anu vyāptirnirṇayasya paścādbhāvi mānam).*[141] Except *Cārvāka* all other systems of Indian philosophy have accepted it as a valid means of knowledge. But they differ from each other with regard to the nature, the process, the components etc. of the inferential cognition. We have discussed the *anumāna pramāṇa* of the *Jainas* in the previous chapter, but still we will reproduce some of these arguments as framed by the Buddhists in this chapter.

In the tradition of *Jaina* logic Akalaṅka has given a comprehensive definition of *anumāna Pramāṇa,* which runs as follows:

साधनात्साध्यविज्ञानमनुमानं तदत्यये
विरोधात्क्वचिदेकस्य विधान प्रतिषेधयोः।[148]

Cognition of *sādhya i.e.* that what is to be known or major term produced by *sādhana i.e.* the instrument to prove the *sādhya* is called *anumāna,* which follows *liṅga grahaṇa i.e.* apprehension of the predicate of proposition and *vyāpti smarana i.e.* remeṃbrance of invariable concomitance. Then he says that because it is *avisariivddin i.e.* non-discrepant in its own subject and removes the obstacles arising due to doubt *i.e. samśaya* perversion *i.e. viparyaya* and indecision *i.e. anadhyavasāya,* it should be considered as *pramāṇa.*

Invariable concomitance *(vyāpti)* is the main feature of *anumāna. Avindbhdva, anyathānupannattva, vipakṣavyāvṛtti and niyatasdhācārya* are well known characteristics of *vyāpti. Akalahka* says it very precisely that *sahabhāvanīyama and kramabhāvanīyama i.e.* having correlation and having successive relation respectively are the main factors of the *vyāpti.*[149] This definition indicates that *anumāna* is not restricted only to *tādātmya* (identical nature) and *tadutpatti* (identical cause of origination), but it can also be applied to those cases, which do not possess of the *tādātmya* and *tadutpati* relation. For instance, we can make an inference about the taste of something looking at its form, which has no *tādātmya* relation.

As regards to *hetu* the Buddhists accept three *hetus* viz. *svabhāva, kārya and anupalabdhi.* The hetus recognized by the Jainas are: *svabhāva, vyāpaka, kārya, karaṇa, purvācara, uttarācara, sahacara, upalbdhirūpa and anupalabdhirūpa.*

Dhrmakirti and Śāntarakṣita have recorded the view of the *Jainas* particularly of Pātrasvāmin regarding the notion of members of inferential cognition and finally refuted his view.

According to him, there are only two members of inferential cognition viz. *pratijñā* (proposition) and *hetu* (reason or middle term). They argue in support of this theory that without accepting the *pratijñā or pakṣa* what is the use of the *hetu* and for what would it be utilized?[150] For instance:

(i) There is fire on the mountain *(pakṣa).*

(ii) Because there is smoke *(hetu).*

This argument of the *Jainas* is recorded in Buddhist literature particularly, in the texts of Śāntarakṣita and Dharmakīrti.

In the context of *hetvābhāṣa,* Dharmakīrti records it and says:

चेतनास्तरव इति साध्ये सर्वत्वगपहरणे मरणं प्रतिवाद्यसिद्धम्, विज्ञानेन्द्रियायुर्निरोधलक्षणस्य मरणस्यानेनाभ्युपगमात्, तस्य च तरुष्वसम्भवात्।[151]

He cited the following examples:

(i) Trees are sentient beings *(pratijñā)*.

(ii) Because they sleep *(hetu)*.

And criticized this idea by stating that this instance is fallacious, since sleep which is manifested by closing of the leaves at night is found only in some trees not in their totality.

Dharmottara explicitly criticizes this issue. He says:

दिगम्बरास्तु साध्येन व्याप्तम् अव्याप्तं वा मरणम् अविविच्य मरणमात्रं हेतुमाह। तद् अस्य वादिनो हेतुभूतं मरणं न ज्ञातम्। अज्ञानात् सिद्धं शोषरूपम् शोषरूपस्य मरणस्य तरुषु दर्शनात्। प्रतिवादिनस्तु ज्ञानम् अतोऽसिद्धम्। यदा तु वादिनोऽपि ज्ञातं तदा वादिनोऽप्यसिद्धं स्याद् इति न्यायः।[152]

Śāntarakṣita, following the footstep of Dhartmakīrti has recorded the theory of members for inferential cognition as proposed by the Pātrasvāmin and finally criticized on the ground that it leads to absurdity.

After giving the definition and division of the inferential cognition he presents the arguments of the Pātrasvāmin regarding the members of inferential cognition.

Before going to see the argumentation between Buddhist and Jaina logicians let us have a precise idea of Buddhist view in this regard. In Buddhist logic ācārya Dignāga has accepted three members viz. *pakṣa, hetu and dṛṣṣānta.*[153] On the other hand, Dharmakīrti includes *Pakṣa* in *Nigrahasthāna* and divided *hetu* into three types[154] viz.

(i) *pakṣadharmatva* i.e. its presence of the reason in the subject totally

(ii) *sapakṣasatva* i.e. its presence in similar instances, although not in their totally,

(iii) *vipakṣavyāvṛtattva* i.e. its absence in dissimilar instances in their totality.

These three are also known as

(i) *ayogavyavaccheda* i.e. impossibility of absence

(ii) *anayogavyavaccheda* i.e. impossibility of otherness in similar, but not in the totality of similar

(iii) *atyntdyogavyavaccheda* i.e. impossibility of others completely, that is absence of totality of the dissimilar instances.

For instance:

(i) What ever *sat,* is *kṣaṇika (pakṣadharmatva).*

(ii) The pot is *sat,* therefore it is *kṣaṇika (sapakṣasattva).*

(iii) Because all entities are *sat (vipakṣavyāvṛtittva).*

Here, *pakṣa and nigamana* are denied and *drstanta and upanaya* are indirectly accepted. Thus, *hetu* is the main feature according to Buddhists. Thus, Dharmakīrti rightly says *viduṣ āṁvācyo hetureva hi kevalaṁ.*[155]

Śāntarakṣita has recorded the view of Pātrasvāmin and ultimately refuted his view. Śāntarakṣita defines *anumāna* as follows:

स्वपरार्थविभागेन त्वनुमानं द्विधेष्यते
स्वार्थ त्रिरूपतो लिङ्गादनुमेयार्थदर्शनम्
त्रिरूपलिंङ्गवदनं परार्थं पुनरुच्यते॥[156]

Inference is of two kinds: Inference for one's own benefit and Inference for the benefit of others. The former should be understood to be that cognition of the inferred object, which is derived from the three featured probans. The hetu that fulfils the three conditions of (a) being present in the subject (b) being present in that wherein the probandum is known to be present (c) being entirely absent where the probandum is known to be absent. The inference for the sake of others should be understood to consist in the verbal expression and the said three featured probans.

In this context, Śāntarakṣita records the arguments of Pātrasvāmin against the notion of *anumāna* as proposed by the Buddhist philosophers, particularly Śāntarakṣita. The argument urged by Pātrasvāmin is presented thus:

अन्यथापनुपन्नत्वे ननु दृष्टा सहेतुता
नासतित्र्यंशकस्यापि तस्मात् क्लीबास्त्रिलक्षणाः॥[157]

The probans is valid only when it is found to be otherwise impossible and not when it has the three features. Because it is found that even when the probans has the three features, it is not valid. When it does not fulfil the condition that it is otherwise impossible as for example, in the case where the probans is cited in the form namely "because he is the son of so and so, therefore he must be dark". Consequently, the three featured probans are inefficient.

Then Pātrasvāmin justifies his own position. He writes:

अन्यथानुपपन्नत्वं यस्यासौ हेतुरिष्यते
एक लक्षणकः सोऽर्थश्चतुर्लक्षणको न वा॥[158]

It means that which is otherwise impossible is held to be the probans, while this is only one featured. It may or may not be regarded as four featured. In other words, the probans is valid only when it is found to be other wise impossible and not when it has the three features. He says:'

अन्यथाऽनुपपन्नत्व एव शोभनो हेतुः न तु पुत्रस्त्रिलक्षः।[159]

It means, *anyathānupapannattva* is the main characteristic of a probans. Through presumption *(arthyāpati)* some characteristic implies three features viz. the *vipakṣavyāvṛttitva, pakṣadharmatva and sapakṣasattva.* But the *vipakṣavydvrtti or anyathdnupapati* can imply all other features, which do not serve any useful purpose. As a matter of fact, the relation is invariable concomitance i.e. *avinābhāva,* which is the heart of *hetu, which* is not present in the three featured reason i.e. *trirupya-hetu,* but found in the one featured *hetu* i.e. *ekarūpya hetu.*

It means, *anyathānupapannatva* is the only probans. There may be three corroborative instances, but they cannot be depended upon. If the *anyathānupapannatva* is not there, what is the use of three features? And if the *anyathānupa-pannatva* is there, what is the use of three features *trairūpyal.* He says:

अन्यथानुपपन्नत्वं यस्य तस्यैव हेतुता
दृष्टान्तौ द्वावपि स्तां वा मा वा तौ हि न कारणम्॥
नान्यथानुपपन्नत्वं यत्र तत्र त्रयेण किम्॥ [160]

He illustrates this point by asserting that the man who has three sons is called *'ekaputraka',* on account of having one good son.

यथा लोके त्रिपुत्रः सन्नेकपुत्रकः उच्यते
तस्यैकस्य सुपुत्रत्वात् तथेहापि च दृश्यताम्॥[161]

Similarly, in the case of the three-featured probans, a single feature would be useful in making inferences. Then, Pātrasvāmin has tried to prove that, there can be no *anyathānupapannatva hetu* in the three featured probans. For instance, one must be dark i.e. *pakṣasatva,* because one is the son of so and so i.e. *sapakṣasatva,* whose other sons are found to be dark i.e. *vipakṣasatvavydvrtti*. This example contains the three featured probans. But then it cannot lead to any valid and definite knowledge and conclusion. For, there is no *avinābhāvasaṁbandha* i.e. relation of invariable concomitance, between his son and his darkness. The climate and eating of vegetables by his mother during the pregnancy is real cause. Therefore, the *trairūpya* is not a correct theory.

He says:

स श्यामस्तस्य पुत्रत्वाद् दृष्टा श्यामा यथेतरे।
इतित्रिलक्षणो हेतुर्न निश्चिनैः प्रवर्त्तते।[162]

Again, Pātrasvāmin has pointed out that the one feature probans has the requisite capacity of leading to valid knowledge. It has no external corroborative instances, either of similarity or of dissimilarity, either in the form of statement or in the form of actual things. Because all things have been included under the subject negative and positive entities and there is nothing apart from these. He says:

भावभावौ कथञ्चित् सदात्मकौ, कथञ्चिदुपलभ्यत्वात्। अत्र न साध ार्म्यवैधर्म्यदृष्टान्तौ वहिर्भूतौ, प्रयोगात्मकावर्थात्मकौ वा विद्यते। भावाभावात्मकस्य सर्वपदार्थराशेः पक्षीकृतत्वात्, तद्व्यतिरिक्तस्य चान्यस्याभावात्।[163]

And, as regards the character of being present in the minor term this is *anyathānupapannatva hetu* and nothing apart from the later. Hence, the probans here is one featured. He says:

तत्रैकलक्षणो हेतुर्दुष्टान्तद्वयवर्जितः
कथञ्चिदुपलभ्यत्वाद् भावाभावौ सदात्मकौ।[164]

Śāntarakṣita, then presented the view of Pātrasvāmin, who cited some examples to establish his own view showing that there are only two members viz. *Pratijñā* and *hetu*. His arguments are elaborate and are presented in the following *Kārikās*. We reproduce his entire text for convenience. His arguments are:

चन्द्रत्वेनापदिष्टत्वान्नचन्द्रः शशलाञ्छनः
इति द्विलक्षणो हेतुरयं चापर उच्यते॥
पतत्कीटकृतेयं में वेदनेत्यवसीयते
पतत्कीटकसंस्पर्शप्रतिलब्धोदयत्वतः॥
चक्षुरूपग्रहे कार्ये सदाऽतिशयशक्तिमत्
तस्मिन् व्यापार्यमाणत्वाद् यदि वा तस्य दर्शनात्॥
कथञ्चिदसदात्मनो यदि वाऽऽत्मघटादयः॥
कथञ्चिन्नो पलभ्यत्वात् खरसम्बन्धिशृंगवत्॥
कथञ्चन सदात्मानः शशशृंगादयोऽपि च
कथञ्चिदुपलभ्यत्वाद् यथैवऽऽत्मघटादयः॥
त्वदीयो वापि तत्रास्ति वेश्यमनीत्यवगम्यते
भावत्कपितृशब्दस्य श्रवणादिह सद्मनि॥
अन्यथाऽनुपपत्त्यैव शब्दादीपादिवस्तुषु
अपक्षधर्मभावेऽपि दृष्टा ज्ञापकतापि च॥
तेनैकलक्षणो हेतुः प्राधान्याद् गमकोऽस्तु नः
पक्षधर्मादिभिस्त्वन्यैः किं व्यर्थैं परिकल्पितैः॥[165]

Following are some of his primary arguments:

(1) (a) The hard-marked is not non-moon or the hard-marked is the *moon (pakṣa)*.

(b) Because it is spoken of as the moon *(hetu)*.

(2) (a) This pain of mine has been caused by the falling insect, *(pakṣa)*

(b) Because its appearance was felt on the touch of the falling insect *(hetu)*.

(3) (a) The eye has the potency of the most effective instrument in bringing about the apprehension of the colour existing at the present time *(pakṣa)*.

(b) Because while it is not damaged, it is that which is used as the instrument by a man who desires to see colour and acts intelligently, or because it is actually found to bring about the cognition of colour *(hetu)*.

(4) (a) The soul, the jar and other things are somehow essentially non-existent (pakṣa)

(b) Because they are somehow not apprehended, like the hare's horn (hetu)

In this case, there is no corroborative instance, for dissimilarity, as the jar and other things include the entire group of positive entities.. And they have been mentioned in the proposition essentially non-existent and the negative entity has been put forward as the instance and apart from the positive and the negative, there is no third category, wherein, it could be pointed out that the exclusion of the probandum implies the exclusion of the probans.

(5) (a) Things like the hare's horn are somehow essentially non-existent (pakṣa).

(b) Because they are somehow non-apprehensible *(hetu)*

(6) (a) This house understood as having your father within *(pakṣa)*

(b) Because your father's voice is heard *(hetu)*

Here also there is no instance for similarity. Hence, the probans is only two featured.

In the case of words, lamps and such things it is found that, even though they do not subsist in the subject, yet they indicate things in the same ways as the inferential probans in the shape of smoke etc. Words and lamps are not properties subsisting in the jar and such things indicated by them. And yet the thing is actually apprehended through them. Hence, in this case the two conditions are present, that of absence where the probandum is known to be absent, and being otherwise impossible. Hence, according to Pātrasvāmin, there are only two members, wherein, other members can be emerged in them. This is the shortest and most well defined ways of making inference.[166]

After presenting the arguments of the Pātrasvāmin, Saritaraksita has refuted his view by stating thus:

तदिदं लक्षणं हेतोः किं सामान्येन गम्यते
जिज्ञासितविशेषे वा धर्मिण्यथ निदर्शने।[167]

It means, is the proposed definition meant to be general? Or in reference to a particular subject on which knowledge is sought? Or in reference to the instance? Śāntarakṣita here analyzed the whole arguments of Pātrasvāmin and has tried to present it. That the whole treatment of Pātrasvāmin can be presented under three heads, which he has quoted in the above, mentioned *kārikās*. And finally he shows the problem related to each of the alternatives and then finally refuted those. Kamalaśila makes this point by asserting thus:

तत्र साध्येनाविनाभावित्वं हेतोः सामान्येन वा स्याद् धर्मिविशेषापरिग्रहाद् विशेषण वा स्याद्, धर्मिविशषपरिग्रहाद, विशेषेऽपि, जिज्ञासितविशेषसाध्यधर्मिण वा स्याद्, दृष्टान्तधर्मिण वा इतीयन्तः पक्षाः सम्भाव्यन्ते।[168]

It means, the proposed definition of the probans is that it is otherwise impossible, which means that it should not exist apart from the probandum. Whether

(i) it means to be general i.e. applicable to all probans or to be applicable to any particular object? And further

(ii) it is meant to be inference to particular object in

which the existence or the otherwise of the probandum is sought to be known, Or

(iii) in reference to that objects which form the corroborative instance.

Out of these three alternative possibilities Śāntarakṣita criticized all the three one by one by pointing out logical difficulties in them. On the first alternative he says:

सामान्येन गते तस्मिन्नेवं चेत् साध्यधर्मिणि
हेतोः सत्त्वं प्रकाश्यते न विविक्षितसिद्धिभाक्।[169]

It means, if it were understood to be general, then what would be indicated would be the existence of the probans in the object where the probandum is present and it would not accomplish what is sought to be accomplished. Kamalaśila makes it clear by saying thus:

न ह्यवनाभावित्वमात्रेणैव विना पक्ष धर्मत्वं शब्दे धर्मिणि चाक्षुषत्वमनित्यत्वस्य गमकं दृष्टिमित्ययुक्तः प्रथमः पक्षः।[170]

Hence, mere fact of its not existing apart from the probandum, without the other fact of its existing wherever the probandum is known to exist, does not make visibility. It does not prove the non-eternality of sound. Thus, the first alternative cannot be accepted. Because for instance, visibility is known to be inseparable i.e. non-existing apart from destruction in a general way and yet it i.e. visibility cannot prove destruction in sound. But then if it is said that its presence in the object is meant, then in that case according to Jainas also, the probans becomes three featured as before. He notes:

तद्यथा चाक्षुषत्वस्य नाशेनाव्यभिचारिता
सामान्येन गता तच्च ध्यनौ तस्य न साधनम्।।
तस्य धार्मिणि सद्भावः ख्याप्यते चेत तथा सति
सैव त्रिरूपताऽऽयाता भवतामपि दर्शने।।[171]

Thus, it might be said that in order to guard against the said objection, recourse might be added to the qualification that the probans should be actually present in the object. If it is the idea of Pātrasvāmin, then Kamalaśila says that there is nothing new in this argument, it is the same as we hold before. Because 'being otherwise impossible included positive and negative concomitance' and by its presence in the object its presence in the minor term becomes admitted.

After rejecting the first alternative, Śāntarakṣita takes the second alternative for analysis; it meant to be applicable to any particular object in which the existence or otherwise of the probandum is. sought to be known. He says:

अथेदं लक्षणं हेतो धर्मिण्येवावगम्यते
यतः प्रमाणात् तत्सिद्धि साध्यस्यापि ततो न तु॥
साध्यस्याप्रतिपतो हि हेतोरपि न निश्चयः
अतो निरर्थको हेतुरन्यतः साध्यसिद्धितः॥
अन्योन्याश्रयदोषश्च हेतोः साध्यस्य निश्चये
द्वेयोरन्यतरासिद्धवन्यस्याप्यनिनिश्चितः॥[172]

It means, if the proposed definition of the probans is meant for one that is found in the minor term only, then that same means of cognition which has made the probans known, would make known the probandum also. If the probandum does not become known, then, the probans also cannot become known. Thus, the probans would be superfluous, the probandum having become known by other means. There would be the incongruity of mutual interdependence also if the definite cognition of the probandum followed from the probans. And between these two, the cognition of one would be dependent upon the cognition of the other.

Kamalaśila makes this point more clearly by citing an example. He says: the probans may be defined as being inseparable from the probandum in the minor term only, as asserted in the following words, "the character of the probans is held by other to exist in the instance and not to be seen apart from the probandum. In my opinion, however, it is that which does not exist in the minor term apart from the probandum. The followers of *Śabara* derive this knowledge from presumption and the followers of *Bhikṣu,* from inference. For us inference is something totally different like *Narasiṁha* i.e. having a dual character".[173]

If such is the definition of the probans, then that same means of cognition by which the probans would be known as inseparable from the probandum, as existent in the object where the probandum is sought to be proved. That same means of cognition would have made known the probandum also, so that, the probans would be entirely redundant.[174]

If the probandum is not known, then the probans is also not known. Because the probans has been defined as what is present in the minor term inseparably from the probandum. And this inseparability from the probandum cannot be known if the probandum is not known. Thus, the probans would ramain unknown', because the cognition of inseparability depends upon the cognition of both.[175]

It might be urged that 'the probans may be known by other means of cognition'; In that case what is the use of probans, the probandum having been known already? Further, if the definite cognition of the probandum were dependent upon the porbans, then there would be the incongruity of mutual interdependence.[176]

Because, the cognition of the probandum would be dependent upon the cognition of the probans as therein lies alone the use of the probans and the cognition of the probans, which is characterized by inseparablity from the probandum. This would amount to a case of clear mutual interdependence.[177]

Faults are also pointed out in the third and the final alternative viz. 'in reference to that object which form the corroborative intance'.

निदर्शनेऽपि तत्सिद्धौ न स्याद् धर्मिणि साध्यधीः
न हि सर्वोपसंहारात् तस्य व्याप्तिर्विनिश्चिता॥[178]

It means, even if the probans were known as existent in the corroborative instance that would not bring about the cognition of concomitance will not have definitely cognized all over. It means, if the inseparability of concomitance of the probans is held to be in the object which forms the corroborative instance and which is something different from the minor term, in which the probandum is sought to be proved, and not all over or everywhere along with the minor term, then how could such a probans bring about the cognition of the probandum in the minor term?[179]

After presenting a general criticism on Pātrasvāmin's theory of members of inferential cognition, Śāntarakṣita tries to point out defects in each and every example cited by Pātrasvāmin.

Firstly, he says: as regards the probans that has been put forward in the form namely 'because it is apprehended somehow', the object of this is not open to uncertainty, he says hence, it is useless.

योऽप्ययं हेतुरत्रोक्तः कथंचिदुपलम्भतः
इति नास्त्येव विषयः सन्दिगधोऽस्येति निष्कलः।[180]

Kamalaśila says that as regards the probans that has been put forward in the form 'because it is somehow apprehended' this is absolutely futile as its object is not open to doubt, that is, it asserts what is already known. And what is already known cannot be the objective of the probans. It is only a doubtful matter that is dealt with by the probans. Because a reason is stated only in reference to what is doubtful. That too is known only in an isolated form cannot be the substratum of the probans, as the probandum would be already known.

Further faults are pointed out in the second example:

चन्द्रत्वेनापदिष्टत्वं सपक्षेऽप्यनुवर्त्तते
क्वचिन्माणवके यद्वा कर्पूररजतादिक।।
चन्द्रत्वसाधने हेतावसाधारणता भवेत्
प्रसिद्धिवयतिरेके च वस्तुरूपसमाश्रये।।[181]

['Being spoken of as the moon' in things where the probandum is known to be present. Or it is also sometimes present in the man who is spoken of as the moon, or in camphor, silver and such other things, which are also called moon.]

Firstly, here, Śāntarakṣita presents the objection and of Pātrasvāmin, regarding the three-featured probans then, he has refuted his objection. The objection is formulated thus: 'if a three-featured probans is possible for the proving of the moon, then how is it that your teacher has asserted that when a man declares that 'the moon is not moon'. For proving of it being the moon against such a person, there can be no inference. He says: in the case where there can be no inference on account of the thing in question being unique, it is excluded by its contrary which is well known in its verbal form. When for example, it is said that the hare-holder is the moon because it is an entity, in a case like this there is no minor term.

Śāntarakṣita gives an answer to the above-cited objection: 'there would be uniqueness only if the probans were meant to prove moon-ness'. As in the absence of any well-known fact regarding it, it would be based entirely upon the nature of the thing itself.

Kamalaśila makes this point by stating that it is with regard to the probans in the shape of the existence or non-existence of things, that uniqueness has been asserted and not with regard to a probans in the form of a well-known fact; because in the case of the latter, as it is dependent upon the wish of the speaker, the necessary concomitance would always be there. The inference without a corroborative instance has been spoken of only in the case, where the other part holds a different opinion and denies all experience, and consequently cannot be convinced of the thing being the moon on the basis of any well-known fact, nor is there any inferential indicative (probans) based upon the capacity of thing by which the moon-ness could be proved with reference to the hare-holder. Because the name 'moon' is based on the mere whim of the speaker and is not an inherent property of the thing concerned. It is for this reason that the inference addressed to him has to be without of a corroborative instance and hence unique, specific.[182]

Further, he goes to show the defect in the example, namely, 'this pain of mine has been cause by the falling insect, because its appearance was felt on the touch of the falling insect'. He writes:

पतत्कीटकृतत्वस्य न विशेषः समीक्ष्यते
पतत्कीटकसंस्पर्शप्रतिलब्धोदयस्य च।[183]

It means, there is no distinction perceived between 'being brought about by the falling insect and having its appearance felt on the touch of the falling insect. Kamalaśila says that there is no distinction perceived between the probans (premises) and the proposition (conclusion). That is, the probans is a part of the proposition itself. In the case in question what is meant to be proved is the fact of the pain being due to a particular insect and the same fact is asserted in different words in the probans. Hence, there is no difference between the premises and the conclusion.

Further, he points out the defect in the citation viz. 'the eyes having the peculiar potency for bringing about the effect in the shape of colour perception'. He shows the problem by stating thus:

चक्षुषो धर्मिरूपस्य सत्ता तावदनिश्चिता
तस्याश्च साधनं युक्तं नासिद्ध्यातिप्रसंगतः।।[184]

As a matter of fact, the very existence of the eyes, which is the subject, is still uncertain. And this proving of existence cannot be valid as it would be open to the defects of inadmissibility and the rest.

What he intends to prove is that if existence is to be proved, then the probans put forward is open to all the three defects of the probans. For instance, if the character cited as the probans is something positive, then it is inadmissible; if it is both i.e. positive and negative, then it is inconclusive. If it is negative, then it is contradictory. Thus, it has been declared that the positive property is not admitted. Both positive and negative would be inconclusive and the negative one would be contradictory. How can existence be proved then?

If what is sought to be proved is the potency in the eye, the subject to bring about visual perception, even the potency, existence etc. are synonyms. The proving of potency would involve the proving of existence. On the negative aspect also, in as much as the potency, being beyond the reach of the senses, would not be well known, the probans would become fallacious as having no well known substratum.

Similarly, the problems in the form namely 'because of the perception of colour' would be something not present in the subject and hence, it should be understood to be inadmissible.

At this point Pātrasvāmin may ask: 'how then the Buddhists prove the existence of the eyes and the other sense organs'. To this question Śāntarakṣita answers:

किन्तु रूपादिभावेऽपि चक्षुर्ज्ञानं न जायते
कदाचित् तेन नन्मात्रं न हेतुरिति गम्यते।।[185]

It means, even though colour and other things are there but sometimes-visual perception does not take place. Hence, it is understood that perception alone cannot be the reason for the existence of the eye directly as ' this is the eye'. What happens is that, it is found that the perception appears only when certain things in the form of colour etc. are there. And it is so found that it is present when these things are there and it is absent when they are absent. And what we seek to prove is that the perception could not have those things alone as its cause, but it must have some other cause, so that the subject of our inference is the said perception, which cannot be said to be unknown. The basis of our conclusion is the practical notion of diversity.

Pātrasvāmin may argue further, 'it may be that in the manner shown, the perception may be the subject even so, the probans remain only two-featured'. To this argument Santarakita replies:

स्वहेतुनियतोद्भूतिरंकुरादिश्च विद्यते
तस्मिन् दृष्टान्त एवं च वैलक्षण्यमतिस्फुटम्।[186]

It means, the sprout is actually found to exist as having its birth inseparably connected with its cause. And this is always available as the corroborative instance. This instance per dissimilarity is clear to be stated.

Kamalaśila makes it clear by stating that, invariably concomitant with its cause is the birth i.e. appearance of the sprout. Things like sprout having their birth dependent upon their cause and hence coming into existence only occasionally, are possible as the corroborative instance i.e. in the proving of the visual perception as being due to the eye. The argument being formulated thus, those things that appear on the presence of something else, only occasionally, cannot be regarded as produced from that alone. They must be regarded as dependent upon their causes. For instance even when the sail and other things are there, the sprout is found to appear or not to appear according as the seed is there or not there.[187]

Even, when colour etc. are there, the visual perception appears only at certain times, according as the eyes are closed or not? Hence, in the case of the denial of the eyes, the argument would point out that the said denial would be contrary to a wider proposition. While in the case of the asserting of the existence of the eyes, it would certain a natural reason.[188]

He points out further defects, in the argument proposed by Pātrasvāmin namely that ' the soul and the Jar are somehow non-existent' etc. by stating that in proving that the jar and the other things are somehow non-existent, the probans is found as in a previous case to be futile and also inadmissible. He says:

कथञ्चिदसदात्मत्वसाधने च घटादिषु
पूर्ववद्धेतुवैफल्यमप्रसिद्धिश्च दृश्यते।[189]

Here, it would amount to proving what is already admitted or proved, as the fact of the jar etc. being 'somehow non-existent[1] is already admitted.

Pātrasvāmin argues that 'there being nothing where the probandum is known to be absent, there can be no corroborative instance per dissimilarity. In replies to this Śāntarakṣita says:

अस्ति चात्रापि विस्पष्टं वैधर्म्यैण निदर्शनम्
तदेवतेषां स्वं रूपं प्रथति हि विपक्षताम्॥
कथञ्चन सदात्मत्वसाधनेऽपि निरात्मसु
इष्टसिद्धिरसिद्धिश्च वैधर्म्याप्तिस्तथैव च।[190]

Here, also there is clear corroborative instance per dissimilarity that same form of the things becomes the thing where the probandum is known to be absent. In proving of the character of being somehow existent in regard to non-entities, there would be proving of what is already admitted, also inadmissibility and the concomitance of the contrary character in that way.

Further defects are pointed out in the argument proposed by Pātrasvāmin : 'your father being present in the house' etc. He says:

पितृशब्दश्रुतैर्याऽपि वेश्मनः प्रतिपाद्यते
पितृसंम्बंधिता तत्र व्यक्तो हेतुस्त्रिलक्षणः॥
क्वचिद् विप्रतिसम्बद्ध स्वरः प्रागुलक्षितः
तस्याननुभवे पूर्वं दुर्द्धरा हेत्वसिद्धता॥[191]

When the presence of the father in the house is sought to be proved by the hearing of the father's voice, the probans in this case is clearly 'three-featured'. As surely at sometime previously the concomitance of the voice has been perceived, then the inadmissibility of the probans would be irresistible. Thus, he proceeds to identify the three-featured character of the probans. He elaborates:

यस्मिन् प्रागुलब्धश्च नोपालब्धश्च यत्र सः
अन्वयो व्यतिरेको वा विस्पष्टं तत्र दृश्यते॥
शब्दास्तु ज्ञापयत्यर्थं नैव वाह्यं कथञ्च
अन्यथासम्भवाभावाद् विवक्षागमकस्त्वसौ॥
तस्यां च प्रतिपाद्यायां वैलक्षण्यमतिस्फुटम्
विवक्षासम्मुखीभावे न हि शब्द प्रयुज्यते॥
दीपस्तु ज्ञापको नैव नीलादेर्लिङ्गभावतः
ज्ञानोत्पादनयोग्यस्य जननात्तु तथोच्यते॥
ज्ञापके लिङ्गरूपे च पक्ष धर्मादि चिन्तयते
अन्यथा चक्षुरादीनां कस्मादेतन्न चोद्यते॥

अन्यथानुपपत्त्यापि चाक्षुषत्वं न साधकम्
पक्षधर्मवियोगेन क्लिबासतेनैकलक्षणाः॥
एकरूपतायोक्तनां द्वैरूप्यं चोपलक्षितम्
द्विरूपत्वेन चोक्तानां त्रैरूप्यं पक्षधर्मतः॥
अन्यथाऽनुपपत्त्येव चाक्षेपादिति चेन्न तत्
शब्दादावन्यथापीष्टे चाक्षुषत्वेन चास्त्यसौ॥[192]

In that house wherein the father had been found before and also in that wherein he had not been found before, there the positive and negative concomitance, is clearly perceived. As regards the word, it does not make known any external object at all, because in this case the character of 'being otherwise impossible' is not present. The word can only be the indicator of the speaker's wish to speak of a certain thing. If speaker's wish were meant to be what is expressed by the word, then its difference is quite clear. Because when the speaker's wish is not there, the word cannot be used.

As regards the lamp, it does not make the blue and other things known by becoming the indicative inferential. All that it does is that it is called a means of cognition. Only in case the word were an inferential indicative, would it be necessary to consider, if it fulfils the conditions of being present in the subject and so forth? Otherwise why cannot the same be urged in connection with the eye and other members as means of cognition? Even through the character of 'being otherwise impossible' 'visibility' cannot prove anything, unless it is present in the subject i.e. the minor term. Thus, 'one featured' probans are all-important. In those that have been cited as 'one featured' probans, the presence of two features becomes clearly indicated. And those that have been cited as two featured, the presence of three features becomes clearly indicated. Because every probans must reside in the subject which therefore is an additional condition that must be fulfilled. If it is argued that the character of 'being otherwise impossible' implies this feature that cannot be so. Because in the case of sound though visibility may be otherwise desired, it is not present in sound which is the subject.

Kamalaśila makes this point clear by stating that in the case of words, the character being otherwise impossible cannot be admissible, with reference to external things. Because it cannot serve as an inferential indicative of these latter, since it is dependent entirely upon the speaker's desire. If the said character is asserted in the case of words with reference to the object that figures in the cognition brought about by the words, then there are all the three features present, as in the case of smoke indicating the fire. Because the speaker's desire is not there, hence, words cannot be used. The usage must be regarded as the effect of that desire. And as such, it is indicative of the thing spoken of, just as the smoke is of fire. And we accept this but not as being expressive of the thing.[193]

As regards the lamp, it is not admitted even as the indicator like smoke. All that is admitted is that it has come to be popularly regarded as the indictor, making things known by reason of its making the jar etc. i.e. objects cognized, capable of bringing about the cognition. But the words are not inferential indicatives. Hence, any discussion as to the indicative subsisting in the subject cannot arise in this case. If it arose in this case, then why could not the same discussion arise in the case of the eye and the rest, which are the means of sense perceptions and not inferential indicatives?

The expression 'Otherwise etc.' sums up the subject matter under consideration. The sense is that, even though visibility is invariably concomitant with non-eternality, it does not prove this non-eternality in sound.

Thus, in all causes the condition of subsisting in the subject must be present by admitting this as a necessary condition. Those probans that have been cited, as 'one featured' must necessarily become two featured', and those cited, as 'two featured' must become three featured'. Thus, on account of the necessity of subsistence in the subject, it is the 'one featured' probans that are really important.

It may be logical to argue that such characters as

subsisting in the subject are all implied by that of 'being otherwise impossible', and hence, they cannot form so many different independent characteristics of the probans. Because, the opponent has himself asserted that there is the character of 'being otherwise impossible' even when subsistence in the subject is not there in the following passage : "through the character of 'being otherwise impossible' the lamp and other things are actually indicative of things, even though they do not reside in the subject".

In the case of visibility, even though 'non-eternality' is 'otherwise impossible', visibility does not subsist in the subject, so that in every way that has been asserted is entirely doubtful.

It has been argued by Pātrasvāmin that in the case of the reasonng 'he is dark because he is the son of so and so' even though the probans has all the three features, yet it is not conductive to certainty of cognition.[194]

To this Śāntarakṣita answers:

तत्पुत्रत्वादिहेतूना संदिग्धव्यतिरेकतः
न त्रैलक्षण्यसद्भावो विजातीयाविरोधतः।[195]

In the case of such probans namely 'because he is the son of so and so, the contrary being open to doubt, the three conditions are not present, because what is cited is not incompatible with the contrary. It may be possible that the child may be the son of the man and yet not dark. There being no incompatibility in this, the absence of the probans where the probandum is known to be absent, is open to doubt and this is one of the three features. So the probans is not three featured, hence, the examples cited by Pātrasvāmin are not relevant.[196]

The entire discussion of Śāntarakṣita and Dharmakirti regarding the theory of inferential cognition of the *Jainas* can be presented in the following manner:

Firstly, the Buddhist philosophers particularly Dharmakīirti and following him Dharmottara *and* Śāntarakṣ ita have presented the *Jaina* notion of inferential cognition;

more precisely they have presented the *Jainas'* idea regarding the members or *avayava vakya* (syllogism) of Pararthanumāna and then the notion of *'hetu'* for the inferential cognition.

In their presentation, they have presented the view of only Pātrasvāmin, but not of other *Jaina* logicians. If we see the *Jaina* tradition and go through the available literature, then it will be clear that the *avayava vakyas* for inferential cognition as accepted by the *Jaina* philosophers are not unanimous. The numbers or the steps are determined with regard to the *Pramātṛ/pramātā* of a particular knowledge. But, there is no doubt that Pātrasvāmin has recorded or rather fixed this number. That is what they have presented the argument of Pātrasvāmin regarding the main cause of the inferential cognition and its principal characteristics. Pātrasvāmin has accepted only *'anyathānupapannatva'* as the principal characteristics of *hetu,* whereas the Buddhists have accepted three characteristics. Finally, Śāntarakṣita has given a logical argument to show the incongruity and irrelevance in the opponent's view and established his own thesis.

On the contrary, in the *Jaina* tradition some philosophers like Prabhachandra and Anantavfrya say that these defects, which are shown by Śāntarakṣita against the view of the *Jainas* i.e. against the idea of one featured probans are not applicable to the *Jainas,* rather these are applicable to the idea of Buddhist philosophers i.e. applicable to the three featured probans, because these can be also applied even to *Hetvabhasa.* And finally they conclude that the one-featured *hetu* is the shortest and the simplest route to make an inference regarding anything.[197]

On Anekāntavāda

Anekāntavāda is the foundation of the *Jaina* philosophy, on which the mansion of *Jaina* philosophy stands. According to Jainism, the reality is dynamic, which is having innumerable characteristics, hence cannot be perceived or known at once by an ordinary man. Different people look at from different aspects of the same reality and therefore, their partial findings seem to be contradictory to one other. Hence, they indulge in debates claiming that each of them was completely true. The *Jaina* philosophers thought over this conflict and tried to reveal the whole truth by establishing a theory of non-absolutist standpoint i.e. *Anekantovada,* based on two theories, namely, *Nayavāda* and *syadvāda.* We have discussed it in detail, in the previous chapter. Here we have to see how Buddhist philosophers have recorded this concept of the *Jainas* and finally refuted that with arguments.

Before attending the Buddhist treatment on the issue, let us have a clear and precise understanding of the concept for better understanding of the Buddhists' argumentation.

To understand the reality there are two mutually distinct and fundamental standpoints from which all things can be considered. They are universalization and particularization. Universalization starts with the observation on a synthetic basis of similarities and gradually reacts the level where distinction exists and finally concludes that any object of consciousness is in reality an element. On the other hand, particularization is based on observation of dissimilarities, which finally leads on to the conclusion that the universe is, but a conglomeration of completely dissimilar existence.

The nature of reality, according to his theory, is permanent in change. It possesses three common characters viz. *utpdda* i.e. origination, *vyaya* i.e. destruction and *dhrauvya* i.e. permanence through birth and decay.[198] It also possesses the attributes i.e. *gunas* which is called *anvayī* and which co-exist with substance *(dravya)* and modifications *(paryāya)* which is called *vyatirekī,* and which succeed each other.[199] And productivity and destructivity constitute the dynamic aspect of an entity and permanence is the enduring factor.[200]

Ankekāntavāda is a theory by which one is able to know the real nature of the many-faced reality. It is defined as:

अनेकेवहवोन्ता अंशा धर्मा वा आत्मनः स्वरूपाणि यस्य तदनेकात्मकम्[201]

Nayavāda i.e. the theory of partial truth is an integral part of the conception *ankekāntavāda,* which is essential to conceive the sole nature of reality. That is why the commentator of *Tattvārthasūtra* says:

जीवादीन् पदार्थान् नयन्ति प्राप्नुवन्ति कारयंति साधयन्ति निर्वर्तयंति निर्भासयन्ति उपलंभयन्ति व्यञ्जयन्ति इति नया:।[202]

It provides for the acceptance of different viewpoints on the basis that each reveals a partial truth about an object. *Naya* investigates analytically a particular standpoint of the problem. It is defined as:

नयो ज्ञातुरभिप्राय:।[203]

अनिराकृतप्रतिपक्षो वस्त्वंशग्राही ज्ञातुरभिप्रायो नय:।[204]

Syādvāda is a theory, which investigates the various standpoints of the truth made possible by *naya* and integrates them a constant and compressive synthesis. Its method is synthetical while *nayavāda* is analytical in character. *Syādvāda* reveals the certainty regarding any problem and not merely by the possibility or probability. More precisely *syādvāda* is the expression of *ankekāntavāda*. This is very clearly stated by *Akalaṅkadeva* namely thus:

अनेकान्तात्मकार्थकथनं स्याद्वाद:।[205]

Let us have the discussion on how *ankekāntavāda* and its two integral parts viz. *nayavāda* and *syādvāda* are presented by the Buddhist philosophers in their respective literatures.

First of all, if we go through the Buddhist literature, we will find the representation of *syadvada* is clearly stated and then it is refuted by the all Buddhist philosophers. Postponing the treatment of *syādvāda* and *nayavdsda* as done by the Buddhists for the time being, we will now discuss some related aspects of Jainism as discussed by the Buddhist, which can be compared with the Jaina concept of *ankekāntavāda* and *nayavāda*.

Let us see first, how *ankekāntavāda* can be compared with Buddhist's philosophical tenets. It can be compared with the concept of answering the question *(vyākaraṇīya)* in the *pāli* literature.[206] *Pāli* literature describes how *Buddha* answered a question in four ways. These four ways are:

(a) *Emaṁśa. vyākaraṇīya,* i.e. answerable categorically.

(b) *Paṭipucchāvyākaraṇīya,* i.e. answerable by putting another question.

(c) *Ṭhāpañīya* i.e. question that should be set aside.

(d) *Vibhajjavyākaraṇīya* i.e. answerable analytically.

Buddha has adopted these techniques and answered the numerous metaphysical and ethical questions put to him by his disciples. Thus, he himself claims to be a *vibhajjavādin* i.e. the person who answers the questions analytically, by breaking the arguments into several compartments and arguing separately to each compartment.[207] In Jainism also, *Jainas* require the *Jaina* monks to explain a problem with the help off *vibhajjavāda.*[208] It shows that both *Jainas* as well as Buddhists followed the analytical method of explanation. It can be assumed further, that the earliest division of the above questions was divided into two ways viz.

(a) *akaṁśavyākaraṇīya pañha*

(b) *anekaṇśavyākararṇīya pañha,*

corresponding to the *Jaina* classification of two kinds of statements viz.

(a) *amaṁśika* dharma

(b) *anekṁśika* dharma.

But in the later period of Buddhism we found that *vibhajja vyākaraṇīya* and *ṭhāpañīya* are the subdivisions of *anekaṁśa vyākaraṇīya pañha* and *paṭipucchāvyākaraṇīya* is a subdivision of *vibhajjavyākaraṇīya.*[209]

One thing should be made clear here that the Buddha used the word *anekaṁśa* in his preaching, for instance, in replying to a question asked *by poṭṭapāda,* Buddha says, "I have taught and laid down doctrines of which it is possible to make categorical assertions and I have taught and led down doctrines of which it is not possible to make categorical assertion". As he says:

एकंशिकापि मया धम्मा देशिता पन्नता, अनेकंशिका पि .... मया ध म्मा देशिता पन्नित्ता।[210]

Here, *anekaṁśikā* like *vibhajjavāda* is similar to *ankekāntavāda* of the *Jainas*. Though the etymology and the meaning of the two terms is same, still there are some differences between these two theories namely, Jainism accepts all statements to possess some relative *(anekānta)* truth, while the Buddhism does not subscribe to this view in toto. All non-categorical statements *(anekāntika)* can be true or false from one standpoint or another. *Anekāntavāda,* unlike *ankaṁsikavāda* c̣onceives of the possibility of knowing reality from one or more standpoints. Durvekamishra in his *hetuvinduṭ ikāloka* summarized this concept as follows:

स्याच्छद्वोनेकान्तवचनो नित्यतोस्तितेन स्याद्वादो अनेकान्तवादो यद्वा स्याद्क्षिणिकः स्याद्क्षणिक इत्यादि।[211]

A developed form of this doctrine is referred to in a later Buddhist philosophical literature. This theory continued still further upto the time of Kundakundācārya. After Kundakunda, Samntabhadra tries to explain it further with some examples, which is referred by Karṇakagomin in his *Pramāṇa vārtikavṛtiṭ īka*[212] and Durvekamishra in his *Hetuvinduṭīkāloka*[213]. According to Samantabhadra, the triple characters abide with a substance at one and the same time. They are not mutually independent. *Utpāda* can never exist without *vyaya* and *dhrauvya*. The other two characters too are mutually dependent. Samatabhadra uses an example to clarify this view. If a jar made of gold is turned into a crown, it will please a man who has an attachment to the crown, but it will displease a man who dislikes the crown but is interested in the gold, will have no objection to it at all. Here, origination, destruction and permanence abide in one reality. Another example is presented to make this controversial point clearer. He says: he who takes a vow to live on milk does not take curd; and he who takes a vow to live on food other than supplied by a cow, takes neither milk nor curd. Thus, Samantabhadra concludes that *utpāda, vyaya* and *dhrauvya* may exist is a relative sense.[214]

The etymology of the word *dravya*[215] itself indicates that a thing is permanent -in-change taking a new form simultaneously with the disappearance of previous form.[216]

On Syādvāda

According to Jainism, an entity is *anantadharmatātmaka* i.e. having innumerable characteristics, which cannot be perceived at once by lay man. To know the real nature of an entity they take resort in *Syādvāda* theory. They conceive the reality, positive and negative aspects i.e. *bhāvābhavātmakatvena,* identity-in-difference i.e. *bhedābhedena,* eternality in non-eternality i.e. *nityanityātmakena,* universal-cum-particular i.e. *sāmānyaviṣeṣātmakena* or substance-in-modes i.e. *dravya paryayatmakena.* These are the main elements of the *Syādvāda* theory. In Buddhist literature, most of the Buddhist philosophers in their respective works have criticized these elements.

Before going to present the criticism of *Syādvāda* theory by the Buddhist philosophers, one thing may be noted here that through *Syādvāda* theory, particularly the seven *bhaṅgas* (sevenfold predications) postulated by the *Jaina* thinkers, still some concepts are not similar to the concept of *Syādvāda* as found in Buddhist literature. What we want to introduce here is that the Buddhists, have also accepted some concepts like *Syādvāda* theory. For example, Sanjay Belatthiputta's four-fold scheme or five-fold formula of denial is based on negative and positive aspects[217], or the founder of *Ājivaka* sect, Ācārya Makkhal Gosālas's three fold standpoint, which is called *trirāśis*[218], or Buddha's *ekamsika* and *anekamśikā* theory[219] and his fourfold schemes to answer to the logical questions[220], are attested the same idea of *Syādvāda* theory.

Thus, Dr. Jayatilleka rightly remarks "But judged by the fact that the threefold schemes of prediction is simpler than the fourfold scheme of the skeptics and Buddhists and the sevenfold scheme of the *Jainas*. It would appear to be earlier than both the Buddhist and *Jaina* schemes, with which the *ājivakas* could not have been acquainted when they evolved theirs. In fact, it can be shown that in the earliest Buddhist and the *Jaina* texts the very doctrine of the *trirāśikas,* which seems to have necessitated the threefold scheme, is mentioned. Thus making it highly probable that it was at least earlier than the

Jaina scheme"[221]. He accounts to this view by saying that the earliest stratum of the *Pāli nikāyas* is known to be of the fourfold scheme. One of the earliest books of the *Jaina* canon, the *sūtrakritānga,* which makes an independent reference to this *trairāśika* doctrine, does not mention the sevenfold scheme, although it was aware of the basic principle of *Syādvāda*.

Buddhist philosophers have criticized the *Jaina* doctrine of *Syādvāda* on the ground that it leads to self-contradiction, commingling and doubt etc. Let us present, one by one, the criticism of the Buddhist philosophers on the *Jaina* concept of *Syādvāda*.

Dharmakīrti's criticism on Syādvāda theory

In the context of refuting the *Saṃkhya* philosophy, which thinks of the nature of reality as absolute difference i.e. *atyantabheda, Dharmakirti* has refuted the *Jaina Arhikas* i.e. the *Digaṁbara Jaina* philosophers, who thinks of the nature of reality as difference-in-non-difference i.e. *bhedābhedabhāva* or *bhedaghaṭitābheda*. In the *Pramāṇavārtika* and its vṛtti Dharmakīrti remarks that the *anekāntavāda* of *Jainas* is a mere non-sensical talk i.e. *pralāpamātra*. He asserts:

एतेनैव यदह्रीकाः किमप्यश्लीलमाकुलम्
प्रलपन्ति प्रक्षिप्तं तदप्येकांतसम्भवात्॥
सर्वस्योभरूपत्वे तद्विशेषनिराकृतेः
चोदिता दधि खादेति किमुष्ट्रन्नभिधावति॥
अथास्त्यातिशयः कश्चिद्येन भेदेन वर्त्तते।
स एव दधि सोऽन्यत्र नास्तीत्यनुभयं परम्॥[222]

Dharmakirti is of the view that the *Jaina* theory of dual character, viz. universal and particular, is so formulated that the character or particularity is relegated to the background and made less significant. He explains this with reference to the famous example of camel and curd. He argues:

दिगंवराणां इदं च किमप्युक्तं अश्लीलमहेयोपादेयमपरिनिष्ठानात् आकुले स्यादुष्ट्रोदधि न स्यादिति यैरुक्तं तेऽपि एतेनैव प्रक्षिप्ताः भावेनैव एकांत

भेदात्। एवं उष्ट्रेऽपि स्याद् दधि। नापि स एव उष्ट्रः येनाऽन्योऽपि स्यादुष्ट्रः, तथा दध्यपि स्यादुष्ट्रः। नापि तदेव दधि, येनान्यत् स्याद् दधि। तदनयोरेकस्यापि वा कस्यचिद् तद्रूपाभावास्य चाभावात्, अतद्भाविनो वा स्वानियतस्य चाभावात्। कस्यचिद् विशेषस्याभावेन दधि खादेति चोक्त उष्ट्रमेव भुञ्जीत। अथानयोरस्ति कश्चिदतिशयः यदत्र तथा चोदितः क्षीरविकारे दध्न्येव प्रवर्त्तते नान्यत्र। अतिशयोऽर्थक्रियार्थिप्रवृत्तिविषयः, स एव तत्फल विशिष्टोपादानभावेन लक्षितस्वभावो हि दधिस्वभावत्वात्। तादृशस्वभावः स च नान्यत्र, अर्थिनः प्रवृत्यभावात्।[223]

He says: if the particularity, which distinguishes camel from curd or vice-verse, is not an important factor. One may as well eat camel when he wants to eat curd. He tries by this argument to demolish the *Jaina* theory as he understood that curd is not only curd by itself *(svarūpena)* but camel in a relative sense *(pararūpena)*. According to Dharamakīrti, there cannot be universal character between camel and curd and even if such a character exists, their mutual difference or particularity is all that matters for both identification and use.

Against the *Jaina* conception of the universal character of a thing he says: if all realities are *sat,* there would be no difference between knowledge and word *(dhī* and *dvani)* that imparts a knowledge, which is quite impossible. Therefore, *Syādvāda* conception is defective.

Prajñākaragupta's Criticism on Jaina concept of *Syādvāda.*

Prajñākaragupta (660-720 AD), in his commentary on *Pramāṇavārttika* of Dharmakīrti, named *pramāṇavārttikālaṁkāra,* criticizes the *Jaina's* view of reality. According to Jainism, origination *(utpatti),* destruction *(vilaya)* and permanence are the three essential characteristics of reality. To this triple nature of reality of the *Jainas* Prajñākaragupta objects:

अथोत्पादव्ययध्रौव्यं युक्तं यत्तत् सदिष्यते
एषामेव न सत्त्वं स्यात् एतद्भावावियोगतः
यदाव्ययस्तदा-स्तदा सत्त्वं कथं तस्यप्रतीयते

पूर्व प्रतीते सत्त्वं तत्तदा तस्य व्ययः कथम्
ध्रौव्येपि यदि नास्मिन् धीः कथं सत्त्वं प्रतीयते
प्रतीतेरेव सर्वस्य तस्मात्सत्त्वं कुतोऽन्यथा
तस्मान्न नित्यानित्यस्य वस्तुनः सम्भवः क्वचित्
अनित्यं नित्यमथवा वस्त्वेकान्तेन युक्तिमत॥[224]

Before criticizing or examining the *Jaina* position he first reproduces the *Jaina* view of the reality in the line *athotpāda* etc., which we have just recorded. His criticism is very much similar to the criticism of Nāgārjuna as we have already noticed. Against this he says: origination, destruction and permanence cannot exit together. If it is destroyed, how can there be the cognition of existence *(yadāvyayaḥ satvakathaṃ)* be a reality. If it is permanent, how can there be destruction and if it is permanent, then it should always be existent? If everything is cognized, then all these would be existence *(satvaṃ)*. How can there be otherwise *(kutonyathā),* that means, how to account for the state of destruction and continuation in one and the same reality? Hence, the reality cannot be realized at both eternal and non-eternal. In conclusion, he observed that it is logical to accept reality as either eternal or non-eternal following the view of *"ekanta pakṣa'*. It means that the triple character of a thing is a self-contradictory theory.

Karṇakagomini's criticism on Syādvāda

Following the footsteps of Dharmakriti, Karṇakagomin in his *Pramāṇavārtikasvavṛittiīkā,* criticizes the view of Digambara *Jainas* on *Syādvāda* theory. He first ridiculed the *Jaina* philosophers particularly the *Digambara Jaina* philosophers that the naked-shameless *Jaina* monks due to their ugliness, speak that 'all in one' and 'all in not one' which is nothing but mere a non-sensical talk."

अह्रीका नग्नतया निर्लजाः क्षपणकाः अयुक्तविधानस्य कुत्सिततत्वात् किमपीत्याह। अश्लीलं ग्राम्यम्। सर्वः सर्वस्वभावो न च सर्व सर्वस्वभाव इति यत् यत् प्रलपन्ति प्रतिक्षिप्तन्तदपि तस्मादेकांतसम्भवात्। एकस्यैवान्तस्यान्तभेदप्रकारस्य सम्भवात्।[225]

Further, he tries to clarify his remark by presenting a traditional example of the Jainas. The Jaina explains their theory of nature of reality with the illustration of a golden jar, where gold is considered the general and not the particular character. To clarify: In a golden jar, the jar is produced *(uptpāta)* the previous mode *(paryāya),* say a *mukuṭa* i.e. crown is destroyed *(vyaya)* and the 'gold' *dravya* is continued *(dhrauvya).* Now, the objection Karṇakagomini wants to point out is: in this theory of reality, with the illustration is 'gold', the *Jaina* treats 'gold' or *sāmānya,* which continued. As a matter of fact, *'dravyatva'* continued to exist in all the three states; hence, it should be treated as general characteristic. But this is not possible in your case due to lack of identical knowledge in all the three states. Even if there is *abhinnakalpanā* i.e. one identical knowledge with regard to gold in the three states, let there be no universal, so far as its modes are concerned, namely *kaṭaka, keyura* etc. Here he points out why the *Jainas* do not recognize the jar or pot itself as a general character, since *dravyatva* is in all of them according to Jainism.

तद्यथा कटकेयूरादिषु सुवर्णप्रत्ययस्यानुयायिनस्सद्भावस्सुवर्णत्वसामान्यं कल्प्यते।

तथा घटपटादिषु द्रव्यत्वादिप्रत्ययस्यान्वयिनः सद्भावाद् द्रव्यत्वसामान्यमेकं किन्नेष्यते।

न चेष्यतेऽभिन्नप्रत्ययसद्भावेऽपि तथा कटकेयूरादिषु सामान्यकल्पना माभूदित्येवम्परमेतत्।[226]

He then criticizes the *Jaina* theory of relativity, according to which they accept the mutual negation i.e. *anyonyābhāva* to distinguish the realities, so that they should not be confused. He then starts to criticize the view that the distinction among things cannot be identified by mutual negation, which is possible in entities produced by causes, which are different. If they are originated from different causes, how does *anyonyābhāva* come into existence?[227] He writes :

दिगम्बरो मन्यते सर्वात्मकमेकं स्यादन्यापोहव्यतिक्रमे तस्माद् भेद एवान्यथा न स्याद् अन्योन्याभावो भावानां यदि न भवेदिति। सोप्यनेन

निरस्तः। अभावेन भावभेदस्य कर्तुमशक्यत्वात्। नाप्यभिन्नानां हेतुतो निष्पन्नानामन्योन्याभावः सम्भवति। भिन्नाश्चेन् निष्पन्नाः कथमन्योन्या-भावकल्पनेत्युक्तम्।[228]

To explain, according to *Jainas 'sarvaṁ ekātmakaṁ* or *ekaṁ sarvātmakaṁ' i.e.* a single entity is identical with many or can be cognized as everything else and vise versa, following the *syādvāda* theory. Now, Karṇakagomin objects to the very idea of maintaining distinction on the basis of absence. He writes : it is not possible for maintaining distinction in case of positive entities on the basis of the absence. (*abhāvena bhāvabhedasya kartumasakyatvāt*). If it is argued that mutual absence or distinction amongst the realities is possible with regard to the realities, which are produced from the causes, which are not different or identical. If they are different, there is no ground to postulate *anyonyābhāva*.

Further, he tries to show the defects in the Jaina's theory of universal-cum-particular of *ūrdhartā sāmānyātatmaka* and *rīryakasāmānyatātmaka vastu*[229]. He then rejects the theory saying that there should be either *abheda* or *atyantābheda*. Both characters cannot co-exist in the same substance. Hence, the ū*rdhatāsāmanya* could be discarded because things are not permanent. And as regarding *fuyksāmānya* that is also defective in character in his opinion. He says: if the universality were in the substance, the *ghaṭa* (pot) and *paṭa* (linen) or *dadhi* (curd) or *usrra* (camel) would be identical. Hence, a shape or a water-pot should be found in cloth and a curd-eater should assume a camel. Therefore, *syādvāda* doctrine is false *(mithyāvāda)* in his opinion. He says:

तेन योऽपि दिगम्बरो मन्यते नास्त्याभिर्घटपटादि सामान्यमिष्यते ......

उभयग्रहणमनेकत्वोपलक्षणार्थान्तस्मिन् सति तद्विशेषस्य उष्ट्र उष्ट्र एव न दधि। दधि

दध्येव नोष्ट्र इत्येवं लक्षणस्य निराकृतेः दधि खादेत्येवं चोदितः पुरुषः किमुष्ट्रं खादितुं नाभिधावति। उष्ट्रेपि दध्यभिन्नाद् द्रव्यत्वाद् अव्यतिरेकात् स्याद् दधि। नापि स एवेति। उष्ट्र एवोष्ट्र इत्येकान्तवादः येनान्योऽपि दध्यादिक स्याद्वुष्ट्रः तथा दध्यापि स्यादुष्ट्रः। उष्ट्रभिन्नेन द्रव्यत्वेन

दध्नस्तादात्म्येनाभिसम्बन्धात् नापि तदेवेति दध्येव दधि। एतेन सर्वस्योभयरूपत्वं व्याख्यातं ..... मिथ्यावाद एव स्याद्वादः।[230]

Thus, Karaṇakagomin makes his refutation following Dharmakirti's arguments and tries to prove that the dual characteristic of an entity is not possible as it invites serious defects in the theory.

Nāgārjuna's Criticism on the Jaina concept of Syādvāda

From the very beginning of the *Jaina* philosophy, the *Jaina* philosophers like *Ācārya* Kundakunda and Umāsvāti established clearly the triple character of reality namely production, destruction and permanence. Nāgārjuna (150-250), the propounder of *śūnyavāda* made the change that the theory of triple character is itself a self-contradictory formula, as it cannot be associated with reality.

In the *Mādhymika sūtra,* in the context of verifying the *saṁsṛta,* he recorded the view of the *Jainas*. Though he does not say whether this view is of *Jainas* or of others, still it is obvious that before *Nāgārjuna* the Jaina philosophers established this triple character of reality. Though Ramachandra Pandeya, in his book Nāgārjuna's philosophy of no-identity has mentioned that this is the view of *Sāmmitya* School of Buddhism, it is the idea as the *Jaina* philosophers hold. Similarly in the *Śūnyatāsaptati* he also recorded this idea of the *Jainas* in the context of establishing the *śūnyatā*. We will discuss here the view of Nāgārjuna regarding the triple character of reality with reference to both the *Mādhyamaka śāshtra* and *Śūnyaśaptati* with the commentary called *prasannadayāvṛtti* of ācārya Chandrakīrti on *Mādhamaka śāshtra*.

According to Nāgārjuna, a thing, which is subjected to origination, destruction and permanence is called *"Saṁskṛta",* which is nothing but the Jaina concept of substance or reality. He firstly presents the *Jaina* position. He says: some philosophers have accepted that the *Saṁskṛta* is the three characteristics of reality viz. origination, destruction and permanence. Then he has developed his arguments by raising the following questions: whether the origination itself is

Saṁskṛta or *asaṁskṛta*. If it is (composite) *Saṁskṛta*, it must have all the three characteristics mentioned above. If it is non-composite *(asaṁskṛta)*, then how would the characteristics of composites be possible? He says:

यदि संस्कृत उत्पादस्तत्र युक्ता त्रिलक्षणी
अथासंस्कृत उत्पादः कथं संस्कृतलक्षणम्।[231]

Secondly, he asked: the origination etc. the three separately are not capable of characterizing composites. If the three together were to characterize it, then how could they exist at one place and the same time? He comments:

उत्पादाद्यस्त्रयो व्यस्ता नालं लक्षणकर्मणि
संस्कृतस्य समस्ताः स्यरेकत्र कथमेकदा।[232]

Ācārya Chandrakīrti makes this point clear by asserting thus: in both ways i.e. either separately *(vyasthā)* or being together *(samastha)*, these three are not capable of characterizing composites. Candrakīrti asserts the triple characteristics viz. *utpāta*, *vyaya* and *dhrauvya* cannot be maintained with regard to the reality. He records two possibilities viz. *vyasthatayā* i.e. separately or individually and *samasthatayā* i.e. collectively. Now resorting to either of the alternatives one cannot explain the triple character of the reality.

With regard to the first alternative i.e. the association of either of the three characteristics individually, he argued: if at the time of origination *(utpādakāle) sthiti* and *bhaṅga* are existent i.e. if a reality is taken to be as associated with the origination only then, this will not be treated as *samskṛta* due to its dissociation with *sthiti* and *bhaṅga*. Further, at the state of *sthiti* i.e. existent there would not be *utpāda* and *bhaṅga* and the *sthiti* should be bereft of *utpāda* and *bhaṅga*. It is illogical to presume any reality bereft *of utpāda and bhaṅga l*ike the fictitious object called *'khapuṣpa'*.

Chandrakīrti finds further faults with this alternative namely that one reality is associated with *sthiti*, which cannot be associated with the *anityadharma* afterwards, due to its contradictory nature, because the one and the same object *śāśvata,* and *aśāśvata dharma* cannot be attributed to one and the same time.

Again, what is not originated and what is devoid of *sthiti* cannot be subject to destruction like *'khapuspa'* or *'bandhyāputra'*. In this manner *utpāda* etc. individually cannot form the definition of reality or cannot present the nature of reality.

Similarly, the other alternative i.e. the three collectively presents the nature of reality is also discarded. Candrakīrti says: In the one and the same object delimited by a particular time contradictory properties cannot be exist. Ridiculing the *Jaina* theory of triple characteristics of reality he comments sarcastically: would any one having mind will entertain the view that the reality is produced, continued to and destroyed in one and the same time in one and the same place. Thus, both the alternatives interpretation of the triple characteristics of reality is discarded and refuted by Chandrakīrti. We have attempted to reproduce his arguments in original for convenience. His arguments runs thus:

तत्र व्यस्ता लक्षणकर्मणि न युजन्ते। यदि उत्पादकाले स्थितिभंगौ न स्यातां तदा स्थितिभंगरहितस्य आकाशस्येव संस्कृतलक्षणत्वेनानुपपद्य एवोत्पादः। अथ स्थितिकाले उत्पादभंगौ न स्तः तदा तद्रहितस्य स्थिति स्यात्। उत्पादभंगरहितश्च पदार्थो नास्त्येवेति न अस्याविद्यमानस्य खुपुष्पवत् स्थितिर्युज्यते। किं च स्थितियुक्तस्य पश्चादनित्यतयापि यागो न स्यात्। तद्विरोधिधर्माक्रान्तत्वात्। अथ स्यात् पूर्वं शाश्वतो भूत्वा पश्चादशाश्वत इति न चैकपदार्थः शाश्वतश्चाशाश्वतश्च युक्त इति नोत्पादभंगरहितस्य स्थितिः। तथा यदि भंग काले स्थित्युत्पादौ न स्याताम्, एवमप्यनुत्पन्नस्य स्थितिहरितस्य खुपुष्पस्य विनाशोऽपि नास्तीति। एवं तावत् उत्पादादयो व्यस्ता नालं लक्षणं कर्मणि नालं न पर्याप्ता इत्यर्थः। इदानीं समस्ता अपि न युज्यन्त इत्याह ..... एकत्र पदार्थे एकस्मिन् काले, परस्परविरुद्धत्वा-द्रागवैराग्यवत्, आलोकान्धकारवद्वा न युज्यन्त इत्यभिप्रायः। यस्मिन्नेव क्षेण पदार्थो जायते, तस्मिन्नेव तिष्ठति विनश्यति चेति कः सचेता प्रपिपद्येत। तस्मात् समस्तानामपि उत्पादादीनां संस्कृतस्य लक्षणकर्मणि नास्ति सामर्थ्यम्।[233]

In the Śūnyatāsaptati, Nāgārjuna clearly says that if origination, permanence and destruction are the three characteristics of composites, then what are the causes for origination of any object? Or in other words, how can they account for the three states of reality? Because the thing which already exists cannot be further originated and the thing which does not exist also cannot be originated and the thing which is in the process of origination *(utpādyamāna* or *jātamāna)* also cannot be originated, as it is included in both created and not created. He writes:

न जायते यदा जातं नाजातमपि जायते
जाताजाताश्च नैवं हि जायमानोऽपि जायते।[234]

Going further, he asked: if the characteristics of composites are another origination, stability and destruction, then this would lead to the fault of infinite regress. If on the other hand, they are not different from it, then they cannot be composites.

उत्पादिस्थितिभंगानामन्यत् संस्कृतलक्षणम्
अस्ति चेदनवस्थैवं नास्ति चेत्ते न संस्कृता:।[235]

Then Nāgārjuna argues that the opponents i.e. the *Jaina* philosophers may contend that the origination of origination is simply the origination of the first origination. The first origination gives rise to the origination of origination. He says:

उत्पादोत्पाद उत्पादो मूल्योत्पादस्य केवलम्
उत्पादोत्पादमुत्पादो मौलो जनयते पुन:।[236]

To this, Nāgārjuna says: if the origination of origination is, for you, originated by the original origination, then how would you account for that origination, not brought about by the original origination, giving rise to the original origination? If according to you, (the *Jainas)* it is originated by the original and originates the original, then how would the original origination having not been originated by it would originate? It is argued further that the original origination, having itself been originated, creates another to originate something. To quote him:

उत्पादोत्पाद उत्पादो मूल्यत्पादस्य ते यदि
मौलनाजनितस्तं ते स कथं जनयिष्यति।
से ते मौलेन जनितो मौलं जनयते यदि
मौलः स तेनाजनितस्तमुत्पादयते कथम्।
अयं उत्पाद्यमानस्ते काममुत्पाद्रयेदिमम्
यदीममुत्पादयितुमजातः शक्नुयादयम्।[237]

Further, Nāgārjuna presents the *Jaina* argument just as a lamp illumines itself as well as others, similarly origination would originate both itself and others. He says:

प्रदीपे नान्धकारोऽस्ति यत्र चासौ प्रतिष्टितः
किं प्रकाशयति दीपः प्रकाशो हि तमोवधः।[238]

To this, Nāgārjuna says: darkness does not exist either in the lamp or at the place where it is located. What could the lamp Fourth Chapter illuminate? Illumination is the destruction of darkness. How could the lamp, which is being originated, destroy darkness? When the lamp being in the process of origination cannot reach darkness? If that is removed by the lamp without having reached it, then that lamp while staying at its own place, would destroy darkness existing in all the worlds. And further he argues: if lamp illumines itself and others, then there would be no doubt that darkness would also cover itself and others. Then, how could this origination itself not originated, originate itself? If it originates after having been originated, then having already been originated how would it be originated again?

Again he says: neither that which is being originated, nor that which has already been originated, nor that which is not yet originated can, in anyway, originate. This point has been stated as in the case of that, which is being traversed, that which has already been traversed and that which is not yet traversed. When that which is being originated cannot be related to origination, how could we say of a thing being originated in relation to origination?

Further, everything that originates relatively is by nature quiet. Therefore, that which is being originated and origination itself are quiet. If there is any un-originated entity anywhere, the same could originate. But it being non-existent, what will originate? If origination were to originate that which is being originated, then which origination would originate the previous origination? If another origination were to originate it, then it would lead to the undesired fault of infinite regress. If it were originated without origination, then every thing would be originated. But it is not proper, therefore, as has been said earlier, to say that an existing thing or non-existing thing or both existing and non-existing thing can originate is not tenable. To quote him:

कथमुत्पद्यमानेने प्रदीपेन तमो हतम्
नोत्पद्यमानो हि तमः प्रदीपः प्राप्नुते यदा।।
अप्राप्यैव प्रदीपेन यदि वा निहितं तमः
इहस्थः सर्वलोकस्थं स तमो निहनिष्यति।।
प्रदीपः स्वपरात्मानौ सम्प्रकाशयते यदि
तमोऽपि स्वपरात्मानौ छादयिष्यत्यसंशयम्।।
अनुत्पन्नोऽयमुत्पादः स्वात्मानं जनयेत् कथम्
अथोत्पन्नो जनयते जाते किं जन्यते पुनः।।
नोत्पद्यमानं नोत्पन्नं नानुत्पन्नं कथञ्चन
उत्पद्यते तथाख्यातं गम्यमानगतागतैः।।
उत्पद्यमानमुत्पत्ताविदं न क्रमते यदा।
कथमुत्पद्यमानं तु प्रतीत्योत्पत्तिमुच्यते।।
प्रतीत्य यद् यद् भवति तत्तच्छान्तं स्वभावतः
तस्मादुत्पद्यमानं च शांतमुत्पत्तिमुच्यते।।
प्रतीत्य यद् यद् भवति तत्तच्छान्तं स्वभावतः
तस्मादुत्पद्यमानं च शांतमुत्पत्तिरेव च।।
यदिकश्चिदनुत्पन्नो भावः संविद्यते क्वचित्
उत्पद्यते स किं तस्मिन् भाव उत्पद्यतेऽसति।।
उत्पद्यमानमुत्पादो यदि चोत्पादयत्ययम्
उत्पादयेत् तमुत्पादमुत्पादः कतमः पुनः।।

अन्य उत्पादयेत्येनं यद्युत्पादोऽनवस्थितिः
अथानुत्पाद उत्पन्नः सर्वमुत्पद्यते तथा॥
सतश्च तावदुत्पत्तिरसतश्च न युज्यते
न सतश्चासतश्चेति पूर्वमेवोपपादितम्॥[239]

Commenting on this, Candraklrti raises an interesting point that though a thing called 'jar' does not exist prior to its origination, even then one can say that the thing to be originated would be called 'jar'. Candrakīrti reacts to this by saying that the thing coming into existence would be called 'jar' only when the act of origination starts. But that which is still in the future cannot be an object of the process of origination. How could then such a thing be the object of the act of origination proceeds in respect of something nor 'jar', then we have to clarify that what is meant by 'non jar' would be a cloth or it would be nothing? If it were cloth in the state of non-origination, how could it be called a 'jar' when originated? If it is nothing, then how could the act of origination proceed in respect of such a thing, which is nothing, and how could that nothing become jar? Therefore, the name to be given to a future cannot establish origination. He says:

यदि कश्चिदनुत्पन्नः उत्पादात् पूर्वं घटो नाम क्वचित्संविद्यते स उत्पत्तिक्रियां प्रतीत्यत्पद्येत। न चैवं कश्चिदुत्पउदात्पूर्वं क्वचिदस्ति। तस्मिन्नसति घटे किमुत्पद्यते। अथस्यात् - यद्युत्पादात् पूर्वं घटो नास्ति, तथापि उत्पन्नः सन् घटसंज्ञा प्रतिलप्स्यते, तदभाविन्या संज्ञया न दोष इति? एतदप्ययुक्त; यदि हि उत्पत्तिक्रिया प्रवर्त्तेत, तदा वर्त्तमानीभूतो भावो घटाख्यां प्रतिलभेत। यदा तु अनागतभावासम्बन्धेन क्रियायाः अप्रवृत्तिः, तदा कुतो वर्तमानता? अथ अघटाश्रयेण क्रिया प्रारभ्येतः, तद्वक्तव्यम् यौऽसौ अघटः स किं भवितुमर्हति पटः? उत नैव किंचित्, कथं तदाश्रया क्रिया प्रवर्त्तते? कथं वा स उत्पन्नः सन् घटो भवेत्? इति सर्वथा भवितत्वकल्पनाप्ययुक्ता। तस्मादुत्पद्यमानमप्युत्पादो नोत्पादयतीति सिद्धम्।[240]

Further, he says that the origination of an entity itself being destroyed cannot be justified. No such entity can be justified which is not being destroyed. Then he examines the element of the *Saṁskṛta* called existence. He says that nothing exists which is existent, nothing exists which is non-existent, and nothing exists which is in the process of existing. How could an un-originated entity have existence? Thus, the existence of an entity, which is being destroyed, cannot be justified. It is not also possible to justify an entity, which is not being destroyed. When all entities always have the characteristics of decay and destruction, what are those entities, which could have existence without decay and destruction? If existence were due to another existence, then that other existence cannot be justified, as origination of origination is not possible by itself or by something else. He writes:

> निरुध्यमानस्योत्पत्तिर्न भावस्योपपद्यते
> यश्चनिरुध्यमानस्तु स भावो नोपद्यते॥
> न स्थितभावस्तिष्ठत्यस्थितभावो न तिष्ठति
> न तिष्ठति तिष्ठमानः कोऽनुत्पन्नश्च तिष्ठति॥
> स्थितिनिरुध्यमानस्य न भावस्योपपद्यते
> यश्चनिरुध्यमानस्तु स भावो नोऽपपद्यते॥
> जरामरणधर्मेषु सर्वभावेषु सर्वदा
> नष्ठन्ति कतमे भावा ये जरामरणं विना॥
> स्थित्यान्यया स्थितेः स्थानं तयैव च न युज्यते
> उत्पादस्य यथोत्पादो नात्मना न परात्मना॥[241]

Further, he examines the element of *Saṁskṛta* called impermanence. He says that which is not destroyed cannot have destruction; that which is already destroyed also cannot have destruction and that which is in the process of destruction is also of the same type. How could that which is not yet produced be destroyed? The destruction of an existing entity cannot be justified. Similarly, the destruction of a non-existing entity also cannot be justified. That very condition which makes the existence of one entity possible cannot destroy the condition of another entity. For example, if the thing has the form of milk, then the form of curd cannot be the cause of destruction of the form of milk. Since milk and curd do not exist simultaneously, the form of curd cannot destroy the form of milk. He says:

तथैव तावत् क्षीरावस्थया सैव क्षीरावस्था न निरुध्यते; स्वत्मनि क्रिया विरोधात्।

नाप्यन्यया दध्यवस्थया क्षीरावस्था निरुध्यते। यदि हि क्षीर दध्यवस्थयोयौगपद्यं स्यात्,

स्यात् तयोर्विनाश्यविनाशकभावः। न तु दध्यवस्थायां क्षीरावस्था अस्ति। यदा च नास्ति, तदा कामसतीं विनाशयेत्।

यदि विनाशयेत्, खरविषाणतीक्ष्णतामपि विनाशयेत्।

तस्मादन्ययाप्यवस्थया नैवान्यावस्था निरुध्यते।[242]

In this way when the origination of all the entities cannot be justified, the destruction of all entities also likewise, cannot be justified. It is not justified to say that an existing entity is destroyed. When the entity is one, existence and non-existence in respect of the same cannot be justified. Candrakīrti explains it by saying that destruction means absence. That which is destroyed does not exist. Therefore, destruction of an existing thing would mean the presence of existence and non-existence together in the same thing. Both of them being contradictory, nothing would be either existent or non-existent.

निरोधो हि नाम अभावः। यस्य भवति, स नैव भवति। ततश्च 'सतो भावस्य निरोधः' इति ब्रवता भावाभावयोरेकाधिकरणता अभ्युपगता भवति। एकत्वे सति उभयं न युज्यते। यदि तदानों भावः स्यात् तदा निरोध नाभावेनावेशाद् भावव्यपदेशोऽयुक्तः। अथ अभावः, सोऽप्यस्य स पदार्थो नैव भावो नाप्यभाव इति युज्यते। अभाव विरोधिना भावरूपेणा वियोगात् तस्मादेकत्वे सति भावा भावयोः स पदार्थो नैव भावो नाप्यभाव। इति युज्यते। अथवा, परस्परविरुद्धत्वादालोकान्धकारवदेकत्वे सति न हि भावश्च नाभावश्चोपपद्यते। एवं तावत् सतो भावस्य निरोधो न युक्तः।[243]

And also the destruction of a non-existing entity cannot be justified, as the second head cannot be cut off. Candrakīrti says that nobody possesses two heads. Therefore cutting of the second head would be like the destruction of non-existence. Thus, there is no destruction by a thing itself, nor there is destruction brought about by another thing, just as the origination of origination is neither by itself not by virtue of something else. Since origination, existence and destruction cannot be established, there is no composite entity. When there is no composite entity established, how could a non-composite entity be established? Thus, Nāgārjuna concludes that origination, existence and destruction are exemplified in the fashion of magic, dream and a city appearing in the sky i.e. *gandharvanagara*. Thus, he concludes:

निरुध्यते नानिरुद्धं न निरुद्धं निरुध्यते
तथापि निरुध्यमानं किमजातं निरुध्यते।
स्थितस्यतावत् भावस्य निरोधो नोपपद्यते
नास्थितस्यापि भावस्य निरोध उपपद्यते।।
तथैवावासीयावस्था न हि सैव निरुद्यते
अन्ययावस्थयावस्था न चान्यैव निरुध्यते।।
यथैवं सर्वधर्माणां निरोधो नोपपद्यते।।
तदैवं सर्वधर्माणां निरोधो नोपपद्यते।।
सतश्च तावद्भावस्य निरोधो नोपपद्यते
एकत्वे न हि भावश्ंच नाभावश्चोपपद्यते।।
असतोऽपि न भावस्य निरोध उपपद्यते
न द्वितीयस्य शिरसंश्छेदनं विद्यते यथा।।
न स्वात्मना निरोधोऽस्ति निरोधो न परात्मना
उत्पादस्य यथोत्पादो नात्मना न परात्मना।।
उत्पादस्थितिभंगानामसिद्धैर्नास्ति संस्कृतम्
संस्कृतस्याप्रसिद्धौ च कथं सेत्स्यत्यसंस्कृत्म्।।
यथा माया स्वप्नो गंधर्वनगरं यथा
तथोत्पादस्तथा स्थानं तथा भंग उदाहृतम्।।[244]

Arcaṭa's Criticism on the Jaina concept of Syādvāda:

Ācārya Arcata (7th or 8th c. A.D.) the author of *Hetubinduṭjkā,* a commentary of Dharmakīti's *Hetubindu* criticizes mainly the arguments of Samantabhadra viz.

dravyaparyāya-yoraìkyaṁ (substance and its mood are the same), *sanjñāsankhyāviśeṣāśca,* which are not being refuted by Dhannakīrti.

Arcaṭa says: origination and destruction cannot exist together in one *dharmi* (substratum) since they are contradictory in nature. The argument, as given by the *Jaina* logicians relatively would not solve the question, because in course of origination and destruction, permanence would not be there, and likewise in the presence of permanent character the other two would be absent. Therefore a triple charactered nature of reality as the *Jainas* assert, is not possible. Here he has attested the *sūtra* of *Tattvārthsūtra* of Umāsvāti and refuted it. He notes:

उत्पादव्ययध्रौव्युक्तं सत्। [245]

इत्येतदप्ययुक्तम्, ध्रौव्येणोत्पादव्ययोर्विरोधात् एकस्मिन् धर्मिण्ययोगात्। कथञ्चिदुत्पादव्ययौ कथञ्चिद् ध्रौव्यमिति चेत्। यथोत्पादव्ययौ न तथा ध्रौव्यम्, यथां च

ध्रौव्य न तथोपदव्ययाविति नैकं वस्तु यथोक्तलक्षणं स्यात्।[246]

In this context Durveka Mishra, the author of *Hetubindu-ṭikāloka,* a commentary on *Hetubinduṭikā* presents the view of the *Jaina* logicians, particularly the view of Samantabhadra. He asked as to, why the *vastu* i.e. reality should be triple charactered. He quotes from Ā*pamīmāṁsā* to present the *Jaina* position:

धटोमौलि सुवर्णार्थो नाशोत्पादस्थितिष्वयम्
शोकप्रमोदमाध्यस्थ्यं जनो याति सहेतुकम्
न नाशेन विना शोको नोत्पादेन विना धृतिः
स्थित्व विना न माध्यस्थ्यं तस्माद्वस्तु त्रयात्मकम्
प्रयोव्रतो न दध्यत्ति न पायत्ति दधिव्रतः
अगोरसव्रतो नोभे तस्माद्वस्तु त्रयात्मकम्।।[247]

He has refuted the view of the *Jainas* regarding the conception of identity-in-difference i.e. *bhedabhedavāda,* which means the substance and its modes cannot be separated from a realistic standpoint, but they are different in name, number, nature, place etc. from the practical view point. It appears as if he does not see much difference between *ubhayavāda* of *Vaiśeṣikas* and *bhedabhedavdda* of *Jainas*. That is the reason why he conceives the substance as being completely different from its modes.

In *Hetubindiṭikā,* in the heading named अह्रीकादिसंमतस्य द्रव्यपर्याययोः भेदाभेदपक्षस्य निरासः[248] ' he refutes the Jaina view. Again the same arguments are repeated in forty-five stanzas in the same book. He argues: the difference between substance and its modes by the name and number etc. and unity of them into one by place, time and nature, is not possible as the nature of reality, since an entity cannot assume more than one character. He says:

द्रव्यपर्यायरूपत्वात् द्वैरूप्यं वस्तूनः किल
तयोरेकात्कत्वेऽपि भेदः संज्ञादिभेदतः॥ [249]

Further, he says that *saṁjñā* is the cause of and intimation *(sariketa),* which depends on desires. How then can one differentiate it by name, since it is also one and not two? Words or descriptions are fictitious; the difference therefore would be imaginative. *Saṁkhyābheda* is also not possible as there is a difference between *vācya* and *vācaka* (i.e. to be spoken and the speaker), which is also imaginative *(kalpita)*. He argues that without the destruction of a substance, there would be no destruction of its modes. Hence, they can be identified neither as *bheda* nor as *abheda*. If the modes were different from the substance, words would not be connected with them? If they were accepted as non-different, their natures would be one. How then could the *Lakṣaṇābheda* be applied or explained? Further *kāryabheda* is also not possible, as there is no difference in nature. We quote here the entire text of arguments, which are very important.

इन्द्रियज्ञाननिर्भासि वस्तुरूपं हि गोचरः
शब्दानां नैव, तत् केन संज्ञाभेदाद् विभिन्नता॥
परमार्थैकतानत्व इत्यादिवचनात् तथा
शब्देनाव्यापृताक्षस्य वुद्धावप्रतिभासनात्॥
अर्थस्य दृष्टाविव तच्छब्दाः कल्पितगोचराः
कल्पितस्यैव तद्भेदः संज्ञाभेदात् भवेद् यदि॥

व्यावृत्तिभेदः कश्चिद् स्यात् वस्तूनो न कथंचन
संख्याभेदोऽपि नैवान्यो मतो वचनभेदतः॥
ततोऽपि कल्पितस्यैव कथञ्चिद् स्यात् विभिन्नता
येषां वस्तुवशा वाच इत्यादेर्न्न तु वस्तुनः॥
अविनाशोऽनुवृत्तिश्च व्यावृत्तिश्च व्यावृत्तिर्न्नाश उच्यते
द्रव्याविनाशे पर्याया नाशिनः किं तदात्मकाः?
नष्टाः पर्यायरूपेण ते चेद् द्रव्यस्वभावतः
किमन्यरूपता तेषां न चेन्नाशस्तथा कथम्?
द्रव्यात्मनि स्थिते पश्चाद् भवन्तश्च तदात्मकाः
विरुद्धधमर्मोध्यासेऽपि, केन, भूतं च किं, यतः॥
पर्यायास्तत्र कल्प्यन्ते, भेदरूपं यदीष्यते
भिन्नं पर्यायरूपं हि द्रव्यरूपाद् भवेद् यदि॥
तदैतत् स्यादभेदे तु नैतत् संबध्यते वचः
एकं जातमजातं च नष्टानष्टां प्रसज्यते॥
द्रव्यपर्याययोरेकस्वभावोपगमे सति
ततो लक्षणभेदेन तयोर्नौव विभिन्नता
कार्यभेदात् स्वभावस्य तयोर्भेदो भवेद् यदि
स्वभावाभेदतो न स्यादभेदस्तु तथा सति॥ 250

The theory 'substance and its modes are different *(abheda)* in place, time, nature, is also defective in prajñākaras' views. He says: position, form, smell, juice, touch etc., are different in modifications. If the nature stays with substance and modes in the form of destruction and otherwise, the substance would be two as *ghaṭa* and *paṭa,* not one which removes *abhedatva* with them. Further, he says: if the *bhedābheda* is accepted the *bheda* (difference) would be fictitious due to not leaving the *abheda* (identity) and hence, *abheda* would be proved as false in character. Here, Arcata thinks in terms of *ubhayavāda,* that if the substance and mode are completely different all the evils of both the 'identity view and difference view' will lay upon this conception. He says:

अभेदस्यारित्यागे भेदः स्यात् कल्पनाकृतः
तस्याऽवितथभावे वा स्याद्-भेदे मृषार्थता॥

अन्योन्याभावरूपाणामपराभावहेतुकः
एक भावो यतस्तस्मान्नैकस्य स्याद् द्विरूपता॥
अन्योन्याभारूपाश्च पर्यायाः स्युर्न्न भेदिनः
तद्विनाशेऽविनाशि स्याद् द्रव्यं वा कथमन्यथा?॥
कूटस्थनित्यता द्रव्ये भेदेषु क्षणनाशिता
कास्मान्नष्टा? विरोधश्चेत् नेष्यते भेदलक्षणम्॥
तदिष्टौ किन्न सामान्यं सर्व्वव्यक्त्यनुयायि च
एकमिष्टं जनन्या च जायायाः किं न चकैता॥
भेदाभेदोक्तदोषाश्व तयोरिष्टौ कथं न वा?
प्रत्येकं ये प्रसज्यन्ते द्वयोर्भावे कथं न ते?॥[251]

Arcata refers to the *Jainas'* view that they analyze through *jātyantara (Sui-geniris),* which exposes the combination of identity and difference, although it makes a distinction between the particular general characters of reality. For instance, *Narasimha* is combination of man and lion, which is not self-contradictory because of the theory of sui-generis.

Opposing this theory, Arcaṭa points out that *Narasiṁha* is compendium of atoms, which cannot be transformed into *narasimha,* due to a combination of the atoms, which is, called *śabalarūpa,* a place of existence of diverse natures. How then could a unity in nature be proved? Arcata finally remarks that this is the philosophy of blockheads.[252]

REFERENCES

1. Tattvasamgraha pañjikā on V. No. 1708.
2. Tattvasamgraha. V. No. 1709.
3. Tattvasamgrapañjikā. On V. No. 1709.
4 *Ibid.*
5 Tattvasamgra. V. No. 1710-12.
6. Tattvasamgra. V. No. 1713-15.
7. Tattvasamgrapañjikā. On the ver. No. 1713-15.
8. *Ibid.*
9. Tattvasamgraha V. No. 1716-18.
10. Tattvasamgraha pañjikā on V. No. 1716-18.

11. Tattvasamgraha V. No. 1719-20.
12. Tattvasamgraha pañjikā on V. No. 1719-20.
13. Tattvasamgraha V. No. 1721 -22.
14. Tattvasamgraha pañjikā/ on the ver.no. 11721-22.
15. *Ibid.*
16. *Ibid.*
17. Tattvasamgraha pañjikā on V. No. 1721-22.
18. Tattvasamgraha V. No. 1723-24.
19. Tattvasamgraha pañjikā on V¿ No. 1723-24.
20. Tattvasamgraha pañjikā on V. No. 1724.
21. Tattvasamgraha V. No. 1725.
22. Tattvasamgraha pañjikā on V. No. 1725.
23. Tattvasamgraha V. No. 1726.
24. Tattvasamgraha V. No. 1727-28.
25. Tattvasamgrahapañjikā.on ver. No. 1727-28.
26. Tattvasamgraha pañjikā on V. No. 1727-28.
27. *Ibid.*on ver. No. 1729.
28. Tattvasamgraha pañjikā on V. No. 1729.
29. Tattvasamgraha V. No. 1730-31.
30. Tattvasamgraha pañjikā on V. No 1732-34.
31 Tattvasamgraha V. No 1735-36.
32. Tattvasamgraha pañjikā on V. No 1735-36.
33. Tativasamgraha V. No.1737-43.
34. Tattvasamgraha pañjikā on V. No. 1737-43.
35. Tattvasamgraha pañjikā. 1737-43.
36. *Ibid.*
37. *Ibid.*
38. Tattvasamgraha V. No. 1711.
39. Taṭtvasamgraha V. No 1749.
40. *Ibid*, on ver. No. 1749.
41. *Ibid.*
42. Tattvasamgraha pañjikā on V. No. 1749.
43. Tattvasamgraha pañjikā on V. No. 1750-51.

44. *Ibid*, on ver.no. 1750-51.
45. *Ibid.*
46. *Ibid.*
47. Tattvasamgraha pañjikā on V. No. 1752-53.
48. Tattvasamgraha V. No. 1754-56.
49. Tattvasamgraha pañjikā on V. No. 1754-56.
50. Tattvasamgraha V. No. 1757.
51. *Ibid.* On ver. No. 1757.
52. Tattvasamgraha pañjikā on V. No. 1757.
53. Tattvasamgraha pañjikā on V. No. 1758.
54. Tattvasamgraha V. No. 1759-61.
55. Tattvasamgraha pañjikā on V. No. 1759-61.
56. Tattvasamgraha V. No. 1762.
57. Tattvasamgraha pañjikā on V. No. 1762.
58. Tattvasamgraha V. No. 1763-74.
59. Tattvasamgraha pañjikā on V. No. 1763-64.
60. Tattvasamgraha pañjikā on V. No. 1765.
61. Tattvasamgraha pañjikā on V. No. 1766.
62. Tattvasamgraha pañjikā on V. No. 1767.
63. Tattvasamgraha pañjikā on V. No. 1768.
64. Tattvasamgraha pañjikā on V. No. 1769.
65. Tattvasamgraha pañjikā on V. No. 1771.
66. Tattvasamgraha pañjikā on V. No. 1772-74.
67. Tattvasamgraha V. No.311.
68. Tattvasamgraha pañjikā on V. No.311.
69. Tattvasamgraha V. No.312.
70. Tattvasamgraha pañjikā on V. No.312.
71. Tattvasamgraha V. No.313-15.
72. Tattvasamgraha pañjikā on V. No.313-15.
73. Tattvasamgraha V. No.316.
74. Tattvasamgraha pañjikā on V. No.316.
75. Tattvasamgraha V. No.317-18.
76. Tattvasamgraha pañjikā on V. No.317-18.

77. Tattvasamgraha V. No.319.
78. Tattvasamgraha V. No.320.
79. Tattvasamgraha V. No.321.
80. Tattvasamgraha pañjikā on V. No.321.
81. Tattvasamgraha V. No.322.
82. Tattvasamgraha pañjikā on V. No.322.
83. Tattvasamgraha V. No.323.
84. Ṭattvasamgraha pañjikā on V. No.323.
85. Tattvasamgraha V. No.324.
86. Tattvasamgraha pañjikā on V. No.324.
87. Tattvasamgraha V. No.325.
88. Tattvasamgraha pañjikā on V. No.325.
89. Tattvasamgraha V. No.326.
90. Tattvasamgraha pañjikā on V. No.326.
91. Tattvasamgraha V. No.327.
92. पृथतरदेशाक्रान्तिरूपेण च, अन्यथैव न प्रतिभासते। मक्षिकापदमात्रेणापि च पिधाने तस्य तथाविधस्यावरणप्रसङ्गश्च Tattvasamgraha pañjikā on V. No.327.
93. Paṃcāsthikāyasāra. 16.
94. Tattvaviniścaya. 2.3.
95. Pramāṇasamuccaya. 1. 47. 9.
96. Majjhima Nikāya. i. 529.
97. *Ibid*.
98. Majjhima Nikāya ii. 31, M. Sayings, ii. p228., i. p50
99. Buddhist legend. Vol.29, p 74 ff.
100. Majjhima Nikāya ii. 31, p 214 ff. , i. p 92 ff; Angutaranikāya. I. 220.
101. Pamāṇavārtika. 1st. Ch. V. No.33-35.
102. Prajṃākaragupta's bhaṣya on it.
103. Pramāṇavārtikālñkāra. 4. 91.
104. *Ibid*. 8. 6-7.
105. Vide the artcle 'the conception of omniscience in Buddhism' by Bhagcahandra Jain. Published in VSMP. 1968.
106. Tattvasamgraha V. No. 1979-82.
107. Tattvasamgraha pañjikā on V. No. 1979-82.
108. Hemacandra's commentary on V. No. 14.

109. Syādvādamañjarī. P. 111-12!, Notes p. 196.
110. Tattvasamgraha V. No 1983-84.
111. Tattvasamgraha pañjikā on V. No. 1983-84.
112. Tattvasamgraha V. No.985.
113. Syādvādamañjarī's Notes.p. 195
114. Syādvādamañjarī, p. 111.
115. Tattvārthsūtra. 2. 9., Aṣṭtī aṣṭasahasri. P. 275.
116. Tattvārthsūtra. I. II. 12.
117. Tattvasamgraha pañjikā on V. No. 1265.
118. Sanmati tarka.p.457.
119. Tattvārthasūtra. V.No. 1213., Tattvasamgraha pañjikā on V. No. 1213.
120. Nyāyakumdacanra. P. 46. Tattvasamgraha pañjikā on V. No.p. 394.
121. Tattvasamgraha V. No. 1264.
122. Tattvasamgraha pañjikā on V. No. 1264.
123. Tattvarthavartika.l. 15. 1.
124. Vide.p. 138. Jainism as presented in Buddhist Literature.
125. Tattvasamgraha pañjikā on V. No. 1264.
126. *Ibid.*
127. Tattvasamgraha pañjikā on V. No. 1264-65.
128. Tattvasamgraha pañjikā on V. No. 1265-66.
129. Jaminisutra. 1.1.4.
130. Jainism As Presented inBuddhist Literature.p. 183.
131. Tattvasamgraha V. No. 1269.
132. Tattvasamgraha V. No. 1273-75.
133. Tattvasamgraha pañjikā on V. No. 1269.
134. Tattvasamgraha V. No. 1270.
135. Tattvasamgraha pañjikā on V. No. 1270.
136. Tattvasamgraha V. No. 1267.
137. Tattvasamgraha V. No. 1268.
138. Tattvasamgraha pañjikā on V. No. 1268.
139. Nyāyaviniścaya. 1. 158, Tattvārthasūtravārtika. P. 185.
140. Nyāyakumudacandra. P. 47, Prameyakamalamārtsṇda. P.8.
141. Aṣṭasahaśrī. P. 75.

142. Tattvasamgraha pañjikā on V. No. 1273.
143. Tattvasamgraha V. No. 1267.
144. Tattvasamgraha V. No. 1268.
145. Tattvasamgraha pañjikā on V. No. 1278-80.
146. Tattvasamgraha pañjikā on V. No. 1279-80.
147. Nyāyaviniścayavivarana. Part. II. P. 1.
148. Nyāyaviniścaya. Part. II. P. I.
149. Sahakramabhāvanīyamovinābhāvaḥ. Pramāṇamīmāṁsā: 3. 16.
150. Siddhiviniścaya. 6. 17.
151. Nyāyabindu. 3. 59.
152. Nyāyabinduṭīkā on 3. 59.
153. Nyāyapraveśa.p. 1.
154. Vādanyāya. P. 61.
155. Pramāṇavārtika. 128.
156. Tattvasaitigraha. V. No. 1361-62.
157. Tattvasamgraha. V. No.1363.
158. Tattvasamgraha pañjikā on V. No.1363.
159. TattvasamgrahaV. No. 1364.
160. TattvasamgrahaV. No. 1367-68.
161. Tattvasamgraha V. No. 1365.
162. *Ibid*. 1369.
163. Tattvasamgraha pañjikā on V. No. 1370.
164. Tattvasamgraha V. No. 1370.
165. *Ibid*. 1371-78.
166. Tattvasamgraha pañjikā on V. No. 1372-78.
167. Tattasamgraha. 1379.
168. Tattvasamgraha pañjikā on V. No. 1379.
169. Tattvasamgraha V. No. 1380.
170. Tattvasamgraha pañjikā on V. No. 1380.
171. Tattvasamgraha V. No. 1381-82.
172. Tattvasamgraha V. No. 1385-85.
173. Tattvasamgraha pañjikā on V. No. 1385-87.
174. *Ibid*.

175. *Ibid.*

176. *Ibid.*

177. *Ibid.*

178. Tattvasamgraha V. No. 1388.

179. Tattvasamgraha pañjikā on V. No. 1388.

180. Tattvasamgraha V. No.1389.

181. Tattvasamgraha V. No. 1394-95.

182. Tattvasamgraha pañjikā on V. No. 1395.

183. Tattvasamgraha V. No. 1396.

184. Tattvasamgraha V. No. 1399.

185. *Ibid.* V. No. 1400.

186. *Ibid.* V. No.1401.

187. Tattvasamgraha pañjikā on V. No.1401.

188. *Ibid.*

189. Tattvasamgraha V. No. 1402.

190. *Ibid.* V. No. 1402-04.

191. *Ibid.* V. No. 1405-06.

192. *Ibid.* 1407-14.

193. Tattvasamgraha pañjikā on V. No.1408-15.

194. Tattvasamgraha V. No. 1369.

195. Tattvasamgraha V. No. 1415.

196. Tattvasamgraha pañjikā on V. No. 1413.

197. Nyāyakumudacandra. Vol. II. P.440., Siddhiviniścayatika. 6. 16.

198. 'Utpādavyayadrauvyayuktam Sat', Tattvārthasutra. 5. 30.

199. 'guṇaparyāyavaddravyam' *Ibid.* 5. 38.

200. The Jiana theory of Reality and Knowledge: p. 131.

201. Nyayavatara. 29.

202. Tattvarthasutra. 1. 35.

203. Laghīyastrayf. P. 55.

204. Prameyakamalamartanda. P. 676.

205. Lghlyasrayi in svapajnabhasya. 3. 62.

206. Angottaranikāya. ii. 46, 196., Milinda pañha. Iv. 2.5.

207. Majjhimanikāya. ii. 46.

208. Vibhajjavādaṁ ca vyāgarjee: Sūṭrakitāṅga. 1. 14. 22.
209. Early Buddhist theory of kbowledge. P. 292.
210. Dīghanikāya. I. 191.
211. Hetubibduṭīkā. P. 284.
212. Pramāṇavārtikasvavṛttiṭīā. P.333.
213. Hetubibduṭīkāloka. P. 369.
214. Āptamīmāṁsā. 5. 9-61.,
cf. Quoted in Pramāṇavārtikasvavṛttiṭīā. p. 333.
cf. Hetubibduṭīkāloka. P. 369.
215. Vide the introduction. P.
216. Laghīyastrayī. P.30, Pramāṇamīṁāsā. P. 24.
217. Dīgha Nikāya. I. 27.
218. Sūtrakṛtāṅga. 1. 3. 11-34., vrtti. P. 45-46, Samavāyāṅga. 224.
219. Dīgha Nikāya. i. 191,
cf. Majjhima Nikāya, ii. 197.
220. For detailed pi. vide 'Jainism in Buddhist Literature' p. 193-201.
221. The Early Buddhist Theory of Knowledge. P. 156.
222. Pramāṇavārtikam. 1. 185.
223. Svapajnavrtti on V. No. 183-85.
224. Pramāṇavārtikalnkara p. 142, 2. 207.
225. Pramāṇavārtikasvapajñavṛttiṭīka on V. No. 183-84.
226. *Ibid.*
227. cf. Tattvasamgraha. V. No. 1733-35.
228. Pramāṇavārtikasvavṛttiṭīka p. 109.
229. Vide. For detail introduction. P.
230. Pramāṇavārtikasvavṛttiṭīka p. 332-342.
231. Mādhyamaśāsthraṁ. Vii. v-i.
232. Mādhyamaśāsthraṁ. Vii. V. No. 2.
233. Prasamapādavṛtti of Candrakīrti on Vii. V. No. 2 of Mādhyamaśāsthram.
234. Sūnyatāśaptatī V. No. 5.
235. Mādhyamaśāsthraṁ. Vii V. No. 3.
236. Mādhyamaśāsthraṁ. Vii V. No. 4.
237. *Ibid.* V. No. 5-7.

238. *Ibid*. V. No. 8.

239. *Ibid*. V. No. 10-20.

240. Prasannapadāvṛtti of Mādhyamakaśāshtra. V. No. 17.

241. Mādhyamaśāsthraṁ. Vii V. No. 21-25.

242. Prasannapadāvṛtti of Mādhyamakaśāshtra. Vii. V. No. 28.

243. *Ibid*. V. No. 30.

244. Mādhyamaśāsthraṁ. Vii V. No. 26-34.

245. Tattvarthasutra 5. 29.

246. Hetubinduṭikā. P. 146.

247. Āptamīmāṁsā. 59-60,
cf. Hetubinduṭīkā. P. 369.

248. Hetubinduṭīkā. P. 98.

249. *Ibid*. p. 104.

250. *Ibid*. p. 104, V. No. 2-13.

251. *Ibid*. p. 105, V. No. 20-25.

252. अथ पुनर्द्रव्यपर्याययोः संमूर्च्छितत्वात् नरसिंहवेदकं शवलरूपत्वात् द्विरूपमुच्यते। तदयुक्तम्। नरसिहम्य शवलरूपत्वासिद्धे। स ह्यनेकपरमाणुसंधातरूपः, ते च प्ररमाणवः प्रत्येकं नरसिंहारूपा न भवन्ति, ऊर्ध्वभागस्तस्य सिंहरूपः अधो भागस्तु नररूपः, जात्यंतरं च स नरसिंहाभ्यां स्यात् न शवलरूपः। विचित्रं हि रूपं शवलमुच्यते। विचित्रता च नानास्वभावतां। नानास्वाभाव्ये चैकत्वं कुत? इति केवलमनेकत्वेऽपि बहुष्वेककार्यदर्शनात् सेनादिवदेकव्यवहार दर्शनकृतोऽयं विपर्यासो जडमतीनाम्।

Ibid. p. 104.

CONCLUSION

We may now record our findings in the form of observations and conclusion. Before doing so, we feel to record the fact that the *Jaina* philosophy and their doctrines have not been taken seriously by the other systems of Indian Philosophy. It is sad to note that even the basic texts of *Jaina* Philosophy are not translated and studied due to this negligence towards the system. Whatever may be the reason of this negligence, the same attitude is noticed in case of ancient texts. For example, though the *Jaina* Philosophers from 9th century onwards have taken great pain to establish their view against the doctrine of other systems of Indian philosophy by refuting those, quoting suitable arguments in thousands of pages in their respective texts, still in none of the texts of Indian Philosophy, the Jaina doctrines have been taken for serious analysis and examination. It is only in few places and few authorities of *Nyāya* like *Vātsāyana Bhāsya* and *prakaraṇa* texts like *Jayanta Bhaṭṭa's Nyāyamañjarī* and *Nyāya Bhūṣaṇa* of *Bhāsarvajṃia* etc. we met with a casual treatment of *Jaina* theories. Further, in one occasion only in some four Sutras of *Brahmasṃtra* and their commentaries by *Śaṅkara, Madhva, Rāmanuja* etc. some of the *Jaina* doctrines have been discussed and refuted. It is only in some of the major texts of Buddhism that Jainism is taken for serious discussion and critical analysis. Therefore, initially we had a major problem to search and identify from the vast literature of Indian Philosophy such as *Nyāya, Vedānta* and Buddhism to first trace the place where Jainism is presented. We are very much aware of our limitations and ability to go through the exhaustive texts of Indian Philosophy and then identify the references. We have tried our best to do justice and it is probable that we might have missed some cases where

Jainism is presented due to negligence and over sightedness. Now we may record our observations under the present study in the following lines under the following heads.

(a) The basic doctrines of Jainism vis-a-vis other systems of Indian Philosophy.

(b) The presentation and the interpretation of the *Jaina* doctrines by other systems of Indian Philosophy.

(c) Some answers from the *Jaina* point of views to the *Nyiyāyīkas, Vedāntins* and Buddhists.

We have noticed that the *Nayāyīkas,* the *Vedāntins* and also the Buddhists have somewhat similar approach against the *Jaina* doctrines. All have objected to the *Jaina* theory of *Anekānta,* their concept of eternity of soul, concept of reality. The arguments developed are almost identical, the basic objection of all being grounded on contradiction and absurdity. Thus, the answers and arguments given by the *Jainas* to one of the systems may be taken as the answer to all those, who do not subscribe to the *Jaina* view.

According to *Jainas, Pratyakṣa* is that type of knowledge, which is able to apprehend the objects with all its permanent and changing qualities and that is possible only by the self. Therefore, *pratyakṣa* means the knowledge arising in the self directly.

The knowledge of the object derived from the sense organs is called *sāṁvyavahārika pratykṣa.* The *Jainas* not only define *sāṁvyavahārika pratyakṣa* but also analyze the process involved in it. The process consists in the four stages of *avagraha, aīhā, avāya* and *dhāraṇā,* which are sometimes treated as four kinds *of pratykṣa.* The idea of four states is original to this system. Though other systems of Indian Philosophy distinguish between *nirvikalpaka* and *savikalpaka* perception, yet their distinction is not as thorough as that of the *Jainas*. No other system has given us such an account of the different states of sense perception.

Regarding the four stages perception, it may be observed that we do not have a definition of *avagraha* in *Nāndisūtra.* It records two types of avagraha viz. *vyañjanāvagraha* and *arthāvagraha*. It is pointed out that *vyañjanāvagraha* is not possible in the case of visual sense organs. *Umāsvātī* records the synonyms of *avagraha* and states that *avagraha* is an indeterminate cognition *(avagrahao-graha-grahaṇaṃ-ālocanaṃ-avagrahaṃ ityanarthāntaraṃ)*. *Pujjapāda* defines it as the first cognition after the contact of the object of sense organs *(vaṣaya viṣayī sannipāte samānāntaraṃ ādyagraha-ṇaṃ avagrahaḥ)*. Two steps are pointed out: when the sense organ is contacted with the object, there occurs *darśana* and in the second stage the cognition arising there after is *avagraha*. He gives the example of the cognition of white colour by the organ of sight *(viṣaya, viṣayl sannipāte sati darśanaṃ bhavati tad anantaraṃ arthagraham avagrahah, yathā caksusā suklam iti rūpam avagmhaḥ)*. It is significant to record that *Pujjapāda* accepts *vyaṃjanāvagraha* as indeterminate cognition. He writes: *arthāvagraha-vyaṃjnāvagrahayor* vyaktāvyakta *kṛto veśeṣaḥ*.

Māṇikyanandi and *Hemachandra* have also defined it as a perfect knowledge arising in the self without the instrumentality of the sense organs. To *Māṇikyanandi 'mukhya'* is that clear, non-sensuous and infinite knowledge of which all veils are removed by special condition *(sāmagrī viśeṣa-viślesita-akhilāvaraṃ atindriyaśeṣato mukhyaṃ)*. On the peculiar nature of such infinite knowledge *Prabhāchandra* notes that it arises when all the veils of *karma* are removed completely under special conditions. Right knowledge, right faith and right conduct are the internal conditions, while space, time etc. are external conditions. When all the conditions are favourable, the karmas are removed completely and there arises *mukhya pratyakṣa*. It is clear and right knowledge, it is *atindriya* i.e. it does not depend on mind and sense organs. So it is perfect and infinite.

The *Jaina* view that the sense organs are not capable to apprehend the objects with all its permanent and changing qualities seems to be reasonable since sense organs have limited capacities.

The concept of non-sensuous knowledge of the *Jaina* Philosophy is based on their metaphysics. According to *Jainas*, knowledge is the essential quality of the self. The pure self possesses infinite knowledge, but due to the veil of the karmic matters, it cannot realize its true nature. When the obstruction of true nature is destroyed, knowledge arises in the self. The self can know objects directly without the help of the sense organs.

Regarding the nature of non-sensuous perception, the *Jainas* are not very clear. They say simply that in *avadhi jñāna* one apprehends material objects directly by the self. In *manaḥparyāya* the knowledge of other mind is acquired and in *keval jñāna,* the self possesses the knowledge of all things past, present and future and also of its own pure nature. It must be recorded that the problem of knowledge of other minds as discussed by *Jainas* can be compared with the western treatments of knowledge of other mind. It is the *Jainas* alone of the Indian Philosophers who singularly have given considerable attention to this problem. The *Jainas* do not say much about the nature of it. How does the self apprehend the object? Does it apprehend the objects as done by the sense organs? Are other objects come in contact with the self only in the shape of ideas, in this knowledge purely subjective experience like the pleasure and pain? These questions are left unanswered.

The *Jainas* hold that every body can become an omniscient, while most other schools believe in God as the omniscient being. According to *Nyāya,* a Yogi can acquire omniscience, which is not permanent because in the stage of final release, there would be no knowledge. Only Gods' omniscience is eternal.

Regarding the nature and process of omniscient or *keval jñāna,* the *Jainas* are not very clear. They simply say that in *kevala jñāna* the self possesses knowledge of all.

In *Nyāya,* there are three types of extra ordinary perception. The first two called *sāmānyalakṣaṇā* and *jñāna-lakṣaṇā* cannot be called *atindnya pratyakṣa* from *Jaina* point of view. *Atindriya pratyakṣa* is not caused by the sense organs and mind whereas *sāmānya lakṣaṇā* and *jñāna lakṣaṇā* arise with the help of the senses. Though there is no direct sense object contact, there is indirect contact. The *Jaina* would also argue that *sāmānya lakṣaṇā* of the *Naiyāyikas* may be in a restricted sense called *atindriya pratyakṣa*. It may be compared with *kevala jṃāna* of *Jainas*. In the *Brahmasūtra* of *Advaitins* it is *atīndriya jṃāna* but there is no knowledge of the object of the past, present and future. There is no question of direct apprehension of all objects of the world in *Brahmajṃāna*. There is the direct apprehension of the self only, which is called *Brahma*. They also accept the direct apprehension of the pure self in the stage of *kevala*. The Yogi *pratyaksa* of the Buddhist may be called *atindriya pratyakāa,* because it is not caused by sense organs. It is the direct intuition of transcendental reality. But the *Jainas* do not accept the *Nirvikalpa* character of it. According to *Jaina,* knowledge must be determinate. As mentioned above, determinate ness is the criterion of right knowledge.

The *Jaina* philosophers though describe the testimony of *Tirthaṅkara* as transcendental or *lokattara,* it is not in fact super mundane and super human. The *Tirthaṅkara* are not otherworldly or super natural deities, but the human beings, liberated from the clutches of the bondage of karma. The idea of *Tirthaṅkara* hood is common to all. Anybody, through self-efforts and self-discipline can queer the karma and can attain the state of *kevalin* and thus, can become "*āpta*" whose statement qualify for being true or valid verbal testimony. In these respects the *Jaina* concept of verbal testimony is more appealing than the orthodox concept in which a super mundane divine Being in the name of God is generally accepted to be the ultimate source of the verbal testimony.

Another most important aspect worth noting in this context is the presentation of the *Jaina* doctrines by the *Nyāya, Vedānta* and Buddhism as *pūrvapakṣa* view. They have been very faithful in presenting the prima-facie arguments of the *Jainas* and it can even be said in appreciation of their presentation that one can read Jainism on the basis of their presentation which we have shown by drawing comparison of their presentation with some original texts of *Jainas* by putting them side by side some times in the main body or at times in the foot notes.

However, it is interesting to observe that though the Buddhist, *Naiyāyikas* and the *Vedāntins* have presented the *Jaina* doctrines very carefully and very authentically, still they have in many cases misinterpreted the *Jaina* doctrines and refuted accordingly. We have already discussed this in the respective places and here we may just note a few cases like their interpretation of the term *'avaktavyatva'* of the third *bhaṅga* of *Syādvāda* theory and the interpretation of the basic concept of *Anekāntavāda* by the *Vedantins* and even by the *Naiyāyikas,* which are misleading and not correct. Though the wordings and the expressions are kept intact, they are interpreted wrongly. No care has been taken either by the *Naiyāyikas* or the *Vedāntins* or the Buddhists to see the real interpretation and implication of the expressions. This has happened in most cases, which we have made clear in the discussion.

We now quote some of the answers from the *Jaina* point of view against the arguments of the *Naiyāyikas, Vedāntins* and Buddhists.

The *Brahmasūtra* read *"naikasminasambhavāt"* to mean that it is not possible to predicate positivity and negativity i.e. *'astitva'* and *'nāstitva'* to one and the same object due to impossibility and non-applicability. The *Jainas* also favour the same reality delimited by the quality of continuation which is one aspect of the reality and 'is not' i.e. non-existent is qualified by the quality of change which is also the essential aspect of the same reality. And making a singular assertion of the reality in the form of either 'it is' or 'it is not' would amount to concealing or suppressing the real nature of reality. Thus, there is no contingency of any kind in the *Jaina* theory of relativity in the statement 'it is' and 'it is not' is the conclusion *of Jainas.*

As regards the objection to the fourth alternative of the *syādvāda* theory viz. *"syādavaktavya"* it may be pointed out that, the concept of inexpressibility should be differentiated from *'avapadesya'* concept as elaborated by *Nyāyasūtra-bhāṣya* (I. I. 4) or from the *'avaktavya'* of the *Vedāntins* with regard to the nature of Brahman.' The *Jainas* do not propose that the reality cannot be verbalized. In fact such a view will go against the supposition of the theory of relativity, which is dialectical and verbalizes the experiences of the reality. What the *Jainas* propose in this *'bhaṅgas'* is that the attribution of two or more contradictory properties or aspects in a single expression is not possible. In other words, *'syādavaktavya'* means the inexpressibility of an expression of experience of existence and the non-existence of a reality in a particular place and time delimited by one and the same property. For example, it is not possible to verbalize the cognition of a pot as being present and absent in a particular space and time delimited by either the aspects of continuity or the aspect of change alone. Thus, one cannot have an expression like 'pot exist delimited by this place and that time delimited further by substance ness, (looking from the point of view of *dravyatva* aspect of reality) and the pot does not exist being delimited by the above mentioned delimiters like the same place, the same time and the same properties. This is the meaning of the term *'avaktavya'*. Thus, the objection that nothing can be verbalized or the realities are inexpressible as posed by the *Vedāntins* and others is misleading and based on the wrong interpretation of the concept *'avaktavya'* which is not intended by the *Jainas*.

As to the objection regarding the size of the soul the *Jainas* have a practical and empirical approach to it. They feel that it is convenient to assume the size of the soul as limited pervaded by the individual, occupied in a given time. The objection that due to the identical size of the various sizes of soul in various states and the stages of the bondage, philosophers hold that the grace of the perfect souls may be helpful to attain salvation, it is not the sole cause to get it. On the contrary, for salvation the *Jaina* philosophers have prescribed fifteen *'guṇastānas'* along with severe penance in mind, body and action. Through these *guṇastānas* one can destroy the *bandhahetus* i.e. the causes of the bondage and the *nirjarās*. Thus, after complete destruction of the *jñānāvaraṇīya karma, darśanāvaraṇīya karma, antarāya* and *mohanīya* karmas a soul can be in its real state; that is what is called salvation in Jainism. Thus, the argument of the *dvaitādvaita* philosophers on the grace of the perfect souls is the cause of attaining salvation is not sound.

The objection that 'atoms as the causes of the creation is not tenable, because it creates a contingency called 'infinite regress' and so on; also looks baseless. The arguments of the *dvaitādvaita* philosophers against the *Jaina* philosophers on atoms as the causes of the creation and the allied arguments related to it, is not the exact position of the *Jainas*. Though the *Jaina* philosophers maintain that atoms are the cause of the creation yet do not persuade any unseen principle i.e. *adṛṣṭa* to create the first motion in the atoms, as pointed out by the *dvaitādvaita* philosopher. According to Jainism, it is the very nature of the atoms i.e. 'the nature of conjunction' and 'the nature of subtraction' which creates the first motion in it. Then they combined with each other to create *skandhas*. In this way the whole creation comes to being. Not only this, they also; say that these atoms are having twenty attributes in it and they are eternal. But as the *dvaitādvaita* philosophers have pointed out that if the *Jainas* accept that atoms are the causes of the creation, then they have to accept that atoms are also having form *(rūpa),* taste *(rasa),* smell *(gandha)* and touch *(sparśa).* This amounts to say that they (atoms) are non-eternal. It is not true; it is the presupposition of the *Vedāntins* or the *Nyāya* philosophers that if something is having forms and touches etc., it would be non-eternal. For the *Jaina* philosophy it makes no problem. Thus, the arguments of the *dvaitādvaia* philosophers against the *Jaina* philosophy are not justified in the philosophical framework of Jainism.

The whole argument of the *dvaita* philosophers start with the problem namely that the '*Jagat*' i.e. universe is created by omnipotent '*Viṣṇu*' which is objected in the *Jaina* philosophy, as they have accepted some eternal causes of the soul like *'dharma'* and *'adharama'* and some external causes like *kāla, ākāśa, pudgala* as the causes for the creation of the universe. In this context they (the dvaita philosophers) have rejected the nature of the universe and the concept of soul as postulated by *Jaina* philosophers.

If we observe the whole analysis by *Vātsyāyana* and his followers we notice that the argument are based on supposing the entire reality, as a whole to be eternal, which is not the position of the *Jainas,* as explained elsewhere. All assertions are partial from the point of view of their material substance. The substance 'gold' continues to exist in all modes in all modifications in all time and space and hence it is eternal. Thus, from the point of view of the continuity of this material substance the *dravya* is called eternal and hence no contradiction and absurdity of any kind can be noticed in *Jaina* position. The *Jainas* never said that *dravyas* or realities are eternal. On the other hand, to them, from the point of view of their changing modes is transitory. It is no surprising to note that even a man is transitory from the point of view of its mode.

Bhāsarvajña in his *Nyāyabhūṣaṇa* has criticized the authoritativeness of the *Jaina* scripture. To us, it appears that whatever arguments *Bhāsarvajña* has provided against the *Jainas* can be forwarded against the *Naiyāyika* as well logically. The only assertion that "the Vedas are '*apauruṣeya*' hence, cannot be liable to any falsehood" is mere a belief and cannot be logically established. The *Naiyāyikas* have accepted along with Vedas, the validity *of āpta vākya,* which is the statement or expression of a trustworthy person. According to *Bhāsarvajña,* validity is common to all, common to a seer as well an ordinary person. If that is true, then how can one accept the *Jaina's* scripture as unauthoritative because they are composed by human being? It must be noted that according to *Jainas,* the scriptures are the statements of *Tīrthaṅkaras* who are identified with the *āptas* of the *Naiyāyikas*. From the above discussion it may be noted that the way *Bhāsarvajña* has presented rather criticized the authoritativeness of the scriptures of the *Jainas* is not adequate, because, without giving very sound and systematic arguments he has criticized the *Jaina āgamas* for the sake of mere criticism.

It may be observed that the *Jaina's* classification of *Pramāṇa* into two kinds namely *pratyakṣa* and *parokṣa* is logical at least as they think. In one case the knowledge is quite independent, hence, direct. In another as for example, in the case of inference etc. they are dependent on perception, hence, indirect. There is nothing wrong in holding so and any opposition to this supposition will be unjustified. And if it is further classified into *anumana* i.e. inference etc. it is also all right. But the acceptance of *smṛti, pratyabhijñāna, tarka* etc. as independent *pramāṇa* does not sound logical. And if the *Naiyāyikas* have to object, they may object these three suppositions. Thus, instead of opposing or objecting the two-fold classification of *pramāṇa,* what *Bhāsarvajña* or the *Naiyāyikas* would have objected to is the independentness of their *pramāṇas,* which they have not done. The reason for such negligence of the logicians, which is noticed throughout their text is not far to seek, which we have observed time and again.

In the context of causality it is stated that contrary to this theory of *'ekānta'* if one follows *anekāntavāda,* these practical verifiable human behaviours cannot be explained. Hence, *anekānta* theory of the *Jaina* cannot be accepted. He gives reason subscribing the view of *anekānta.* No causality between the agent and its result can be explained, for, in *anekānta* theory the doer is different and the enjoyer will be different. There would not be any inclination towards taking food, for, it would not satisfy one's hunger. If the king is well fed, the naked monk will have the satisfaction of eating. And if not, this will amount to *ekāntavāda* not *anekāntavāda.*

As can be seen, *Bhāsarvajña* interprets *anekānta* as lack of causality between the doer and enjoyer of any action.

According to him, in *anekānta* theory the doer of an action and the enjoyer of that will be different. There would not be any guiding principle if 'a' does an action, he will attain its fruits for certain. And if he gets or if causality is established, that would be *ekāntavāda* to the pleasure of the *Naiyāyikas*. As a matter of fact, the *Jainas* do not interpret *anekānta* in the way *Bhāsarvajña* has interpreted. The *Jainas* always establish causality between the doer and the enjoyer and this does not affect that position of *anekāntavāda*. To explain, *Bhāsarvajña* notes: the *Jainas* have prescribed the process of attaining *saṁbara, nirjara* and *mokṣa* and also the avoidance of *āsrava* and *bandha* gradually. By employing *syādvāda* or *saptabhaṅgī* to this, no consistency will be maintained with regard to the performance and non-performance of the prescribed observation, because by employing *sapptabhaṅgī* the prescription will be *syād viśiṣṭa, syādaviśiṣṭa* etc. for both the cases viz. in case of *mokṣa* as well *bandha*. This means that no distinction can be maintained between *saṁbara, nirjarā* and *mokṣa* or *āśrava* and *bandha*. This is not correct. In the *anekāntavāda* as understood and explained by the *Jainas,* the theory of causality and the distinction between *saṁbara* and *nirjarā* etc. can be well maintained.

We may conclude the present discussion with the following observation: We are not in favour of accepting or rejecting any doctrine of any system following the true spirit of *Jaina* theory of *anekānta* where every modal assertion or judgment are relative and conditional. Still at places where we have tried to defend the *Jainas* and offend the opponents, is just to show how the doctrines of the *Jainas* are correct in the arena of philosophical speculation in the *Jainas* philosophy only.

BIBLIOGRAPHY

Primary Sources

1. Abhinava Dharmabhuṣaṇa Yati: Nyāya Dīpikā, Patibhāprakāśan, Delhi, 2001.

2. AbhinavacārūkTrtī: Prameyaratnālṅikāra, Paṇḍit Oriental Research Institute, Mysore, 1948.

3. Anantavīrya: Prameyaratnamālā, Chaukhambā Vidhyā Bhavana, Váraṇāsi, 1964.

4. Arcaṭa: Hetubinduṭfīā, Barodā Oriental Institute, Barodā, 1949.

5. Ballhabhācārya: Bhāratīya Vidyā prakāśan, Vāraṇāsi, 1971.

6. Ballhabhācārya: Vikram Saṁvat. Aṇubhāṣya, Srināthadvārā Taipalboard, Rajasthan, 2038.

7. Bhāsarvajña: Nyāyabhūṣaṇa, "addarśana prakāśana Pratiṣ ṭānaṁ, Vāraṇāsi, 1968.

8. Cakradhara: Nyāyamajmarīgranthibhaṅga, L. D. Institute of Indology, Ahmedabad, 1972.

9. Dharmakīrti: Pramāṇa Vārtika, Bauddha Bhāratī, Vāraṇāsi, 1984.

10. Dharmakirti: Nyāyavindu, Bauddha Bhāratī, Vāraṇāsi, 1985.

11. Dharmottara: Sāhitya Bhaṇāra, Merath, 1975.

12. Durveka Mishra: Dharmottara Pradīpikā, Kāśi prasad Jayaswal Research Institute, Patna, 1971 .

13. Gotama: Nyāyadarśanarṁ, ed. Dhundirāj Shasthri, Caukhmba Sanskrit Series, Vāraṇāsi, 1970.

14. Hemacandra: Pramāṇamīmārhsā, Tārā publication, Vāraṇāsi, 1970.

15. Hemacandra: Granthatayī, Sri Yośobhārati Jaina prakāśana Samiti, Mumbai, 1982.

16. Śaṅkarācārya: Brahmasūtrabhāṣya, Motilal Banarasidass, New Delhi, 1980.

17. Śāntarakṣita: Tattvasaṁgraha, Bauddha Bhāratī, Vāraṇāsi, 1964.

18. Jayantabhaṭṭa: Nyāyamajṃarī, vol. I&II, Oriental Research Institute, Mysore, 1983.

19. Keśava Kāśmīra: Vedānta Kauthbha Prabhā, Vṛndāvan, 1905.

20. Madhyācārya: Śakāvda. Brahmasūrabhāṣya, Śukruvārā, Pune. 1848.

21. Malliseṇa Sūri: Syādvādamajṃari, Motilal Banarasidass, Delhi. Vikrarh Samvat 2452.

22. Nāgārjuna: Mūlamādhyamikakārikā, Louis de la vallee paussin, 1903.

23. Nemicandra Siddhānta Cakraborthi: Dravyasarhgraha, Motilal Banarasidass, Delhi, 1989.

24. Nimbārkācārya: Vedāntapārijāta Saurabha, ed. Dhuṇḍiraj Shasthri, Vṛndāvan, 1932.

25. Prabhācandra: Prameyakamalamārtaṇḍa, Sri Sadguru publication, New Delhi, 1990.

26. Prabhācandra: Nyāyakumudacandra, Sri Sadguru. publication, New Delhi, 1991.

27. Pujjyapāda: Sarvārtha Siddhi, Mánikachaṇdra Digambrara Jaina Granthamālā Parikṣalāya, Mumbai, 1939.

28. Purusottama: Saṁ vat. Vedāntādikaraṇamālā, Pusti Prakasan, Rajasthan, 2038.

29. Rāmānuja: Śribhāṣya, Sanskrit Samśodhana Saṁsat, Melukot,2038.

30. Samantabhadra: Āptamīmāṁsā, Sanskrit- Sanskrit Granthamālā, ' Ahmedabad, 1999.
31. Siddhasena Divākara: Sanmatī prakaraṇa, Jṇānodaya Trust,Ahamedabad, 1963.
32. Siddhasena Divākara: Nyāyāvatāra, Shri Jaina Swetāmbra Conference, Mumbai, 1928.
33. Sri Śántisūri: Nyāyāvatāravārtikavṛtti, Bhāratīya Vidyābhavana, Mumbai, Vikram Saṁvat. 2005.
34. Srimad Vidyābhuṣaṇasimha Súri: Syādvāda Siddhi, Sri Mānikachandra Digambrara Jaina Granthamālā Samiti, Mumbai, 1950.
35. Umāśvāti: Tattvārthasūtra, Pārśvanātha Vidyāśrama Śodha Santhā, Vāraṇāsi, 1976.
36. Vasubandhu: Abhidharmakośa, Bauddha Bhāratī, Vāraṇāsi, 1971.
37. Yaśovijaya: Jaina Tarka'Bhāṣā, Motilal Banrasidass, Delhi, 1973.

Secondary Sources

1. Bhattacharyya, Hari Mohan: 1992, Jaina Logic and Epistemology, K. P. Bagchi and Company, Calcutta.
2. Bijalwan, C. D. :1977, Indian Theory of Knowledge, Heritage Publication, New Delhi.
3. Bothra, Puspā: 1996, The Jaina Theory of Perception, Motilal Banarasidass, New Delhi.
4. Dalai, B.K. : Samavayavada of Tattvacintamani (Eng. Trans. with notes and Critical Edition), Pratibha Prakashan, Delhi, 1999.
5. Dalai, B.K. : English trans. Of Nyaya Siddhantadipa (Containing Mangalavada, Karanatavada, Andhakaravada, Saktivada and Padasaktivada of Sasadhara), with study, Pratibha Prakashan, Delhi, 2000.
6. Dalai B.K. : Bibliography of Jainism, Vedavidya Prakashana, Poona.

7. Dalai B.K. : In defence of Jain concept of Pramāṇa, Tulsi Prajñā, Jain Visva Bharti, 1999.
8. Dalai B.K. : Jain Concept of Śabda Prasmāṇa, Proceedings of National Seminar on Śabda khaṇḍa of Prasthānaratnakara, Gandhinagar, 2000. pp. 173-200.
9. Dalai B.K. : Concept of Anyathāsiddha, Prof. P.G. Lalye Fel. Vol. pp. 150-161.
10. Dalai B.K. : Jain Concept of Error, Proceedings of National Seminar on Theories of Error, 2002.
11. Dalai B.K. :Jain concept of Mind, MM Kaul Fel. Vol. 2003.
12. Dalai B.K. : Śaśadhara's Theory of casuality, Journal of R.V. University, Calcutta, 2003. pp. 10-31.
13. Dalai B.K. : Concept of Avaktavya, Vanī Jyoti, Journal of Utkal University BBSR, 2003. pp. 212-219.
14. Dalai B.K. : Speakers Intention according to Jain Philosophy, Proceedings of the National Seminar, CASS, Poona, 2003.
15. Dalai B.K. : Sankaras on Jain Theory of Soul and Anekāntavada, A Critique Calcutta, 2003. pp. 13-28.
16. Dalai B.K. : Jain Theory of Causality, Proceeding of the National Seminar on Causality Shri Vallabha Trust, 2004. pp.577-590.
17. Dalai B.K. : Concept of Parokṣa Pramāṇa, Prof. Thite Fel. Vol 2004.
18. Dalai B.K. : Jain Concept of Darkness, Proceeding of National Seminar, Shri Vallabha Trust, 2004.
19. Dixit, K. K.: 1971, The Jaina Ontology, L. D. Institute of Indology, Ahmedbad.
20. Gopalan, S.: 1991, Jainism as Meta Philosophy, Sri Sadguru Publication, Delhi.
21. Jain Bhaskar, Bhagchandra: 1972, Jainism in Buddhist Literature, Alok Prakāśan, Nagpur.

22. Jain, Ramacandra: 1973, Jaina Darśana me niścaya aur vyavahāra naya: eka anuśilana, Pārśvanśtha Vdyā Patiṣṭ āna, Vāraṇāsi.

23. Kalgatgi. G. T : 1988, f Jainism, Prakrit BhāratI Academi.

24. Marathe, M. P.: 1984, Studies in Jainism, I. P. Q. Publication, University of Pune.

25. Mehta, Mohan Lai: 1971, Jaina Philosophy, P. V. Research Institute, Vāraṇāsi.

26. Mukharjee, Satkari: The Jaina philosophy of Non-Absolutism, 1978, Motialal Banarasidass, Delhi.

27 . Muni, Devendra: 1997, Jaina Darsana, University Publication, New Delhi.

28. Muni, Dulharaja: 1973, Jaina Darsana: Manana aur Mimārhsā, Adarśa Sāhitya Samgha, Rajathan.

29. Nahara, P. C. and Ghosh, K. C: 1988, An Encyclopedia of . Jainism, Sri Sadguru Publication, Delhi.

30. Padmarajiah. Y. J : 1963, Comparative studies of Jaina Theory of Reality and Knowledge, Motilal Banarasidass, Delhi.

31. Batairiya, Mukta prasad: 1973, darśana me atma dravya vivecana, Prācyavidyā śodha academi, Delhi.

32. Potter, Karl H.: 1991, Presuppositions of Indian Philosophy, Motilal Banarasidass, Delhi.

33. Rampuria, Sreechand: 1996, of Jaina philosophy Religion and Culture, Jaina Viśva Bhāratī Institute, Ladnun.

34. Sanghvi, Sukhlalji: 1961, Advanced Studies in Indian Logic and Metaphysics, Indian Studies, Calcutta.

35. Schubring, Walther: 3 995, ctrine of the Jainas, Motilal Banarasidass, New Delhi.

36. Sikdar, Jogendra Chandra: 1987, The concept of Matter in Jaina philosophy, P. V. Research Institute, Vāraṇāsi.

37. Singh, Ramjee: 3 993, Jaina perspective in Philosophy and Religon, Párśvanātha Śodhapīṭha, Váraṇāsī.

38. Tatia, Nathmlal: 1951, s of Jaina philosophy, P. V. Research Institute, Vāraṇāsi.

Research Bulletins

1. Anekānta (quarterly): Vīrasiva Mandir, Delhi.
2. Annals of Bhandarakar Research Institute, Pune.
3. Śramaṇa: (Monthly): Párśvanātha Vidyāśrama, Vāraṇāsi.
4. Jaina Siddhānta Bhāṣkara: D. K. Jaina Institute, Jaina Bhavana, Arha, Bihar.
5. Jaina Vidyā (Half yearly): Jaina Vidyā Santhan, Jajasthan.
6. Jinavāṇī (quarterly): Samayajmāna Maṇdala, Jaipur.
7. Journal of the Asiatic Society of Bombay: Asiatic Society of Bombay.
8. Philosophical Quarterly: Department of Philosophy, University of pune. Pune.
9. Prakrit Vidyā (quarterly): Kunda Kunda Bhārati, Delhi.
10. Saṁbodhi: L. D. Institute, Ahmedabad.
11. Tírthaiṅkara (Monthly): Haribhaiyā Prakāśana, Indor.
12. Tulsi Prajñā: (quarterly): Jaina Viśva Bhārati, Ladnun.

INDEX

A

B